IDEAS OF JEWISH HISTORY

IDEAS OF JEWISH HISTORY *Edited, with introductions and notes, by* MICHAEL A. MEYER

BEHRMAN HOUSE, INC. | PUBLISHERS | NEW YORK

ACKNOWLEDGMENTS

The editor and publisher thank the following for permission to reprint or translate:

Charles Scribner's Sons for a selection from Ellis Rivkin, *The Shaping of Jewish History*, © 1971 by Ellis Rivkin.

Columbia University Press for a selection from Salo Wittmayer Baron, *A Social and Religious History of the Jews*, Second Edition, Volume I, © 1952 by Columbia University Press.

Doubleday & Company, Inc. for a selection from Theodor H. Gaster, tr., *The Dead Sea Scriptures*, © 1956 by Theodor H. Gaster.

The Dvir Co. Ltd. for a selection from Yehezkel Kaufmann, *Gola ve-Nekhar*, © 1929 by the Dvir Co. Ltd.

Harvard University Press and the Loeb Classical Library for selections from H. St. J. Thackeray, tr., Josephus, *The Jewish War* and *Jewish Antiquities*, © 1967, 1961 by Harvard University Press.

The American Jewish Congress for Michael A. Meyer, tr., Leo Baeck, "Theology and History," *Judaism*, XIII, © 1964 by the American Jewish Congress.

The Jewish Publication Society for selections from Gerson D. Cohen, tr., Abraham ibn Daud, *The Book of Tradition;* Martin Cohen, tr., Samuel Usque, *Consolation for the Tribulations of Israel;* Ernst J. Schlochauer, tr., Abraham Geiger, "A General Introduction to the Science of Judaism" and "On the Spiritual Life of Israel," in Max Wiener, ed., *Abraham Geiger and Liberal Judaism;* Henrietta Szold, tr., Simon Dubnow, "Jewish History: An Essay in the Philosophy of History" and Koppel S. Pinson, tr., Simon Dubnow, "The Sociological View of Jewish History," in Koppel S. Pinson, ed., Simon Dubnow, *Nationalism and History;* Merton B. Dagut, tr., Ben Zion Dinur, *Israel and the Diaspora.* © 1967, 1964, 1962, 1958, 1969, respectively, by the Jewish Publication Society of America.

The Leo Baeck Institute for Lionel E. Kochan, tr., Immanuel Wolf, "On the Concept of a Science of Judaism," *Leo Baeck Institute Year Book,* II, © 1957 by Leo Baeck Institute.

The National Council of the Churches of Christ in the U.S.A. for selections from the *Revised Standard Version of the Apocrypha,* © 1957 by the Division of Christian Education of the National Council of the Churches of Christ in the U.S.A.

Sifriat Poalim Ltd., for a selection from Raphael Mahler, *Divre Yeme Yisrael: Dorot Aharonim,* Volume I, © 1952 by Sifriat Poalim Ltd.

Library of Congress Cataloging in Publication Data

Meyer, Michael A   comp.
  Ideas of Jewish history.
  360 p.
  (Library of Jewish studies)
  Bibliography: p.
    1. Jews—History—Philosophy—Addresses, essays,
  lectures.   2. Jews—Historiography—Addresses, essays,
  lectures.   I. Title.
  DS115.5.M48   909'.04'924   73–19960
  ISBN 0–87441–202–1

For Margaret
  and for
Daniel, Jonathan, and Rebecca

CONTENTS

*F*OR MODERN JEWS, a conception of their past is no mere academic matter. It is vital to their self-definition. Contemporary forms of Jewish identity are all rooted in some view of Jewish history which sustains them and serves as their legitimation. Judaism itself provides the source for this significance attributed to historical perception. Traditional Jewish faith rests neither on abstract speculations nor on a revelation given to a single prophet: it is a people's collective and continuing response to a Divine will manifest to it in the early stages of its historical existence and determining its fate down to the present time. But the importance of the historical dimension lies as well in the widely variegated and extraordinary nature of the Jewish past; Jews have been a part of so much of world history, and yet this very participation has made them unique. The history of the Jews has reached into all the phases of Western civilization: the ancient Near East, the Greco-Roman world, the cultures of medieval Christianity and Islam, modern Europe, the Americas, and again the Near East. Jewish existence has taken the forms of a seminomadic clan, a wandering band in the Sinai wilderness, a monarchy, a hierocracy, a worldwide diaspora, and a modern, almost wholly secular state. Jews have defined themselves or been categorized by others as a people chosen by God, a corporative religious community, a denomination on the Christian model, a race, and a nationality. Among them have been mystics, religious rationalists, agnostics, and atheists. For nearly two thousand years they possessed no land of their own and even today 80 percent continue to live among the nations, outside the State of Israel. The great diversity of their historical experience has enabled modern Jews, themselves representing a variety of Jewish identities, to choose particular strands as paradigmatic of their own form of Judaism or even to declare their Jewishness basic or normative for all ages past. But it has also raised serious questions regarding the totality of that past. How is it to be conceived as a whole?

Christians, Muslims, and Jews themselves have supplied conceptions in accordance with the religious principles that guided their understanding of the historical process. All have had to come to terms with the fact, that despite the vicissitudes of their anomalous historical experience, the Jews survive as an identifiable entity. They have withstood one challenge after another—both physical and intellectual—somehow maintaining an historical continuity. How Jewish writers have dealt with this enigma—in all of its aspects and its components—serves as the subject of this volume.

Until the modern period, Jews invariably perceived their history as the consequence of God's relation to the people He had chosen as His own. This theological conception, originating in the Bible, remained dominant until the nineteenth century and continues among many religious Jews to the present. Though the relevance of nonreligious factors had been recognized some time earlier, it was only during the last hundred years that fully secular ideas of Jewish history emerged. Yet the persistent notion of God's will as the ultimate cause of Jewish history should not be taken to imply that conceptions of Jewish history assume a diversity of forms only with the advent of modernity. Despite the common theological framework which has characterized Jewish historical writing for two and a half millennia, attitudes both to individual events and to the nature of Jewish history as a whole have undergone change all along. An understanding of Jewish ideas of history therefore requires nothing less than a history of those views beginning with the Bible and continuing down to contemporary historians.

In my general introduction to the readings in this volume, I have attempted briefly to present such a history. It is intended to provide a survey of conceptual development over the course of time so that the major themes and problems—those common to all ideas of history as well as those specific to the history of the Jews—may be generally understood before they are examined within the context of individual writings. Here, too, I have tried to indicate what I consider to be the strong points and the shortcomings of each conception, particularly for those of more recent times.

The far briefer introductions which precede the individual selections present the specific background for each work and, by way of pointing out certain highlights, suggest why a particular selection was chosen for inclusion. Although ideas of Jewish history obviously originate with the Bible, the ready availability of this basic volume made the inclusion of selections from it seem superfluous. Nonetheless, any study of the texts of Jewish historiography must, of course, begin with its historical sections. It is only against the background of the biblical writers that the first deviations from their approach, brought about by the influence of Hellenism, can be properly understood.

In making the selections for this volume I have been guided by certain criteria. First, I have tried to choose writings which do not merely reformulate earlier notions but represent some clear novelty of conception. In some cases, however, I did select a later example to represent a particular type if the presentation seemed clearer or more concise. Second, I considered it important, wherever possible, to choose comprehensive views or at least, where that was not realizable (as in the case of some of the medieval material), an excerpt which presupposed a more general conception. Only for the earlier periods have I included some selections which deal with specific historical subjects and where the underlying idea must be inferred from the application. By far the greater part of the selections are themselves conceptual, and to some extent methodological. Third, especially for the contemporary period, I have confined myself—with the exception of Leo Baeck—to the writings of individuals known principally for their work in Jewish history, although I realize that a number of other Jewish thinkers—philosophers, essayists, and theologians from Judah Halevi to Ahad Ha-Am to Franz Rosenzweig—did indeed develop conceptions of Jewish history. Some of their writings are included among the "Suggestions for Further Reading" at the end of this volume. Finally, I have felt an obligation to offer the English reader selections hitherto unavailable in his own language. About half of the material presented here appears in English for the first time.

Such a collection will not, of course, satisfy everyone. Important modern Jewish historians have been omitted, although their work has done much to advance Jewish historiography. In each instance, however, careful study of their writings showed either that they did not differ markedly from one or another conception which was included or that their contribution was rather to specific questions of Jewish historiography than to an overall view. Finally, in some cases, omission was simply due to the fact that a view had not been succinctly formulated in a manner which permitted coherent excerption.

The brief notes, placed at the foot of certain pages, are strictly explanatory in character and are intended for the reader with little background in Jewish or general history. No attempt has been made at a textual analysis of the readings, nor have I documented my introductory essay with any of the numerous specific writings on Jewish historiography which served me in composing it; those in English are listed in the back of the volume. While I have thus drawn upon the work of other scholars, I believe that the task of tracing ideas of Jewish history from the Bible to our own time in terms of their principal components has never previously been attempted in any language.

The biblical quotations used in this volume in nearly every case follow the Jewish Publication Society version of 1917; spelling of proper nouns is generally according to the new *Encyclopaedia Judaica*.

Thanks are due to a number of colleagues at Hebrew Union College in Cincinnati who took time from busy schedules to read portions of the manuscript and who made valuable suggestions. I am grateful also to the students in my Jewish historiography course, both in America and in Israel, who by their questions and comments forced me to examine my own historical conception and to refine my understanding of the views of others. Mrs. Marsha Bernstein and Mrs. Rose Weinstein skillfully and diligently typed parts of the manuscript. From Neal Kozodoy I received the idea for this volume; he also, along with the Advisory Committee of the Library of Jewish Studies, provided helpful advice and criticism. I can only hope that publication of this book will impart a greater appreciation for the fascinating and perennial enigma which is the history of the Jews.

JEWISH HISTORY, as Simon Dubnow noted some eighty years ago, is characterized by a unique duality. On the one hand, it is so "intimately interwoven" with the history of the Western world that it cannot be understood apart from it. On the other hand, it possesses specific characteristics which differentiate it sharply from the history of the nations with which Jews have come into contact. This same duality also characterizes the questions which, consciously or unconsciously, Jewish historians have had to answer in formulating a conception of the Jewish past, or in trying to write an account of it. Certain issues affect the writer of Jewish history no less than they do his colleagues in other branches of the discipline. Of these, the most basic are the determination of causality, the affirmation or denial that history possesses a goal, the rendering or withholding of moral judgments, and the division of the historical continuum into identifiable periods. To these general issues, Jewish historiography adds the unique problem of dealing with a protean entity—the Jews—which seems to bear few if any constant characteristics and which for the far greater part of its history has been scattered and without a land of its own.

Before attempting to trace the ideas of Jewish history which have been developed from the biblical writers down to the present, it will be well to delineate these basic issues, the common and the specific, so that the significance of the changing positions taken on each of them will be more readily apparent.

The problems shared by all historians fall into two realms: the philosophical and the historiographical. In the former, the initial questions are epistemological: How can the past be known when it is not present to our senses? Do the individual data which make up the past constitute knowledge in the same sense as do generalizations in the social sciences? These issues are basic to the entire historical enterprise, for the value of its conclusions depends upon the degree of success we achieve in establishing our cognition of the past as a valid form of human knowledge. But such epistemological questions are independent of the actual content of any specific history and hence play no role in a conception of the particular Jewish past. Insofar as Jewish writers have dealt with them, they have done so as philosophers of history, apart from any specific historical context.

This is not true of the issue of causality. The authors of nearly all the selections which follow either explicitly express a view of this question or permit its easy determination from their interpretation of historical events. They have variously and to varying extents tried to understand their people's history as the working out of a transcendent or immanent Divine plan; as the product of the will of powerful individuals; as the result of impersonal social and economic forces; or as a combination of some or all of these. Among historians in the modern period, religious interpretations of Jewish history have generally given way to secular ones, but the will of God as a determinative force in Jewish and world history was still an important explanatory principle for specific phenomena as late as the work of Heinrich Graetz in the second half of the nineteenth century and it continues to be significant for many religious writers to the present time.

An historian may believe God's role in history to be one of two kinds or both. He may regard God's influence as constant and hence indiscernible, every human act being a manifestation of God's will. Thus even an apparently secular historian, one who attributes no specific event directly to God, may believe in the ultimate, all-embracing influence of Divine Providence. Thereby he, of course, raises the concomitant philosophical problem of reconciling this influence with human freedom, but as in the case of epistemological issues, the historian's answer to this question is usually not evident from his historical work. The other possibility is to allow of Divine intervention at specific points of Jewish or general history—either arbitrarily or in direct response to some human action. In this case God's will becomes an independent and immediate determinative factor of particular events either instead of, or more commonly in addition to, His continuous influence as it is mediated through the deeds of men.

Strictly secular Jewish historians have limited causality entirely to immanent factors with no transcendent references, either stated or assumed. But here, too, there are basic differences, not only as to the role of the individual in history, but as to the question of whether ideal or material factors are basic to a determination of human motivation, and hence to the understanding of history. Jewish and general historians alike remain divided on this philosophical question, which borders on the psychological. The modern period has produced Jewish historians who insist upon the force of ideas in determining Jewish history, economic determinists who deny it, and advocates of multiple-factor theories of causality who refer to the influence of both ideal and material causes.

No less universal a question is that which inquires about the goal of history. The Greeks, wedded to a cyclical theory of development, denied the existence of historical teleology. History simply repeated itself with appropriate variations; it did not lead anywhere. By contrast, Jewish writers have since biblical times viewed world history as moving toward an ultimate consummation: the advent of an End of Days (later associated with the figure of the Messiah) when life as we know it will be transformed. Christians, too, have viewed history as God's preparation of His world for the Parousia, the second and final coming of Christ. But especially for the Jews, for whom messianism became so central to religious belief, the endeavor to perceive direction in world history, as well as specifically in their own past, has been a continuing and conspicuous preoccupation. With the modern age, the idea of a messianic end was for many writers transmuted into a secular equivalent: the philosophically grounded notion of inevitable historical progress toward the realization of an optimal condition of man. As Jewish writers came under the influence of Hegelian (idealist) or Marxist (materialist) versions of this doctrine, they formulated conceptions of Jewish history correlated to the operation of such an immanent force. To some extent, religious and secular messianism continues to play a role in historiography even today. But during the last century most academic historians, including those of the Jews, have turned away from this idea of necessary movement toward a predetermined, as yet unrealized, goal.

Along with the philosophical questions, the Jewish historian also shares with his colleagues certain historiographical (or methodological) ones. Of these, one is closely related to his decision on causality, though that decision is not necessarily determinative: Is rendering moral judgment upon the past a proper activity of the historian? The question is related to causality since an individual who is deemed an unwitting tool of God's will or an object of inexorable historical forces cannot, without some philosophical reconciliation, be blamed or praised for his actions. Still, moral judgment involves a methodological question as well: Is it the historian's task to evaluate the character and actions of his subjects, or does his discipline demand a commitment to impartiality? As we shall see, most Jewish historians have not withheld judgment, especially when dealing with matters about which they felt strongly. Their religious or ideological convictions have almost invariably left an imprint upon their historical writings.

Periodization, though once again not unrelated to the question of causality, is more strictly a historiographical issue, arising from the need to establish some temporal framework within which to arrange historical data. In the history of nations, a period may be defined by a war, the reign of a ruler, a cultural efflorescence, a religious transformation, or an economic crisis. In Jewish history, too, it has been necessary to locate natural divisions in the long course of the Jewish past. But the task of Jewish historians has been especially difficult. Because Jews have lived simultaneously under a variety of political, economic, and social conditions, no single scheme of periodization can do full justice to the historical experience of Jews in all the lands of their dispersion. The expulsion of the Jews from Spain in 1492 was without question of crucial and long-term significance for Sephardic Jewry, but it represented no watershed for the Jews in Germany. The French Revolution, in some respects a turning point for West-European Jewry, was of little immediate consequence to the far larger concentration of Jews living in Poland and Russia. Periodizing Jewish history has, therefore, been a hazardous venture with results that can never be fully satisfactory. Yet the directly opposite alternative to a single scheme, namely, separate periodizations for Jewish communities in different lands, destroys the possibility of a unified treatment. No major Jewish historian has yet chosen that extreme.

The general problem of periodization leads us necessarily to the issues specific to the historiography of the Jews. Once the Jews became scattered among the nations—a process which began long before they ceased to exist as a national entity in Palestine—their history no longer possessed the unity of a nation dwelling upon its own soil. In the ancient world, Alexandrian Jewry came to differ radically from the Jewry of Palestine, medieval Jewish communities existing under Islamic rule from those in Christian lands, Jews in modern Germany from those in Czarist Russia, and today Israeli Jewry from Jews in America. Jewish historians have had to search for the common bond which united Jews undergoing very different historical experiences. We may call this the problem of spatial connection. The answers to it have been varying and contradictory.

Equally basic to any conception of Jewish history is the question of continuity in time. Given geographical dispersion, wide variations in cultural development, and distinct differences in Jewish self-definition, the Jewish historian has been pressed to come up with some thread running the entire length of Jewish history from Abraham to the present, some belief or hope or form of consciousness which was always and everywhere present. Without such a thread of continuity it has often seemed that Jewish history would break apart into discrete segments, geographically and temporally divided portions of an irreparably fragmented whole. The threads of continuity which have been chosen were in each instance determined by the way a particular historian viewed the nature of the entity he was studying. Thus, the first modern Jewish historians, living in Germany at a time when Judaism was being redefined in purely religious terms, saw Jewish history as the history of a religious idea, while later writers, of the period of Jewish nationalism, determined that the subject of Jewish history was the people itself and not its religious faith. Continuity was thus achieved by declaring a certain religious or moral idea consistently present or by deciding that the Jews unfailingly preserved the subjective attributes of nationhood.

But even today the question of definition, and hence of continuity, remains unsettled. Contemporary confusion and disagreement about who the Jews are in the present have also prevented any common view of their past. Indeed, it seems most likely that the wide variety of conceptions which have been formulated until now will spawn an increasing number of variations in the years ahead.

The first Jewish historians whose work has come down to us were the writers who composed and edited the historical sections of the Bible. Most likely drawing upon earlier written and oral accounts, they produced a coherent narrative of the origins of the world and of the history of Israel down to their time. We find their work in the books of Joshua, Judges, Samuel, Kings, Ezra, Nehemiah, and Chronicles as well as in the narrative portions of the Pentateuch and other biblical books. Their writing reveals a philosophy of history strikingly original in the Near Eastern context and of long-term influence upon the historical thinking of the Western world.

A particular historiographical tradition did exist in the empires of Mesopotamia and Egypt long before the time of the biblical writers. It produced historical writings that may be divided into three principal categories: king lists, which present the royal succession and sometimes relate the major events of each reign; annals describing the exploits of a particular monarch year by year; and detailed accounts of victorious military campaigns. The authors seem to have been scribes in the service of the ruler, men whose principal task it was to record the glory of their master for posterity. Their writings present the official view of events; they record only victories, never defeats. At no time do they criticize their sovereign or presume to render judgment upon his deeds. The victories and successes which they recount are invariably ascribed to the greatness of the rulers and of the deities who favor them. Indeed, it is often the king himself who relates the events in the first person. No attempt is made to comprehend the events according to any religious principle which might give meaning to disaster as well as to triumph.

Such official chronicles seem to have existed in ancient Israel, too, but they have not been preserved. The "Acts of Solomon," the "Chronicle of the Kings of Israel," and the "Chronicle of the Kings of Judah," which are mentioned in the Bible, probably belonged to the typical Near Eastern genre. What is remarkable is that the biblical historians broke so completely with this pervasive historiographical tradition and produced a radically different conception of history based on their unique religious faith.

This faith rested upon a single God who controlled the destinies of all nations, yet had established a special relationship with His chosen people. Though transcendent, He entered directly into history in order to reveal His will, to reward and to punish. Given moral responsibility to choose between obedience to God's commands and rejection of them, human beings were regarded as free historical agents, but the outcome of their actions—victory and defeat, success and failure—was invariably to be explained as God's response to their deeds: as reward for a pleasing act, as punishment for an offense.

Although rulers continue to play a central role in biblical historiography and to serve as a basis for periodization, the subject of Israelite history—in contrast to the rest of the ancient Near East—is the people as a whole; their consciousness of God provides continuity from Abraham onward, despite changing forms of political existence (cf. Neh. 9:6-37). Because of its special relationship to God, Israel stands at the very center of human history. The other nations exist principally as instruments by which God may exercise His will upon Israel; the significance of their history is contained in that of Israel.

The biblical historians are best understood as men of religion who were not interested in historical events for their own sake. They were mainly content to leave details of battles and the like to courtly writers of annals. Their criterion of significance was a religious one. They wanted to show from the experience of the past that God was faithful to His covenant, that He punished the wicked and rewarded the good, whether they were kings or common men or the people as a whole. History thus came to assume immense meaning as the arena in which faith was subjected to continuous trial. It was also invested with an a priori explanatory principle for every major event: Israel suffered defeat only when it had sinned; it was victorious in battle only when it had been upright before God. The biblical writers viewed history as the ongoing illustration of religious truth. Here God's relation to Israel, established in the days of the Patriarchs and renewed at Sinai, was ever verified anew. It is thus not surprising that Moses, speaking in the desert shortly before his death, should have exhorted the people never to forget its past:

> Remember the days of old,
> Consider the years of many generations;
> Ask thy father, and he will declare unto thee,
> Thine elders, and they will tell thee (Deut. 32:7).

By enabling the people to remember, the biblical historians were performing a sacred task; they were proving through history the faithfulness of their God.

In the Greek world this close connection between history and ultimate truth simply did not exist. Hellenic religion was focused upon a pantheon of deities who frequently quarreled with one another and sometimes used men to further their conflicting ambitions. Mortals might strive to appease the gods and attempt to divine their desires, but they could never be certain of their favor. History, far from being the response to a single known Divine will, consisted only of the chaotic schemings of gods and men. It possessed no fixed structure. Even the later philosophical tradition introduced no change in this regard. It, too, ascribed no ultimate significance to history. For Plato the realm of truth lay beyond history in the eternal and unchanging world of ideas; salvation came through thought and contemplation, not through historical deed. So, too, Aristotle's god, the "unmoved mover," existed apart from history, exercising no moral will upon it. It is not surprising, therefore, that the Greek philosophers could find little cognitive value in a discipline which spoke only of the specific and never rose to the level of the universal concept. Even the arts, though outside the realm of philosophical thought, represented a higher level of significance. In his *Poetics* Aristotle wrote:

> The distinction between historian and poet is not in the one writing prose and the other verse—you might put the work of Herodotus into verse, and it would still be a species of history; it consists really in this, that the one describes the thing that has been, and the other a kind of thing that might be. Hence poetry is something more philosophic and of graver import than history, since its statements are of the nature rather of universals whereas those of history are singulars.

Yet, because the Greeks separated religion and philosophy from history, they were able to develop a historiographical tradition very different from that of the Bible and much closer to the historical writing of modern times. Since the historical world was subject to no prior religious principle of explanation, Greek historians could develop a historiography based upon inquiry rather than illustration. Moreover, as men of predominantly secular concerns, they could turn their attention to the details of political and military events, hoping thereby to serve the leadership of their city-states.

While they did recognize the force of a supervening fate upon the outcome of events, they focused upon the multifaceted world of human affairs. Emptying the historical realm of transcendent meaning, the Greek historians began to investigate it independently of any religious considerations and thus to lay the foundations of a secular historiography. In the instance of Herodotus (early fifth century B.C.E.) the shadow of the gods still loomed over human history and there was little escape from the force of destiny. But a generation later the far more secular Thucydides scarcely attributed any determinative influence to gods, oracles, omens, and the like. With remarkable psychological insight, he delved into the motivations of his protagonists, realizing that the reasons men gave for their actions were seldom their real motives.

No Jewish historians were influenced directly by the Hellenic model. Sustained contact between the Greek and Hebrew worlds did not come until the Hellenistic period and following Alexander the Great's conquest of the Near East. But although Hellenistic and later Roman historiography was less exclusively political and military, serving to edify by example as well as to explain, it did transmit, as well, the heritage of Herodotus and Thucydides. Some aspects of that heritage can be detected in the first post-biblical work of Jewish history, the book of I Maccabees, written some time after 135 B.C.E. Here is a sober account limited almost exclusively to a detailed narrative of military and political events. Unlike much of the Bible, this apocryphal work does not dwell upon miracles; God is remote from the narrative. Nor does the author explicitly ascribe the victory of the Maccabees to their faith in God, although he doubtless believed in its efficacy. In fact he is so reluctant to speak directly of God that he does not even mention Him by name, preferring "Heaven" or "He." Thus, both in terms of his focus of interest and his approach, the anonymous author bears distinct evidence of Greek historiographical influence.

II Maccabees, probably written about the same time, is in certain respects closer to biblical historiography and in others more distant. As in the Bible, God intervenes directly and miraculously in history; He punishes sin and maintains a special relationship with Israel. Religious matters play a more prominent role here than they do in I Maccabees: the gruesome martyrdom of a mother and her seven sons who refuse to eat swine's flesh receives particularly dramatic treatment. Yet in other respects II Maccabees moves away from the biblical mode. Here for the first time a Jewish historian addresses his readers directly and explains to them the purpose of his work. Like the Hellenistic writers, he wishes to edify and even to entertain. Thus, although his conception of Jewish history is traditional, the form he employs is distinctly Greek.

It is not, however, until the first century C.E. that we have a Jewish historian who is fully heir to the traditions of Greco-Roman historiography. Josephus Flavius, onetime Judean general and later imperial pensioner at the Roman court, for the first time among Jews explicitly puts forward the goal of historical truth for its own sake. He thus sets his work sharply apart from both the biblical writers who precede him and from all subsequent Jewish historical writing until the modern epoch.

Josephus sought to understand the events he portrayed without reference to a religious framework. He does state his belief in God's providence and His punishment of the wicked, and he can hardly avoid referring to God when he presents the history of the biblical period in his *Antiquities,* but wherever possible God's direct action is minimized. Thus, confronted with the explicit biblical account of the sea dividing before the children of Israel, Josephus feels compelled to make some excuse:

> For my part, I have recounted each detail here told me just as I found it in the sacred books. Nor let anyone marvel at the astonishing nature of the narrative or doubt that it was given to men of old, innocent of crime, to find a road of salvation through the sea itself, whether by the will of God or maybe by accident, seeing that the hosts of Alexander, king of Macedon, men born but the other day, beheld the Pamphylian Sea retire before them and, when other road there was none, offer a passage through itself, what time it pleased God to overthrow the Persian empire; and on that all are agreed who have recorded Alexander's exploits. However on these matters everyone is welcome to his own opinion.

Moses, in Josephus' account, is not merely the servant of the Lord, bringing His word to the people. Instead, he appears as lawgiver, statesman, philosopher, and military hero. Perhaps Josephus purposely transposed biblical history into terms more readily comprehensible to his Greco-Roman readers, but it is also possible that he had himself come to view the history of Israel as following a pattern little different from that of other nations.

While Josephus reiterates his impartiality and quest for truth, the account he presents of his own time bears evidence of two ulterior concerns: to justify the actions of Rome and to vindicate himself. Invariably, he judges Roman intentions and methods as both noble and humane in putting down the Judean revolt. Despite contrary evidence, he contends that the Temple was burned *against* the will of Titus, the Roman general. He invariably blames extremist factions among the Jews for bringing suffering upon their people, while portraying his own defection from the Judean cause in a fashion that not only clears him of any charge of treason or military incompetence, but makes it appear that he was motivated by concern for the common good. His description of his rival, John of Gischala, as "the most unscrupulous and crafty of all who have ever gained notoriety by such infamous means," gives clear evidence of his inability to free himself from his passions. Yet when he deals with events in which he did not himself directly participate he is indeed capable of a high degree of impartiality. Even Eleazar, the leader of the extremist Sicarii holding out to the end against the Romans at Masada, is furnished with a noble and eloquent speech in which he exhorts his followers to choose martyrdom over surrender.

Josephus' work, though standing out as a major application of Greco-Roman historiographical method to Jewish history, does suffer from a failure to adhere to the highest standards of that method. His writing lacks the depth of insight which characterized Thucydides; it mostly confines itself to a relation of surface events in their chronological sequence. Josephus fails to probe underlying forces, and he is unable to distinguish a datum of major significance from one with little historical effect. His great advance over biblical historiography is that he draws causality into the sphere of the human and frees it from the religious drama of reward and punishment; he does not, however, display an awareness of causal complexity.

Josephus' interest in the empirical truths of history could find no emulation in the centuries that followed, either among Christians or among Jews. With the triumph of Christianity in the Mediterranean world, attention was increasingly drawn away from the temporal sphere to the eternal, from this world to the next. Eyes turned up toward heaven, ceasing to glance backward or forward along the continuum of profane events. The most extreme formulation of this otherworldliness was given by the third-century bishop Tertullian who insisted: "Now that Jesus Christ has come, no longer do we need curiously to inquire, or even to investigate. . . . To be ignorant of everything outside the rule of faith is to possess all knowledge."

To a great extent Tertullian's attitude was shared a century later by the much more influential Saint Augustine whose writings left the deepest imprint upon Christian thought during the medieval period. In dividing the universe into an earthly city of the flesh characterized by the love of self and a heavenly one of the spirit marked by the love of God, Augustine bifurcated man's historical life. Secular existence was seen to be rooted in the earthly city, religious life in the heavenly one. The supreme good for man was to renounce the *civitas terrena* and strive through life in the church to anticipate as fully as possible a future life in the eternal City of God. Necessarily, a true Christian whose desire was to flee the profane world, whose life on earth was to be "rather called death than life," could hardly be expected to take any serious interest in the history of that world. The one significant historical event had already occurred with the coming of Jesus Christ. Moreover, all men were predestined to sin and some were predestined to be saved by the grace of God. Thus history could not assume the profound religious meaning that it had possessed in the Hebrew Bible. As Augustine's otherworldly ideal began noticeably to wane in intellectual circles only toward the end of the Middle Ages, the Christian environment could provide medieval European Jewry with no stimulus to be concerned with its own nonsacred past. And in the East, too, where the Sassanian and later the Muslim civilizations were likewise basically uninterested in understanding the course of profane events (though the Muslims lavished much attention on genealogies), Jewish thinkers received no outside impetus to study their history beyond the biblical period.

There were, however, internal reasons as well for the Jews' turning away from contemporary history; for them, too—but for other reasons—history had ceased to possess clear meaning. The last centuries before the Common Era witness the rise of an apocalyptic tendency in Judaism which produces such works as Enoch, Syriac Barukh, and some of the Dead Sea Scrolls. The authors of these works, despairing of their own age, share the belief that evil presently reigns in this world and therefore that their own time is removed from God. Yet their purposeful distance from the present is balanced by the conviction that the end of the rule of wickedness will soon be at hand, history as presently known will be violently consummated, and a new aeon, lived in direct relation to God, will commence. The apocalyptic writers turn their attention to the End and to the mysterious signs which herald its coming. When they do refer to history, their words are veiled in the language of allegory, as in the book of Daniel, which is the closest approximation of apocalypse in the Hebrew Bible. History is not a realm of significant human action or of collective moral consequence. God has determined its course in advance. The End of Days must come at the time which God has preordained for it.

The dominant Pharisaic tradition, which became normative for medieval Judaism, was not, however, apocalyptic. The Pharisees and their successors, the Rabbis, did not put their faith in the mystical vision of a cataclysmic End of Days as did the apocalyptic sectarians. In fact, they discouraged such speculations. Nor did they view history as preordained. Although they did elaborate a concept of life after death, their attachment to the life of the Written and Oral Law bound them fast to a this-worldly existence in the service of God. But for the Rabbis as well, the historical events of their own time came to assume a lesser importance than they had for the biblical authors.

After the destruction of the Second Temple by the Romans in 70 C.E. and the loss of political independence, Israel ceased to be the subject of history in the normal sense. It was no longer a force among nations but a scattered people without a political or cultic focus. The *halakhah*, Jewish law, in a sense became the Jew's City of God, and the city of men became as alien to his religious consciousness as it was to Saint Augustine. The destruction of the Temple, which was ascribed to Israel's sinfulness, came to serve as a dividing line between an earlier sacred history in which God's will had been clearly manifest and the following period in which God had distanced Himself from His people, punishing them for their sins. Thus the Rabbis lavished their attention upon the biblical narratives, elaborating them with midrash and fanciful commentary, but they paid little attention to the historical events which followed. Bereft of a continuing political history extending into their own time, they immersed themselves in the sacred history of a closed period which they continually experienced anew.

Yet even their biblical studies testify to a distinctly nonhistorical view of the past. The Rabbis seem to have possessed no conception of the development of ideas or institutions; they were willing to assume that the Patriarchs adhered to a Judaism little different from their own. So, too, they insisted that the Oral Law embodied in the Talmud, no less than the written word of the Torah, had its origins at Sinai. When medieval Jews turned to historical narratives of the Bible, it was to find support by concrete example for their own religious and ethical concepts.

The principal Jewish creation of the early Middle Ages, the Talmud, therefore confines its historical interest to anecdotes, some with a basis in fact and some without, but it presents no integrated narrative. Only in the unique tractate "Ethics of the Fathers" are we presented with a chain of tradition by which the law was transmitted through the generations from Moses down to Rabbi Judah the Prince, compiler of the Mishnah. Outside the Talmud, one chronological work was written, probably in the second century C.E., called *Seder Olam* ("The Order of the World"). It calculates the dates of major biblical events and for the first time establishes a chronology according to the creation of the world; a final summary chapter briefly notes, as well, events from Alexander the Great to the Bar Kokhba revolt of 132–135 C.E. The author, presumed to be R. Yose ben Halafta, gives no explicit reason for writing the book. However, his endeavor to establish a single consistent chronology, reconciling apparent variations in the biblical text, would place his work very much in the rabbinic tradition of seeking to resolve scriptural contradictions which might otherwise create some doubt about the accuracy of the text. Though he confined himself almost entirely to biblical history, mixed chronicle with midrash, and sometimes departed from chronological sequence, the author of *Seder Olam* did evince a desire to establish a sequential framework for Jewish history. His concern was unusual for that time. With the exception of the *Seder Olam Zuta* ("Small Order of the World") of uncertain date, which carries its chronology to the Jewish Babylonia of the sixth century, there are virtually no works like it for the next eight centuries. For the most part, historical considerations remained inessential to the rabbinic view of the world.

The Jewish philosophers of the Middle Ages were hardly more interested in Jewish history than were the halakhists. The best known of them, Moses Maimonides, shared his mentor Aristotle's contemptuous attitude toward historical study. He deemed it "a sheer waste of time," which produced neither wisdom for the mind nor profit for the body. His view of the Jewish past was in general uncritical, enabling him to accept those legends and fanciful elaborations of the Bible which did not overtly contradict philosophical principles. He did have some knowledge of Jewish history and he attributed an importance to chronological sequence which was unusual for his time. But Maimonides did not devote himself to writing Jewish history nor to developing a comprehensive idea of its nature.

For Judah Halevi, the twelfth-century philosopher and poet, Jewish history was of considerably greater significance. In his *Kuzari*, Halevi developed a biblical, and hence historical rather than philosophical, foundation for Jewish faith. He based his claim for the truth of Judaism upon the public revelation at Sinai, witnessed, according to biblical account, by 600,000 Israelites. According to Halevi, the presence of God descended upon the Jewish people and gave it a religious preeminence which makes the special governance of Divine Providence a unique possession of Israel until the messianic age. But though, like the biblical writers, Halevi attributed redemptive meaning to history, he was, again like them, interested in history only as the most telling argument for religious truth, not in history for its own sake. God's relationship to Israel he found illustrated by the period of ancient prophecy in the Land of Israel and by the promise of messianic redemption. The detailed history of the Jews lying between these points of origin and goal—the Diaspora—was for him, no less than for his contemporaries, of merely peripheral concern.

Only in the tenth century is there a revival of interest in nonbiblical history, marked by the appearance of a number of historical and semihistorical works. Yet these writings are of very different kinds and were prompted by unrelated considerations.

Most scholars are agreed that the book of *Josippon* was composed in Southern Italy about 950. Its anonymous author, a man of apparently broad erudition, drew upon a Latin translation of Josephus and other sources to present a Hebrew account mainly of the period of the Second Temple. He claimed to have done no more than to excerpt and translate his sources: "I have collected stories from the book of Joseph b. Gorion [Josephus Flavius] and from the books of other authors who wrote down the deeds of our ancestors and I compiled them in one scroll." Yet in the process, the author did inject his own variations; in particular, he expressed far greater sympathy for the Judeans in their battle against the Romans than had Josephus. In the course of time, his work became immensely popular, especially in an expanded edition of the twelfth century which added legendary material. The writing of the book does not attest to the revival of a historiographical tradition within medieval Jewry, but the wide readership it attracted does reflect a greater interest in the post-biblical Jewish past.

A very different motive prompted the *Igeret Rav Sherira Gaon,* a letter written in 987 by the head of the Babylonian academy in Pumbedita. It is unlikely that Rav Sherira would have delved into Jewish history at all were it not for the arrival of a question addressed to him by the community of Kairouan in North Africa. He was asked for information regarding the correct succession of the tradition and how the Talmud came to be written. Though no explicit reason for the inquiry is given, it seems not to have been prompted by idle curiosity. More likely, it was a response to the polemical challenge of the Karaites. For more than a century, the schismatic Karaite movement had been dividing Islamic Jewry into Rabbanites, who maintained the continuity and reliability of the Oral tradition, and Karaites, who accepted only the written Torah as the word of God. Already a hundred years earlier a new work of chronology, the *Seder Tannaim ve-Amoraim* ("The Order of the Talmudic Authorities") had sought to legitimize Rabbanite claims. During the following generations vigorous polemics were carried on between the two factions. The question to Rav Sherira was in all likelihood motivated by the need to refute Karaite arguments against rabbinic tradition. Sherira's reply is therefore little more than a laconic presentation of the claim of succession, which supplies the relevant names and dates. But this was just the information that was sought. His responsum achieved great currency and became the model for similar chains of tradition, such as Abraham ibn Daud's *Book of Tradition* of 1160–1161, and others that were composed as late as the sixteenth century.

Still other considerations underlie additional works preserved from this period. Ahimaaz ben Paltiel, the author of the *Chronicle of Ahimaaz* and the scion of a proud and influential family in Southern Italy, recounted in verse the exploits of his illustrious ancestors. Nathan ha-Bavli, in a contemporary chronicle of which only fragments are extant, described the institutions of Babylonian Jewry as they existed in the tenth century, and detailed the disputes which flared up among its leaders.

In Ashkenazic Jewry during this period we find none of these types of historical writing. When we do encounter a form of historiography among German Jews in the eleventh century, it stems from intentions quite apart from those which brought forth the *Josippon, The Chronicle of Ahimaaz,* and the chains of tradition in the Sephardic world. German Jewry was awakened to historical consciousness by a shattering event which left it in need of accounting and explanation: the First Crusade of 1096. The chronicles which have been preserved recounting the massacres crusaders wrought upon the Jewish communities of the Rhineland dwell upon attack, attempts at escape and self-defense, and martyrdom. Their authors were motivated by the desire to commemorate the courage of that generation as an example to their readers and to provide a theological justification for the innocent victims. A similar account was written when the Second Crusade of 1146 once more forced martyrdom upon the Jews. Thus it was catastrophe, suddenly impinging devastatingly upon lives otherwise impervious to the course of history around them, that called the Jews' attention to the events of their own time. But the interest was strictly ephemeral. As far as we know, Northern European Jewry for centuries thereafter evinced little curiosity in its own physical or literary history. Only occasionally did it recount new instances of persecution and note the names of martyrs and the genealogy of scholars in *Memorbücher,* books of recollection, such as were kept by various Jewish communities in Germany.

Not until the sixteenth century do we witness a revival of Jewish historical writing. It is prompted by two new factors, one an event within Jewish history and one an influence from the outside: the expulsion of the Jews from Spain and the impact of the Renaissance.

Just as the Crusade massacres had abruptly drawn the attention of Ashkenazic Jewry to an external world impinging upon their fate, so the traumatic expulsion from Spain in 1492 aroused among the Sephardim a need to recount and explain the ensuing dislocation and suffering. This great anguish in their own time led Jewish writers to collect accounts of other persecutions which Israel had suffered in generations past. Awareness of them would intensify the longing for an end to the Diaspora and make even more fervent the Jews' hopes for the Messiah. Joseph ha-Kohen recounted these sufferings in a work he called *The Vale of Tears,* written in 1558. He explained his choice of title in this way:

> I have called it *The Vale of Tears* for that is its content. Whoever reads it will gasp with astonishment; tears will roll down from his eyes. He will put his hands on his hips and exclaim: "How much longer, O Lord! I will

entreat my God that the days of our sorrow come to an end and He send our righteous Messiah to redeem us speedily for the sake of His mercy."

About halfway through the text, Joseph interrupts the narrative to set forth his reasons for writing the volume:

The expulsions from France and this bitter and impetuous expulsion [from Spain] aroused me to compose this book so that the children of Israel might know what they did to us in their lands, their courts, and their castles. For, behold, days will come!

The same desire to assuage the pain of suffering and kindle the messianic hope for a sudden reversal of Jewish fortunes also prompted Samuel Usque to compose his *Consolation for the Tribulations of Israel*, written in Portuguese and published at Ferrara in 1553. By linking the biblical prophecies of doom with succeeding events, Usque perpetuated the traditional notion that Israel suffered for its sins, but he also called attention to events down to his own time as the fulfillment of God's will. The prophecies of consolation he associated with the coming redemption, especially in the concluding section of his work where he did not hesitate to alter biblical verses to make them refer specifically to the present. Usque's work still fits entirely within the traditional theological scheme of causality. Though dealing with the past, it remains untouched by the secularization of historical writing which was advancing in the surrounding intellectual world of the Renaissance.

The Italian Renaissance could not, however, fail to have an effect upon the Sephardic Jews living in Italy. The Italian humanists, who sought to free themselves from the intellectual shackles of medievalism by reasserting the norms of the classical world, had rediscovered as well the Greco-Roman tradition of historiography. Their historical writing soon took on a sophistication which set it clearly apart from earlier chronicles. They abandoned the medieval habit of seeking supernatural causes for historical events and instead began probing the motives of men. Unlike their immediate predecessors in the writing of history, the Renaissance historians were not secluded monks; they were politicians and diplomats intimately familiar with worldly affairs. The best known of them, Machiavelli, employed totally secular explanations in trying to understand the history of his native Florence. As non-Jewish historiography was thus desacralized and serious attempts made to conceive the past in terms of an immanent causality, Jewish writers who came within the Renaissance orbit were influenced to revise their own conception of history. The Renaissance impact made itself felt in a broadening of historical horizons, in a turn to secular interpretation, in historical criticism of traditional texts, and in a new regard for chronological sequence.

In the earlier period, with very few exceptions, Jews had not devoted themselves to studying the history of the nations in which they lived. In the sixteenth century, however, such an interest became widespread. Under the influence of the Renaissance and prompted by a variety of considerations—some messianic, some secular—Jews produced in Hebrew a number of works of general history. On the island of Crete, Elijah Capsali wrote histories of both Venice (1517) and the Ottoman Empire (1523) in which specifically Jewish matters alternate with non-Jewish affairs. In Italy in 1554, Joseph ha-Kohen published a history of the kings of France and Turkey. And toward the end of the century, in Prague, David Gans issued a Hebrew chronicle of world history from the Creation to his own time. To be sure, this widening of historical horizons within the Jewish community still faced the opposition of narrower minds and was deemed of only the slightest consequence when compared to halakhic studies. But because the histories of other nations could be viewed with less theological presupposition than that of Israel, increased awareness of them must have played a role in the eventual secularization of Jewish history as well.

The first traces of such secularization can be found in the work of Solomon ibn Verga. Like Usque's Consolation, his Shevet Yehuda ("The Staff of Judah"), written during the 1520's, devotes attention to persecutions of the Jews; and he, too, in the first instance acknowledges Divine punishment as their cause. But he is willing to move beyond theological explanations and to suggest the relevance of secular factors in explaining these catastrophes. In two instances he proposes that, at least in part, Jews themselves directly brought on persecution by their pretentious, envy-inspiring behavior. His enumeration of multiple causes indicates a desire to approach a pressing historical question from something larger than a single predetermined viewpoint. It marks the beginning of investigative probing into the dynamics of Jewish history. God's providence is no longer a sufficient explanation. Living among the nations whose own histories allow of secular explanation, Israel, too, is subject to the human factors that determine the course of events. Recounting its history, therefore, demands a devotion to seeking out empirical truth. Thus, alongside the motives of consolation, theodicy, and literary enjoyment, there emerges the desire to present an accurate account. Introducing his work on the general and Jewish history of the Ottoman Empire, Elijah Capsali announces in the tenor of Josephus: "I proclaim with certainty to the Tribes of Israel that my mouth will speak truth in all of the tales which I shall recount; I shall not turn to lies."

Until this time Jewish writers had made little distinction between fact and legend. The two are seamlessly interwoven in works like *Josippon* and the *Chronicle of Ahimaaz*. It is only in the sixteenth century that Azariah dei Rossi, the first truly critical Jewish scholar of the modern period, makes the effort to separate them. Rossi's historical work, more than that of his contemporaries, clearly reflects the inquiring spirit of the Renaissance. In his *Meor Enayim* ("Light to the Eyes") we find the same criticism of venerated texts as in Lorenzo Valla's attack upon the authenticity of the Donation of Constantine, which allegedly had bestowed secular power upon the Church. In the process of investigating a problem in Jewish history, he draws abundantly upon non-Jewish sources, even when they seriously question accepted beliefs. He impugns the reliability of unsubstantiated legendary material within the rabbinic literature and finds reason to cast grave doubt upon the accuracy of the chronology accepted by the Rabbis. His work was sufficently controversial to encounter severe opposition on the part of Jewish leaders, though mostly outside of Italy. Yet in many ways Rossi's book was closer to earlier Jewish writings than to the historiography of secular Renaissance historians. He still believed in miracles and that history was the manifestation of God's will; he did not attempt to produce a connected narrative, but only to solve certain problems that perplexed him. The importance of his book lies in the novel elements it contains, as an example of the inroads made by the critical temperament of the Renaissance upon an essentially medieval mind.

In Eastern Europe the Renaissance spirit eventually reached cities like Cracow and Prague, which experienced an efflorescence of the sciences and arts. For the Jews in Poland and Bohemia the sixteenth century was likewise a period of great creativity. Though their writings were mostly limited to the traditional realm of Jewish law, here, too, there was a spark of interest in astronomy, mathematics, and history. In 1592 David Gans, who had combined secular learning with extensive study of Talmudic law, published in Prague a two-part chronicle consisting of Jewish and world history. Perhaps as a result of his mathematical training, he chose to emphasize precise dates and exact chronological sequence, thus putting all the facts at his disposal into a neat order. In this respect he differed from writers like ibn Verga, Usque, and the earlier medieval chroniclers who had not consistently presented their material in chronological sequence. Gans gave the Jewish past a definite temporal framework stretching from Creation to the year of his work's publication. Content was on the whole restricted to names, books, and instances of persecution, and he pointed to no causal connections among the facts he inserted in their proper slots. But his chronology did provide a structure. What was early and what was late could no longer be so easily confused.

The following two centuries witness no major advances in the writing of Jewish history. In Eastern Europe, political strife and economic decline are accompanied by spiritual stagnation; the period of greatest creativity is past. A firmly traditional outlook upon the world, rooted in Jewish law and tradition, comes to dominate a community dwelling within an intellectually unchallenging environment. After Gans, there is little further historiographical innovation, only a few additional examples of traditional forms: thus, the massacres at the time of Chmielnicki's Cossack revolt in 1648 call forth Nathan Hannover's narrative account, *Yeven Metzula* ("Deep Mire"). But basically the Jew in Eastern Europe retains the medieval conception that only biblical history is directly revelatory of God's plan and that, for the present age, elaboration of His law, not a study of worldly events, is the proper manner of doing His will.

In Western Europe also there are fewer works dealing with history and no important advances. Only in the nineteenth century did Jews begin to produce integrated and comprehensive histories, not merely fragments or chains of tradition. The first such all-embracing account was in fact published by a Gentile. Beginning in 1706, Jacques Basnage, a French Protestant living in exile in Holland, brought out a history of the Jews from the time of Jesus to his own. His *L'histoire et la réligion des Juifs,* intended as a continuation of Josephus, served for more than a century as a basic historical source for both Jews and Christians.

Even increasing exposure to the European Enlightenment of

the eighteenth century could not awaken serious interest among Jews either in their own history or in that of their host countries. To some extent they did take pleasure in the iconoclasm of writers like Voltaire whose historical works cast obloquy upon the Christian Middle Ages and the power of the Church. But the chief appeal of the Enlightenment lay in its search for liberation from the past. To the Jew entering the modern world, history was a divisive force separating and differentiating him from the surrounding society in which he now sought acceptance. History recalled the alleged role of the Jews in the crucifixion of Jesus, as well as the various crimes of which Jews had been accused throughout the Middle Ages: well poisonings, blood murder, and the like. History also depicted the Jews as living isolated within their own world—an image the acculturating stratum of Western Jewry wanted forgotten. Little wonder, therefore, that the intellectual appeal of the Enlightenment for the Jews lay in its philosophy and literature, not in its historiography. The philosophically based natural religion which dominated the thought of the eighteenth century provided universal truths that could be shared by Jews and Christians. Thus the chief figure of the Jewish Enlightenment in Germany, Moses Mendelssohn, was drawn to a variety of intellectual pursuits, but could muster no enthusiasm for the study of history. His spiritual disciples, who published *Ha-Measef,* the first important Hebrew periodical, were likewise basically uninterested in history. Their general concerns ran to the sciences and poetry. Among Jewish subjects, biblical studies were their main preoccupation. Their closest approximation to history lay in the biographies they wrote of prominent individuals—from Moses Maimonides to Mendelssohn himself—who might serve as exemplars of enlightened Judaism for their own time.

It was not until the nineteenth century that a reflective conception of Jewish history became central to the consciousness of the Jew. The reasons for this new concern lay first of all in a transformation of the cultural environment. The Romantic movement which gradually replaced the Enlightenment at the beginning of the century came to regard as shallow and inadequate whatever was grounded in man's reasoning faculties alone. Genuine truth was now seen to inhere in the historical experience of mankind and to be reflected variously in different cultures. Writers in the fields of theology, literature, politics, and philosophy all sought to root their doctrines in the soil of the past. Values and concepts were seen to have evolved gradually from distant origins via a continuous and organic process of growth. Proper conclusions could be drawn only from a controlled, empirical examination of available data, guided by maximum objectivity. Whereas philosophy, independent of any historical foundation, had reigned supreme in Germany during the Enlightenment, the new ideal of *Wissenschaft*, scholarly discipline, came to dominate intellectual life by the 1820's.

In relation to historical study, *Wissenschaft* meant first of all the application of critical philological methods to the source materials of the past. Beyond this, it meant a reluctance to deliver easy judgments on former ages, a hesitation to declare one period superior to another as the writers of the Enlightenment had done. For Leopold Ranke, the leading German historian of his age, the disinclination to praise or to blame produced a non-evaluative attitude where "each period is immediate to God" and hence to be judged by no external standard; the historian seeks only to show what actually happened.

The first Jew consciously to apply the approach of *Wissenschaft* to Jewish studies was Leopold Zunz. Early in his career he insisted upon the importance of investigating the Jewish past for its own sake, without regard for its relevance to the present. Jewish literature, he wrote, should be studied "in its fullest compass as an object of research, without worrying whether the total contents should be or can be also a norm for our own judgments." When he came to write a brief biography of Rashi, the foremost of the medieval Jewish commentators, he insisted on understanding him in terms of Rashi's own eleventh century, ridiculing other writers who had tried to make him into a modern man. However Zunz remained basically a philologist rather than an historian, devoting himself principally to rediscovering, identifying, and analyzing the Jewish literature of the Middle Ages.

The ideal of *Wissenschaft* alone was insufficient to produce a synthetic conception of Jewish history. Another element was needed, and it was supplied in the first instance by a new current in German philosophy: the system of historically grounded metaphysical idealism, beginning with Herder on the eve of the nineteenth century and achieving its most developed form in Hegel. What was most important in idealistic philosophy for awakening a conscious attempt to grasp the Jewish past as a totality was the conception of history as taking place fundamentally in the realm of ideas: of basic consequence were not events but the development of human thought. Within such a view of world history, the history of the Jews, though bereft of a normal national character, could be understood to play a significant role in the advance of the human spirit as the bearer of its own peculiar idea.

In 1819, when a group of Jewish university students in Berlin (some of whom had been pupils of Hegel) gathered to form a society for the purpose of propagating culture and a disciplined study of Judaism among their fellow Jews, they necessarily considered what the significance of Jewish existence could be in the present, based upon a particular understanding of the role played by Judaism in history. One of their number, Immanuel Wolf, composed a document, "On the Concept of a Science of Judaism," which not only affirmed the importance of applying the approach of *Wissenschaft* to the Jewish domain, but also declared that Jewish history was essentially the development of a single, unique religious idea: the idea of the unity of God. This idea of the one God stood at the beginning of Israel's history though it was realized only imperfectly by the Jews themselves. The course of Jewish history became the constant struggle of the idea to develop within the Jewish consciousness and to attain universality; the historical existence of the people was determined by its role as the bearer of the idea. Because Jewish history was not basically concerned with political institutions, the collapse of the Jewish state did not sever the continuity of development. The idea was carried forward regardless of material circumstances (though adverse external events might hinder its full understanding). Thus Wolf was able to contradict Hegel within the latter's own sphere of discourse by arguing that Judaism did not represent, as the philosopher held, an idea of limited importance which had been fully realized and superseded long ago, but an idea "founded on the essence of humanity itself" and hence of the greatest significance and importance for the thinking spirit even in the present.

The conception of Jewish history as the history of a religious idea possessed another appeal as well, aside from that afforded by its conformity with intellectual fashion. The nineteenth century was the period during which German Jewry, gradually and not without setbacks, gained political emancipation and the status of civil equality. One of the principal obstacles in the path of full rights was the belief that Jewish identity was national in character and hence that the Jews could not be absorbed within another national entity.

To suggest that Jewish continuity lay in the realm of nationality or peoplehood would have meant to raise serious questions regarding the place of the Jew in German society; religious belief, on the other hand, was a recognized area of acceptable difference even in a modern state. The desire for equal political status thus contributed its share to confining Jewish history to the history of Judaism.

Finally, a role in this definition was played by the movement for Jewish religious reform. Systematic change of customs and ceremonies depended upon a conception of the Jewish past which was centered on the faith of an ever-evolving religious community. Because Abraham Geiger, the most important of the nineteenth-century reformers, could define Jewish history as the history of the idea of ethical monotheism, he could also regard Jewish law as essentially secondary, no more than a means for the preservation of the idea—and one which might no longer be needed in the same form in the modern world. Study of the past was of great importance because it helped to determine which elements of the Jewish tradition were central and hence should be preserved, and which were peripheral, and hence might be discarded. Thus *Wissenschaft* could provide an objective basis for religious change.

This conviction that Jewish history was basically the history of Judaism, and only secondarily that of a physical entity, continued to be influential among Jewish thinkers in Western Europe for most of the nineteenth century. Yet from the beginning, the history of the flesh-and-blood Jews was not entirely ignored, and in the course of time it gradually displaced the idealistic approach. The first Jewish writer to attempt such a history was Isaac Marcus Jost. His interest in the subject was less philosophical or scholarly than it was apologetic. Jost was concerned with a scientific (*wissenschaftlich*) account of Jewish history because only such an approach would yield an accurate picture of who the Jews really were and thus provide a basis for deciding the burning issue of how they might best adapt to a life of integration within the modern state. In the introduction to his *History of the Israelites* Jost wrote: "It is time to close the files on the value or lack of value of the Jews and Judaism and to begin with an analysis of the phenomenon itself, its origin and development, in order to understand its essence and whether it be desirable to change it."

Although Jost did focus upon the Jews, it was their religious doctrine—which Jost defined in rationalist terms to the exclusion of the mystical tradition—that for him provided continuity from age to age. Their change in status from a political entity to a "religious society" at the end of the period of the Second Temple did not, therefore, constitute a real break in Jewish history. Moreover, this religious continuity made it possible for Jost to arrange his material principally according to geographical units, allowing for a large range of difference between Jews in Palestine and Hellenistic Egypt, in the Roman Empire and in the Parthian, in Christian Europe and in the civilization of Islam. Jost did not bind himself to a strict chronological sequence, but allowed his account to move back and forth in time as he took up each area of Jewish settlement. Nor did he develop a single periodization for all of Jewish history, allowing what seemed to be major turning points in the history of each Jewish center to constitute units of division for that particular Jewry. Jost was not a philosopher, and he did not seek out any inner structure of Jewish history. He was content to gather neglected sources and to put them together into as coherent an account as his limited material permitted. His objectivity and good historical sense exceeded those of the men who followed him, though their work became the more well known.

The first systematic philosophy of Jewish history was devised by a Galician Jew who did not write a comprehensive history of the Jews. Nahman Krochmal's Hebrew *Guide of the Perplexed of the Time* (published posthumously in 1851) contains philosophy and discrete historical studies, but most importantly it presents a definite structure and dynamics of Jewish history within the context of a general theory of historical development. According to Krochmal, the nations of the world each undergo a process consisting of three organic stages: growth, blossoming, and decay. While every national culture is unique, all gain their historical life from their participation in the Absolute Spirit, which is for Krochmal, in the language of idealist philosophy, to be equated with God. Each such culture must eventually pass away leaving no more than traces of what was once an integrated whole; each represents only a *partial* manifestation of the Absolute Spirit in that nation's particular national spirit and hence it is doomed to evanescence. But unlike all other nations, Israel's national spirit is free of such one-sidedness. Its culture reflects a *full* manifestation of the Absolute Spirit. Israel's God is this Spirit itself and hence Israel shares in its eternity. Israel, too, undergoes stages of growth, blossoming and decay, but unlike the other nations, it always rises again to begin the cycle anew and, at least after the first renewal, on a higher level of spiritual consciousness. Krochmal outlines three such cycles through which Jewish history had passed, and he apparently regarded his own time as the beginning of a fourth.

Krochmal's philosophical structuring of Jewish history had a number of important ramifications. No less than for Wolf, Jewish history was for him the history of an idea, not the history of individuals or institutions. He, too, wished to justify continuing Jewish existence as against the idealist philosophy which consigned Judaism to a past phase in the history of the world spirit. The result was that he ascribed all change to ideal, not material factors. Israel's history was totally explainable in terms of its relationship to God. In Krochmal's words: ". . . The entire history of this people, its origins and its prosperity as well as its decline and fall, is explicable by an encompassing spiritual cause: the Divine power which resides in our midst." Though Krochmal's Absolute Spirit is conceived of as an impersonal, scrutable force rather than as the transcendent being of the Bible, for him as well historical change is not determined by man.

In addition, Krochmal's philosophy of Jewish history placed severe constraints upon the free interpretation of the Jewish past. His unitary periodization according to stages created a Procrustean bed into which facts had somehow to be fitted. Like the Bible, it makes historical phenomena conform to an unquestioned pattern. Thus, the Hebrew prophets must be seen as atypical of their age since they appear in a period of decline, and the same must hold for the Jewish creativity of sixteenth-century Poland. Yet, in an age of perplexity among Jews who were beginning to question the future of Jewish existence, Krochmal's philosophy of history provided confidence that the eternity of the Jewish people was assured by its unique adherence to the Absolute Spirit. Israel's future was rooted in the metaphysics of history. It also meant, once again, that because the subject of Jewish history was spiritual, changing political circumstances could not affect the continuity of its existence. On the contrary, Krochmal repeatedly insisted that Israel's centrality in the scheme of world history, its chosenness expressed in these new philosophical terms, presented it with the ongoing mission of becoming "teachers of the great multitude of nations."

With Heinrich Graetz, whose *History of the Jews,* translated into many languages, is still widely read today, we arrive at the major Jewish historian of the nineteenth century. Graetz's conception of Jewish history has enjoyed enormous influence and is regarded by some scholars as unsurpassed even today. His historiographical method, while in certain respects resembling that of the great German historian Leopold Ranke, was essentially his own. Both conception and method are deserving of a somewhat extended analysis.

In his early essay, entitled "The Construction of Jewish History," Graetz begins with a seemingly inappropriate question: "What is Judaism?" One would think, on the basis of the essay's title, that his question should have been: "How does one construe or structure Jewish history?" But in fact Graetz realized correctly that his own question must be the prior one. It raises the basic issue—the nature of Judaism—to which a number of Jewish thinkers had already addressed themselves in his time, each one coming up with some particular essence. Yet each of their philosophical definitions failed to account for the full complexity of the phenomenon; invariably one aspect was emphasized to the exclusion of others. Thus Graetz determined to give his own answer to this fundamental question. It is the answer of an historian: the totality of Judaism can be understood only through a study of its development, for an idea becomes fully known only by having its operation in history traced over a long period of time. The historian who empirically investigates the Jewish past, with particular attention to its crucial turning points, will be in a better position to determine the nature of Judaism than will the philosopher.

For Graetz, a glance at Jewish history reveals a number of salient characteristics. First, Judaism has its origins in the negation of paganism and in the counter-assertion of its own transcendent God-idea: a God of spirit, not contained within nature. Second, this God-concept was concretely embodied in political and social institutions and intimately conjoined with the Land of Israel. These two elements, the religious and the political, became the basic constituents of Judaism. Third, the Jewish faith is a religion of the future, which looks forward to the messianic age when at last its history will be fulfilled. It may, of course, be argued that these characteristics which Graetz regards as basic are no less arbitrary than the ones adduced by his philosophic predecessors. But for him they are grounded in the very substance of Jewish history, and hence bear the stamp of objective truth.

On the basis of this early essay, it seems that for Graetz, as for Wolf, Geiger, and Krochmal, Jewish history was essentially the reflection of an idea. And indeed, the idea of Judaism as he here outlined it—somewhat redefined to stress the rationalism of the God-concept and the strict moral imperative—did become normative for him when he wrote his history a few years later; all phenomena not conforming to it were judged aberrant. But when the Jewish people absorbed this idea, Graetz maintained, a unique "folk-soul" (*Volksseele*) was formed to carry the idea through time. It may be said, that rather than the history of Judaism, Graetz wrote the history of this collective soul. His attention was not given to the idea apart from the people that embodied it, but neither was he primarily interested in the purely physical aspects of the Jewish past. In this respect, Graetz's conception of Jewish history represents an intermediate stage between the earlier view, which paid little regard to the people that brought forth and developed the Jewish idea, and the national historiography of Simon Dubnow who follows him. For Graetz the focus is on the Jewish people, but as bearers of the idea.

Though Graetz's history is distinctly modern in its application of critical analysis, it repeatedly reflects the author's belief in a transcendent causalty. For Graetz, Jewish history, and to a lesser extent world history, is reflective of God's will, which is the ultimate determinant of all events; scarcely less than the biblical historians, Graetz conceives history as a drama of Divine reward and punishment. Yet for Graetz, no less than for the Bible, there is a human component in historical causality as well. Peoples and individuals remain free moral agents and hence, despite their ultimate attribution to Providence, causal questions must still be addressed to the immanent process of historical development. Here Graetz proves to be basically an idealist, ascribing the survival of the Jews—as against the demise of the ancient Greeks—to a sense of their mission to be holy through a higher morality. It was this consciousness of their task, according to Graetz, that unified, strengthened, and preserved the people even under the worst circumstances. Although from the providential perspective individuals are insignificant, Graetz in fact attributes causal centrality to their role in Jewish history. Biography is a basic component of his historical writing, and he explains the course of events more by the will of powerful men than by the operation of impersonal historical forces.

For Graetz, the understanding of Jewish history required more than defining a normative and unchanging Judaism to provide continuity throughout its entire span and a doctrine of causality to explain its dynamics. It also demanded a deliberate periodization so that the structure and the turning points would be apparent. Graetz's first attempt at periodization was made in the above-mentioned essay. Here he suggested a division into three periods, each in turn neatly divided into a prelude and three stages, and each possessing a definite character. Prelude to the first period was the wandering in the desert, its first stage the interval from Joshua through the Judges, the second from Samuel through Solomon, the third from the division of the kingdom to the destruction of the First Temple. Its principal characteristic was the dominance of the political principle over the religious. The second period is introduced by the Babylonian Exile, followed by a first stage running from Ezra to the Maccabees, a second from the Maccabees through the reign of John Hyrcanus (135–104 B.C.E.), and a third from the split between Pharisees and Sadducees to the destruction of the Second Temple. This period was marked by its cultic-religious character. The last period, the period of the Diaspora, has as its prelude the study of Jewish law, as its first stage the aggadic effort to find meaning in the law, as its second the philosophical systematization which commences with Saadiah in the tenth century, and as its last stage, the speculative-philosophical outlook which begins with Mendelssohn. Graetz calls it the theoretical-religious period and sees it continuing into his own time.

A number of points are worth noting in regard to this periodization. First, unlike in Krochmal's scheme and unlike in Graetz's own later conceptualization, there are no stages of growth, blossoming, and decay. On the contrary, there is from the beginning an upward progression from the political to the religious, which marks one stage off from another. Only in the messianic state (which will presumably commence a fourth period) will the political reappear in closest conjunction with the religious—and hence, until then, Judaism must always remain the religion of the future. Second, the periodization is determined by factors internal to Jewish history, not by the course of general history. For the Diaspora period, modes of reflection upon the idea of Judaism, not the passing of world empires, become determinative of the internal boundaries between stages. Finally, it is a single, nonoverlapping scheme which posits a unified development over all areas of Jewish settlement.

When he came to write the history of the Jews, Graetz did not hold himself to his early scheme of division. In fact, he changed his mind on a number of boundaries even during the process of publishing the various volumes. He refined his periodization further and allowed nonintellectual changes to determine some of the divisions. The principal innovation came with his adoption of Krochmal's scheme of rise and decline for all three major periods and his eventual decision that a fourth period began with Mendelssohn, following the decline which characterized the preceding epoch of "one-sided rabbinism."

Despite the tendency to view Jewish history as a single continuous whole, which is reflected in his periodization, Graetz was certainly aware of the differences among Jewish communities in different lands. But he argued that there were always focal points which provided a degree of unity and from which historical life spread out over the wide periphery. This conception anticipates Dubnow, though it does not become the cornerstone of Graetz's historiography as it does for the later historian. In fact, Graetz at times seems quite unaware of the need to divide the history of each area of settlement according to the factors relevant to it. Moreover, he does not separate external history from internal, but allows material development to mingle freely with literary creativity.

For Graetz, as for Zunz, Diaspora Jewish history consisted essentially of passive suffering and active spiritual endeavor. The former could not be omitted in a history of the Jews, but the latter was its true subject. A spiritually stagnant Jewish community, to Graetz's mind, could not be considered a center of Jewish life regardless of its size. ("According to population," Graetz wrote, "the Asian Jews were more significant than the European Jews. But the contents of their heads made the latter superior, so that Europe must be considered the main seat of Judaism.") For the same reason Graetz devoted two-thirds of his last volume to the 400,000 Jews of Germany, though there were five times as many living in the Russian empire. He was generally little interested in demography; considerably neglected social history; and ignored economic history almost completely.

Among Graetz's shortcomings are also his undisguised prejudices: he seldom withholds his own moral and aesthetic judgments.

His dislikes are manifestly clear. Outside of the Jewish sphere, he detests Greek morality and has scarcely more regard for Christianity, which he terms the "arch-foe of Judaism." Within Jewish history, he cares little for narrow talmudism and even less for mysticism. By attributing such phenomena to suffering imposed from the outside, he absolves normative Judaism from the responsibility for creating them. Yiddish is for him an "ugly mongrel tongue" and Hasidism a "daughter of darkness." Both represent a contradiction of the westernization process which Graetz affirmed. No less vicious is his treatment of the contemporary Reform movement, though, ironically, toward the end of his life Graetz's own views approach those of Geiger. On the other hand, he is willing to treat favorably and at length prominent cultural figures like the poet Heinrich Heine and the essayist Ludwig Börne even though both converted to Christianity. According to Graetz—who admired them—they were nonetheless "imbued with true Jewish spirit."

These prejudices contributed to the liveliness of Graetz's account, as did his focus upon personalities, his expanded treatment of particularly dramatic episodes, and his great ability as a writer. Above all, his readers felt that he was totally committed to his subject. Small wonder, therefore, that despite all of its shortcomings, his conception of Jewish history attained such widespread and lasting influence.

It was among East European Jews that the inadequacies of Graetz's view became most clearly apparent. Not only had Graetz given short shrift to the major developments in Poland and Russia, but the philosophical basis of his conception of Jewish history was foreign to this different historical context. His notion of the Jews as a religious people bearing a single God-idea throughout four thousand years was unable to strike deep roots in an environment as rife with anti-metaphysical positivism and secular nationalism as with religious piety. Yet so authoritative was Graetz's historiography, that even Simon Dubnow, the greatest of the Jewish historians who appeared in Eastern Europe during the last decades of the ninteenth century, was at first unable to free himself from its influence.

Dubnow's own Jewish identity differed sharply from that of Graetz. At an early age he had ceased to believe in God and for a time became a cosmopolitan universalist. It was only because he came to realize that the tie among Jews need not be primarily

religious that he found his way back into the Jewish community as a
Diaspora Jewish nationalist. His belief that Jewish national
consciousness, existing apart from political institutions, could best
be sustained by a knowledge of the Jewish past led him into the
study of Jewish history. Indeed, this became his life's mission and
his substitute religion: "Historiography," he wrote in his diary, "is
for me like a temple which in reverent silence I help to build."

From the beginning, therefore, Dubnow rejected Graetz's
notion that Jewish history was guided by Divine Providence, and he
never took recourse to transcendent explanations. In his work,
Jewish historiography became entirely secular; it was still in large
measure religious history, but it was no longer itself sacred. Still,
Dubnow did not go over to materialism. From Graetz he adopted
the designation of Israel as a "spiritual nation" and he held to this
conception. Although he defined "spirit" more broadly than Graetz,
he judged that it was this spirituality, rather than any material
factors, which accounted for Israel's survival. When, in his various
historical writings, he came to determining causes for the individual
events of Jewish history, he usually allowed himself to be guided by
the nature of the instance. Persecution of the Jews in fifteenth-cen-
tury Italy, for example, he decided stemmed from a genuine
religious motive in the South, but was due to economic interests in
the industrial North.

At first Dubnow had fully shared Graetz's idea that the
substance of Jewish history in the Diaspora consisted of "thinking
and suffering." He therefore also accepted his predecessor's scheme
of periodization according to the major shifts in intellectual activity.
His initial innovation was only to suggest that the various periods of
Diaspora existence were each dominated by a particular Jewish
community which because of its central importance exercised
hegemony over other areas of Jewish settlement. In unspoken
contradiction to Graetz, he also insisted that these centers "must
perforce coincide with the numerical center of the dispersed
people."

It was only after he had been active as a Jewish historian for a
number of decades that Dubnow's conception of the structure of
Jewish history became clearly differentiated from that of Graetz.
Unlike his predecessors in the West, he ultimately rejected the
concept of a single idea running the entire length of Jewish history.
In 1897 he wrote: "In the history of Judaism . . . there is no single
definite idea which runs through all periods like a silk thread." With

this empirical observation, Dubnow called into question the accepted continuity and unity of Jewish history. From a strictly idealist standpoint, such a denial made impossible the writing of an integral account. But Dubnow concurrently discovered a new strand of continuity: the people itself. The "national thread" was woven through all the periods of Jewish history and among the various areas of Jewish settlement. Defined as a nation through the entire extent of their history, the Jews were not mere bearers of an idea. Israel was not a vessel, but itself the subject of Jewish history. Its national consciousness, expressed in a variety of ways, constituted the basis of its continuing creativity.

Dubnow's national conception of Jewish history had a profound influence upon his historiography. Somewhat inaptly, he came to term his view of Jewish history "sociological," not on account of any influence from contemporary sociology, but since his national orientation extended his interest beyond the works of individuals to the social institutions which Jews had created: their autonomous communities in Muslim and Christian lands. Unlike works of literature, these latter were manifestly the creation of the group rather than of individuals, and consequently highly expressive of the national spirit. But even literary achievements were, if possible, to be viewed as collective accomplishments. The Talmud became for Dubnow the national expression of a particular phase of Jewish history. He saw it as the surrogate for the old Sanhedrin and the other organs of self-government which preceded it. This national view also produced a degree of tendentiousness in his historical writing. His ideological commitment did not allow him to treat centrifugal forces with dispassion. Whatever was supportive of Jewish national consciousness he treated favorably, whatever served to weaken that consciousness was judged harshly—in the instance of the post-Mendelssohn Germanizers, as "treason against the national cause." In addition, his profound commitment to the indivisible unity of the Jewish people blinded him to social and economic tensions among conflicting interests. A class analysis of Jewish society at any stage of Jewish history would have been destructive of its national foundation which, for want of a territory, had to depend on a subjective consciousness. Further, his emotional attachment to the Jewish people made it impossible for him to ascribe any responsibility to the Jews for their woes. Invariably, in Dubnow's account the Jews are the innocent victims of persecutions even when, as in the case of the Chmielnicki massacres of 1648, some of them served the interests of the Polish nobility and played a role in the oppression of the Ukrainian peasants. Lastly, despite his avowed recognition of the close relationship between world history and Jewish history, Dubnow's view of the Jewish people as always and everywhere the subject of its own history led him to minimize external influences upon the spiritual life of the Jews; his tendency was to stress the originality and independence of Jewish achievements.

Dubnow's departure from the conception of his predecessors is most apparent in the structure he gave to his *World History of the Jewish People*, written in the 1920's. His periodization is not controlled by religious and literary developments, but by political and demographic changes. The basic division is into two: an Oriental Period (1200 B.C.E.–eleventh century C.E.) followed by a Western Period. Within the earlier epoch the period of Israel's statehood is divided according to the various empires that controlled the land. Thereafter, the smaller divisions are all made according to the hegemonic influence exercised successively by one or a number of Jewish communities. Dubnow's time boundaries, for the most part, are only loosely fixed. He recognizes major historical changes as coming about through a gradual process rather than as the immediate result of an event that can be precisely fixed in time. He solves the problem of organization by a compromise between the country-by-country and the strictly chronological approaches: within each of the hegemonic eras he begins with the focal point and moves from the center to the periphery. When a major occurrence, cutting across Jewish community lines, makes necessary a unified treatment of that phenomenon, there is sufficient flexibility to allow for a departure from the usual method. Such events were, for example, the Crusades and the Shabbatean messianic movement of the seventeenth century. Within the treatment of each area of settlement, Dubnow proceeds sequentially from the political conditions under which the Jews lived to their organs of self-government and finally to their intellectual life and literature. Thus he achieves a degree of coherence unmatched by both his predecessors and successors. Within this scheme his writing takes on evenness and breadth; it does not suffer from the episodic quality of Graetz's work. But by the same token, because it reduces the biographical element, it also lacks dramatic appeal. In addition, Dubnow was a poor stylist. Taken together, these two factors would help to explain why his major work did not enjoy the popularity of Graetz. Yet Dubnow's secular conception of Jewish history and his historiographical methodology are far closer than those of Graetz to the suppositions of nearly all Jewish historical writing in the present.

Dubnow was a Jewish nationalist, but not a Zionist. He believed that it was possible for Jews to live creatively in culturally autonomous, national communities within the political framework of other nations. An ever-present desire for expression of the national spirit was for him the motivating force of Jewish history. But he did not connect national consciousness with a perpetual wish to return to the Land of Israel. Zionist historians, by contrast, have insisted upon the constancy and centrality of this theme.

Among the Zionists, the late Yehezkel Kaufmann's conception of Jewish history is unique in that he viewed this love of the Land as but a component within a more comprehensive religious consciousness. He argued that without the conception of Israel as the people of God, the nation could not have survived under the corrosive conditions of the Diaspora. "Religion," wrote Kaufmann, "was the sole source of its national will." And religion continued to operate as the chief constituent of national unity even after the widespread breakdown of faith within modern Jewry.

By thus subordinating the national impulse to the religious conception, Kaufmann placed himself outside the mainstream of Zionist historiography, which has regarded religion as but one expression of national feeling. The latter, as best exemplified by Ben Zion Dinur, has insisted upon the primacy of the attachment to Zion, which existed in a religious form during the Middle Ages and assumed a secular character in the modern world. For Dinur the entire course of Jewish history is Palestinocentric. Love of Zion ever sustained and preserved the Jewish nation; this love constitutes its essence and the basis of its unity in all the lands of dispersion. While, for Dubnow, Palestine served as the hegemonic center for but one particular period, for Dinur it is consistently the focal point. His view leads him to select a single, nonoverlapping scheme of periodization, abandoning completely Dubnow's conception of shifting concentrations of Jewish creativity. By this means—though at the expense of coherence—Dinur is able to build into the division itself his belief that regardless of the varying civilizations under which it lived, the Jewish people was always essentially one, and always focused upon its land. It also influences him to lay heavy emphasis upon the political circumstances of the Land of Israel and the people's relationship to it. The Diaspora, according to Dinur, did not begin until 636 because only in that year, with the Arab conquest of Palestine, did the Land of Israel cease to be a land of Jews. He insists on this boundary although the majority of Jews had long lived outside of Palestine and spiritual direction for at least four centuries had come from Babylonia. Similar thinking produces the suggestion that the major break at the other end of the continuum occurred when Rabbi Judah the Pious led an immigration of some one thousand Jews to Palestine in the year 1700, thus beginning the resettlement of the Land and the modern period of Jewish history. Dinur also developed a scheme of alternating periods of stability and crisis which he thinks inevitably characterize Diaspora existence. The rigid pattern could be broken only once the people was again gathered in its land. Not surprisingly, American Jewry, which cannot at all be forced into the scheme, plays no role in this periodization whatsoever.

Raphael Mahler agrees with Dinur in insisting upon the ubiquity of the Zionist motive. He, too, finds in every generation the desire for national redemption through return to the Land, and he deems it the ever-present source of the nation's creativity. What sets Mahler apart from other contemporary Jewish historians is his understanding of the Jewish past from the perspective of Marxist dialectical materialism. This means, first, that the history of the Jews is to be understood within the framework of the general advance of the nations through the stages of feudalism, capitalism, and socialism. Thus Jewish creativity in the Diaspora was dependent upon existence within a feudal or semifeudal society where Jews performed special economic functions or even constituted a third class alongside nobility and peasantry. As soon as Europe emerged into capitalism and this special role was taken away, independent spiritual existence necessarily gave way to assimilation as Jews were integrated into the economy of the various states. The conclusion to be drawn is the Zionist one, that in the modern world Jewish individuality can be preserved only in a Jewish state. The second implication of Mahler's Marxism does not, however, dovetail so easily with his Zionism. For his commitment to an economic analysis of historical causalty leads him to explore class antagonisms within the Jewish community. Nationalist historians had shied away from this subject, which could only serve to weaken the collective identity. Mahler, however, has relentlessly pursued these conflicts and in his emphasis upon them exposed an unquestionably significant element. The same is true for his proper stress upon external cultural influences which had affected Judaism. Yet, to the extent that he has seen economic considerations as virtually the sole motivating factor for the Jewish upper classes and allowed for the operation of only one ideal motive—the Zionist-socialist one—the Marxist perspective has severely distorted his view. His materialist conception of spiritual life also makes it difficult for him to see religion as anything other than a reactionary element in the modern world or a cover for class interest. For Mahler, Jewish history is driven by an immanent force which determines the destinies of mankind: the necessary progress toward a classless, but nationally differentiated society. Since he believes this progress is not only inevitable but also desirable, he is given a criterion by which he can be not only analyst of the phenomena of Jewish history, but also judge.

In the United States, Jewish historiography, for the most part, has not followed either the Zionist or the materialist interpretations. Salo Baron, the dean of Jewish historians in America, has perceived the desire for return to Zion as only one motif, alongside the contrary affirmation of Diaspora existence as a positive value. Denying that the material factor is necessarily crucial, he has preferred to weigh all potential causes according to their relative explanatory value in each historical instance. Baron's own conception is based on his understanding of Jewish history as an ongoing relationship between Judaism, broadly defined as both religion and culture, and the Jewish people which bears it. The two in their interdependence, to his mind, constitute the subject of Jewish history, much as they did for Graetz, though Baron does not accept Graetz's view that a single religious idea dominated Judaism all along. On the contrary, antinomies and contradictions have always been present. Diaspora Jewish history, therefore, consists of a religious/cultural component (Judaism in its manifold variety) combined with a social one (the physical history of a people without political institutions) and of the interplay between them.

Baron's conception, though having the advantage of balance and freedom from ideological bias, suffers from an apparent lack of overall coherence. Certainly the application of his approach in his great, as yet uncompleted *A Social and Religious History of the Jews* gives the reader that impression. Critics have pointed out that the work lacks any obvious conceptual framework which might give shape to the substance of the Jewish past. Baron here abandons Dubnow's periodization according to hegemonic centers and reverts instead to a single unitary scheme of division which includes all phenomena between the years 500 and 1200 in a category called "High Middle Ages" and those between 1200 and 1650 in what is called "Late Middle Ages and Era of European Expansion." Within these large and nonrelevant time units the material is divided topically. In general, Baron does follow Dubnow's approach of sequentially dealing first with the status of the Jews, then with their institutions, and finally with their creativity. But he does so within temporal boundaries that are not related to the phenomena themselves and which are so wide as to obviate coherence. As biography plays virtually no role in what is largely a sociological approach, the activities of prominent individuals are distributed among the nonpersonal categories of topical division. Also, complex matters, which require for their understanding a number of the themes which Baron here explores separately, do not appear as part of a configuration and thus cannot easily be evaluated. Therefore, while Baron's work enhances our knowledge of the particular themes he has chosen, his methodology is not conducive to revealing the dynamics of Jewish history and the connections among its diverse elements. Having contributed much to preparing the way for a profound new, synthetic view of Jewish history, his conception and its execution have not been able to provide that synthesis.

Other scholars have attempted to find the basis for such a comprehensive view. A most interesting recent suggestion is Ellis Rivkin's "unity concept." In every period of Jewish history, Rivkin maintains, Jews have consistently adhered to a unified view of the world, whether expressed within the framework of monotheism or, in more recent times, by a secular equivalent. In some of his writings, he goes further to suggest that Jewish adherence to one or another form of the unity concept indicates the operation of a trans-historical principle analagous to the evolutionary principle in biology. For Rivkin, it is the operation of this principle which explains the ability of the Jews to adapt repeatedly to foreign influences without the loss of Jewish identity. Their unique capacity to respond integratively to every new challenge posed by the surrounding world has enabled them to survive the most radical transformations of their environment and to continue as an historical entity despite thoroughgoing changes in their own structure of belief and self-understanding. For Rivkin, it is the capacity to discern unity in the midst of diversity which represents the vocation of the Jews and the key to Jewish history.

Yet a suggestion like Rivkin's must raise certain questions. First, while it may be easy enough to accept the notion that Jews have consistently rejected various forms of polytheism, old and new, it does not follow—certainly not empirically—that a metaphysical principle has been operative which explains this adherence to unity. Second, it remains in doubt whether the unity concept does indeed characterize all ages of Jewish history, especially the most recent period where fragmented and differentiated views of reality seem increasingly to characterize modern Jews. Third, a concept of the unity of all existence, as Rivkin admits, has not been peculiar to Jewish history, and hence it has only limited value in setting the Jews apart. As monotheism spread to the West, the capacity to unify experience ceased to be a unique differentiating feature of Jewish history. The cultures of Christianity and Islam, as well as modern scientific conceptions, also proved capable of integrating new influences into a unified view of the world. The special relation of the unity concept to the Jewish experience seems to lie only in its origin within Jewish history and its long relationship to it. Though basic to an understanding of this history, it neither comprehends its entirety nor does it single out Jewish history as unique.

Are we left, then, with the dilemma of, on the one hand, having to choose some constant (a God-idea, a spiritual nationhood, a yearning for Zion, a unity concept) which seems either too narrow or too wide to encompass the Jewish historical experience or, on the other, of giving up the hope of finding some basis for continuity and pursuing instead individual themes chronologically arranged? Perhaps there is no simple scheme or conception which can render a full account of the immense complexity of Jewish history. But there may be some value in considering the relevance of a simple metaphor which, while it does not constitute a single key to understanding the Jewish past, may help to explain its continuity. It is the paradigm of a rope. In a rope few if any strands run fully from one end to the other yet the rope itself does not pull apart. So, too, Jewish history contains many and diverse material and spiritual strands running for some portion of its entire length. Occupational and political status, rationalism and mysticism, religious self-conception and national self-conception, succeed and complement each other along the continuum, varying geographically and according to different strata and competing ideologies within the Jewish communities. No segment of the rope contains exactly the same strands; if each strand were of a distinctive color, their combined appearance at any one point of Jewish history would be different from that at any other juncture. But the overlap is so great that each remains bound up with the others. Thus American Jewish life in the present is surely very different from that of twelfth-century Germany, but its component strands link it backward to other strands, some reaching as far as the Middle Ages and even beyond. Viewed in this way, the Jewish past would possess historical continuity and yet remain unfettered by attachment to a single constant which must always be proven present.

Such a solution to the question of continuity, however, can be fully adequate only for the secular Jewish historian who rejects transcendent causality. It cannot completely satisfy the Jewish thinker who is committed to perceiving the persistent influence of God upon human history in general and upon Jewish history in particular. For the latter it is necessary to find some reconciliation between his theological concern with God's relation to His people and the account he presents of the course which that people's history has taken. For Jews, the question of God's presence in history has taken on a particular urgency in the wake of the mass murder of millions of their brethren in the Nazi holocaust. That immense tragedy has brought some Jewish thinkers to a further distancing of God from man and a reaffirmation of the incomprehensibility of His ways, others to a complete denial of God's Providence, and still others—most notably Emil L. Fackenheim—to the discernment of a divine imperative to Jewish survival arising out of the catastrophe itself.

Living within Nazi Germany during the 1930's, Leo Baeck, who was concurrently a rabbi and teacher in Berlin and the official leader of German Jewry, occupied himself with just this question of God's relationship to history. He formulated his own view in terms of the then current intellectual debate over the impact of historicism upon theology. In an essay which he wrote at that time, entitled "Theology and History," Baeck argued that the historicist tendency to regard all historical phenomena as relative to time and place and as evolving one out of another need not conflict with the Jewish conception of transhistorical revelation. For God's influence on history, as Baeck here conceived it, was the ever-present divine imperative to which Jewish history was an unfolding response. The continuity of Jewish history lay in the continuity of its chain of religious teachers, its uniqueness in the acceptance of the revelation. Baeck was thus able to allow for a source of human initiative beyond history while limiting to the temporal realm the determination of specific events and their causes. Though writing before the Nazi holocaust, he was in this way able to provide at least one possible solution to the problem of God's role in human and Jewish history: the spiritual and moral imperative is rooted in the divine, but the course of history is the work of men.

Finally, a word should be said about the difficulty of conceptualizing the Jewish history of our own time. The establishment of the State of Israel in 1948 has raised serious questions regarding the proper subject matter of Jewish history following that watershed event. Does Jewish history encompass all aspects of the history of the State of Israel, or only those which are also of significance to Jews outside its borders? Or does it henceforth limit itself to Diaspora existence alone, declaring the history of the State of Israel "Israeli history"? Does an Israeli who feels no connection with Jews outside Israel belong within the purview of Jewish history any more than a Jew who has converted to Christianity? These new questions relate themselves to the older one: What constitutes Jewish history in the Diaspora? Is it everything noteworthy done by Jews (sports, politics, etc.), or only what was done by Jews (or to Jews) because of their Jewishness? These questions have yet to be confronted seriously by Jewish historians. All that can be stated with certainty is that today Jewish existence stands bifurcated into the life of a political state with a large degree of cultural independence and the life of Diaspora communities for whom Jewishness constitutes only a portion of total identity. Any new, comprehensive idea of Jewish history will have to encompass these two highly dissimilar forms of present-day Jewish life.

HELLENISM AND APOCALYPTICISM

INTRODUCTION TO II MACCABEES

ALTHOUGH it was not included in the biblical canon and contains no verbal revelation, II Maccabees shares the Bible's idea of history. No less than the biblical writers, its author is committed to the notion of God's will determining the fate of His chosen people. He preserves the religious tone of the Bible and emphasizes God's power to intervene miraculously, interrupting the natural order. Like the Bible, his work views history as a testing ground where good is rewarded and evil brings speedy retribution. It is for him a moral and religious saga, not a course of secular events.

Yet at the same time II Maccabees introduces a number of features not present in biblical historiography. The writer addresses his readers directly, informs them of his source, and of the aims of his work. He tells us that he has, in fact, done no more than provide an epitome of the work of Jason of Cyrene, abbreviating and recasting it to have a wider appeal. He is not interested in conveying details, but rather in inspiring his readers. His purpose is also to entertain, as these concluding verses of his last chapter indicate:

So I too will here end my story. If it is well told and to the point, that is what I myself desired; if it is poorly done and mediocre, that was the best I could do. For just as it is harmful to drink wine alone, or, again, to drink water alone, while wine mixed with water is sweet and delicious

and enhances one's enjoyment, so also the style of the story delights the
ears of those who read the work.

*This explicit self-consciousness of the writer's task and objective
puts the author of II Maccabees very much into the tradition of the
popular Hellenistic writers, even while his conceptions sharply
distinguish him (and his source, Jason of Cyrene) from the analytic
historical tradition of Thucydides.*

*The work was written in Greek during the latter part of the
second century* B.C.E. *Its main portion begins with the ascent to
power of the Seleucid monarch Antiochus Epiphanes (175* B.C.E.*)
and continues to Judah Maccabee's defeat of the Syrian general
Nicanor (variously dated from 164 to 160* B.C.E.*) The first passage
which follows contains the epitomist's introduction in which he sets
forth the purpose of his work. The second, the tale of Heliodorus, is
the most imaginative and detailed instance of Divine intervention to
be found in the book. The last passage presents an obvious example
of theologizing, or drawing a religious lesson from history: from the
course of events which have been described the reader is expected
to take comfort in God's mercy, but also to note that God
unhesitatingly disciplines Israel for its sins. Thus the book serves to
exhort the reader as well as to overwhelm him with religious awe.*

THE HISTORIAN OUTLINES HIS TASK

The story of Judas Maccabeus and his brothers, and the purification of the great temple, and the dedication of the altar, and further the wars against Antiochus Epiphanes and his son Eupator, and the appearances which came from heaven to those who strove zealously on behalf of Judaism, so that though few in number they seized the whole land and pursued the barbarian hordes, and recovered the temple famous throughout the world and freed the city and restored the laws that were about to be abolished, while the Lord with great kindness became gracious to them—all this, which has been set forth by Jason of Cyrene* in five volumes, we shall attempt to condense into a single book. For considering the flood of numbers involved and the difficulty there is for those who wish to enter upon the narratives of history because of the mass of material, we have aimed to please those who wish to read, to make it easy for those who are inclined to memorize, and to profit all readers. For us who have undertaken the toil of abbreviating, it is no light matter but calls for sweat and loss of sleep, just as it is not easy for one who prepares a banquet and seeks the benefit of others. However, to secure the gratitude of many we will gladly endure the uncomfortable toil, leaving the responsibility for exact details to the compiler, while devoting our effort to arriving at the outlines of the condensation. For as the master builder of a new house must be concerned with the whole construction, while the one who undertakes its painting and decoration has to consider only what is suitable for its adornment, such in my judgment is the case with us. It is the duty of the original historian to occupy the ground and to discuss matters from every side and to take trouble with details, but the one who recasts the narrative should be allowed to strive for brevity of expression and to forego exhaustive treatment.

*Nothing is known of Jason beyond the reference to him here.

THE MIRACULOUS PUNISHMENT OF HELIODORUS

While the holy city was inhabited in unbroken peace and the laws were very well observed because of the piety of the high priest Onias and his hatred of wickedness, it came about that the kings themselves honored the place and glorified the temple with the finest presents, so that even Seleucus* the king of Asia, defrayed from his own revenues all the expenses connected with the service of the sacrifices. But a man named Simon, of the tribe of Benjamin, who had been made captain of the temple, had a disagreement with the high priest about the administration of the city market; and when he could not prevail over Onias he went to Apollonius of Tarsus, who at that time was governor of Coelesyria† and Phoenicia. He reported to him that the treasury in Jerusalem was full of untold sums of money, so that the amount of the funds could not be reckoned, and that they did not belong to the account of the sacrifices, but that it was possible for them to fall under the control of the king. When Appollonius met the king, he told him of the money about which he had been informed. The king chose Heliodorus, who was in charge of his affairs, and sent him with commands to effect the removal of the aforesaid money. Heliodorus at once set out on his journey, ostensibly to make a tour of inspection of the cities of Coelesyria and Phoenicia, but in fact to carry out the king's purpose.

When he had arrived at Jerusalem and had been kindly welcomed by the high priest of the city, he told about the disclosure that had been made and stated why he had come, and he inquired whether this really was the situation. The high priest explained that there were some deposits belonging to widows and orphans, and also some money of Hyrcanus, son of Tobias, a man of very prominent position, and that it totaled in all four hundred talents of silver and two hundred of gold. To such an extent the impious Simon had misrepresented the facts. And he said that it was utterly impossible that wrong should be done to those people who had trusted in the holiness of the place and in the sanctity and

*Seleucus IV Philopater, ruler of Syria (187–176 B.C.E.).

† Those portions of Palestine and southern Syria captured by the Seleucid monarch Antiochus III from the Egyptian Ptolemies (c. 200 B.C.E.).

inviolability of the temple which is honored throughout the whole world. But Heliodorus, because of the king's commands which he had, said that this money must in any case be confiscated for the king's treasury. So he set a day and went in to direct the inspection of these funds.

There was no little distress throughout the whole city. The priests prostrated themselves before the altar in their priestly garments and called toward heaven upon Him who had given the law about deposits, that He should keep them safe for those who had deposited them. To see the appearance of the high priest was to be wounded at heart, for his face and the change in his color disclosed the anguish of his soul. For terror and bodily trembling had come over the man, which plainly showed the pain lodged in his heart to those who looked at him. People also hurried out of their houses in crowds to make a general supplication because the holy place was about to be brought into contempt. Women, girded with sackcloth under their breasts, thronged the streets. Some of the maidens who were kept indoors ran together to the gates, and some to the walls, while others peered out of the windows. And holding up their hands to heaven, they all made entreaty. There was something pitiable in the prostration of the whole populace and the anxiety of the high priest in his great anguish.

While they were calling upon the Almighty Lord that He would keep what had been entrusted safe and secure for those who had entrusted it, Heliodorus went on with what had been decided. But when he arrived at the treasury with his bodyguard, then and there the Sovereign of spirits and of all authority caused so great a manifestation that all who had been so bold as to accompany him were astounded by the power of God, and became faint with terror. For there appeared to them a magnificently caparisoned horse, with a rider of frightening mien, and it rushed furiously at Heliodorus and struck at him with its front hoofs. Its rider was seen to have armor and weapons of gold. Two young men also appeared to him, remarkably strong, gloriously beautiful and splendidly dressed, who stood on each side of him and scourged him continuously, inflicting many blows on him. When he suddenly fell to the ground and deep darkness came over him, his men took him up and put him on a stretcher and carried him away, this man who had just entered the aforesaid treasury with a great retinue and all his bodyguard but was now unable to help himself; and they recognized clearly the sovereign power of God. While he lay prostrate, speechless because of the divine intervention and deprived of any hope of recovery, they praised the Lord who had acted marvelously for His own place. And the temple, which a little while before was full of fear and disturbance, was filled with joy and gladness now that the Almighty Lord had appeared.

Quickly some of Heliodorus' friends asked Onias to call upon the Most High and to grant life to one who was lying quite at his last breath. And the high priest, fearing that the king might get the notion that some foul play had been perpetrated by the Jews with regard to Heliodorus, offered sacrifice for the man's recovery. While the high priest was making the offering of atonement, the same young men appeared again to Heliodorus, dressed in the same clothing, and they stood and said, "Be very grateful to Onias the high priest, since for his sake the Lord has granted you your life. And see that you, who have been scourged by heaven, report to all men the majestic power of God." Having said this they vanished.

Then Heliodorus offered sacrifice to the Lord and made very great vows to the Savior of his life, and having bidden Onias farewell, he marched off with his forces to the king. And he bore testimony to all men of the deeds of the supreme God, which he had seen with his own eyes. When the king asked Heliodorus what sort of person would be suitable to send on another mission to Jerusalem, he replied, "If you have any enemy or plotter against your government, send him there, for you will get him back thoroughly scourged, if he escapes at all, for there certainly is about the place some power of God. For He who has His dwelling in heaven watches over that place Himself and brings it aid, and He strikes and destroys those who come to do it injury."

GOD'S SPECIAL RELATION TO ISRAEL

Not long after this, the king sent an Athenian senator to compel the Jews to forsake the laws of their fathers and cease to live by the laws of God, and also to pollute the temple in Jerusalem and call it the temple of Olympian Zeus, and to call the one in Gerizim* the

*The Samaritans had a sanctuary on Mount Gerizim near the city of Shechem.

temple of Zeus the Friend of Strangers, as did the people who dwelt in that place.

Harsh and utterly grievous was the onslaught of evil. For the temple was filled with debauchery and reveling by the Gentiles, who dallied with harlots and had intercourse with women within the sacred precincts, and besides brought in things for sacrifice that were unfit. The altar was covered with abominable offerings which were forbidden by the laws. A man could neither keep the sabbath, nor observe the feasts of his fathers, nor so much as confess himself to be a Jew.

On the monthly celebration of the king's birthday, the Jews were taken, under bitter constraint, to partake of the sacrifices; and when the feast of Dionysus* came, they were compelled to walk in the procession in honor of Dionysus, wearing wreaths of ivy. At the suggestion of Ptolemy† a decree was issued to the neighboring Greek cities, that they should adopt the same policy toward the Jews and make them partake of the sacrifices, and should slay those who did not choose to change over to Greek customs. One could see, therefore, the misery that had come upon them. For example, two women were brought in for having circumcised their children. These women they publicly paraded about the city, with their babies hung at their breasts, then hurled them headlong from the wall. Others who had assembled in the caves nearby, to observe the seventh day secretly, were betrayed to Philip‡ and were all burned together, because their piety kept them from defending themselves, in view of their regard for that most holy day.

Now I urge those who read this book not to be depressed by such calamities, but to recognize that these punishments were designed not to destroy but to discipline our people. In fact, not to let the impious alone for long, but to punish them immediately, is a sign of great kindness. For in the case of the other nations the Lord waits patiently to punish them until they have reached the full measure of their sins; but He does not deal in this way with us, in order that He may not take vengeance on us afterward when our sins have reached their height. Therefore He never withdraws His mercy from us. Though He disciplines us with calamities, He does not forsake His own people.

*An annual or semiannual orgiastic celebration in honor of Bacchus, god of wine.

†Probably Ptolemy son of Dorymenes, a friend of the Seleucid king.

‡A Syrian general appointed by Antiochus Epiphanes.

JOSEPHUS FLAVIUS

INTRODUCTION TO JOSEPHUS FLAVIUS

SINCE, in addition to his other works, Josephus also composed an autobiography, we are fairly well informed on his life. He was born into a priestly family in Jerusalem and was descended on his mother's side from the Hasmonean dynasty. Proud of his lineage, he also possessed a strong sense of his own worth and dignity. He was apparently well educated, became acquainted at first hand with the various religious groupings in Judea, joined the Pharisees, and at the age of twenty-six was chosen to embark on a mission to Rome. With the outbreak of the Judean revolt against the country's Roman overlords (66–70 C.E.), Josephus became commander of the Jewish forces in the Galilee. Faced with a rival faction, led by John of Gischala, he nevertheless managed to maintain his authority and to fortify the various cities of the region. But the attack of the Roman army, under the command of Vespasian, quickly put an end to the Jewish defenses and Josephus chose flight to the Roman camp over martyrdom with his comrades. Though at first held captive, he was released when Vespasian was proclaimed emperor. After accompanying Vespasian's son, Titus, on his successful campaign against Jerusalem, he settled in Rome where he enjoyed the privilege of Roman citizenship and an annual pension. Though denounced by fellow Jews as a traitor, he continued to identify with Judaism and to

52

defend it against hostile detractors. It was in Rome that he wrote his historical works.

Josephus composed The Jewish War in Aramaic shortly after the events it describes, events which Josephus largely witnessed himself. It is likely that Vespasian commissioned him to write the book as a warning to Jews living in Babylonia lest they embark upon a similar path of revolt against Rome. A Greek version followed, and it is this one which has been preserved. The Jewish War begins with the Maccabean period and runs down to the fall of the desert fortress of Masada in 73 C.E. Most of the narrative, however, is concentrated on the period from the invasion of Vespasian (67 C.E.) to the destruction of the Temple by Titus (70 C.E.). In the Preface, which is presented here, Josephus dedicates himself to the ideal of objectivity and to the quest for historical truth. He wants to follow in the tradition of Greek and later Hellenistic historiography as it had come down to him, especially perhaps through Polybius, a Greek historian who lived in Rome two centuries earlier and whose work was known to Josephus. It is worth noting how in this Preface Josephus claims the ability to separate his passions from his narrative and requests the reader to "credit the history with the facts, the historian with the lamentations." He thereby admits to his emotional involvement with his subject, but believes he has succeeded in separating it from his understanding of events. For his paramount ideal is to "hold historical truth in honor."

The Jewish Antiquities, written around 93 C.E., is a larger work both in length and in scope. It runs from the Creation down to the beginning of the Jewish revolt during the procuratorship of Florus. About half of it is devoted to the biblical period; the remainder concentrates especially upon the final years of the Second Temple, beginning with the reign of Herod. Josephus embellishes the biblical account with added details and with stories taken from the aggadic literature of the Pharisaic teachers. The only major event completely omitted from his version is the uncomplimentary incident of the golden calf. Josephus wrote The Jewish Antiquities in order to explain Judaism and evoke respect for it on the part of non-Jews. He is concerned to point out the venerability of Jewish tradition and to make it as comprehensible as possible to the Greek reader. He also wants to entertain him with a drama. But, once again, it is principally zeal for the truth, understood as adherence to facts and opposition to those who do it outrage, that Josephus mentions in his Preface (presented below) as the explicit motive for writing the book. Although in many respects it parallels the Preface to The Jewish War, this later introductory statement contains certain additional elements worthy of note: especially the portrayal of Moses as "lawgiver" on the Greek model and the commitment to chronological sequence (setting forth the details "each in its place") which, as we shall see, ceases to be significant for most of the writers who follow him.

The war of the Jews against the Romans—the greatest not only of the wars of our own time, but, so far as accounts have reached us, well nigh of all that ever broke out between cities or nations—has not lacked its historians. Of these, however, some, having taken no part in the action, have collected from hearsay casual and contradictory stories which they have then edited in a rhetorical style; while others, who witnessed the events, have, either from flattery of the Romans or from hatred of the Jews, misrepresented the facts, their writings exhibiting alternatively invective and encomium, but nowhere historical accuracy. In these circumstances, I—Josephus, son of Matthias, a Hebrew by race, a native of Jerusalem and a priest, who at the opening of the war myself fought against the Romans and in the sequel was perforce an onlooker —propose to provide the subjects of the Roman empire with a narrative of the facts, by translating into Greek the account which I previously composed in my vernacular tongue* and sent to the barbarians in the interior.

I spoke of this upheaval as one of the greatest magnitude. The Romans had their own internal disorders. The Jewish revolutionary party, whose number and fortunes were at their zenith, seized the occasion of the turbulence of these times for insurrection. As a result of these vast disturbances the whole of the Eastern Empire was in the balance; the insurgents were fired with hopes of its acquisition, their opponents feared its loss. For the Jews hoped that all their fellow-countrymen beyond the Euphrates would join with them in revolt; while the Romans, on their side, were occupied with their neighbors, the Gauls,† and the Celts‡ were in motion. Nero's death,§ moreover, brought universal confusion; many were induced by this opportunity to aspire to the sovereignty, and a change which might make their fortune was after the heart of the soldiery.

I thought it monstrous, therefore, to allow the truth in affairs of

*Aramaic.

†The French.

‡The Germans.

§Nero, who became Roman Emperor in 54 C.E., died in 68.

such moment to go astray, and that, while Parthians* and Babylonians and the most remote tribes of Arabia with our countrymen beyond the Euphrates and the inhabitants of Adiabene† were, through my assiduity, accurately acquainted with the origin of the war, the various phases of calamity through which it passed and its conclusion, the Greeks and such Romans as were not engaged in the contest should remain in ignorance of these matters, with flattering or fictitious narratives as their only guide.

Though the writers in question presume to give their works the title of histories, yet throughout them, apart from the utter lack of sound information, they seem, in my opinion, to miss their own mark. They desire to represent the Romans as a great nation, and yet they continually depreciate and disparage the actions of the Jews. But I fail to see how the conquerors of a puny people deserve to be accounted great. Again, these writers have respect neither for the long duration of the war, nor for the vast numbers of the Roman army that it engaged, nor for the prestige of the generals, who, after such herculean labors under the walls of Jerusalem, are, I suppose, of no repute in these writers' eyes, if their achievement is to be underestimated.

I have no intention of rivaling those who extol the Roman power by exaggerating the deeds of my compatriots. I shall faithfully recount the actions of both combatants; but in my reflections on the events I cannot conceal my private sentiments, nor refuse to give my personal sympathies scope to bewail my country's misfortunes. For, that it owed its ruin to civil strife, and that it was the Jewish tyrants who drew down upon the holy temple the unwilling hands of the Romans and the conflagration, is attested by Titus Caesar‡ himself, who sacked the city; throughout the war he commiserated the populace who were at the mercy of the revolutionaries, and often of his own accord deferred the capture of the city and by protracting the siege gave the culprits time for repentance. Should, however, any critic censure me for my strictures upon the tyrants or their bands of marauders or for my lamentations over my country's misfortunes, I ask his indulgence for a compassion which falls outside an historian's province. For of all the cities under Roman rule it was the lot of ours to attain to the highest felicity and to fall to

*Inhabitants of the mountainous region southeast of the Caspian Sea.

†The region of the upper Tigris River; present-day northern Iraq.

‡Roman Emperor (79–81 C.E.) and destroyer of the Second Temple in 70.

the lowest depths of calamity. Indeed, in my opinion, the misfortunes of all nations since the world began fall short of those of the Jews; and, since the blame lay with no foreign nation, it was impossible to restrain one's grief. Should, however, any critic be too austere for pity, let him credit the history with the facts, the historian with the lamentations.

Yet I, on my side, might justly censure those erudite Greeks, who, living in times of such stirring actions as by comparison reduce to insignificance the wars of antiquity, yet sit in judgment on these current events and revile those who make them their special study—authors whose principles they lack, even if they have the advantage of them in literary skill. For their own themes they take the Assyrian and Median empires, as if the narratives of the ancient historians were not fine enough. Yet, the truth is, these modern writers are their inferiors no less in literary power than in judgment. The ancient historians set themselves severally to write the history of their own times, a task in which their connection with the events added lucidity to their record; while mendacity brought an author into disgrace with readers who knew the facts. In fact, the work of committing to writing events which have not previously been recorded and of commending to posterity the history of one's own time is one which merits praise and acknowledgment. The industrious writer is not one who merely remodels the scheme and arrangement of another's work, but one who uses fresh materials and makes the framework of the history his own. For myself, at a vast expenditure of money and pains, I, a foreigner, present to Greeks and Romans this memorial of great achievements. As for the native Greeks, where personal profit or a lawsuit is concerned, their mouths are at once agape and their tongues loosed; but in the matter of history, where veracity and laborious collection of the facts are essential, they are mute, leaving to inferior and ill-informed writers the task of describing the exploits of their rulers. Let us at least hold historical truth in honor, since by the Greeks it is disregarded.

To narrate the ancient history of the Jews, the origin of the nation and the circumstances of their migration from Egypt, the countries which they traversed in their wanderings, the extent of the territory which they subsequently occupied, and the incidents which led to their deportation, would, I considered, be not only here out of place but superfluous; seeing that many Jews before me have accurately recorded the history of our ancestors, and that these records have been translated by certain Greeks into their native tongue without serious error. I shall therefore begin my work at the point where the historians of these events and our prophets conclude. Of the subsequent history, I shall describe the incidents of the war through which I lived with all the detail and elaboration at my command; for the events preceding my lifetime I shall be content with a brief summary.

I shall relate how Antiochus, surnamed Epiphanes,* took Jerusalem by storm and, after holding it for three years and six months, was expelled from the country by the Hasmoneans; next how their descendants, in their quarrel for the throne, dragged the Romans and Pompey† upon the scene; how Herod,‡ son of Antipater, with the aid of Sosius,§ overthrew the Hasmonean dynasty; of the revolt of the people, after Herod's death, when Augustus was Roman Emperor and Quintilius Varus provincial governor; of the outbreak of war in the twelfth year of Nero's principate, the fate which befell Cestius‖ and the success which attended the Jewish arms in overrunning the country in the opening engagements.

Then I shall proceed to tell how they fortified the neighboring towns; how Nero, apprehensive for the Empire in consequence of the reverses of Cestius, entrusted the conduct of the war to Vespasian;¶ of his invasion of Jewish territory, accompanied by his elder son; of the strength of the forces, Roman and auxiliary, with which he penetrated into Galilee, and of the towns of that province which he captured either by main force or by negotiation. In this connection I shall describe the admirable discipline of the Romans on active service and the training of the legions; the extent and nature of the two Galilees,** the limits of Judea, the special features

---

*Seleucid ruler of Syria (175–164 B.C.E.) who endeavored to hellenize Judea by force.

†General who in 64–63 B.C.E. established Roman rule throughout Syria and Palestine.

‡King of Judea (37–4 B.C.E.).

§Roman general and governor of Syria.

‖Cestius Gallus, Roman governor of Syria who was defeated by the rebellious Judeans after an unsuccessful siege of Jerusalem in 66 C.E.

¶Roman Emperor (69–79 C.E.) who took over command of the Roman army in Judea after the defeat of Cestius and succeeded in conquering most of the country.

**Upper and Lower Galilee.

of the country, its lakes and springs. I shall give a precise description of the sufferings of the prisoners taken in the several towns, from my own observation or personal share in them. For I shall conceal nothing even of my own misfortunes, as I shall be addressing persons who are well aware of them.

I shall next relate how, at the moment when the Jewish fortunes were on the decline, Nero's death occurred, and how Vespasian's advance upon Jerusalem was diverted by the call to imperial dignity; the portents of his elevation which he received, and the revolutions which took place in Rome; his proclamation by his soldiers as Emperor against his will; the civil war which, on his departure for Egypt to restore order to the realm, broke out among the Jews, the rise of the tyrants to power and their mutual feuds.

My narrative will proceed to tell of the second invasion of our country by Titus, starting from Egypt; how and where he mustered his forces, and their strength; the condition to which civil war had reduced the city on his arrival; his various assaults and the series of earthworks which he constructed; further, the triple line of our walls and their dimensions; the defenses of the city and the plan of the temple and sanctuary, the measurements of these buildings and of the altar being all precisely stated; certain festival customs, the seven degrees of purity, the ministerial functions of the priests, their vestments and those of the high priest, with a description of the Holy of Holies. Nothing shall be concealed, nothing added to facts which have been brought to light.

I shall then describe the tyrants' brutal treatment of their fellow-countrymen and the clemency of the Romans toward an alien race, and how often Titus, in his anxiety to save the city and the Temple, invited the rival parties to come to terms with him. I shall distinguish between the sufferings and calamities of the people, culminating in their defeat, as attributable respectively to the war, the sedition, and the famine. Nor shall I omit to record either the misfortunes of the deserters or the punishments inflicted on the prisoners; the burning of the Temple, contrary to Caesar's wishes, and the number of the sacred treasures rescued from the flames; the taking of the whole city and the signs and portents that preceded it; the capture of the tyrants, the number of the prisoners and the destiny allotted to each; nor yet how the Romans crushed the last remnants of the war and demolished the local fortresses; how Titus paraded the whole country and restored order; and lastly his return to Italy and triumph.

All of these topics I have comprised in seven books. While I have left no pretext for censure or accusation to persons who are cognizant of the facts and took part in the war, my work is written for lovers of the truth and not to gratify my readers.

⚜

PREFACE TO THE JEWISH ANTIQUITIES

Those who essay to write histories are actuated, I observe, not by one and the same aim, but by many widely different motives. Some, eager to display their literary skill and to win the fame therefrom expected, rush into this department of letters; others, to gratify the persons to whom the record happens to relate, have undertaken the requisite labor even though beyond their power; others again have been constrained by the mere stress of events in which they themselves took part to set these out in a comprehensive narrative; while many have been induced by prevailing ignorance of important affairs of general utility to publish a history of them for the public benefit. Of the aforesaid motives the two last apply to myself. For, having known by experience the war which we Jews waged against the Romans, the incidents in its course and its issue, I was constrained to narrate it in detail* in order to refute those who in their writings were doing outrage to the truth.

And now I have undertaken this present work in the belief that the whole Greek-speaking world will find it worthy of attention; for it will embrace our entire ancient history and political constitution, translated from the Hebrew records. I had indeed ere now, when writing the history of the war, already contemplated describing the origin of the Jews, the fortunes that befell them, the great lawgiver under whom they were trained in piety and the exercise of the other virtues, and all those wars waged by them through long ages before this last in which they were involuntarily engaged against the Romans. However, since the compass of such a theme was excessive, I made the War into a separate volume, with its own beginning and end, thus duly proportioning my work. Nevertheless, as time went on, as is wont to happen to those who design to attack large tasks, there was hesitation and delay on my part in rendering

*In The Jewish War.

so vast a subject into a foreign and unfamiliar tongue. However, there were certain persons curious about the history who urged me to pursue it, and above all Epaphroditus,* a man devoted to every form of learning, but specially interested in the experiences of history, conversant as he himself has been with large affairs and varying turns of fortune, through all of which he has displayed a wonderful force of character and an attachment to virtue that nothing could deflect. Yielding, then, to the persuasions of one who is ever an enthusiastic supporter of persons with ability to produce some useful or beautiful work, and ashamed of myself that I should be thought to prefer sloth to the effort of this noblest of enterprises, I was encouraged to greater ardor. Besides these motives, there were two further considerations to which I had given serious thought, namely, whether our ancestors on the one hand, were willing to communicate such information, and whether any of the Greeks, on the other, had been curious to learn our history.

I found then that the second of the Ptolemies,† that king who was so deeply interested in learning and such a collector of books, was particularly anxious to have our Law and the political constitution based thereon translated into Greek; while, on the other side Eleazar,‡ who yielded in virtue to none of our high priests, did not scruple to grant the monarch the enjoyment of a benefit, which he would certainly have refused had it not been our traditional custom to make nothing of what is good into a secret. Accordingly, I thought that it became me also both to imitate the high priest's magnanimity and to assume that there are still today many lovers of learning like the king. For even he failed to obtain all our records: it was only the portion containing the Law which was delivered to him by those who were sent to Alexandria to interpret it. The things narrated in the sacred Scriptures are, however, innumerable, seeing that they embrace the history of five thousand years and recount all sorts of surprising reverses, many fortunes of war, heroic exploits of generals, and political revolutions. But, speaking generally, the main lesson to be learned from this history by any who care to peruse it is that men who conform to the will of God, and do not venture to transgress laws that have been

---

*The historian's patron during the last part of his life.

†According to *The Letter of Aristeas,* Ptolemy II (called Philadelphus), who ruled Egypt from 283 to 245 B.C.E., initiated the Greek translation of the Hebrew Bible.

‡The high priest in the Aristeas story.

excellently laid down, prosper in all things beyond belief, and for their reward are offered by God felicity; whereas, in proportion as they depart from the strict observance of these laws, things otherwise practicable become impracticable, and whatever imaginary good thing they strive to do ends in irretrievable disasters. At the outset, then, I entreat those who will read these volumes to fix their thoughts on God, and to test whether our lawgiver has had a worthy conception of His nature and has always assigned to Him such actions as befit His power, keeping his words concerning Him pure of that unseemly mythology current among others; albeit that, in dealing with ages so long and so remote, he would have had ample license to invent fictions. For he was born two thousand years ago, to which ancient date the poets never ventured to refer even the birth of their gods, much less the actions of the laws of mortals. The precise details of our Scripture records will, then, be set forth, each in its place, as my narrative proceeds, that being the procedure that I have promised to follow throughout this work, neither adding nor omitting anything.

But, since well-nigh everything herein related is dependent on the wisdom of our lawgiver Moses, I must first speak briefly of him, lest any of my readers should ask how it is that so much of my work, which professes to treat of laws and historical facts, is devoted to natural philosophy. Be it known, then, that that sage deemed it above all necessary, for one who would order his own life aright and also legislate for others, first to study the nature of God, and then, having contemplated His works with the eye of reason, to imitate so far as possible that best of all models and endeavor to follow it. For neither could the lawgiver himself, without this vision, ever attain to a right mind, nor would anything that he should write in regard to virtue avail with his readers, unless before all else they were taught that God, as the universal Father and Lord who beholds all things, grants to such as follow Him a life of bliss, but involves in dire calamities those who step outside the path of virtue. Such, then, being the lesson which Moses desired to instill in his fellow-citizens, he did not, when framing his laws, begin with contracts and the mutual rights of man, as others have done; no, he led their thoughts up to God and the construction of the world; he convinced them that of all God's works upon earth we men are the fairest; and when once he had won their obedience to the dictates of piety, he had no further difficulty in persuading them of all the rest. Other legislators, in fact, following fables, have in their writings imputed to the gods the disgraceful errors of men and thus furnished the wicked with a powerful excuse; our legislator, on the contrary, having shown that God possesses the very perfection of virtue, thought that men should strive to participate in it, and inexorably punished those who did not hold with or believe in these doctrines. I therefore entreat my readers to examine my work from this point of view. For, studying it in this spirit, nothing will appear to them unreasonable, nothing incongruous with the majesty of God and His love for man; everything, indeed, is here set forth in keeping with the nature of the universe; some things the lawgiver shrewdly veils in enigmas, others he sets forth in solemn allegory; but wherever straightforward speech was expedient, there he makes his meaning absolutely plain. Should any further desire to consider the reasons for every article in our creed, he would find the inquiry profound and highly philosophical; that subject for the moment I defer, but, if God grants me time, I shall endeavor to write upon it after completing the present work.

INTRODUCTION TO THE DEAD SEA SECT

THE MEMBERS *of the Qumran community, living in the caves by the shore of the Dead Sea during the last two centuries of the Second Temple, had fled there from the more populated regions of the land, purposely removing themselves from the surrounding world. Although scholars are not fully agreed as to the group's identity (most today identify the sect with the Essenes described by Josephus), the scrolls which were discovered beginning in 1947 leave no doubt as to its view of history. To these sectarians, God rules the world according to a fixed scheme which human beings cannot hope to alter. In His wisdom He has allowed evil to be active in the world, but He has also determined its ultimate defeat. In the end, God's elect, the "sons of light," will triumph over the "sons of darkness." They will receive their due reward while their opponents suffer eternal damnation. The history of the present, therefore, has little significance; it consists merely of variations of wickedness. Only the final consummation of history will be of genuine consequence.*

This eschatalogical outlook is basic to the Manual of Discipline, perhaps the most revelatory document of the sect. In addition to describing the rules and rites of the community, the manual gives us an insight into the sect's view of the world. The

64

selection which follows best illustrates the author's belief in the unchangeability of the present order. Mankind is divided into those under the domination of the Prince of Light and those subject to the Angel of Darkness. The former are possessed by the spirit of truth; the latter by the spirit of perversity. While the author does seem to allow for some individual freedom in choosing which of the two spirits to follow, perversity will continue to beset Truth until the end of the term God has appointed for it. Then the sect, which has withdrawn itself from history to await the end, will finally be vindicated.

OF THE TWO SPIRITS IN MAN

This is for the man who would bring others to the inner vision, so that he may understand and teach to all the children of light the real nature of men, touching the different varieties of their temperaments with the distinguishing traits thereof, touching their actions throughout their generations, and touching the reason why they are now visited with afflictions and now enjoy periods of well-being.

All that is and ever was comes from a God of knowledge. Before things came into existence He determined the plan of them; and when they fill their appointed roles, it is in accordance with His glorious design that they discharge their functions. Nothing can be changed. In His hand lies the government of all things. God it is that sustains them in their needs.

Now, this God created man to rule the world, and appointed for him two spirits after whose direction he was to walk until the final Inquisition.* They are the spirits of truth and of perversity.

The origin of truth lies in the Fountain of Light, and that of perversity in the Wellspring of Darkness. All who practice righteousness are under the domination of the Prince of Lights, and walk in ways of light; whereas all who practice perversity are under the domination of the Angel of Darkness and walk in ways of darkness. Through the Angel of Darkness, however, even those who practice righteousness are made liable to error. All their sin and their iniquities, all their guilt and their deeds of transgression are the result of his domination; and this, by God's inscrutable design, will continue until the time appointed by Him. Moreover, all men's afflictions and all their moments of tribulation are due to this being's malevolent sway. All of the spirits that attend upon him are bent on causing the sons of light to stumble. Howbeit, the God of Israel and the Angel of His truth† are always there to help the sons of light. It is God that created these spirits of light and darkness and made them the basis of every act, the [instigators] of every deed and the directors of every thought. The one He loves to all eternity, and is ever pleased with its deeds; but any association with the other He abhors, and He hates all its ways to the end of time.

*The Last Judgment when the spirit of perversity will finally be destroyed.

† Possibly Gabriel, who is the champion of the sect against the powers of evil.

This is the way those spirits operate in the world. The enlightenment of man's heart, the making straight before him all the ways of righteousness and truth, the implanting in his heart of fear for the judgments of God, of a spirit of humility, of patience, of abundant compassion, of perpetual goodness, of insight, of perception, of that sense of the Divine Power that is based at once on an apprehension of God's works and a reliance on His plenteous mercy, of a spirit of knowledge informing every plan of action, of a zeal for righteous government, of a hallowed mind in a controlled nature, of abounding love for all who follow the truth, of a self-respecting purity which abhors all the taint of filth, of a modesty of behavior coupled with a general prudence and an ability to hide within oneself the secrets of what one knows—these are the things that come to men in this world through communion with the spirit of truth. And the reward of all that walk in its ways is health and abundant well-being, with long life and fruition of seed along with eternal blessings and everlasting joy in the life of eternity, and a crown of glory and a robe of honor, amid light perpetual.

But to the spirit of perversity belong greed, remissness in right-doing, wickedness and falsehood, pride and presumption, deception and guile, cruelty and abundant insolence, shortness of temper and profusion of folly, arrogant passion, abominable acts in a spirit of lewdness, filthy ways in the thralldom of unchastity, a blasphemous tongue, blindness of eyes, dullness of ears, stiffness of neck and hardness of heart, to the end that a man walks entirely in ways of darkness and of evil cunning. The wage of all who walk in such ways is multitude of afflictions at the hands of all the angels of destruction, everlasting perdition through the angry wrath of an avenging God, eternal horror and perpetual reproach, the disgrace of final annihilation in the fire, darkness throughout the vicissitudes of life in every generation, doleful sorrow, bitter misfortune and darkling ruin—ending in extinction without remnant or survival.

It is to these things that all men are born, and it is to these that all the host of them are heirs throughout their generations. It is in these ways that men must walk and it is in these two divisions, according as a man inherits something of each, that all human acts are divided throughout all the ages of eternity. For God has appointed these two things to obtain in equal measure until the final age.

Between the two categories He has set an eternal enmity. Deeds of perversity are an abomination to Truth, while all the ways of Truth are an abomination to perversity; and there is a constant jealous rivalry between their two regimes, for they do not march in accord. Howbeit, God in His inscrutable wisdom has appointed a term for the existence of perversity, and when the time of Inquisition comes, He will destroy it for ever. Then Truth will emerge triumphant for the world, albeit now and until the time of the final judgment it go sullying itself in the ways of wickedness owing to the domination of perversity. Then, too, God will purge all the acts of man in the crucible of His truth, and refine for Himself all the fabric of man, destroying every spirit of perversity from within his flesh and cleansing him by the holy spirit from all the effects of wickedness. Like waters of purification He will sprinkle upon him the spirit of truth, to cleanse him of all the abominations of falsehood and of all pollution through the spirit of filth; to the end that, being made upright, men may have understanding of transcendental knowledge and of the lore of the sons of heaven, and that, being made blameless in their ways, they may be endowed with inner vision. For them has God chosen to be the partners of His eternal covenant, and theirs shall be all mortal glory. Perversity shall be no more, and all works of deceit shall be put to shame.

Thus far, the spirits of Truth and perversity have been struggling in the heart of man. Men have walked both in wisdom and in folly. If a man casts his portion with Truth, he does righteously and hates perversity; if he casts it with perversity, he does wickedly and abominates Truth. For God has apportioned them in equal measure until the final age, until He make all things new.* He foreknows the effect of their works in every epoch of the world, and He has made men heirs to them that they might know good and evil. But [when the time] of Inquisition [comes], He will determine the fate of every living being in accordance with which of the [two spirits he has chosen to follow].

*Cf. Isaiah 65:17 and Matthew 19:28.

THE MEDIEVAL JEW AND HISTORY

INTRODUCTION TO THE HISTORICAL VIEW OF THE RABBIS

THE BIBLICAL VIEW that Jewish history consists of the people's response to God's commands and His consequent reward or punishment is continued in Rabbinic literature. Here, too, obedience and rebellion are seen as determinative of Israel's fate. The Greek tradition of seeking secular explanation, which was present in Josephus, failed to establish itself among the Rabbis. Medieval Jews even went beyond the Bible in their disregard of temporal development. Unlike the biblical writers, who worked within a chronological framework, however schematized, and produced a minimal number of anachronisms, they believed that the Judaism of their own time, in its essential beliefs and practices, had been normative ever since Abraham. When they discussed the past, particular incidents, rather than its totality, caught their attention.

In the following selection from the Talmudic tractate Gittin, the Rabbis contemplate the reasons for the destruction of the Second Temple. The tale which they relate in explanation indicates their belief that so great a catastrophe could not have come about by chance. It can only be understood by the principle which governs Jewish history at all times: the law of religious/moral cause and effect. To be sure, the Rabbis are not all agreed that the anecdote of

Kamza and Bar Kamza was indeed the actual cause—there are various possibilities, and this is only one of them—but there can be no doubt as to the nature of the cause which brought about the calamity. And what is true for the destruction of the Temple is no less true for the other major events of Jewish history, as the passages from the tractates Shabbat and Yoma make clear.

The Talmudic outlook is perpetuated among the Jews of Christian Europe. In the biblical commentary of Rashi (Rabbi Solomon ben Isaac, 1040–1105), the most famous of the medieval Jewish exegetes, we can find the belief, still widespread in his day, that Judaism had remained basically unchanged from earliest times, that the Patriarchs had in fact instituted the morning, afternoon, and evening prayers. The excerpt chosen for presentation here attests to Rashi's acceptance of the belief that Jacob studied Torah in a school conducted by his ancestor Eber, an institution Rashi probably conceived of as little different from the Talmudic academies of much later times. This passage also exemplifies the attitude of veneration toward the biblical text which made necessary a reconciliation of apparently contradictory references. It was assumed that discrepancies could not exist in Divine revelation. The calculations which Rashi here undertakes are therefore not prompted by historical interest, but by the religious motive of defending the integrity of the text while at the same time vindicating Jacob's filial piety.

THE DESTRUCTION OF THE TEMPLE

The Tale of Kamza and Bar Kamza

The destruction of Jerusalem came through a Kamza and a Bar Kamza in this way. A certain man had a friend Kamza and an enemy Bar Kamza. He once made a party and said to his servant, Go and bring Kamza. The man went and brought Bar Kamza. When the man [who gave the party] found him there he said, See, you tell tales about me; what are you doing here? Get out. Said the other: Since I am here, let me stay, and I will pay you for whatever I eat and drink. He said, I won't. Then let me give you half the cost of the party. No, said the other. Then let me pay for the whole party. He still said, No, and he took him by the hand and put him out. Said the other, Since the Rabbis were sitting there and did not stop him, this shows that they agreed with him. I will go and inform against them to the Government. He went and said to the Emperor, the Jews are rebelling against you. He said, How can I tell? He said to him: Send them an offering and see whether they will offer it [on the altar]. So he sent with him a fine calf. While on the way he made a blemish on its upper lip, or as some say on the white of its eye, in a place where we [Jews] count it a blemish but they do not. The Rabbis were inclined to offer it in order not to offend the Government. Said R. Zechariah b. Abkulas to them: People will say that blemished animals are offered on the altar. They then proposed to kill Bar Kamza so that he should not go and inform against them, but R. Zechariah b. Abkulas said to them, Is one who makes a blemish on consecrated animals to be put to death? R. Johanan thereupon remarked: Through the scrupulousness of R. Zechariah b. Abkulas our House has been destroyed, our Temple burnt and we ourselves exiled from our land.

Idolatry, Immorality, and Bloodshed

Why was the first Sanctuary destroyed? Because of three [evil] things which prevailed there: idolatry, immorality, bloodshed. Idolatry, as it is written: "For the bed is too short for a man to stretch himself and the covering too narrow when he gathereth himself up" (Is. 28:20). What is the meaning of "For the bed is too short for a man to stretch himself"? R. Jonathan said: It is: This bed* is too short for two neighbors to stretch themselves. And [what is the meaning of] "the covering too narrow when he gathereth himself up"?—R. Samuel b. Nahmani said: When R. Jonathan [in his reading] came to this passage, he would cry and say: To Him, concerning Whom it is written, "He gathereth the waters of the sea together like a heap" (Ps. 33:7), the cover became too narrow!

Immorality [prevailed] as it is written: "Moreover the Lord said: Because the daughters of Zion are haughty, and walk with stretched-forth necks and wanton eyes, walking and mincing as they go, and make a tinkling with their feet" (Is. 3:16). "Because the daughters of Zion are haughty," i.e., they used to walk with proud carriage. "And wanton eyes" i.e., they filled their eyes with kohl.† "Walking and mincing as they go," i.e., they used to walk with the heel touching the toe. "And make a tinkling with their feet," R. Isaac said: They would take myrrh and balsam and place it in their shoes and when they came near the young men of Israel they would kick, causing the balsam to squirt at them and would thus cause the evil desire to enter them like an adder's poison.

Bloodshed [prevailed] as it is written: "Moreover Manasseh shed innocent blood very much, till he had filled Jerusalem from one end to another" (II Kings 21:16). They were wicked, but they placed their trust in the Holy One, blessed be He. For it is written, "The heads thereof judge for reward, and the priests thereof teach for hire, and the prophets thereof divine for money; yet will they lean upon the Lord and say: 'Is not the Lord in the midst of us? No evil shall come upon us'" (Micah 3:11). Therefore the Holy One, blessed be He, brought them three evil decrees as against the three evils which were their own: "Therefore shall Zion for your sake be plowed as a field, and Jerusalem shall become heaps, and the mountain of the house as the high places of a forest" (ibid., 3:12). But why was the second Sanctuary destroyed, seeing that in its time they were occupying themselves with Torah, [observance of] precepts and the practice of charity? Because therein prevailed

---

*Manasseh, the faithless king, introduced idols into the Temple (here represented by the bed and its covering). The idols left no room for the God of Israel.

† A powder used for painting the eyelids.

hatred without cause. That teaches you that groundless hatred is considered as of even gravity with the three sins of idolatry, immorality, and bloodshed together.

Religious and Moral Shortcomings

Abbaye said: Jerusalem was destroyed only because the Sabbath was desecrated therein, as it is said, "and they have hid their eyes from My sabbaths, therefore I am profaned among them" (Ezek. 22:26).

R. Abbahu said: Jerusalem was destroyed only because the reading of the shema* morning and evening was neglected [therein], for it is said, "Woe unto them that rise up early in the morning, that they may follow strong drink" [etc.]; and it is written, "And the harp and the lute, the tabret and the pipe, and wine, are in their feasts: but they regard not the work of the Lord;" and it is written, "Therefore my people are gone into captivity, for lack of knowledge" (Is. 5:11–13).

R. Hamnuna said: Jerusalem was destroyed only because they neglected [the education of] schoolchildren; for it is said, "pour it out [sc. God's wrath] because of the children in the street" (Jer. 6:11). Why pour it out? Because the child is in the street.†

Ulla said: Jerusalem was destroyed only because they [its inhabitants] were not ashamed of each other, for it is written, "Were they ashamed when they committed abomination? nay, they were not at all ashamed [. . . therefore they shall fall]" (Jer. 6:15).

R. Isaac said: Jerusalem was destroyed only because the small and the great were made equal, for it is said, "And it shall be, like people like priest"; which is followed by, "The earth shall be utterly emptied" (Is. 24:2–3).

R. Amram son of R. Simeon b. Abba said in R. Simeon b. Abba's name in R. Hanina's name: Jerusalem was destroyed only because they did not rebuke each other: for it is said, "Her princes are become like harts that find no pasture" (Lam. 1:6): just as the hart, the head of one is at the side of the other's tail, so Israel of that generation hid their faces in the earth,‡ and did not rebuke each other.

*The twice-daily recitation of Deuteronomy 6:4: "Hear, O Israel: the Lord our God, the Lord is One."

†There is no school provided for him.

‡They shut their eyes to evil.

RASHI / CHRONOLOGY AND CHARACTER

"So Esau went unto Ishmael, and took unto the wives that he had Mahalath the daughter of Ishmael Abraham's son, the sister of Nebaioth, to be his wife" (Gen. 28:9).

The Sister of Nebaioth—From the statement in the text that she was "the daughter of Ishmael" would I not know that she was the sister of Nebaioth? Rather, it teaches us that Ishmael died after he had betrothed her to Esau, but before her wedding, and her brother Nebaioth gave her away in marriage. It also teaches us that at that time Jacob was sixty-three years old. For Ishmael was seventy-four years old when Jacob was born. Ishmael was fourteen years older than Isaac, and Isaac was sixty years old when [Esau and Jacob] were born, making a total of seventy-four. [Ishmael] lived to be 137, as it is said: "And these are the years of the life of Ishmael, a hundred and thirty and seven years" (Gen. 25:17). Thus when Ishmael died, Jacob was sixty-three years old. Here we further learn that [Jacob] concealed himself for fourteen years in the house of Eber, and afterward he went to Haran. For he remained in the house of Laban for only fourteen years before the birth of Joseph, as it is said: "I served thee fourteen years for thy two daughters, and six years for thy flock" (Gen. 31:41). And he received the flock as wages only after Joseph was born, as it is said: "And it came to pass when Rachel had borne Joseph . . ." (ibid., 30:25) [that he received the flock as wages]. Now Joseph was thirty years old when he came to power. Nine years elapsed from then until Jacob went down into Egypt (seven of plenty and two of famine). Jacob said to Pharoah: "The days of my sojournings are a hundred and thirty years" (ibid., 47:9). Add it up: fourteen years before the birth of Joseph plus thirty years of Joseph's life, and nine years that he ruled until Jacob came, gives us a total of fifty-three years. But when he left his father he was sixty-three years old, making a total of 116 years. But [Jacob] says [to Pharoah] that he is 130 years old. Fourteen years are missing! From this you learn that after he received the blessings, he concealed himself in the house of Eber for fourteen years. But he was not punished [on that account]* because of the merit [of his studying] the Torah [during that time]. For Joseph was separated from his father for only twenty-two years, i.e. from his seventeenth year to his thirty-ninth, corresponding to the twenty-two years that Jacob was separated from his father [Isaac] and was unable to honor him—twenty years in the house of Laban and two years on the road, as it is written: "And he built him a house and made booths for his cattle" (ibid., 33:17). Our Rabbis interpreted this verse to mean that he spent eighteen months on the way since the house was for the rainy season and the booths for the summertime. According to the calculation based on scriptural verses which we made above, from the time he left his father until he went down into Egypt at the age of 130 we find a surplus of fourteen years. But on his way to Laban he surely concealed himself in the house of Eber in order that he might study the Torah with him, and on account of the merit of [studying] the Torah he was not punished for them. . . . .

*As he might have been for not serving the needs of his father during that fourteen-year period.

INTRODUCTION TO ABRAHAM IBN DAUD

*I*BN DAUD (c. 1110–1180), who lived first in southern Spain and then in Toledo, is known to us for his philosophical writing no less than for his historiography. In both these fields, his aim was basically the same: to argue for the validity of the Jewish tradition. In one case he drew his evidence from philosophy, in the other from history. The overt purpose of his Book of Tradition, as he clearly expressed it in the Prologue which follows as the first selection, is to establish the continuity of the chain of transmission whereby the Oral Law, held coeval with the written Torah, was faithfully handed down from biblical times to the present. The author was prompted to this task by the challenge of the Karaite sect, which had broken off from Rabbinic Judaism a few centuries earlier and had denied the solidity of that chain. To confute the Karaites, his book presents the kabala, the passing on of the tradition from generation to generation through a sequence of seven eras of teachers: the men of the Bible, the leaders of the Second Temple period, the Tannaim, Amoraim, Savoraim, Geonim, and Rabbis. Never during all the generations, according to ibn Daud, did any serious differences of opinion arise which might impugn the authority of the tradition.

While primary, his polemical motive seems not, however, to have been his only one. He may also have desired to prove the symmetry of Jewish history as indicated by equivalent periods stretching from Abraham to the end of prophecy and from that point to the coming of the Messiah. If so, Jewish history would attest to the continuous Providence of God and hint at the coming messianic redemption. As Gerson D. Cohen, the work's recent editor, has pointed out, such numerical speculation and its consequent consolation would be deemed worthy of a contemporary intellectual in the Spanish Jewish milieu, while concern with the historical events for their own sake would not.

To be sure, ibn Daud's account is not entirely limited to a dry recitation of names. Here and there information extraneous to the basic purpose of the work is given as well. Especially as the narrative comes closer to his own time, ibn Daud expands his horizons to include material which would reflect favorably upon the stature of the Spanish Jewish community and justify its spiritual independence from the academies of Babylonia. In the final chapter, he relates in some detail a probably fictitious tale of four rabbis from southern Italy who were taken captive by a Muslim sea captain and then sold into slavery in North Africa and Spain. Once freed by their fellow Jews, they became legal authorities for their respective communities, considerably raising the level of learning. However, it is the underlying polemic against the Karaites which remains basic. It returns again explicitly in the Epilogue, the beginning of which is the second selection below.

THE RELIABILITY OF THE RABBINIC TRANSMISSION

The purpose of this *Book of Tradition* is to provide students with the evidence that all the teachings of our rabbis of blessed memory, namely, the sages of the Mishnah and the Talmud,* have been transmitted: each great sage and righteous man having received them from a great sage and righteous man, each head of an academy and his school having received them from the head of an academy and his school, as far back as the men of the Great Assembly,† who received them from the prophets, of blessed memory all. Never did the sages of the Talmud, and certainly not the sages of the Mishnah, teach anything, however trivial, of their own invention, except for the enactments which were made by universal agreement in order to make a hedge about the Torah.‡

Now should anyone infected with heresy§ attempt to mislead you, saying: "It is because the rabbis differed on a number of issues that I doubt their words," you should retort bluntly and inform him that he is "a rebel against the decision of the court";‖ and that our rabbis of blessed memory never differed with respect to a commandment in principle, but only with respect to its details; for they had heard the principle from their teachers, but had not inquired as to its details, since they had not waited upon their masters sufficiently.¶ As a case in point, they did not differ as to whether or not it is obligatory to light the Sabbath lamp; what they did dispute was "with what it may be lighted and with what it may not be lighted." Similarly, they did not differ as to whether we are

*The Mishnah is the first authoritative compilation of Rabbinic law, completed in Palestine in the early third century, C.E. Later it was expanded by the addition of the Gemara (here simply called Talmud) to form the Talmud.

†The first of the Rabbis, in the second century B.C.E.

‡ Laws which made trespassing against the written commandments of the Bible less likely.

§ A Karaite, who denies the authority of the Rabbinic tradition.

‖ That is, he has rebelled against the binding authority of the Rabbis.

¶ Had the contact of students with teachers been more extended, there would have been no differences even with regard to details.

required to recite the *shema* evenings and mornings; what they differed on was "from when may the *shema* be recited in the evenings" and "from when may the *shema* be recited in the mornings."* This holds true for all their discussions.

THE UNBROKEN CHAIN

Thus there were ten generations from the prophets Haggai, Zechariah, and Malachi until Rabban Johanan b. Zakkai,† five generations of Tannaim‡ and seven generations of Amoraim,§ giving a total of twenty-two generations until the end of the Amoraic period. Then there were five generations of Savoraic rabbis, ‖ eight generations of the Gaonate¶ and three generations of the Rabbinate: the generation of R. Nissim, R. Hananel, and R. Samuel the Nagid; the generation of the five rabbis named Isaac; and the generation of R. Joseph ha-Levi** and R. Barukh b. R. Isaac. Thus, there were sixteen generations from the sealing of the Talmud until the demise of R. Joseph ha-Levi, of blessed memory. This gives a grand total of thirty-eight generations from Haggai, Zechariah, and Malachi until R. Joseph ha-Levi, of blessed memory. All of them were trustworthy witnesses, who received [the tradition] on the testimony of trustworthy witnesses, and their sacred chain of tradition has never been broken.

Such is not the case with the heretics.†† The fact is that Anan

*The question of determining the times of day for proclaiming God's unity opens the first tractate of the Talmud.

†Johanan ben Zakkai (first century C.E.), the leading sage at the end of the Second Temple period and immediately thereafter.

‡The sages of the period of Mishnah (first and second centuries C.E.).

§The scholars of the period of the Gemara (third through fifth centuries).

‖Babylonian sages of the period immediately following the compilation of the Babylonian Talmud (sixth and seventh centuries).

¶The institution of highest religious authority in Babylonia (end of the seventh to middle of the eleventh century).

**Joseph Ha-Levi ibn Migash (1077–1141), outstanding Talmudic scholar of Spanish Jewry who died twenty years before ibn Daud wrote his book.

††The Karaites.

the wicked* and his son Saul, may the name of the wicked rot, were disciples of R. Yehudai,† who broke with him and his tradition without any substantive ground whatever, but only out of the envy that overcame them. Hence, they cannot possibly say: "Thus have we received on the testimony of So-and-So [who received] from the prophets." Instead, they fabricate things out of their own hearts.

---

*Anan ben David (eighth century), regarded as the founder of the Karaites.

†Yehudai ben Nahman, head of the Babylonian Talmudic academy at Sura (c. 757–761).

INTRODUCTION TO THE CHRONICLE OF AHIMAAZ

AHIMAAZ BEN Paltiel (1017–c. 1060) the descendant of a distinguished Jewish family, lived in southern Italy during the last years of Byzantine rule. In 1054 he moved from Capua to Oria, where his ancestors had first settled. Proud of his lineage, he determined to compose a "Scroll of Genealogies" which would contain not only his line of descent but also as much as was still known about the exploits of each generation. His motive was filial piety, his scope almost entirely limited to the leading members of his own family. As it was probably intended for his children and their progeny, the work seems to have received little circulation and only a single manuscript has survived. Yet it possesses considerable historical value for the light it sheds on the otherwise sparsely documented Jewish life of southern Italy from the the ninth to the eleventh centuries. Its historiographical importance lies in the author's turning to the past for a purpose which is neither polemical nor, despite the prayerful tone at the beginning and end, basically religious.

Ahimaaz was a man of letters, but in no sense a critical historian. He allowed the supernatural and the natural, the fantastic and the factually credible, to dwell side-by-side without making any endeavor at differentiation. The selection which follows aptly

83

illustrates this characteristic. It relates how R. Shephatiah, one of the most illustrious members of the clan, succeeded in saving his community from the proselytizing ambitions of Emperor Basil I. The outline of his account, based on written or oral sources, rings true; the splendor of the Byzantine court and the Emperor's missionary zeal to convert the Jews are confirmed from other documents. But at the same time Ahimaaz does not doubt that his ancestor was able to converse with demons as easily as with emperors. Indeed, this supernatural capacity redounds to the glory of the family no less than Shephatiah's more mundane achievements.

The chronicle is written in the rhymed Hebrew prose which had been adapted from the model of Arabic writers and it embodies a number of acrostics. Aesthetically pleasing literary form was apparently as important a consideration for Ahimaaz as the narrative itself. The translation given here preserves the line division of the original, but no attempt has been made to reproduce the rhyme.

RABBI SHEPHATIAH, DEFENDER OF HIS PEOPLE

At that time and in those days
A king reigned over the Edomites,*
A man of injustice, deceit, and bloodshed.
In his heart he devised a scheme to silence
The proclaiming of the unity of God (Whose work is perfect)
By the seed of holy and upright men.
With the passing of eight hundred years
Since the Holy City's ruin,
The Exile of Israel and Judah,
The destruction of the exalted sanctuary,
There arose a servant of Haman†
To extirpate the unforsaken people—
A king, and his name was Basil.‡
He meant to lead it astray,
To wipe out its memory and remnant,
To exterminate the survivors of Israel,
To turn them away from the Torah
And make them err in the religion of despair.
He sent out swift couriers
To all of the provinces
And riders on horseback
He sent to all parts
Of his realm,
That were subject to him:
To turn the Jews from their faith
And make them follow in error.
The messengers ranged
Even beyond Otranto,§
Where they embarked on a ship

*The Christians of the Roman Empire.

† The villain of the book of Esther.

‡ Basil I, Byzantine Emperor (867–886).

§Town in southern Italy, site of a fairly large and learned Jewish community.

And crossed to the province of Apulia.*
When the news arrived
The land did tremble.
They traversed the province from end to end
And came to the environs of Oria,†
Bringing epistle with seal:
The seal of the king.
And the seal was of gold—
On the letter sent by the king to R. Shephatiah.‡

And these are the words of the letter,
Written and inscribed therein:
"I, Basil the king, have sent for you;
You are to come unto me,
And refuse not your presence.
For I have heard of your wisdom,
The depth of your understanding,
And the vastness of your learning.
It is my desire to see you,
And I swear by my life
And by the crown on my head
That your coming will be in peace
And I shall certainly return you to your home.
I shall show you honor
As I would do to my own kin;
Any request you may seek of me
I shall grant with abounding affection.

Then he embarked on the vessel
And came up to Constantinople,
Which King Constantine§ had built.
(May God shatter its power
And that of all its inhabitants.)

*In southern Italy.

† Small town near Brindisi in southern Italy containing an important Jewish community.

‡ Shephatiah ben Amittai (d. 886), religious poet and leader of the Jewish communities of southern Italy.

§ Constantine I (c. 288–337), Roman Emperor who founded Constantinople as the capital of the Roman Empire in the East in 330.

But God's grace availed him before the king
And he found favor in his eyes and in the eyes of the court.

Then the king conversed with him about the Torah;
He asked him regarding the Temple's construction
And the building of the house of impurity
That is called by the name "Sophia."*
"Which one demanded more funds?"
Inquired the king.
He insisted it was the construction of Sophia,
For into this one building
Had gone untold wealth.
But R. Shephatiah's word of response
Was correct and considered:
"Let the king command
That Scripture be brought before him.
There he will find the answer
As to which structure cost the more."
Immediately it was done,
And he found that the funds
Used by David and Solomon
Exceeded the measure
Weighed out for Sophia:
By 120 talents of gold
And by five hundred talents of silver and more.
Thereupon said the king:
"R. Shephatiah has excelled me in wisdom."
But he responded and said: "Sir,
Scripture has prevailed against you, not I."

Then they sat down to eat,
And refresh themselves at the table
With delicacies and with fruits.
Bowls made of gold
Were set before him
That he might eat his food pure,
In accordance with the Torah's command.
With chains of exquisite silver
The bowls were lowered from above;

*The cathedral of Hagia Sophia in Constantinople.

And from whence they descended before him
No man was able to see.

Now Basil had a daughter
Whom he loved as the apple of his eye.
But a demon tormented her
And he could find no cure.
So he spoke to him in secret
And entrusted him with a plea:
"Help me, Shephatiah,
Cure my daughter of her affliction."
He responded: "I shall surely do it
With the help of God Almighty."
He asked him: "Have you some special place
In which there is no impurity?"
The king answered: "I have Bukoleon,*
The beautiful garden."
So they inspected it
And he liked Bukoleon
(Which literally means: "mouth of a lion").
There he brought the maiden
And exorcised the demon in the name of the Dweller on High
And the name of the Creator of heaven and earth,
Who founded the earth in His wisdom,
Maker of mountains and seas,
Who suspends the world upon nothing.
Then the demon cried aloud:
"Why will you bring comfort
To the daughter of the wicked
Whose sinful rule
Has multiplied evil
For the people redeemed?
God has delivered her to me
To humble and to break her.
Now leave me,
For I shall not come out from my place."
Then he answered the demon:
"To your words I will not respond.
Come out in the name of the Lord,

*Palace and gardens of the Byzantine emperors, built overlooking the Sea of Marmora.

That he may know God is with Israel."
Immediately it came forth
And fled away in haste.
But he seized it
And thrust it in a vessel of lead.
The vessel he closed tight
And sealed it in the name of his Master.
He cast it into the sea
That it sank in the flood of waters,
While the maiden went, tranquil and calm,
In peace to the king and the queen.

Then he came to the king for dismissal
And the king came forward to greet him,
He placed his arm on his neck
And led him into his chambers.
Then he began to lure him from his faith
And tempt him with the bounty of his gifts
To stray after vanity.
He took him outside
And pressed him with urgency.
He approached him with a bribe
And appointed him companions.
When Shephatiah beheld this insolence and zeal,
He cried out in loud voice:
"Mighty sir,
You overwhelm me with violence!"
Thereupon the king arose from his throne;
He lifted him up from among the people
And gave him permission to go.
He sent him to the queen
That she give him blessing and gift.
The queen asked him of his affairs:
"Have you daughters or sons?"
He answered her readily:
"Your servant has one son and two daughters."
She gave him the rings in her ears
And the belt around her waist.
She urged him: "As tribute to your learning—
Give them to your two daughters.
For in costliness they are without parallel

And their value is beyond measure."
The weight of the rings was a liter of gold
And the belt was equal in price.

When he was ready to leave,
The king called him aloud
And said: "Shephatiah, request of me
And I shall give you of my wealth.
But should you desire no money,
I shall leave to you cities and towns;
For thus did I write you,
That I would fulfill your desire and wish."
But he answered him downcast,
Bitterly weeping and sad:
"If my lord would favor Shephatiah,
Let those who seek wisdom find peace;
Do not make them abandon God's Torah
Nor drive them to the desert
Of mourning and grief.
But if in this wise you refuse
To fulfill so completely my wish,
Do this much for me—
Let no persecution come to my city."
The king, from deep in his throat,
In anger exclaimed:
"Had I not sent you my seal
And sworn to you by my own self,
I would wreak evil upon you
At this very moment, right now.
But how can I harm you,
Having sent you my word?
I am unable to retract
What I have said in my letter."
So he set forth a decree, sealed in gold,
That no persecution occur in Oria,
And he sent him back to his city in honor,
In peace to his house and his parlor.

INTRODUCTION TO THE CRUSADE CHRONICLE OF SOLOMON BAR SIMEON

THE FIRST CRUSADE of 1096 proved a traumatic experience for Ashkenazic Jewry which had hitherto enjoyed a relatively tranquil existence in Western and Central Europe. As the Crusaders moved eastward to conquer the Christian holy places from the Muslims, they turned first to the Jewish communities in their path, pillaging and murdering the infidels who dwelled in the midst of Christendom. The Jewish communities of the Rhineland and those further to the east responded by choosing martyrdom over submission to the baptism which was offered them as the only alternative.

Unless earlier chronicles have perished, these massacres seem for the first time to have prompted Ashkenazic Jewry to record for posterity the events of their own age. The account from which excerpts are presented below is one of three which have come down to us in whole or in part. It was apparently written about a generation after the events it describes. The author, Solomon bar Simeon, probably relied on an earlier written account as well as on the oral testimony of witnesses. Whatever his sources, his presentation is vivid and rich in detail, though the chronological sequence is notably faulty.

Since the beginning of the account is not extant, we do not know what reasons, if any, the author gave at the outset for committing his tale to writing. But the primarily, or even exclusively, religious character of his intent is abundantly clear: God chooses the martyrs to sanctify His name so that succeeding generations might benefit from the merit of their acts. For this reason their death has relevance for all Jewry. In addition, it serves as an example to others should God at some future time choose them for the same purpose.

Though the author speaks of the Crusaders in the vilest epithets, they are to his mind really but agents of God's will, the rod of His anger as Babylonia and Rome had been. Solomon, no less than his protagonists, realizes that attempts at escape must in the end be futile. Since he can find no obvious sin among the "holy men" of the communities, he must ascribe their calamity to the collective burden of wrongdoing going back as far as the golden calf. The sins of the past affect the present no less than the merit of the martyrs will be accounted to all Jewry in the future.

The first excerpt presented here is taken from the beginning of the account and relates the persecutions in the Rhenish cities of Spires, Worms, and Mainz. The second selection recounts the martyrdom of R. Kalonymus ben Meshullam, the leader of the Mainz community. It also reveals how the author treats contradictory accounts of the manner of his hero's death: he presents each opinion but concludes that the significant fact is the freely chosen martyrdom itself, not the manner in which it came about. The brief final excerpt supplies the author's theological interpretation.

{ornament}

MASSACRES IN THE RHINELAND

Now I shall relate how the persecution also spread to the remaining communities which were slain for the name of the One, and how they clung to the Lord, God of their fathers, proclaiming His unity with their last breath.

It was in the year 4856,* the year 1028 of our exile, in the eleventh year of the 256th lunar cycle, at a time when we hoped for salvation and consolation according to the word of the prophet Jeremiah: "Sing with gladness for Jacob, and shout at the head of the nations . . ." (31:7). But it turned instead into grief and lamentation, weeping and screams. We were afflicted with the many evils that are mentioned in all of the [biblical] threats of punishment;† both those which are written and those which are not, came upon us.

At first there arose against us insolent men, a foreign people, a bitter and impetuous nation, French and Germans. They had planned to travel to the Holy City, desecrated by robbers, in order to seek there the grave of the hanged bastard,‡ to chase out the Muslims who dwelled in the land and to conquer the land for themselves. They set up their own signs for emblems and fastened a detestable symbol, a Cross, upon their garments, all the men and women whose hearts prompted them to travel the road of error to the grave of their messiah, until they were more numerous than locusts upon the face of the earth: men, women, and children. Of them it is said: "The locusts have no king . . ." (Prov. 30:27). Now as they passed through the towns where the Jews lived, they said to one another: "Here we are going on a long journey to search out the House of Idolatry§ and to seek vengeance against the Muslims, when, behold, the Jews are dwelling in our midst, they whose ancestors slew him and crucified him without cause. Let us first take

*According to the Era of Creation. It is the equivalent of 1096 C.E.

† Deuteronomy 28:15–69.

‡ Jesus. Impotent anger drove the writer to express references to everything connected with Christianity in the most derogatory terms.

§ The Church of the Holy Sepulchre in Jerusalem.

vengeance upon them and eradicate them from among the peoples so that the name of Israel not be remembered; or let them become like us and acknowledge the son of the menstruant woman."

When the communities heard of their words, they resorted to the response of our ancestors: repentance, prayer, and acts of charity. But the members of the holy people were powerless, their hearts melted, and their strength ebbed. They hid themselves in the most secret places against the threatening sword; they afflicted their souls with fasting and abstained from drink for three consecutive days, night and day, aside from their daily penances, until their skin shriveled upon their bones and became as withered as a stick. They shouted and raised a great and bitter cry, but their Father did not answer them. He shut out their prayer and covered Himself with a cloud, so that no prayer might pass through; He despised the tent of Israel and removed them from His presence. It was His decree stemming from "In the day when I visit . . ." (Ex. 32:34).* This was the generation that He chose to be His portion. For they possessed the strength and courage to stand in His Temple, to fulfill His word, and to sanctify His great name in His world. Of them David says: "Bless the Lord, ye messengers of His, ye mighty in strength, that fulfill His word . . ." (Ps. 103:20).

In that year the Passover fell on Thursday and the New Moon of Iyar on Friday. On the Sabbath of the eighth of Iyar, the enemies rose up against the community of Spires and slew eleven holy souls. They were the first who sanctified their Creator on the holy Sabbath, as they refused to reek of their stench.† Among them was one esteemed and pious woman who killed herself in sanctification of God's name; she was the first of those who slaughtered themselves or were slaughtered in all of the communities. The remainder were saved by the bishop without having to change their faith.

On the 23rd of Iyar they attacked the community of Worms, which had divided itself into two groups. A portion remained in their houses and a portion fled to the bishop. Then desert wolves rose up against them who were in their houses and despoiled men, women, and children, young and old. They ripped down the stairs and destroyed the houses; they plundered and took booty; they

*Later generations of Jews, as well, share some guilt for the sin of the golden calf related in Exodus 32.

†To submit to the odium of the ceremony of baptism.

seized the Torah scroll and trampled it in the mud, tore and burned it; they devoured Israel with open mouth. After seven days, on the New Moon of Sivan, the day on which Israel arrived at Sinai to receive the Torah, those who still remained in the bishop's palace were placed in terror. The enemy treated them cruelly, just like the first group, and put them to the sword. But they were strengthened by the example of their brothers; they allowed themselves to be killed and they sanctified the name of God in the sight of all. They stretched out their necks and permitted their heads to be cut off for the name of their Creator. There were those among them who raised a hand against themselves. They fulfilled the verse: "The mother was dashed in pieces with her children" (Hos. 10:14); and fathers fell on their sons, for they were slain on top of them. Men slaughtered their brothers and relatives, their wives and children; also bridegrooms their brides and the compassionate woman her beloved. All of them accepted the judgment of Heaven with a whole heart. Consigning their souls to their Maker, they cried aloud: "Hear, O Israel: the Lord our God, the Lord is One" (Deut. 6:4). The enemies stripped them, dragged and threw them about; they left alive only the very few whom they baptized forcibly and against their will in their reeking waters. About eight hundred was the number of the slain who were killed in those two days, and all of them were brought naked to the grave. Of them Jeremiah laments: "They that were brought up in scarlet embrace dunghills" (Lam. 4:5). May God remember them for the good.

When the holy men, the pious ones of the Most High, the sacred community of Mainz, shield and protector of the communities, whose fame is spread throughout all lands—when they heard that part of the community in Spires had been slain, and the community of Worms had been attacked for the second time, and that the sword was reaching toward them, then their hands weakened, their hearts melted and became as water. They cried to the Lord with all their heart: "Lord, God of Israel, wilt Thou totally destroy the remnant of Israel? Where are all Thy awesome miracles of which our fathers told us? Didst Thou not bring us up out of Egypt and Babylonia and so frequently save us? How is it that now Thou hast left and abandoned us, O Lord, to deliver us into the hand of wicked Edom* that it might destroy us? Distance not Thyself from us for trouble is near and there is none to help us." So

*A designation for the Christians.

the leaders of Israel gathered together to formulate a plan whereby they might be saved. They said one to another: "Let us select some of our elders to decide what we should do, for this great evil will swallow us up." They agreed to offer ransom for their lives, to scatter their money, bribing princes, nobles, bishops, and governors. Thereupon the heads of the community, those esteemed by the bishop, arose and went to the bishop, his officials and retainers, in order to speak with them. They said to them: "What shall we do about the news we have heard, that our brothers in Spires and in Worms have been slain?" They replied to them: "Listen to our advice! Bring all of your money to our treasury. Then you, your wives, sons, and daughters, and all that belong to you may stay in the palace of the bishop until these bands will have passed through and thus you will be able to save yourselves from the hands of the errants." But they gave this advice only in order to gather us together and have us delivered into their hand, to seize us as fish that are caught in an evil net and to take our money—which they finally did. The end proves the beginning. But then the bishop did gather his officials and retainers, mighty nobles, gentry of the land, in order to aid us, for in the beginning it was his will to save us with all his power; and we gave him, his officials, and retainers a large bribe to save us. But in the end all of the bribing and all of the conciliation were of no use in shielding us from calamity on the Day of Anger.

At this time there arose an obstinate duke by the name of Gottfried*—may his bones be pulverized—who was led astray by the spirit of harlotry to join those going to their Idolatry. He took an evil vow not to set out on his way until he had avenged the blood of the Hanged One with the blood of Israel and not to leave remnant or refugee from those who bore the name Jew; and he was filled with anger against us. But there was raised up a repairer of the breach, the paragon of the generation, a fearer of God, worthy of the offering upon the innermost altar, R. Kalonymus,† leader of the community of Mainz. While there was still time, he sent a messenger to King Henry‡ in the Kingdom of Apulia,§ where he

*Godfrey of Bouillon, leader of a German contingent of Crusaders numbering some 40,000 men.

†Kalonymus ben Meshullam ha-Parnas, scion of the eminent Kalonymus family of Germany which flourished from the ninth to the thirteenth century.

‡Henry IV, German Emperor (1056–1106).

§Usually refers to southern Italy, but here probably Italy as a whole is intended.

had been staying for nine years, and he reported to him all of the incidents. The king became angry and sent letters to all the lands of his kingdom, to princes, bishops, governors, and to Duke Gottfried, words of peace: to protect the Jews so that no one do them bodily harm and to assist them and give them refuge. Thereupon the evil duke swore that he had never intended to do them any harm. Nonetheless, in Cologne they paid him five hundred pieces of refined silver. Likewise in Mainz they gave him money, and he promised to be their support and to act peaceably toward them. But the Maker of Peace had departed from them and turned His eyes away from His people; He turned them over to the sword. No prophet or seer, no man of wisdom and understanding can determine the root of it, how it was that the sin of the very numerous community [of Israel] was so heavy that the holy communities were punished with their lives as if they had been spillers of blood. Yet surely He is the Righteous Judge and ours is the guilt.

Then the treacherous enemies prevailed, and they slandered the people of the Lord, saying: "You are the descendants of them who slew the object of our worship and hanged him upon a tree. He [Jesus] himself has said: 'There will yet be a day when my sons will come and avenge my blood.' We are his sons and it is incumbent upon us to seek his vengeance upon you, for you rebelled and sinned against him. Your God, who promised to deal well with you, has never been satisfied with you for you did evil before Him. On that account He forgot you and no longer favors you, for you are stiff-necked. He separated Himself from you, shed His light upon us and took us for His portion." Hearing this, our hearts trembled and stuck in our throats. We fell silent and sat in darkness like those long dead, waiting for the Lord to look forth and behold from heaven.

Also the Adversary, the pope of wicked Rome,* sent word to all the nations who believed in the Offspring of Adultery, namely the descendants of Seir† that they should gather themselves together, go up to Jerusalem and conquer the city. Thus the errants‡ might travel easily on their way to the grave [of him] whom they accepted as their God. The Adversary came to intervene among the nations, and they all gathered together as a man to fulfill his command.

*Pope Urban II at the Council of Clermont in November, 1095.

† The Edomites (Gen. 36:20, 43), who are equated with the Christians.

‡ The Crusaders.

Their number was like the sand upon the shore of the sea, their voice was like the roaring of whirlwind and tempest. When the embittered of heart had gathered, they put forward wicked plans regarding the people of the Lord, and asked: "Why should we trouble to fight against the Muslims in the vicinity of Jerusalem? Is there not a people among us that does not share our faith, whose ancestors even hanged our God? Why should we let them live and dwell among us? Let our swords begin with their heads and afterward we will go upon our way of error." Thereupon the heart of our God's people grew faint and they could muster no spirit, for these were severe plagues which smote them again and again. They came and laid their supplication before the Lord; they fasted, diminishing their blood and flesh; and the heart of Israel melted within it. But the Lord did as He had spoken, for we have sinned against Him. He forsook the tabernacle of Shiloh, the tent which He had made to dwell within His people among the nations. His anger was kindled and He bared His sword against them until they remained only as a beacon upon the top of a mountain and as an ensign upon a hill. And He delivered His strength into captivity and trampled it under foot. See O Lord, and consider, to whom Thou hast done thus! Is not Israel, the robbed and despoiled people, Thy lot and Thy portion? Why hast Thou raised the shield of its foes and why has their force triumphed? They have heard that I sigh, and the ears of all that hear me do tingle. How the mighty rod is broken, the glorious staff, like fine gold, the holy community of Mainz! It was the Lord's doing, therewith to test His worshipers in the yoke of His pure faith.

One day a Gentile woman came bringing a goose which she had raised since it was a gosling so that it went everywhere the woman went. She proclaimed to every passerby: "Behold, this goose understands by itself that I have decided to go in error* and she wants to come along too!" Then the errant, the burghers, and the country folk assembled themselves against us and said to us: "Where is your security and how will you save yourselves now? Look at these miracles which the Crucified One has performed before our eyes in order that we seek vengeance upon our enemies." Then they all came with swords to slay us, but a few of the important burghers came and stood against them and did not let them harm us. At that point the errants arose with a single heart against the burghers and each smote the other until they killed one of the errants. They then

*To join the Crusaders.

said: "The Jews are responsible for all of this!" Nearly all united
against them [the burghers] and spoke to them harshly, intending to
fall upon and assault them. When the holy men* saw all of these
things and heard their words, then their hearts melted. Great and
small, they said: "O that we might die by the hand of the Lord and
not by the hand of the Lord's enemies, for He is a merciful King, the
One in His world!" They left their houses deserted and they did not
go to the synagogue except on the Sabbath before the New Moon of
Sivan. It was the last Sabbath before our slaughter. A few went
there to pray, including R. Judah bar Isaac, and they wailed a great
lament until they were totally exhausted, for they saw that it was a
decree of the King of Kings which none can contravene. There was
one distinguished student there, R. Barukh bar Isaac, who said to
us: "Know in truth and honesty that a decree has been leveled
against us from Heaven and we cannot save ourselves. For last night
I and my father-in-law Judah, heard dead souls praying by night in
the synagogue with loud voices like wailing. When we heard the
sound, we thought that perhaps some of the community had come
from the court of the bishop to pray in the synagogue at midnight.
With anguish and bitterness of heart we ran to the entrance of the
synagogue to see who was praying. But the door was closed. We
heard the voices and the great wailing but we did not understand a
word of what they were saying. Frightened, we returned to our
home, as the house was near the synagogue." When we heard these
words, we fell on our faces and said: "Ah Lord God! Wilt Thou put a
full end to the remnant of Israel?" Then they [Barukh and Judah]
went to relate the occurrence to their brothers in the court of the
governor and in the chambers of the bishop. So they recognized
that it was the Lord's decree and they raised a great lament. They
accepted God's will and said: "Righteous art Thou, O Lord, and
upright are Thy judgments" (Ps. 119:137).

THE MARTYRDOM OF R. KALONYMUS

Now I shall relate the slaying of the pious leader R. Kalonymus, and
of his company. May the Lord avenge him speedily and in our days.

* The Jews destined to become martyrs.

It was on that day regarding which the Lord said to His people: "Be ready against the third day" (Exod. 19:11). On that very day they prepared themselves, stretched out their necks, and offered their sacrifice for a sweet savor unto the Lord. On that day there were slain for the sake of His great name—for Him who is One in His world and aside from whom there are no gods—one thousand and one hundred holy souls, excepting only the righteous leader, R. Kalonymus, who escaped on that day together with a few of the chosen men of Israel, fifty-three souls. They fled through the chambers of the bishop until they came to the vestry of the house of idolatry,* which was the treasury, called *secretarium*. There they remained in distress and anguish because of the sword hanging over their heads. The entrance to the vestry was narrow and dark, so that none of the enemies had noticed them; and they kept perfectly still. As the sun went down, gloom and distress settled upon them. Their tongues cleaved to their palates out of thirst. So they approached the window to speak with the monk who was in charge of the treasury that he might give them water to restore their souls. But he refused until they gave him ten pieces of fine silver for a pitcher full of water. Thus was the biblical verse fulfilled: "Thou shalt serve thine enemies . . . in hunger and in thirst . . . (Deut. 28:48). When he brought the pitcher to the window, its opening was narrow and he was unable to get the water inside. Finally, he took a lead pipe to convey the water, and they drank a measured quantity, not satisfying their thirst.

Now I shall relate the incident in which these righteous men were slain. In the middle of the night the bishop sent someone to the window of the vestry to the leader, R. Kalonymus. He called to him and said: "Hear me, Kalonymus! The bishop has sent me to find whether you are still alive. He has commanded me to save you and all those with you. Come out to me! He has three hundred soldiers, swords drawn and wearing armor. We are ready to give our lives for yours. If you do not believe me, I will swear to you that this is what my lord the bishop has commanded me. He is not in the city but has gone to the village of Rüdesheim; he has sent us here to save the remnant of you that remains and he desires to be of assistance." They did not believe him until he swore to them. Then R. Kalonymus and his company went out to him. Their chief put them on boats, transported them across the Rhine river, and brought them by night to the village of Rüdesheim where the bishop was

*The Cathedral of Mainz.

staying. The bishop was very pleased that R. Kalonymus was still alive and he promised to save him and the men that came with him. But the sword of the enemy pursued them, the anger of the Lord had not turned away from them. He whose hand directs the hearts of kings and princes like watercourses at first inclined the heart of the bishop favorably toward them. But later the bishop went back on his word. He called R. Kalonymus and said to him: "I am not able to save you. Your God has turned away from you and it is not His will that a remnant among you survive. I no longer have the strength to save you or to assist you further. Now know what you and the company with you must do: either you must believe in our faith or you must bear the sin of your ancestors." The pious R. Kalonymus answered him and cried out with bitterness of soul: "It is true that the will of our God is not to save us. Thus your words are true and correct. You have not the power to assist any further. Now give us time until tomorrow to reply to your proposal." Then R. Kalonymus returned to his pious companions and told them the words of the bishop. Thereupon they all arose together and blessed their sacrifice; with single voice and single heart they acknowledged God's justice and received the yoke of His worship. Then, before he returned to the bishop, the pious R. Kalonymus first took his son Mar Joseph, kissed him, and slew him. When the bishop heard that he had slain his son, he became very angry and said: "Henceforth I surely have no desire to assist them further." When the villagers heard what the bishop had said, they assembled, along with the errants, to slay the Jews. Meanwhile, on the same day R. Kalonymus returned to the bishop and on the way discovered what the bishop had said. When he returned to the bishop's presence, R. Kalonymus took a knife in his hand, pressed toward him, and wanted to kill him. But the bishop's men, and even the bishop himself, had detected the intention, and he commanded that R. Kalonymus be removed from his presence. The servants of the bishop assaulted him and slew him with a wooden pole. But some said that he did not return to the bishop a second time and that immediately after slaying his son, he took his sword, planted it in the ground, and fell upon it so that it was driven into his stomach. There are also those who say that the enemies slew him upon the way. In any case, the great man was slain for the unity of the name of the King of Kings, the Holy One, blessed be He. And he was completely and wholly with the God of Israel. Thus the righteous man fell and was slain together with his community.

THE MERIT OF THE MARTYRS

And in the same manner as the enemies carried out the devices of their hearts in those communities of which we have told, so did they do in other communities: in Trèves, in Metz, in Regensburg, in Prague, . . . and in Pappenheim. All of them sanctified the great and awesome name of God out of love and attachment. It all happened in the same year and during one season. For God had chosen all that good generation to be His portion in order to bring merit through them upon succeeding generations. Thus may it be the will of God, supreme and exalted, that He credit their descendants after them with the reward of their acts. May their merit, their righteousness, piety, and integrity stand by us forever to bring us Redemption and to guide us for eternity in the Land of the Living.

JEWISH HISTORIOGRAPHY OF THE SIXTEENTH AND SEVENTEENTH CENTURIES

INTRODUCTION TO SAMUEL USQUE

*S*AMUEL USQUE *(sixteenth century) was a Portuguese Marrano, a Jew forcibly converted to Christianity, who after extensive wanderings settled in Ferrara near the eastern coast of Italy. He was well versed in the classics as well as Hebrew, though his knowledge of rabbinics seems to have been meager. His* Consolation for the Tribulations of Israel, *written in literary Portuguese and published in 1553, consists of three pastoral dialogues (a popular Renaissance form) in which a certain Ycabo, representing Jacob/Israel, relates his historical sufferings to two fellow shepherds who try to comfort him. Dialogue I covers the biblical period; Dialogue II the Second Temple; and Dialogue III the succeeding period down to the author's own time. It concludes with a final lament and with consolations.*

Usque's purpose in relating these misfortunes is not historical; it is religious: he offers a theodicy, comfort, and hope. To his mind, the great events of history are still to be understood as Divine recompense for human deeds. He suggests that Israel has not suffered innocently, but on account of its sins; that recounting the sufferings of the past makes the present ones, seen in perspective, appear less horrendous; and that the afflictions of recent times give assurance of the speedy advent of the Messiah.

With the exception of the last thirteen sections of the final dialogue, Usque's relation of historical events is based on uncritical acceptance of earlier sources, both Jewish and Christian. Even the final sections, which contain an original account of incidents which the author experienced himself, are more in the nature of description than attempts at critical understanding. Yet these last chapters also reveal Usque's great talents as a writer. Here his highly imaginative approach to his material is most apparent, and it is above all this element which gives his work a place in the history of Jewish historical literature. In the selection which follows, Ycabo vividly characterizes the Spanish Inquisition as a terrifying wild monster which brings devastation upon the Christians of Jewish extraction.

§♦§

Those whom Brother Vincent* left as *confesos*† in Spain thrived so that they joined the ranks of Spain's grandees and noblest lords; they were therefore soon united in marriage with its leading families. They occupied posts of distinction and importance in the court: they held the titles of count, marquis, bishop, and obtained other high dignities which the material world bestows upon those who court it. Those who remained Jews enjoyed their secret favor and also flourished and prospered.

This happiness lasted until the time of King Ferdinand and his wife, Queen Isabel.‡ And like an uprooted flower, which speedily dries and withers, so did this prosperity perish, like all my others. For the enemies of good fortune found the king, and much more so the queen, Isabel, inclined to persecute me; and they began to encourage them to destroy the *confesos*. Little effort was required to win the sovereigns' minds, for their stock, it seems, has produced the greatest enemies of my people in the history of the world.

They turned their power against the Jews who were already within the Christian fold. As *confesos*, they were no longer recognized as Jews, and their minds were at ease and their hearts secure, since they were Christians. The king and queen sent to Rome for a wild monster, of such strange form and horrible mien that all Europe trembles at the mere mention of its name.§

Its body, an amalgam of hard iron and deadly poison, has an adamantine shell made of steel and covered with enormous scales. It rises in the air on a thousand wings with black and poisonous pinions, and it moves on the ground with a thousand pernicious and destructive feet.

Its form is like both the awesome lion's and the frightful serpent's in the deserts of Africa. Its enormous teeth equal those of the most powerful elephants. Its whistle or voice kills even more

*Vincent Ferrer (1350–1419), a successful Christian converter of Jews.

†Christians whose parents, or they themselves, converted from Judaism.

‡The Catholic monarchs who established the Inquisition in Spain (1480) and later expelled the Jews (1492).

§The Inquisition.

quickly than the venomous basilisk. Its eyes and mouth spew continual flames and blazes of consuming fire, and the food it eats is the fire in which human bodies burn.

Its flight is swifter than the eagle's, but wherever it passes its shadow spreads a pall of gloom over the brightest sun. Finally, in its wake it leaves a darkness like the darkness visited upon the Egyptians in one of the plagues.

And when it arrives at its destination, the green grass which it treads or the luxuriant tree on which it alights dries, decays, and withers, and then is uprooted by the monster's devastating beak. It desolates the entire countryside with its poison until it is like the Syrian deserts and sands, where no plant takes root and no grass grows.

Such an animal was brought against the entire *confeso* community (who were supposedly unrecognizable in Christian garb). The monster burned a great many of these children of mine* with the fire from its eyes and strewed the land with countless orphans and widows. With its mouth and powerful teeth it wrecked and swallowed all of their worldly riches and gold. With its massive, poison-laden feet, it trampled their renown and their greatness, and with its awesome and misshapen countenance it disfigured and marred comely faces [which were forced to gaze upon it], and darkened hearts and souls with its flights. And it still continues its vile deeds in Spain, against the limbs which were severed from my body. And though my children are parading their Christianity, their lives are not saved.

I do not want to be remiss in telling you that in addition to the enemies, there were at that time some *confesos* who delivered their own brothers into this cruel monster's power. Poverty was the spur and the reason for most of their evil acts. Many poor *confesos* went to the houses of their richer brothers to ask for a loan of fifty or a hundred *crusados*† for their needs. If any refused them, they accused him of Judaizing with them.

These misfortunes lasted for four years. Then the sovereigns determined to uproot the *confesos* completely from Judaism, and remove them from contact with the Jews. They exiled from their domains all the Jews whom the wrath of Brother Vincent had not reached, and those whose constancy had kept them within the Law

*The children of Israel. It is Ycabo (Jacob-Israel) who is the speaker.

†Portuguese coins bearing the figure of a cross.

of Moses. Both groups wandered in great tribulation and hardship through many lands. Some passed over to the Kingdom of Portugal, others to the lands of the Moors,* while some dispersed to the Kingdom of Naples and other parts of Europe.

Here many of Your judgments, O Lord, were fulfilled, which You pronounced against me through the lips of Your prophets. Concerning this wild beast and a similar one in Portugal it was said by Jeremiah: "I shall send among you serpents, basilisks, which cannot be charmed, and they shall bite you with an incurable bite" (8:17). For with these I shall bring it about that "what comes into your mind shall not be at all, in that you say: 'Let us be like the nations and like the families of the countries to worship wood and stone.' As I live, saith the Lord, surely with a mighty hand and outstretched arm and poured out fury will I be king over you" (Ezek. 20:32–33). "And then the great and notable treasure of yours in which you place all your hope will be converted into tow, and the one who acquired it into a spark, and they shall both burn together, and none shall quench them" (Is. 1:31). Because "they who depart from Me shall be written in the earth, for they have forsaken the well of living waters, who is the Lord" (Jer. 17:13). "At the time of their afflictions they will say to me, 'Rise up, save us,' and I shall answer them, 'Where then are your gods now whom you worshiped? Let them arise and save you in the time of your affliction'" (ibid., 2:27–28).

*Lands under Muslim rule.

INTRODUCTION TO SOLOMON IBN VERGA

SOLOMON IBN VERGA, the principal author of the Shevet Yehuda ("The Staff of Judah"), was a Spanish Jew, born in the latter half of the fifteenth century. With the expulsion of the Jews from Spain in 1492, he was among those refugees granted the right of residence in Portugal. But along with his fellows, he was forcibly baptized there five years later and lived ostensibly as a Christian until he was able to leave the country in 1506. He composed his work during the 1520's, and it was first published, with some additions by his son Joseph, in 1554.

The Shevet Yehuda is principally composed of two types of material: accounts of persecutions, beginning with the Hellenistic period but concentrating mostly on the last few centuries up to his own period; and conversations conducted in the courts of Christian monarchs. The latter are entirely imaginary, serving ibn Verga as a suitable vehicle for the expression of his own views on a variety of religious, philosophical, and historical questions. There are a small number of statements made by the author in his own name and also a few chapters describing past glories of the people, such as Solomon's Temple and the ceremony of installing a new exilarch in Babylonia.

Ibn Verga states at the outset that he composed the work so that his fellow Jews, noting all these persecutions, would turn to God, petitioning Him to consider these sufferings atonement for their sins and to bring an end to their afflictions. This pious purpose remains fully in keeping with the earlier historical literature. Likewise, the author's lack of concern for chronological sequence and his juxtaposition of diverse kinds of material are medieval characteristics.

The novelty of ibn Verga's conception of Jewish history is found in his understanding of historical causality. Without abandoning belief in the influence of the Divine, he allows for the operation of secular determinants. Even an event of such great consequence as the expulsion from Spain is at least partially explicable by the specific actions of his fellow Jews not vis-à-vis God, but vis-à-vis the Gentiles. To be sure, ibn Verga's purpose is exhortatory no less than explanatory, and he does not consider historical factors which are independent of the behavior of the Jews themselves. But he does provide a very early limited example of an empirical approach to the dynamics of Jewish history.

This shift in the traditional manner of interpretation is less obvious in the historical sections of ibn Verga's work, where he is dealing with persecutions, than in the imaginative and reflective portions. The two selections below parallel each other to some extent. They both deal with the need to explain the sufferings of the Jews which reached their climax with the expulsion of 1492. The first is taken from an imaginary conversation between a Spanish monarch, Alfonso, and a Christian scholar, Thomas. It contains the latter's answer to the king's question: Why are the Jews despised? The second selection consists of ibn Verga's further reflection upon the same subject, except that here the question is posed in traditional Jewish terms: Why this great anger? And here ibn Verga answers in his own name. Especially noteworthy is his comment: "When the merit is not great, the tribulation of the Exile is prolonged as a result of natural causes. . . ." Allowing for the superior force of Divine intervention when the Jewish people is truly righteous, he exposes its history to the operation of natural forces once Israel's "merit" is lacking.

WHY THE JEWS ARE HATED

The answer of Thomas*: I have never seen an intelligent person who hates the Jews. They are hated only by the masses—and for good reason. First, the Jews are proud and are always seeking to domineer. They do not consider that they are exiles and serfs, driven from land to land. On the contrary, they try to present themselves as lords and nobles, and therefore the people envy them. The Sage† has said that the hatred which is caused by envy can never be overcome. My lord will find empirical confirmation in the fact that when the Jews came to his kingdom they came as serfs and exiles, wearing tattered clothes. For many years they neither put on an expensive garment nor evinced any haughtiness. In those days did my lord hear that any blood accusations were made against them? If such had been made, they would have been recorded in the chronicles of the kings of Spain, as is the good and proper custom, in order to learn from them for the future. There can thus be no question that as long as they gave no cause for envy, they were beloved. But now the Jew is ostentatious. If he has two hundred pieces of gold, he immediately dresses himself in silk and his children in embroidered clothing. This is something that not even nobles who possess an annual income of a thousand doubloons would do. Therefore accusations are leveled against them, which may perhaps lead to their expulsion from the kingdom. In the city of Toledo their pride brought them to such presumption that they struck Christians, and their leaders were constrained to proclaim that whoever struck a Christian would be punished by their laws. In this regard we can apply Solomon's statement: "For three things the earth doth quake . . . for a servant when he reigneth . . ." (Prov. 30:21–22).

A second reason for the hatred is that when the Jews came to my lord's kingdom they were poor and the Christians were rich. Now it is the opposite, since the Jews are clever and achieve their purposes with cunning. Moreover, they became very rich by lending on interest. My lord will note that three-quarters of all the

*A fictitious Christian sage who here answers the question of the Spanish king regarding hatred of the Jews.

† King Solomon, traditional author of the book of Proverbs (cf. Prov. 27:4).

lands and estates of Spain are all in the hands of the Jews*—and this on account of the heavy interest.

THE CAUSES OF JEWISH SUFFERING

Said Solomon [ibn Verga]: If a man will reflect upon these great afflictions,† he will be dumbfounded and ask, "Why this great Divine anger? He has not done the like to any of the other nations, despite their being burdened with sins more than the Jews!" All these questions and others like them have for their answer a single verse which says: "You only have I known of all the families of the earth; therefore I will visit upon you all your iniquities" (Amos 3:2). In addition, there are seven causes for what happened to us. First—the sins of our fathers; even as our Sages, may their memory serve as a blessing, revealed when they commented on the verse: "Nevertheless in the day when I visit, I will visit their sin upon them" (Exod. 32:34)—there is no affliction [which is not in small part a punishment for the sin of the golden calf]; and the Elegist has said: "Our fathers have sinned, and are not; and we have borne their iniquities" (Lam. 5:7). Second—when the merit is not great, [the tribulation of] the Exile is prolonged as a result of natural causes: religious hatred and the desire of the ruler to convert everyone to his religion and faith; and our Sages said: "Why is the mountain called Sinai? Because from it descended hatred [sina in Hebrew]!" How much the more so when our religion prohibits eating and drinking with others, which draws people together. As our Sages said: "Drinking together is a great thing because it brings close those who are distant;" and as they explained the verse: "For Thou hast done it" (Lam. 1:21).‡ Third—the slaying of Jesus of Nazareth; Moses' statement should not be taken lightly: "Lo, if we sacrifice the abomination of the Egyptians§ before their eyes, will they not stone

*A gross exaggeration.

†The persecutions of the Jews, and especially their expulsion from Spain.

‡In the Midrash to Lamentations (I, 56) God's relation to Israel is likened to a king who married a lady after insisting that she break off relations with her former companions. Subsequently, he became angry with her and drove her from the palace. But now she could find no friends. So, too, God prohibited marital relations with the Gentiles and therefore He is responsible for their rejection of Israel in exile.

§The god of the Egyptians.

us?"* (Exod. 8:22). Fourth—a high degree of jealousy or envy exists with regard to these three: religion, women, and money; and each of them is involved in the relationship between Israel and the nations. While still in Spain [the Jews] began, as a result of frequent contact, to cast their eyes upon the daughters of the land. Some of them justified their action by saying that it was punishable only by whipping, without realizing that religious zealots might assault them and that according to Jewish tradition they were subject to Divine punishment. Furthermore, with regard to all such sins, if the woman becomes pregnant, they will have begotten a child to [serve] a foreign cult. Envy based on money resulted when the Jews began to interfere in the professions and commerce of the land. Above all, when a cheat or robber was found among the Jews, the usual procedure was to cast the blame upon all. As a result, the name of God was desecrated, for it was said that we have no religion. As Rabbi Moses of Coucy[†] noted, this one matter [of having cheats and robbers] among our people would in itself be sufficient to prolong our Exile. And in the Prophets it is said: "The remnant of Israel shall not do iniquity, nor speak lies" (Zeph. 3:13). Fifth—the people became accustomed to swearing falsely. Ibn Ezra[‡] wrote that this alone would suffice to postpone the end of our Exile. Sixth—the pride with which some of our people thought to lord it over the Gentile inhabitants of the land, although the latter were the actual masters. As a result of this pride it happened in the year of the expulsion [from Spain] that on the eve of the Day of Atonement a quarrel broke out among the worshipers in the synagogue, whereupon everyone seized a torch from in front of the Ark in order to hit his neighbor with it. There are numerous instances of this kind that take place among us—and the Lord, He is righteous!

But since these matters are most depressing, I have seen fit to present in what follows something more heartening: the splendor of the Temple and the building of it as I have found them described by the great Versoris[§] upon the request of the pious king Alfonso.[||] I have translated his description from the Latin into our holy tongue.

*Moses' intention to sacrifice to God an animal held sacred by the Egyptians is equated with what the author regards as the Jews' crucifixion of Jesus.

† Thirteenth-century French codifier of Jewish law.

‡ Abraham ibn Ezra (1089–1164), biblical commentator, poet, and grammarian.

§ Johannes Versoris (fifteenth century), French philosopher and scientist. Such a description of the Temple is not to be found in Versoris' works.

|| Alfonso is a common name of Spanish kings. Since the matter is fictitious, no particular monarch is intended.

INTRODUCTION TO AZARIAH DEI ROSSI

With Azariah Dei Rossi (c. 1511–c. 1578) a modern critical
approach enters Jewish historiography for the first time. Though
not the writer of a connected Jewish history, he prepared the way
for such histories by pioneering the analytic and comparative
treatment of sources upon which they would be based.

Rossi, who was born in Mantua, belonged to a distinguished
Jewish family of scholars and musicians. He spent his life in various
Italian cities, earning his living as a physician, but at the same time
acquiring a remarkable erudition in Jewish, classical, and Renaissance literature. In addition to Hebrew and Aramaic, he knew
ancient and medieval Latin well, had some knowledge of Greek,
and was fluent in Italian. In 1571, while living in Ferrara, he
experienced an earthquake, which he described in the first part of
his Meor Enayim ("Light to the Eyes"), entitled "The Voice of
God." While acknowledging that earthquakes are a manifestation of
God's power, Rossi was driven by his experience to consult all
available sources on the subject, both Jewish and non-Jewish, and
to compare them. In the wake of the earthquake, Rossi took refuge
in a neighboring village. There he met a Christian scholar who
asked him questions about a Hellenistic work, The Letter of
Aristeas, dealing with the Greek translation of the Hebrew Bible. To
the Christian's surprise, Rossi was forced to admit that the Letter

did not exist in Hebrew and was unknown among the Jews. To remedy that situation, he forthwith translated it into Hebrew and made it the second part of his book, called "The Glory of the Elders."

However, it is the third and longest portion of Meor Enayim, the "Words of Wisdom," which is of the greatest significance. It consists of sixty chapters treating a variety of historical subjects in no particular sequence and in no relation to the preceding two parts of the book. Here Rossi discusses questions of Jewish chronology, finds contradictions among various sources, and concludes that the rabbinic chronology according to the creation of the world is of relatively recent origin. In discussing the garments worn by the Priests in the Temple, he utilizes not only The Letter of Aristeas, Philo, Josephus, and Rabbinic writers, but also Christian scholars—a revolutionary departure from previous Jewish practice.

Not surprisingly, his work, which was published 1573–75, aroused a great deal of opposition on the part of the rabbinic leadership. The outstanding legal authority, Joseph Caro of Safed, was prepared to issue a ban against it, and only his death prevented its execution. Even in Rossi's own city of Mantua, no one under twenty-five years of age was allowed to read it. The book was definitely in advance of its time. Only in the late eighteenth and early nineteenth ceturies did the advocates of Jewish enlightenment and the movement for the scientific study of Judaism recognize a great precursor in Azariah dei Rossi.

The excerpt given here, taken from the third part of Meor Enayim, reveals both Rossi's critical approach to Jewish literature and his comparative method. While recognizing the authority of the legal tradition, Rossi refused to accept without question the validity of the aggadot, the largely legendary accounts contained in the Talmud and Midrash—especially insofar as these conflicted with the course of nature and with other, patently more reliable sources. The tale of the gnat which entered into the head of Titus, the Roman commander who destroyed the Temple, is an instance of such an aggadah.

THE GNAT WHICH ENTERED TITUS' BRAIN

In the *Pirke Rabbi Eliezer,** a work earlier than most of the Tannaitic literature known to us, you will find in Chapter 49 the following account. "Titus,† the wicked, entered the Holy of Holies and said, 'No enemy or adversary can prevail against me.' What did the Holy One, Blessed be He, do? He sent a gnat which entered his nose and went on until it reached his brain. Thereupon it became as large as a young pigeon, weighing two selahs. This occurred in order to make him aware that his power amounted to nothing." You will find the story at greater length in *Bereshit Rabba* 10, in *Vayikra Rabba* 22, and in the Gemara (*Gittin* 56b).‡ There are differences between the Midrashic accounts and the passage in the Gemara, but this much is common to both: When Titus was on his way home to Rome after destroying the Temple, while traveling on board ship, he profaned and blasphemed. Thereupon, a gnat entered his nose and pecked away at his brain for seven years. Finally, he screamed: "Break open my brain so that you may know how the God of the Jews has punished me."

The Talmudic version continues: "It has been taught, R. Eleazar son of R. Yose§ said, 'I was with the great men of Rome, and when he died they broke open his brain and found something about the size of a sparrow weighing two selahs.' A Tanna taught, 'About the size of a young pigeon, a year old, weighing two liters.' Said Abbaye,‖ We have a tradition that its proboscis was of brass, its claws of iron, and they placed it in a bowl.'" The versions agree that when the gnat was removed, Titus died. And in the Midrash *Tanhuma*¶ to the Torah portion "Hukat ha-Torah" (Num. 19:1–22:1)

*A collection of aggadot (tales, narratives, legends), which purports to be early in composition, but was in fact compiled in the eighth century, well after the Tannaitic period (first and second centuries C.E.)

†The Roman emperor who destroyed the Second Temple in 70 C.E.

‡In interpretive (Midrashic) works on Genesis and Leviticus and in the Talmud.

§Palestinian sage of the second century who traveled to Rome where he allegedly was shown the gnat which penetrated Titus' brain.

‖Babylonian Talmudic sage (278–338).

¶A homiletical commentary to the Pentateuch.

you will find it related very differently with regard both to details and to the duration of time. I have not bothered to copy here completely all of the texts mentioned since the books are available. Whoever will examine all of them will easily see that there are many points on which they do not agree. This great divergence will make the intelligent person wonder why, if it is a true incident, the reports mentioned do not tend to greater coincidence. Moreover, will not any man of understanding have to consider a number of things? To begin with, the tale is full of particulars contrary to nature. Although they would indeed be possible by God's will, their combination is in truth so extraordinary that one would have expected an effect and notoriety appropriate to so extensive and remarkable a miracle. Now it may be supposed that when the gnat entered by way of the nose, it ascended to above the cerebral cortex for this is indeed an open channel, as anatomists have, in fact, maintained. In particular, the sage Fernelius,* in his *Paths of Medicine*, Chapter 49, says that the proper way to unclog the upper parts of the brain is not by means of medicine taken orally but by draining it via the nose, ears, or neck, or via the seams of the skull. It may also be supposed that it did not perforate the brain. . . . But should we not be amazed at there being an empty space between the skull and the brain so large as to contain something the size of a young bird, and that the bird would not press upon the brain and make it contract even more? In the above mentioned passage from *Bereshit Rabba* it is explicitly stated that the gnat pecked away at his brain and, what is more, it did so for a long time. And in *Hullin* 58a † there is a clear statement that animals without bones cannot live for more than a year. And what of its proboscis being of brass and its claws of iron? According to natural scientists, all metals are produced in the bowels of the earth by the interaction of primary qualities with the heat of the sun. Iron, in particular, is formed from thick sulphur heated together with a small amount of unrefined mercury; brass, from refined mercury mixed with red, turbid sulphur. You will find all this easily in Ibn Latif, ‡ *The Gate of Heaven* (II,2). . . .

Furthermore, the question of time presents a severe problem. If you will look in any of the chronicles of the emperors, or even in

* Johannes Fernelius (sixteenth century), noted French physician.
† In the Babylonian Talmud.
‡ Isaac ben Abraham ibn Latif (c. 1210–c. 1280), Spanish philosopher and mystic.

the *Book of Tradition* of R. Abraham ibn Daud,* you will find that the destruction of the Temple occurred in the second year of Vespasian's reign. Vespasian ruled for about ten years and his son Titus after him for less than three years. Thus, at the end of the seven years, when, according to the Rabbis, Titus died, he in fact mounted the throne. In some of my leisure moments, I looked through all the important historical works, for in this regard I apply the words of Jeremiah (18:13), "Thus saith the Lord: Ask ye now among the nations," in order to know what they wrote regarding the death of Titus and the nature of his illness. I found eight noted writers who agree that the fatal disease was ague. . . . Each wrote concerning our subject in its proper place. In addition, two other writers have provided us with further testimony and clarification. The writer Dio Cassius,† in narrating that Titus at the point of death said he regretted not having done one thing which he might have done, notes that in his opinion the regret concerned his not having slain his brother Domitian, since Titus believed that Domitian had poisoned him in order to take over the throne— which was in fact the case. And Philostratus‡ the Greek, in the seventh book of his *Life of Apollonius,* wrote that Domitian killed him by pricking his flesh with the sharp tailbone of a certain fish, which treatment being thought a cure for his chills. In the same way the warrior Ulysses,§ king of the Isle of Ithaca, was slain by his son Telemachus. Thus there are ten examples from all the languages of the Gentiles, each of them innocently controverting the story of the Rabbis. Those who respect the truth will have to admit that it seems they know the specific details of such stories better than our Sages.

On the other hand, I have seen that the contemporary writer Ferentillus‖ in his account of the Hellenistic kings ascribed this form of death, via a gnat entering the nose, to Antiochus Epiphanes, the enemy of the Jews in the days of the Hasmoneans. (As is known, it is because God delivered us from his hand that we celebrate Hanukkah.) It is true that he did not relate the incident in the extraordinary fashion that the Rabbis did [when they wrote of Titus]. Moreover, II Maccabees 9 does mention that Antiochus

*See introduction to the selection from this work above.

†Roman historian (c. 150—235).

‡Flavius Philostratus "The Athenian" (c. 170–245), Greek scholar resident in Rome.

§ The hero in Homer's *Odyssey.*

‖Augustinus Ferentillus, Italian historian at time of Rossi.

blasphemed and spoke arrogantly, whereupon, while the words were still in his mouth, he was afflicted with severe and odious pains, worms entered his flesh, and he died in his ailment. (All this is related at length.) But there is no mention there of the gnat which Ferentillus wrote about, and I have no idea where he got it from. In sum, from all that has here been mentioned, it seems very clear that this story about Titus, related by the Rabbis, occurred neither wholly nor in part.

Now it is not my intention to appear overwise by thus proclaiming that there are stories of the Rabbis which cannot be understood literally. Such Talmudic tales as that of Og, the King of Bashan, uprooting a mountain the size of three parasangs (*Berakhot* 54b) and that of Rabba son of bar Hana (*Baba Batra* 73a)* have long been acknowledged to be fables by all except fools, as is noted by Maimonides† in the Introduction to his *Guide of the Perplexed*. However, I know men whom I consider well versed in the Torah who take these stories in their literal sense and who express themselves vehemently against those that do not believe them. I shall therefore render an opinion for the sake of the man who drinks thirstily the words of the Rabbis, but following Maimonides has accepted the value of human reason—lest when he read of the curse of Titus or any similar matter he be astonished and perplexed, unable to force himself to believe the story. We have treated our subject innocently and with no base intention, bowing to sources with superior knowledge. Further, I would say that Gentile writers in their own poetry and rhetoric multiply incidents which did not occur and invent stories on the spur of the moment in order thereby to inspire emotion, fire the imagination, provide knowledge, and produce initiative (for example, Cicero‡ in his *First Philippic* and in his *Pro Roscio*). Thus, too, our Sages, who were truly wise, recognized clearly that such incidents had no foundation whatever or did not occur in the manner in which they told them. That did not prevent the Sages from telling and embellishing them as if they had really happened just as related. But it was done in order to implant in the hearts of the multitude the goodness and honesty

*Rabba son of bar Hana claimed to have seen a number of "wonders," among them an antelope the size of a mountain and a frog as large as a fortress.

† Moses Maimonides (1135–1204), the greatest of the medieval Jewish legists and philosophers.

‡ Marcus Tullius Circero (106–43 B.C.E.), Roman orator and politician.

which they desired to take shape in their souls. The purpose was moral or religious instruction. . . . With regard to the story of Titus, therefore, you are free to say that it is an invention, a way of teaching the simple multitude that our Lord is great, mightily inflicting punishment by means of even the smallest of His creatures upon those who rise up against Him, and especially upon every arrogant doer of evil. With great wisdom they referred their invented tale of the wicked man to Titus who acted so wickedly toward us. . . . Now may not such a story justifiably be told in that it brings us closer to our Heavenly Father? . . . All the embellishments of the Rabbis concerning the gnat, strange and impossible as they are, nonetheless fully represent a piece of splendid wisdom on their part. By telling the tale they accomplish two things: they imbue the multitude with increased wonder and amazement, and they cause men of understanding to comprehend what the simile represents. . . .

My reader, I hope this explanation will be acceptable to you. But be careful to apply it—or similar explanations which you may hear from me—only where it may be of value, lest you requite my desire to be of help to you by doing harm both to me and to yourself. For not all the sayings of the Rabbis are to be interpreted in the same way. . . .

Now I will not refrain from informing you, my dear reader, that when some learned men of our people heard of what I have written concerning the gnat of Titus, they spoke out against me. They charged that I had found fault with the holy words of our Sages and that God would not fail to bring a more than fitting punishment upon such an enemy as I. Nevertheless I have not held back from writing it down in this book. Aside from what I suggested at the beginning of the chapter, I may say in the spirit of Maimonides (*Guide*, Introduction and I,5) that there are two possibilities: If the reader wants to believe literally every word that the Rabbis wrote, thinking thereby to bring every distant thing near to the glory of Heaven, let him regard this chapter as if it had never been written, either for good or for ill. If, on the other hand, he wants to explain the tales rationally but has been unable to do so, then I think he will act wisely by selecting the way I have outlined. Praised be He who apportioned to the Rabbis from His wisdom, and praised be He by their lips which speak from the grave.

INTRODUCTION TO DAVID GANS

DAVID GANS (1541–1613) presents the rare example of an Ashkenazic Jew in the premodern world who was very much interested in intellectual life and events beyond the Jewish community. He spent his early years in Germany and in Poland studying with the leading rabbinic authorities of his day before settling in the Bohemian city of Prague. His interest in astronomy brought him into contact with such leading figures in the early history of modern science as Johann Kepler and Tycho Brahe. He wrote an astronomical work in which he held, against Copernicus, that the ancient Ptolemaic system, by which the sun is held to revolve around the earth, was still the correct one.

Gans's importance for Jewish historiography rests upon his Tzemah David ("Offspring of David"), which he published in two sections in 1592. The first part is a chronicle of Jewish historical events from Adam down to the year of publication. It consists mainly of the names of prominent rabbis and the dates on which they published their most important works. There are also a few references to persecutions. By and large, Gans compiled it from earlier writers and perhaps also from the title pages of rabbinical writings available to him. The second part is a chronicle of world history, again going back as far as Genesis and coming down to his own time. Here the events recorded are predominantly of a political nature. The author drew them mainly from the contemporary German chroniclers with whom he was familiar.

The novelty of Gans's work lies in his strict fidelity to chronological sequence, which is perhaps related to his mathematical interests. Each entry in the first part is listed by its date according to the chronology of Creation. In the second part, Christian dates are added for all events after the birth of Jesus. Gans, however, fails to examine his sources critically and makes no attempt at historical interpretation.

In the two introductions, which are given below, Gans is at pains to justify his decision to write on such a seemingly insignificant subject as past events. He is particularly hard pressed to legitimate a study of secular history, and he does so with arguments of both a religious and practical nature. The selections which are given from the two parts of the chronicle itself are representative of the kinds of entries found throughout the work.

WHY A JEWISH CHRONICLE?

Wise reader, you must not think that the first part of this book is of no value simply because most of what it contains may already be found in earlier volumes—especially in the important and lovely *Book of Genealogies,** to which the author of the *Chain of Tradition*† has already added information on recent generations to the extent that hardly a single figure is missing. Rather, I would maintain that there are a number of responses to such a contention. First, there has not been an author before me who followed the chronology according to the age of the world from the Creation down to his time, year by year, as I have done in this book. Even the authors of the *Book of Genealogies* and the *Chain of Tradition* almost entirely omitted the dates of the Judges and the Kings, mentioning them only in the slightest. Second, I have added the sequence and the dates of the Hasmonean kings during the period of the Second Temple, as also the sequence and dates of the Herodian kings, each one in his proper place and with the proper year. Third, I have added the sequence of the Geonim which I have taken from the responsum of Rabbi Sherira Gaon,‡ who is more reliable than other authors regarding their order and dates. I have converted the dates from the Document Chronology§ used in his book because most people are not sufficiently familiar with it. I have arranged the Geonim in my book each in his proper place according to the Chronology of Creation with which we are most familiar today. Aside from the opportunity to make these innovations, earlier writers left me sufficient room to demonstrate my ability. Therefore, I have toiled and, praise be to God, I have found things that I gathered from books and writers as well as a very small

*Written by Abraham Zacuto (1452–c. 1515) and first published in Constantinople in 1566.

† Written by Gedaliah ibn Yahya (1515–1578) and first published in Venice in 1586.

‡Sherira Gaon (c. 906–1006), noted legal authority of the Geonic period (end of seventh to middle of eleventh century). In response to a question from the North-African Jewish community of Kairouan, he composed a chronology of the Rabbinic authorities known as the *Igeret Rav Sherira Gaon.*

§A chronology beginning with the start of the Seleucid Era (312 B.C.E.) widely employed by the Jews for official purposes as late as the Geonic period.

amount which I have added from my own knowledge. This is not surprising since our Rabbis already said in the first chapter of Tractate *Hullin* and in the Jerusalem Talmud in the second chapter of Tractate *Demai*: "Did there arise no righteous man from Moses to Hezekiah [who would have destroyed all forms of idolatry] . . .? Rather, his ancestors left room for him to distinguish himself."* So, too, my predecessors have left me room to show my capacity. This matter has already been compared to a giant who lifts a dwarf on his shoulders and the dwarf sees farther than the giant himself. However, in my case, I have not stood upon the shoulders of the author of the *Book of Genealogies* with regard to wisdom and intellect, for even if I should take an extraordinary leap upward, I would not reach the bottommost parts of his intellect. For who am I and what is my life in such matters? THE WORD OF DAVID.

Know further that it is not my intent in Part One of this book to expatiate upon matters dealt with by earlier writers. It has rather been my purpose to abbreviate. For previous authors wrote at length on many matters in such excellent fashion that there is no need to correct their words. It is only because, as is already known, most people in our generation want to learn the entire Torah while standing on one foot, that I decided to satisfy their desire with a short book that leaves out more than it includes but obviates the necessity of spending much time and effort in searching through the works of the older writers. Therefore, know that Part One of this book does not claim to be more than a general chronological outline. Whoever would like to know the details can quench his thirst by consulting the earlier volumes mentioned and they may serve him as shields of mighty men in an armory, as THE TOWER OF DAVID.

I have also decided to copy from the chronicles of non-Jewish writers the history of the four kingdoms—Babylon, Persia, Greece, and Rome—and all the kings who ruled over them from the time of Nimrod son of Cush,† the first king of Babylon, up to the time of our lord, Emperor Rudolph II‡ (may his glory be exalted), as well as numerous incidents which occurred during their days. However, in order to separate the holy from the profane, I have set aside for these matters a special section of this book. Thus, that which deals with the living God will not be mixed with secular events. As for the

*The idols were not destroyed until the time of King Hezekiah.

† Genesis 10:8–12.

‡ Holy Roman Emperor (1576–1612).

usefulness of such information and my reasons for presenting it, I shall make them clear in Part Two of this book, with the help of my Rock, THE SHIELD OF DAVID.

Thus I have composed for you a chronicle from the year of Creation to this year 5452.* Above each entry I have indicated the appropriate year, according to the Chronology of Creation, when that particular individual lived or that event occurred. I have done so for two reasons. First, it may be that typographical errors will occur in the dates given in the text itself, and thus a major confusion might result. In such a case the date written above the entry will immediately correct the error. Second, even though the date is given within each entry, the date given above will facilitate finding a particular year speedily and with no effort; this will be of general usefulness. It will not be considered superfluous, but rather on account of it readers will commend and give PRAISE TO DAVID.

I cast my supplication before every reader of this book that if he find in it any mistake in content, in chronology, or in any other respect, he do me the favor of correcting it out of love, not pride or scholarly envy. The Psalmist has already said: "Who can discern errors?" (Ps. 19:13). Moreover, it is known that even Daniel, "the greatly beloved," about whom Scripture says that he was skillful in all wisdom, cunning in knowledge, and discerning in thought— even he erred in his calculation of dates. How much more so a simple man like myself, tossed about a hundred times by the storms of the era and the waves of his own tribulation. Therefore, sir, do not seek occasion to write against me with animosity. Rather judge me with leniency for many and great are the divergences of opinion with regard to chronology, not to speak of numerous variant versions. And where my excuse is not adequate, stretch your hands over me in favor and friendship and correct my mistakes. Do not despise and do not RUIN DAVID.

However, I can see in advance that many will raise their voices against me, contending that I have no right to deal with matters beyond my capacity, to compose books in competition with our Rabbis, the great men of the earth. But since this volume is not concerned with legal decisions, I have decided to undertake its authorship. The Lord God knows that it is not my intention to magnify or glorify myself through this book, for even children are capable of compiling and composing such a volume. I have not

*1592.

written it for scholars, who are filled with Torah like a pomegranate, but only for average people, young and insignificant students like myself. . . .

MOSES ISSERLES, SOLOMON LURIA, AND A PERSECUTION

5332 [1572] Rabbi Moses Isserles, the fully pious man whose writings have enlightened the eyes of the Exile. They include *Torat ha-Olah,** *Torat ha-Hattat,*† and *Shulhan Arukh.*‡ He raised up many disciples and disseminated knowledge of the Torah in Israel. He taught in the holy community of Cracow for about twenty years, and in the year 5332 he passed away.

5333 [1573] Rabbi Solomon Luria of Ostrog.§ He is the great luminary, the crown of Israel, model to the age, in whose light our people walks and from whose waters all the Diaspora of Israel drinks. His fame has gone out to the entire world. He taught many students and exceeded all the men of his generation. He wrote his great work on the whole system of the Talmud—incomparable in size, depth, and acuity. He called it: *Yam shel Shelomo,*‖ but it has not yet been published. He also wrote responsa. He was called to the Academy on High¶ in the year 5333. . . .

5334 [1574] A time of trouble for the Jews of Moravia. A number of them died as martyrs in sanctification of God's name, until the Emperor Maximilian, may the memory of the righteous be for a blessing, took pity upon them out of the abundance of his righteousness and compassion, and he saved them.

* A philosophic work.

† A legal work on forbidden foods.

‡ Actually an adaptation of the legal compendium, *Shulhan Arukh* ("The Prepared Table"), of Joseph Caro to the customs of Ashkenazic (Central and East-European) Jewry.

§ City in Volhynia, at the time belonging to the kingdom of Poland.

‖ That is, "Sea of Solomon."

¶ A euphemism for the death of scholars.

THE BENEFITS OF STUDYING WORLD HISTORY

I see in advance that many will speak out against me, condemn me, and consider me sinful because I have taken material from non-Jewish writers. Moreover, Part Two of my book contains tales of war and similar events which in their eyes have no religious value. At the very least, they will regard it as forbidden reading on the Sabbath. However, I shall not make lengthy excuses since many of the great men of Israel can serve as my defense. For all the religious philosophers already took from the works of Aristotle and from the other philosophers what was correct and true; they ate the kernel and threw away the husk. In our own time, as well, there have been Jewish writers who have transmitted to us information concerning historical events which they took from non-Jewish sources: for example, Abraham Zacuto in his *Book of Genealogies,* Joseph ha-Kohen* in his *Chronicles of the Kings of France and the Ottoman Empire,* Abraham Farissol† in his *Ways of the World,* and others. And if the objection be to the secular contents of Part Two, note well what the illustrious Rabbi Moses Isserles, model of piety for our time, wrote in his glosses on *The Prepared Table,* in the section "Way of Life," 307a: "People who derive enjoyment from reports and tales of historical events are permitted to relate them on the Sabbath as on weekdays." Further on, in Paragraph 16, he wrote: "The prohibition against reading about profane matters and tales of wars, if taken precisely, refers only to works written in other languages, but in the holy tongue it is permitted. Thus it appears to me from the Tosafot‡ to Chapter 'All the Holy Writings' in the Talmud, and thus it has been the custom to be lenient in this matter."

I further contend that Scripture has allowed us to search in non-Jewish books for accounts of events which can be of some use

---

*Joseph ha-Kohen (1495–1578), who lived mostly in Italy, wrote a chronicle of Jewish persecutions called *The Vale of Tears* (1558) in addition to the work of general history (1554) mentioned by Gans.

†Abraham Farissol (c.1451–c.1525), biblical commentator, geographer, and polemicist, active in Ferrara, Italy. His *Ways of the World* is the first modern Hebrew work on geography.

‡Comments on the Talmud dating from the twelfth to fourteenth centuries.

to us. Thus it is written at the end of the Scroll of Esther: "And the full account of the greatness of Mordecai . . . is it not written in the book of the chronicles of the kings of Media and Persia?" Likewise in Jeremiah 18 it is written: "Ask ye now among the nations. . . ." Also in the weekly portion, Ve'ethanan, Scripture says: "For ask now of the days past, which were before thee, since the day that God created man upon the earth . . ." (Deut. 4:32). Therefore, since many pious men, who desire to know the events of history, have urged me to write them down, I have written Part Two of my book for this generation, weary of the Exile. I hope to bring joy to householders who earn their bread in sorrow and by the sweat of their brow, so that after their toil and effort they may be able to rest from their labors by reading of matters old and new.

I have perceived many benefits to be derived from the accounts contained in this book:

1. The incidents related here give abundant evidence of Divine Providence watching over the people of Israel. For great and mighty kings conquered other states and kingdoms—destroyed, uprooted, and annihilated them so that not even their memory remained. But God, the Blessed and Exalted, protected us and did not let us be devoured by them. He always fulfilled His promise to defend us. Consider what happened when many and great wars arose on account of differences of religion, or even merely on account of differences in customs. As is known, the difference between the Papal party and the Lutheran one is only concerned with practices, yet they have been fighting each other these last fifty years and have killed more than a million Christians. But for all that, "Against any of the children of Israel shall not a dog whet his tongue" (Ex. 11:7). Praised be the Lord who has bestowed His wondrous love upon us.

2. A person should beware, if he rise to greatness and power, that he be humble, contrite, and beloved by the people. He should not trust in his power and might, thinking: "My hand is raised; who is lord over me?" Nor should he doubt divine punishment, for although there was never a power like that of the Roman Empire, yet we find that more than fifty emperors were slain by the sword, a number were poisoned, and some were driven to suicide. Others were blinded and their eyes poked out; still others had their noses chopped off, were flayed, drowned, or eaten by vermin. All such you will find written in this book with regard to each of them.

3. A person should take care to be on his guard against a minor and insignificant enemy no less than against a powerful one. He

should consider that several emperors and kings were poisoned by enemies of low station and little consequence.

4. A person should learn not to quarrel with more powerful than he, nor to incite or dispute with one that fortune smiles upon, for most who opposed great rulers fell beneath their feet.

5. These tales reveal God's justice, that He metes out punishment to the wicked even in this world, where most of the evil emperors and kings were slain and perished from the earth.

6. You will find a number of moral maxims among the words of the emperors, and they make a much greater impression upon the masses when you tell them that the maxim originated with a particular emperor.

7. From these accounts it is possible to derive evidence for several dates and sayings of our Sages. Thus Rabbi Moses Isserles wrote in his gloss on Chapter 18 of the book *Foundation of the World** (included on Page 156 of the *Book of Genealogies*): "I have noted the names and dates of renowned non-Jewish philosophers in order to determine the chronology from past generations to the present day, since from non-Jewish sages one may derive evidence for our own Sages."

8. I have seen fit to mention some celestial signs, new stars, and eclipses which took place in certain years and what occurred in consequence of them. The value thereof lies in arousing the attention of the reader to the saying of our Sages in Chapter "He Who Sleeps" of the Talmud: that when an eclipse occurs it is an evil sign for the world. The saying is to be understood according to the interpretation of Rashi, the foremost of the commentators, on the verse in Ecclesiastes (3:14): "God hath so made it, that men should fear before Him." Here Rashi says: "All that the Holy One, blessed be He, did in the work of Creation was to remain forever . . . and when something changes, it is God who acted and commanded the change in order that men should fear Him." Therefore, should there again be such phenomena, let us pray to the Lord God to cause the evil of the constellation to pass over us. For in this regard our Sages said: "Israel is not affected by the constellations."† And Rashi interpreted this statement to mean that repentance changes the effect of the constellation.

*Written by Isaac ben Joseph Israeli (early fourteenth century) and dealing with the geometrical problems of the earth.

†Talmud *Shabbat* 156a.

9. We dwell among the nations and are strangers and sojourners among them. When they tell us or ask us about ancient times and earlier kingdoms, we are forced to put our hand over our mouth and do not know what to answer. We seem to them like dumb animals who do not know the difference between left and right. It is as if we were all born yesterday. However, by means of this book it will be possible to respond with a tiny bit [of information] about every historical period. Thus we may find favor and goodwill in their eyes. And even if this is not an absolute benefit, I have nonetheless seen fit to mention it among the others.

10. As I already indicated in the introduction to Part One, when the reader of this second part comes upon the might and power of kings and emperors, while we in our exile have neither king nor ruler, he will pray to God to restore our judges as of old and to bring about the messianic redemption. So may it be His will, amen.

FOUR ITEMS WORTHY OF NOTE

4782 (1022) The Muslims came up against Italy to despoil it. And [the Italians] called out to the emperor* for help. The emperor came to Italy and fought against the Muslims, smiting and destroying them completely. He wrought a great deliverance for Italy at that time. It took place in the year 4782, which is the Christian year 1022.

4970 (1210) Genghis Khan, King of Tatary, the great and terrible monarch, the mighty destroyer. The beginning of his rule was in the Muslim year 617, which equals the year 4970, and the Christian year 1210. (See *Book of Genealogies*, p. 151.) And how historians have dwelt upon the power, might, and greatness of this king!

4972 (1212) Frederick II, Duke of Swabia, King of Sicily, the twenty-fourth German emperor. He was nineteen years old when he was crowned in the year 4972. He was the son of Emperor Henry

*Henry II, Holy Roman Emperor (1014–1024).

II and the grandson of Emperor Frederick Barbarosa. He loved justice, was wise, humble, and merciful to his people. But he was most cruel to his enemies. He was successful in his wars. He had frequent feuds and quarrels with the pope. They both loved and hated each other.

4987 (1227) Emperor Frederick traveled to Asia in the year 4987, 1227 of the Christians, and conquered the Land of Israel from the King of Egypt. When Corderius, the son of the Egyptian king, saw that the emperor was winning, he tore down the wall of Jerusalem and escaped. The emperor thereupon took Jerusalem as well as many other cities in the Land of Israel. . . .

INTRODUCTION TO NATHAN HANNOVER

ALTHOUGH IT was written some five hundred years after the Jewish Crusade chronicles, Nathan Nata Hannover's Yeven Metzula ("Deep Mire") more closely resembles these medieval works than it does later historiographical writings. Like the Crusade chroniclers, Hannover deals with a series of persecutions, following the plundering and murdering bands from one Jewish community to another. He, too, writes a short time after the events, basing his narrative mainly on the experiences of others which he heard or found in written form. And he, too, is far from being a critical historian. Content for the most part simply to relate the course of events, he ascribes their cause to sin and divine chastisement. Only the breadth of his knowledge, extending to various classical and modern languages, and his interest in general history, as background for his tale of persecutions, links Hannover to the tradition of David Gans.

Hannover was born in the Polish province of Volhynia but wandered extensively through Central Europe. In Italy, he published his small volume at Venice in 1653. Following the Introduction, it contains a chronological presentation of the events which led up to the union of Ukrainian Cossacks, under their chieftain Bogdan Chmielnicki, with Tatar warriors against the

Polish king. Although it then proceeds to recount the warfare between the Polish forces and those of the Cossacks and Tatars, Hannover concentrates on the Jewish communities, relating their attempts to save themselves and their subsequent fate at the hands of the rebels. Throughout the narrative, he repeatedly expresses his high regard for the Polish monarch and nobility—this, despite Polish betrayals of the Jews. The final chapter is devoted to a description of the inner life of Polish Jewry before the catastrophe, presenting an idealized portrait arranged by the pillars upon which, according to two Talmudic rabbis, the world is based: Torah, divine service, deeds of lovingkindness (as Simon the Just designated them); and truth, judgment, and peace (as R. Simon ben Gamaliel taught). The book became extremely popular, was soon translated into Yiddish, and was often reprinted.

In the Introduction, which is given here, Hannover attempts to prove from Scripture that the catastrophe of his day was already foreseen by King David, traditionally considered the author of the book of Psalms. His method is the common technique of gematria: the discovery of a significant correlation between the meaning of certain words and coincidences in the numerical value of the Hebrew letters which compose them. Thus he is able to find a numerical intimation of the date of the persecutions, of the Ukrainians and Tatars, and of the name of the Cossack chieftain—all in three verses from Psalms. He also gives us his reasons for writing the book and why it is worth buying. This introduction, but not the work as a whole, is written in a rather belabored rhymed Hebrew which the translation does not attempt to reproduce.

JEWISH HISTORY AS PROPHECY FULFILLED

"I am the man that hath seen affliction by the rod of His wrath" (Lam. 3:1). For the Lord smote His people Israel, His firstborn. From heaven to earth He cast down His glorious and lovely land of Poland, "fair in situation, the joy of the whole earth" (Ps. 48:3) and His ornament. "The Lord hath swallowed up unsparingly the habitations of Jacob" (Lam. 2:2), destroyed His inheritance, "and hath not remembered His footstool on the day of His wrath" (ibid., 2:1) and His anger.

All of this did King David (may he rest in peace) foresee in his prophecy: that Tatars and Greeks* would join together to destroy Israel, His chosen, in the year zot† of His creation. The Greeks said, as is their custom: "Whoever wants to stay alive must change his faith and make a public statement renouncing Israel and its God." But the Jews paid no heed to their words; they stretched out their necks for the slaughter, sanctifying the name of God. These were the land's great scholars and the other men, women, and children: all of His community. "The Lord is a God of vengeance" (Ps. 94:1). May He wreak His vengeance and return us to His land.

King David (may he rest in peace) forewarns of this [zot] persecution in Psalm 32 (vs. 6): "For this [zot] let everyone that is godly pray unto Thee in a time when Thou mayest be found [le'et metzo] . . ." so that the calamity will not come about. The letters of the words le'et metzo have the same numerical value as yavan vekedar yahdav hubaru [Greece and Tatary joined together]. Dog and cat joined to uproot the people of Israel, which is compared to a straying lamb. It happened in the year five thousand and zot [408] of the Creation.

Psalm 69 (vss. 2–3) also refers to this persecution: "Save me, O God. . . . I am sunk in deep mire . . . and the flood overwhelmeth me" etc. Tavati biven metzula [I am sunk in deep mire] possesses the numerical value of hemil vekedar beyavan yahdav

*Ukrainians of the Orthodox Chruch.

†The letters of the Hebrew word zot have the numerical value of [5]408, the year of the persecution according to the Era of Creation.

hubaru [Chmiel and Tatary joined together with Greece], scorpion and wasp. *Shibolet* [the flood] is numerically equivalent to *hemiletzki, hayavan, vekedar* [Chmielecki,* Greece, and Tatary]; thus wrath and anger overwhelmed me. (In the Polish language his name was changed to Chmielecki to indicate his nobility, but in Russian he was called Chmiel.) The great scholar, our teacher R. Jehiel Michel, judge and head of the academy in the holy and precious community of Nemirov,† whose soul departed in purity for the santification of God's name, said that *hemil* was an acronym for *havle mashiah yavi le'olam* [he will bring about the birth pangs of the messiah]; and after him will come the feet of Elijah.‡

Therefore I have called my book dealing with this incident *Yeven Metzula* ["Deep Mire"] for the Psalmist alludes to the catastrophe and speaks of the enemy nation, Tatars and Greeks, and of the enemy Chmiel (may his name be blotted out; may the Lord send a curse upon him). This book shall preserve the tale for future generations. I have dwelt at length upon the causes which initiated this brutish design: that the Greeks revolted against the kingdom of Poland like a rebellious cow, that Greeks and Tatars joined together although they had always hated each other. I have related all of the battles and persecutions, large and small. Likewise, the dates on which the major persecutions occurred have been recorded so that everyone might be able to note the day on which his father or mother died and to observe the memorial properly. The book will also describe all of the good and just practices of the glorious Jewish community of Poland—all in the pure fear of the Lord. I based these practices upon the six pillars which support the mighty world.§

I have written it all in lucid, clear language and printed it upon fine, clean paper. Therefore, buy this book without delay. Do not withhold your money. Thus I will be able also to publish the book *Plant of Delights*‖ containing homilies I have composed on all of the Torah. For this merit, God, fearful and awesome, will preserve you

*A variant form of Chmielnicki.

†A city in the Ukraine whose Jewish inhabitants were slaughtered when it fell to the Cossacks.

‡ Elijah the Prophet is regarded by Jewish tradition as the harbinger of the Messiah.

§ The pillars are mentioned in Mishnah *Avot*, ch. 1.

‖ It did not appear.

from every anguish and distress. And may He speedily send us the Messiah. Amen; thus may God do, who dwelleth in splendor. These are the words of the author, Nathan Nata, son of our teacher, R. Moses Hannover Ashkenazi (may the memory of the righteous be for a blessing; may the Lord avenge his blood) who lived in the holy community of Zaslav, which is near the large holy community of Ostrog in the province of Volhynia in the great land of Russia.*

*Not politically a part of Russia, but inhabited by a non-Polish Ukrainian population.

SCIENTIFIC STUDY OF
THE JEWISH PAST

INTRODUCTION TO IMMANUEL WOLF

THE "Society for Culture and Science among (or: of) the Jews," which was initiated at Berlin in 1819, set itself a number of goals. Some of these were apologetic, some educational, some political. But its principal objective was to develop a scientific approach to the study of Judaism, following the canons of German scholarship with which its members had become familiar. The chief vehicle was to be the first Jewish periodical devoted almost exclusively to impartial and objective study of the Jewish past and present: the Zeitschrift für die Wissenschaft des Judentums. Its editor, Leopold Zunz, was convinced that the journal must maintain itself on the highest level, descending neither to polemics nor to ephemera.

The first issue of the short-lived Zeitschrift (only one volume was published) appeared in 1822. It opened with a statement by Immanuel Wolf, one of the founders of the Society, which had originally been delivered in a series of two lectures. This essay, presented here in its entirety, consists of two elements, each important for the development of Jewish historiography: a conception of the substance of Jewish history and an outline of the nature of Jewish scholarship.

In the first part of his statement, Wolf's debt to German idealist philosophy is most apparent. Here he defines the object of Jewish history as "the fundamental idea of Judaism," its unifying concept of God. He traces this idea through time as it was carried forward by the Jewish people, the "guardians of the idea of God." In the course of its history, the idea encountered various influences and challenges but always managed to maintain its vitality and to act continually as an important factor in the history of the human spirit. Paradoxically, Wolf suggests that in the premodern world the Jewish idea of unity was best understood by Spinoza, although this philosopher had renounced (and was excommunicated from) the Judaism of his day. That he could see Spinoza as a great representative of "pure" Judaism is the best indication of the degree to which Jewish history was for Wolf the history of a concept, one not even necessarily present at all times in the consciousness of the people.

The second part of Wolf's essay is devoted to outlining the proper study of Judaism. Wolf discusses the sources and the scientific criteria, and he suggests a division into sub-disciplines: the philology, history, and philosophy of Judaism. In discussing the history of Judaism, he notes that the division into periods will accord with the different aspects of the spiritual principle or the levels at which the idea has appeared. Thus he sets forth the criterion by which Jewish history will be periodized by most writers in the nineteenth century. His conclusion indicates most clearly what motivated Wolf, Zunz, and some of their associates to undertake a reexamination of the Judaism which they had inherited: their desire to bring Jewish study into the orbit of science, and thus to achieve a place for it in the modern Western world.

ON THE CONCEPT OF A SCIENCE OF JUDAISM

If we are to talk of a science of Judaism, then it is self-evident that the word "Judaism" is here being taken in its comprehensive sense—as the essence of all the circumstances, characteristics, and achievements of the Jews in relation to religion, philosophy, history, law, literature in general, civil life and all the affairs of man—and not in that more limited sense in which it only means the religion of the Jews. In any event, it is the religious idea which conditions all the ramifications of Judaism and the one on which they are based. But the more this idea has everywhere penetrated human life and combined and incorporated itself with life, the more difficult it is to recognize and comprehend it as a whole, unless one strives to understand it in all its forms and modifications. In the diverse unfolding of the whole life of a people there do of course exist aspects and tendencies which are remote from the sphere of religion; but in Judaism, more than anywhere else, the influence of the basic religious idea is visible in all the circumstances of human life.

From its first formation until our own time, i.e., for a period of at least three millennia, Judaism has preserved itself as a characteristic and independent whole. Admittedly, alien views from outside have often exercised their influence on Judaism, for in the world of the spirit, no more than in the world of matter, do two bodies exist side by side without exercising a mutual influence. But those alien elements that Judaism has absorbed had to submit to the fundamental idea of Judaism in order to assimilate themselves to it and become one with it. Similarly, all that has come forth from Judaism everywhere bears the imprint of this basic idea and reveals it in every form. But infinitely more significant is that influence on humanity Judaism has exercised, as history incontestably reveals. Founded in alien surroundings, under Egyptian influence, but taking an altogether different course from the Egyptian people, Judaism as a result of its own inner characteristics, has always remained strange and isolated in relation to the rest of the world. But the spiritual content, the idea of Judaism, has communicated itself to the most varied peoples of the world.

What is this idea that has existed throughout so much of world history and has so successfully influenced the culture of the human race? It is of the most simple kind and its content can be expressed in a few words. It is the idea of unlimited unity in the all. It is contained in the one word YHVH which signifies indeed the living unity of all being in eternity, the absolute being outside defined time and space. This concept is revealed to the Jewish people, i.e., posited as a datum. But this took place at a time when man's mind was far from ready to grasp it in all its universality. For man needs time in order to raise himself from the world of the physical and the many to that of the universal unity, the all-embracing and all-existing Monas.* Thus the idea of the unity of God, as taught by Judaism, could only gradually be comprehended and recognized by a people which had not yet raised itself from the physical world. At first, therefore, the idea of God had to be conveyed in personal and individual shape and could only gradually be revealed in its full universality. Therefore the idea of God, if it was to continue and develop among mankind, had to be clothed in a body and thus brought nearer to human understanding. In this way Judaism intimately united the world of the spiritual and the divine with the world of human life. But it depicted the divine in its first revelation as a living, spiritual entity, incommensurable with the world of matter and incapable of physical representation. But the body surrounding the divine idea, in which its gradual unfolding and development proceeded, was Mosaic theocracy. Thus the Jewish people became a nation of priests in the sense of guardians of the idea of God—a people of God.

But because the idea of Judaism, as a purely spiritual principle, was at the time of revelation by no means in harmony with the concept of the world and cultural level of the Jewish people, nor of any other, it never came to rest since it was first manifested and has remained in constant struggle. But peace and permanence are alien to the realm of the spirit, which is truly living. It is in the nature of the spiritual world to be in constant motion, and never to cease development.

Now as the spiritual principle continued to grow in the Jewish State, of which it provided the foundation, the Jewish people were led to an ever more living knowledge of it. But the struggle of the idea of God against the world of the senses in which the Jewish people was still confined and to which all the neighboring peoples

*From the Greek, here meaning a single spiritual entity.

enticed it, the constant activity of this idea, which, once proclaimed, was bound to overcome all obstacles, must unfold itself continuously and rise to a universal level. This ferment manifested itself in the division of the Jewish State, in its never-ending inner and outer struggles. The prophets in Israel recognized that the continued existence of the State was bound up with the fundamental religious idea and they would not therefore tolerate a second temple alongside the one which was a symbol of unity. They prophesied incalculable misfortune if all maxims of State were not made in conformity with the basic religious principle. But they proclaimed infinite bliss for mankind once the idea of God were acknowledged.

The constant dissensions and disturbances, however, were bound to weaken the small Jewish State to such an extent that it could no longer maintain itself against the neighboring peoples striving for universal dominion. The Jewish people lost its external independence and only found its internal, characteristic independence, its nationhood—in the unique world of religion. That is the reason why the Babylonian exile was so uncommonly favorable to the development of the idea of God. Not until then did it intertwine and become fused with the whole inner life of the Jews. Incidentally, the influence exercised by the Chaldean on Jewish culture is well known. When another powerful race of people seized dominion over the peoples of Asia, when a new victorious conqueror, in accordance with the manner and spirit of the time, began to force the majority of the then known peoples of the world into one universal monarchy and to unify them under one scepter, the Jews, as enemies of the previous dynasty, could not be regarded as enemies of the new: they were permitted to return to their own country. But behold a remarkable event! Hundreds of thousands remained in the dispersion and were not incorporated a second time into the Jewish State. But everywhere they preserved the selfsame idea on which their nationhood depended. They remained adherents of Judaism and thereby links in a chain.

But a Jewish State arose anew, a temple was built anew as a symbol and rallying point for Judaism. The struggle of the idea had nearly ceased internally, the Jews had come to terms with the true spirit of their laws in which the political and moral principles were bound into an indissoluble unity by the religious principle, and had thereby become incapable of ever again falling away from the fundamental idea of Judaism. The separation of the Samaritans from the true Jews was the cause of unceasing disputes, and the conflict between religious and worldly power which should have been united, soon began to bring about recurrent disturbances. The conflict with the outside world, however, became more and more violent. Later a principle that was utterly different from Judaism came into conflict with it—Hellenism. In Judaism the divine idea is present as a given, revealed idea. In Hellenism all knowledge has developed from the human spirit itself. Both in their very different ways are the most momentous factors in the cultural history of the human spirit. When it came into contact with Judaism, Hellenism had already won its triumph over the hitherto dominant Asiatic world. Different principles are hostile to each other. They seek to penetrate and dissolve one another. In most cases a new product emerges, a distinctive third entity. The originality and inner consistency of Judaism might well be shaken but was not to be destroyed. Moreover, the Hellenistic principle here, remote from its native soil in the Syrian empire, was not present in its original power and dignity. It had no wish to inject other peoples with its own spirit and to force it on them. The encounter between the Greek and Jewish principles was more peaceful in Egypt, especially in Alexandria, because here the two principles did not confront each other in obstinate contradiction, but were attenuated by a third principle, the Egyptian principle, which stood between them. In time new principles were formed here combining these three in different proportions but in a way that the different components remained visible: the philosophy of Philo,* Gnosticism, neo-Platonism.

Judaism, meanwhile, was continuously attacked from outside and soon shaken internally by even more damaging tendencies. Different methods of comprehending and interpreting the religious principle, which was now closely bound up with the life of the people, and the different hopes based on these for the future of the gravely threatened state, divided the worshipers of divine unity into as many sects as political parties. The unfolding religious idea was in a state of ferment which caused all minds to turn to the imminence of a decisive event. Then Judea began its final struggle against the all-powerful Romans and the Jewish State succumbed, astonishing the world by its vast strength even while dying. But the Roman Empire, this largest and last universal dominion of antiquity, the

*Philo Judaeus (c.20 B.C.E.–50 C.E.), Jewish Platonic philosopher of Alexandria, Egypt.

guiding principle of which now began to weaken, represented a vast organization capable of absorbing the idea which had hitherto lived among a small people and had developed to a certain level, so that the universal idea might become universal. This took place in the shape of Christianity.

The life of the peoples of antiquity, generally moving out of the world of the senses and the infinite, reflected higher and eternal values only in vague and surmised form, truly and spiritually perceived only by a few outstanding sages. Yet this life which practiced and encouraged individual virtue and which will always remain of great interest historically, as the childhood of the human race, had completed one cycle and was now to become a more serious and advanced spirit. The idea of God spread among the peoples and raised them to a higher level of being, but it was inwardly understood and shaped differently, according to different aspects and clothed in different forms. The Jewish State, however, had fulfilled its mission; and together with the Temple in which the pure idea of God had reigned without being represented in physical images but only to be comprehended by the thinking spirit, together with this lofty Temple, the foundation of the whole edifice, the Jewish State collapsed. Thus a people was robbed of freedom and independence, which it could and would enjoy to the fullest extent or not at all. A people whose every circumstance, public and domestic life, science and art, was conditioned and ordered by one and the same principle; a people whose literature is nothing but the representation of a religious idea at an ever more advanced stage of development, whose poetry is nothing but the glorification of this idea.

The Jewish State collapsed but not Judaism. Hundreds of thousands still acknowledged their adherence to the selfsame idea. Misfortune only attached them to it more firmly; they carried it with them throughout the world. Everywhere the Jew preserved his national characteristics and remained a Jew. The greater the misfortunes the people underwent, the more confidently did they give themselves up to the childlike hope for reunification and renewed glory. The expectation of a messianic end of time which would resolve all injustice, and bring all truth to light, is as natural to humanity, especially when humiliated and downcast, as the legend of a blissful golden innocent dawn. Misfortune, suppression, and persecution—the more they are intensified, the more lively the conviction on the part of the sufferer that his present state will not endure; the more closely do the fellow-sufferers cling together and the more firmly do they hold fast to everything that yet remains to them as testimony of a blissful past. But the scholars among the Jews in the first centuries after the destruction of their state were once again able to bind the idea of Judaism and life closely together, modified to accord with the changed circumstances of the times. Even under the Mosaic constitution all public institutions were a reminder of this fundamental idea but the same concept was bound up with domestic life, even extending to clothing (ritual fringes and phylacteries). But now everything that referred to the public life of the people, to the sanctified soil of the national territory, had lost its significance. Temple and priest were no more. What was now necessary was to unite with domestic life everything that had formerly been significantly bound up with public life. A profound knowledge of human nature was the foundation of this scheme. Family life is the source and training ground of morality and, when customs and habits are bound up with the domestic hearth, they grow deep and indestructible roots in the minds of men. That is why the Rabbis have interwoven the whole life of the Jews with religious reminiscences and customs. The mysterious meaning which the Rabbis attributed to most of these, the pious cast of mind in which they struggled and decided every atom of this world of ceremony, filled the people not only with holy reverence at every religious action and popular custom which it had preserved, but the people also accepted the new decrees of the Talmudists with eagerness and with the same reverence. The Talmudists succeeded in complementing the age-old decrees artificially, as an oral tradition running parallel to the scriptures, thus with the most minute care but with the best of intentions, erecting a fence around the Law (as they themselves put it) in order that this might remain all the more inviolable and pure. This unique mode of life, everywhere surrounded by a veil of sacredness and piety, founded on a single and an essentially extremely simple idea, preserved by the Jews with anxious care, transmitted from generation to generation, and held together even more consistently and more firmly by continued outside pressure, is what has preserved Judaism for so long.

Without the vitality of the original religious idea indwelling in Judaism, the spirit would inevitably very soon have succumbed to the pressure of external events. But the active inner principle developed ever-new life, ever-new strength. Judaism also developed alongside its Pharisaic and Rabbinic manifestation, a purely intellectual and speculative outlook, already to some extent in evidence in the sects of the Essenes, Therapeutics,* and Sadducees, and then in the systems of Jews familiar with Greek philosophy and, finally, and notably, in the Kabbalah.† Thus we see the Jews, even in the Middle Ages, together with the Arabs, energetically tilling the fields of scholarship, particularly in Spain. This was at a time when Islam, which had borrowed its finest dogmas from Judaism, seemed willing to make amends for the damage previously done to scholarship. The Jews became the interpreters of Arab learning to the European world and with the re-establishment, or rather the beginning of real scientific life in Europe—dying Greece bequeathing its inheritance to the Western world—Judaism also influenced the shaping of the new literary life. Only when modern history began were the Jews overtaken in the life of culture. Fanatical violence which had raged most cruelly against the Jews, particularly from the beginning of the Crusades until Ferdinand the Catholic,‡ had succeeded in producing that effect which continuous hostile pressure and subjugation never fail to produce, and which only the vitality of the idea basic to Judaism had been able to avert for so long. In the end the spirit too had necessarily to succumb to the fetters which deprived the body of freedom of movement. Excluded from public life, restricted to certain fields of activity, the Jews were more and more pushed back into their own unique world, handed down to them by their fathers and forefathers. But the life of this world, that had been preserved from antiquity, became more and more constricted and hollow, for the living spirit could no longer move freely within it. Since then, and until the present day, the rabbis confined themselves to their scholastic preoccupations. But that is the nature of scholasticism: to follow the letter of a tradition assumed to be holy and inviolable, to develop from within it every aspect of human knowledge in all directions and thus to hamper every free, individual, and living movement of the human mind, and to preclude any rational and independent understanding of infinite truth.

Thus the Jews in general now live, and most of all their scholars, i.e., their rabbis, in hollow isolation, in self-imposed

*A sect of Jewish ascetics, similar to the Essenes, which existed near Alexandria during the first century C.E.

†The Jewish mystical tradition.

‡King of Spain when the Jews were expelled in 1492.

constraint, in peaceful brooding over the letters of vanished centuries. But no one familiar with history should be surprised at this. For the history of the European Jew in the Middle Ages for the most part consists only of a series of experiments arranged by the enemies of this unfortunate people in order to oppress and to exterminate them. The history of European greed in America and Africa can show deeds of greater shame. Yet from time to time benevolent Northern light brightens the darkness into which Judaism finally fell.

In the inner family life of the Jews there were preserved, together with old customs and habits, ineradicable traces of a more noble human nature and an active mind. But what is of the highest importance is this: that Judaism, in succumbing, so to speak, beneath the weight of years and external violence into a debilitating lethargy, was yet depicted in accordance with its unique, vital, and eternal idea, in the latter's highest degree of definition, consistency, and freedom—as though this were the last, exhausting act of its manifestation—in the manner of the pure speculative thinking, i.e., purely scientifically. This was in the system of Benedict de Spinoza,* a man whose subtlety and profundity were centuries in advance of his time, whose highly significant influence on the more consistent and profound philosophies of the present day is unmistakable, who did indeed renounce the external rites of Judaism but who had understood all the more its inner spirit.

Thus Judaism shows itself to be for most of the history of the world an important and influential factor in the development of the human spirit. The only person who can fail to recognize this is the man who looks at history, as he looks at everything else, with preconceived notions; or the man who only sees in the history of the world an aggregate of individual events, to whom the random succession of diverse events is a mere source of amusement, and for whom only bloody battles, bold conquests, and miraculous coincidences of fate are of importance. The annals of world history could only offer us the satisfaction of our curiosity, mere food for our yearning for the miraculous and empty play for our fantasies if they contained nothing besides this. But events are only manifestations of the moving and developing spirit and it is indeed the gradual unfolding of the living spirit which constitutes the instructive

*The great philosopher of the seventeenth century who was excommunicated by the Amsterdam Jewish community.

element in world history, which alone makes possible a true understanding of the past and the present. History, considered from this point of view, would be just as instructive and as meaningful if it were to give us a complete record of the dreams of the greatest men of every age, as these could tell us just as much as their actions about the development of the spirit.

An idea, such as Judaism, which has developed and remained in existence for so many centuries, which has been alive and productive for such a long period in the history of the world must for this very reason be founded on the essence of humanity itself and thus be of the greatest significance and importance for the thinking spirit.

Judaism presents itself to us in a dual form—first, in the documents of history and literature, in an extensive set of writings; and second, as a still living principle, acknowledged by millions of people dispersed all over the world. To the latter the original simple idea has, so to speak, turned rusty under the influence of the oxygen in a hostile atmosphere. The fence with which the Law was surrounded gradually spread wider and wider, so that it grew into a challenging barrier, barring the path to the inner sanctuary, and even burying the sanctuary. But the free spirit of science breaks through the weeds of a ceremonial that a thousand years of habit have made mechanical and lifeless; and within, it sees the selfsame idea of God, that was formerly revealed in all its clarity. The influence of the irresistible progress of spirit already begins to make a powerful impact on Judaism. Where external pressure has ceased, the spirit can begin to develop more freely. The idea strives to free itself from the unyielding walls in which it has been imprisoned, and must once again reveal itself in its own inner, spiritual essence.

Judaism, as a whole, as here presented, based on its own inner principle and embodied, on the one hand, in a comprehensive literature, and, on the other, in the life of a large number of human beings, both can be—and needs to be—treated scientifically. Hitherto, however, it has never been described scientifically and comprehensively from a wholly independent standpoint. What Jewish scholars have achieved, especially in earlier times, is mostly theological in character. In particular, they have almost completely neglected the study of history. But Christian scholars, however great their merit in the development of individual aspects of Judaism, have almost always treated Judaism for the sake of a historical understanding of Christian theology, even if it was not their intention to place Judaism itself in a hateful light, or, as they put it—to confute Judaism. Even though some important scholarly works written from a general literary standpoint and interest have emerged not merely as vehicles or propaedeutics for Christian theology (which is admittedly difficult to separate from Jewish theology), these achievements apply only to individual aspects of the whole. But if Judaism is to become an object of science in its own right and if a science of Judaism is to be formed, then it is obvious that quite a different method of treatment is under discussion. But any object, no matter of what type, that in its essence is of interest to the human spirit, and comprehensive in its diverse formation and development, can become the object of a special science.

The content of this special science is the systematic unfolding and representation of its object in its whole sweep, for its own sake, and not for any ulterior purpose. If we apply this to the science of Judaism, then the following characteristics emerge:

1. The science of Judaism comprehends Judaism in its fullest scope.

2. It unfolds Judaism in accordance with its essence and describes it systematically, always relating individual features back to the fundamental principle of the whole.

3. It treats the object of study in and for itself, for its own sake, and not for any special purpose or definite intention. It begins without any preconceived opinion and is not concerned with the final result. Its aim is neither to put its object in a favorable, nor in an unfavorable, light, in relation to prevailing views, but to show it as it is. Science is self-sufficient, is in itself an essential need of the human spirit. It therefore needs to serve no other purpose than its own. But it is for that reason no less true that each science not only exercises its most important influence on other sciences but also on life. This can easily be shown to be true of the science of Judaism.

Every science falls into several parts according to the essential differences in the material, and this will also apply to our science. This, however, in accordance with the above-mentioned twofold revelation of its object, will fall initially into two main divisions:

1. Study of Judaism in its historical and literary writings.

2. Statistical study of Judaism in relation to the present-day Jews scattered throughout all the countries of the world.

The aim will be to depict Judaism, first from a historical

standpoint, as it has gradually developed and taken shape; and then philosophically, according to its inner essence and idea. The textual knowledge of the literature of Judaism must precede both methods of study. Thus we have, first, the textual study of Judaism; second, a history of Judaism; third, a philosophy of Judaism.

1. The textual study of Judaism is the interpretative and critical understanding of the whole literature of the Jews, as the literature in which are defined the special world of the Jews and their unique way of life and of thought. Textual study will make use of varying methods inasmuch as this literature is in different languages, embraces different themes, and belongs to different ages.

2. The history of Judaism is the systematic description of Judaism, in the forms it has assumed at any special time, and in all its aspects. In particular, there are three such tendencies: the religious, the political, and the literary which are everywhere, however, intimately bound up with each other. When depicted as a whole they yield the general history; when depicted individually, they yield the history of religion, politics, and literature.

The history of the Jews will fall into several periods in accordance with the many different aspects in which the spiritual principle of Judaism has manifested itself in the course of time, or in accordance with the different levels at which the idea, the formative spirit of the whole, has appeared.

3. The philosophy of Judaism has as its object the conception of Judaism as such. This it must unfold and reveal in all its truth in accordance with its inner rationality. It will teach the understanding of the idea of God as it has gradually been revealed in Judaism. Furthermore, it will point to the connection between external historical events and the inner development of the living idea. Whereas history concerns itself only with what has happened, with the past, the interest of philosophy also extends to the state of the idea in the present, in the Judaism of today. The history of the past is directly followed by the second main division of the subject, i.e., Judaism in the living form in which it lies before us—the general statistical position of the Jews in every country, with special reference to their religious and political circumstances.

This would be, in general outline, the framework of the science of Judaism—a vast field embracing literary researches, compilations, and developments! But if the object as such is important to science and the human spirit in general, its progressive development is bound to follow. The truly scientific spirit therefore cannot on account of the multifariousness and the vast scope of the field doubt the possibility that such a science might be established. The essence of science is universality, infinity, and therein lie the spur and the attraction which it has for the human spirit whose nobler nature rejects any limitations, any rest, any standing still. But should the question be asked: what advantage will accrue to science as a whole from a scientific treatment of Judaism on these lines? It is obvious once again that such a question cannot emanate from anyone who has grasped the true spirit of science. How could it be that an object, which in any way at all had its place within the field of scientific research, could be examined and discussed without shedding some light on other objects of science and thus indirectly over the whole field of the sciences? In the realm of the sciences nothing stands on its own, nothing is isolated. On the contrary, all the sciences are subject to mutual influence, are bound to each other by an inner harmony. But it is above all the task and the obligation of our age to summarize these main branches of human knowledge, which are manifestations of a principle, in their whole extent, together with all connected and related fields and to trace their general development back to its basic principle. Thus everything that the admirable diligence of earlier ages had achieved and gathered together in detail would be assembled into a unity of meaning. But today the attention of the scholar, in his attempt to obtain a thorough insight into the history of the development of the human spirit from the earliest ages of man, is directed, above all, toward the Orient, this cradle of human culture, this source of so much that is great and sublime. As this is so, would it not be timely to subject Judaism, this richest and most widespread fruit of the Orient, to a thorough examination from a purely scientific point of view? Or are we to neglect, in our attraction toward the more unknown and more remote world of the Hindus and Persians, the treasures of a Judaism that is closer and more accessible? Or indeed do the latter promise no yield? Are they perhaps already exhausted? Anyone who supposes this to be the case is ignorant of the wealth of material available.

But Judaism is not only of historical interest. It is not a principle that belongs to the past, that has already lived and is now preserved merely in the pages of history. It lives on, acknowledged by a not inconsiderable portion of humanity, even of European humanity, on a numerical basis alone. And yet the position of these living witnesses of antiquity among the peoples of Europe is still the subject of debate. The institutions of the Middle Ages have here, as elsewhere, ceased to function. The situation of humanity has changed but is not yet settled. No universally valid principle has yet been found for the relations of the Jews; and if there is ever to be a just decision on this issue, then this can clearly only be done through the ways of science. Scientific knowledge of Judaism must decide on the merits or demerits of the Jews, their fitness or unfitness to be given the same status and respect as other citizens. This alone will make known the inner character of Judaism and separate the essential from the accidental, the original from the later addition. Science alone is above the partisanship, passions, and prejudices of daily life, for its aim is truth. I mean genuine science, free and infinite, not that pseudoscience which only consists of empty reasoning, in an arbitrary combination of different opinions which number among them prejudice due to selfishness, love of power, envy, and vanity. It deals in assertions, it relies on the authority of concepts which happen to be currently accepted by the masses, instead of being founded on the inner concept of its objects. True science will ignore an opponent of this kind, for the latter will vanish at its sight, as night before the day.

It remains to indicate in a few words that aspect, in the light of which the establishment of a science of Judaism seems to be a necessity of our age. This is the inner world of the Jews themselves. This world, too, has in many ways been disturbed and shaken by the unrelenting progress of the spirit and the associated changes in the life of the peoples. It is manifest everywhere that the fundamental principle of Judaism is again in a state of inner ferment, striving to assume a shape in harmony with the spirit of the times. But in accordance with the age this development can only take place through the medium of science. The scientific attitude is the characteristic of our time. But as the formation of a science of Judaism is an essential need for the Jews themselves, it is clear that, although the field of science is open to all men, it is primarily the Jews who are called upon to devote themselves to it. The Jews must once again show their mettle as doughty fellow workers in the common task of mankind. They must raise themselves and their principle to the level of science, for this is the attitude of the European world. This attitude must banish the relationship of strangeness in which Jews and Judaism have hitherto stood in relation to the outside world. And if one day a bond is to join the whole of humanity, then it is the bond of science, the bond of pure reason, the bond of truth.

INTRODUCTION TO LEOPOLD ZUNZ

FOR LEOPOLD ZUNZ (1794–1886), Jewish history was the history of Jewish literature. Trained in philology at the University of Berlin, Zunz saw it as his task to apply the modern critical approach of Wissenschaft to the vast store of Jewish creativity. Since he was not a practicing rabbi or a theologian, his motives for undertaking this project were freer of nonscholarly considerations than those of most of his colleagues. He was not principally interested in studying the past for the sake of religious reform. His main concern was to win respectability for Jewish studies in the German academic community. He thought this might best be done by proving that the literature of the Jews constituted a fruitful field for research and that it could be explored with the same critical scrutiny as any other domain of scholarly investigation. To this end also, he defined Jewish literature broadly, to include writings on every conceivable subject, not merely those of religious content.

Zunz was little interested in the physical history of the Jews. To his mind—as to that of the historian Heinrich Graetz—the Middle Ages had brought the Jews only suffering and anguish. Their chief tormentor had been the Church, constantly confronting them with persecutions, humiliations, and unabating efforts to bring about their conversion. When Zunz touches upon this subject at all—as he does in the following selection taken from his The Synagogal Poetry of the Middle Ages—it is only to explain why the medieval literature of the Jews is so harsh in its treatment of Christians. The modern reader, he maintains, needs to know the plight of the Jews in order to gain a sympathetic understanding of the vengeful sentiments which appear in their liturgy. The substance of Jewish history is the inner spiritual life of the Jews; their external history—their suffering—is significant only insofar as it helps to explain some characteristic of their literary creativity.

THE SUFFERING OF THE JEWS

If there be an ascending scale of sufferings, Israel reached its highest degree. If the duration of afflictions, and the patience with which they are borne, confer nobility upon man, the Jews may vie with the aristocracy of any country. If a literature which owns a few classical tragedies is deemed rich, what place should be assigned to a tragedy which extends over fifteen centuries, and which has been composed and enacted by the heroes themselves?

The dispersion of the Jews, sufficiently disastrous in itself, but especially so when considered in connection with their desire for reunion, might have filled a sympathetic heart with charity and respect; and the Jews were the more entitled to proper treatment, since among themselves the stranger had always been protected. Lowly and powerless, they should have received protection; it was preferred, however, to exact from them heavy taxes and tolls, even to impose monetary penalties upon their poor. . . .

As long as oppression and exclusion had not subjected the Jews from infancy to habitual contempt, and as long as fanaticism had not yet pervaded the masses, the Jews lived on peaceful terms with their fellow citizens, for no real antagonism was entertained against them by the people. But the priests strained every nerve to crush the Jews morally, and to withdraw all sympathy from them by declaring that "Jewish" and "diabolical" were synonymous terms. In Syria, as in France, many Christians had visited the synagogues, joined in the celebration of Jewish festivals, and often preferred Jewish to Christian preachers and judges; Jews and Christians visited one another, feasted together, and even intermarried. This drove the Fathers of the Church to frenzy: they had recourse to tyrannical edicts and councils. When the authority of monasticism became prevalent, when canonizations and pilgrimages to the tombs of saints were on the increase, when finally Hildebrand* secured the ascendancy of the priests in Europe, the Jews sank lower and lower; and after they had been reduced by legislation and custom to extreme contempt, it was easy for the populace to persecute the helpless with abusive names. Men called them dogs, and heaped

*Pope Gregory VII (1072-1085).

upon them every insult. "We are abused," says a Selihah,* "spat upon, and treated like mire in the streets"; "we sit speechless in the corner, like witnesses taken in a lie"; "we listen to provocation and answer nought". . . .

The Middle Ages are the period of barbarism, that is, of the united sway of physical force, ignorance, and priestcraft. These were the halcyon days of certain precious inventions, such as auricular confession, celibacy, disallowance of the Bible, Carthusian monasticism,† crusades and trials for witchcraft, inquisitions, and the burning of heretics. Priestcraft and rapacity crushed the prosperity of Provence, impoverished Spain, depopulated Asia and America. Despots and priests left in their track more misery and desolation than had been caused by all the Scythians, Huns, and Vandals‡ together. The Jews unquestionably fared better among Poles, Bohemians, Magyars, and Khazars, Franks and Bulgarians, Bedouins and Mongols, than among medieval Christians. The ecclesiastics, whose butcheries were on the increase in England about and after 1150, sufficiently proved their temper upon the slaughtered Albigenses, Waldenses,§ Protestants, and other heretics; and Israel's Selihah furnished but a single page in that record.

The Jews, who in England, France, and Germany passed like merchandise from hand to hand, were required, now by priests and rulers, now more truculently by the populace, to submit to baptism. Often, in the case of refusal, blood was shed. Amid such scenes a thousand-voiced echo of loyal professions burst forth from the poetry of the synagogue: "Beware of denying the Only One, of forsaking your religion and of breaking your faith," and other such admonitions. Under oppression, the noble-minded sufferers uttered their fairest sentiments. The bruised flowers sent forth a sweet odor. The enchained proved more free than his torturer. . . .

The mournful road . . . from Constantine‖ to Charles V¶ sustains the opinion that in the Middle Ages the history of the European Jews principally exhibits a mere series of hostile

*A penitential poem.

†A monastic life of extreme asceticism instituted by St. Bruno in 1084.

‡"Barbarian" tribes who spread over Europe in ancient times.

§Albigenses and Waldenses were Christian heretical sects of the twelfth century.

‖Roman Emperor during the early fourth century who was the first to become a Christian.

¶Holy Roman Emperor (1515-1558).

experiments for the extermination of these sufferers. It also justifies the opinion which was naturally formed concerning the authors of such horrors. The Christians were held to be venal, perjured, covetous, cruel; their priests unchaste, rapacious, and heartless; their princes the scourge of God. . . .

An historical survey of the Jewish Middle Ages explains the motives of wrath and exasperation [in the synagogue liturgy], it lays open the source of complaints, it reveals both the pangs and their causes. We feel the sufferings, we hear the imprecations, we share the hopes. The stern words uttered in these Jewish psalms,* by which no Christian ever lost his life, rise as the dying cry of myriads of murdered human beings; only love, not derision—justice, not oppression—could have turned them into words of conciliation.

*The Jewish liturgical poetry of the Middle Ages.

INTRODUCTION TO ABRAHAM GEIGER

THE LIFE of Abraham Geiger (1810–1874) was divided between two great interests: scholarship and the active rabbinate. Though he tried to integrate the two, they often created a tension which he was unable fully to resolve; his desire to shape the future of Judaism inevitably affected the way he viewed the Jewish past. As a reformer of Jewish religious life in Germany, Geiger looked to scholarship to provide the basis for practical changes in worship and Jewish law. His conception of Jewish history stressed the continuous presence of spiritual development as precedent for the ongoing evolution of Judaism. A universalist in his religious outlook, he held that Judaism was not restricted within the confines of a narrow nationality, that its true aspirations always included the entirety of mankind.

Thus in the first two selections below, which are taken from lectures Geiger gave at the Academy for the Science of Judaism in Berlin during the years 1872–74, the universality of Judaism is a basic theme. The Jewish idea was once clothed in the garments of a language and national institutions, and these lent it vitality. But it was never dependent on them. Nationality characterizes only the origins of Israel, not its essence. Indeed, Judaism survived primarily because it did not require a political framework. It lived by its universal faith in the one God. And it is the dynamics of this faith which, for Geiger, constitutes Jewish history. Thus, too, his periodization is according to successive religious and intellectual forms: revelation, tradition, legalism, and critical study—the last no less legitimate a relation to the Divine than the first.

The third selection is taken from a sermon which Geiger delivered in 1869 at the dedication of a new synagogue in Wiesbaden. Noteworthy here is Geiger's description of the Jews as a spiritual people, imbued by divine revelation with a unique creative spirit. This spirit manifests itself in the faith of Israel which, according to Geiger, is strictly rational in character, eschewing dogma and mystery.

THE DEVELOPING IDEA OF JUDAISM

The introduction to the Science of Judaism which is to be given here aims at bringing about a full understanding of the religious thought and ideal content which pervades Judaism and which dwells within it as its unique life-giving force. The only method by which such understanding can be acquired is the study of the manner in which the idea first entered into the physical world, of the way in which it has found expression in language and literature and in which it has manifested itself in practice in the course of history. Only when the spiritual motive behind Judaism has thus been traced inductively will it be possible for us to gain a true conception of its full content and its philosophical and religio-ethical tenets. It is true that they will then be isolated from the time-bound forms in which they have been expressed at various periods, but they will still bear within themselves vital forces which have not yet achieved their full development. The Science of Judaism may thus be divided into three aspects:

1. Philological.
2. Historical, particularly as regards the history of Jewish literature and culture.
3. Philosophical and religious.

To begin with, there will be some who will count against Judaism the fact that it has a philological aspect at all, which is supposed to be no less important than its history, and who will view this as proof of its narrowness. There will be those who will compare Judaism with Christianity. They will point out that, while Christianity has exerted some influence on the development, or rather on the style, of language, it did not make its appearance in a language of its own, but in Greek which was then the idiom of world culture. The fact that, soon thereafter, Christianity came to employ Latin, the tongue of the Romans who held sway over the civilized world, will be taken as an indication of the universal nature of this faith. On closer examination, however, one will find that what seemed an advantage for Christianity is actually a shortcoming and that what first appeared to be a weakness in Judaism is actually one of its strong points.

A new idea can originate only in a strong personality. It is only by a strong individual that a universally acceptable idea can be conceived. It will then mature into consummate expression only in one who is especially qualified and endowed for this purpose by his active participation in the general natural tendencies of mankind. Wherever a superior form of development of the universal human type is in evidence it will manifest itself in superior, distinctive individuality. In such persons the idea which can embrace all of mankind will shine forth in the form of a conviction that pervades all of that person's life; the idea will carry with it both the demand that everyone else allow himself to be imbued with it to the same extent and the awareness that this demand is possible of fulfillment, especially here. This conviction will dominate such an individual. Moreover, while the conviction will, on the one hand, constitute the whole essence of that individual, his personality, sharp and distinct as it is, will, on the other hand, impress the seal of its subjective nature on the idea. It is impossible to separate the two influences from one another.

If this is true with regard to one individual, it must certainly be even more so in the case of a whole nation. It is only in a nation with special potentialities that science, art, and religion will manifest themselves in a refined form. Just because they are so completely dominated by the idea, the people, its views, and its language, will also impress their full individual character upon the thoughts and creations which are supposed to represent that which is universally human. Only a people which has a healthy vitality and which constitutes a closed entity will be able to produce ideas that are viable, comprehensive, and of abiding value. These ideas will, of necessity, bear the imprint of the definite and unique physiognomy of that people. This physiognomy is the vessel that will contain the idea and will perforce limit its manifestations. It will detract nothing, however, from the general validity of its contents. Thus the idea must come to the fore in full individual definiteness and in accordance with the language and concepts of the people with whom it originated; indeed, it must come forth as the particular expression of that people. Only later may it become transfigured into a greater spirituality, as it becomes independent of the soil in which it first matured. If it is not to fall victim to that curse which adheres to every unhealthy outgrowth of romanticism, it must not be the product of vague and hazy perceptions. Thus, we will not cast aspersions on the universal value of ancient Greek art just because its themes were derived from mythology and its characters bear Greek features. True, the artist of today no longer carves idols, nor does he mold his figures in terms of Greek beauty, but the fact remains that the idea of art was fully realized by the ancient Greeks and this will be understood by everyone who is receptive to it.

The strength of Judaism lies precisely in the fact that it has grown out of a full national life and that it possesses both a language and a history as a nation. The idea of Judaism was an all-embracing one. Hence, if it was not to be a drifting shadow, it had to find expression in a healthy national individualism which, on the one hand, saw all of mankind epitomized within itself, but, on the other hand, sought to embrace all the world of mankind beyond its own confines. Thus it is a strong point of Judaism that it originally revealed itself in a language which was entirely imbued with the idea and which was the noblest fruit of a full national life. Judaism was not, however, dependent upon language and nationality; indeed, it survived in all its vitality even after being deprived of both. When its vessel was smashed, its survival was not affected thereby. Because it always had to engage in violent struggle, Judaism remained a closed and separate entity; and yet it has succeeded in transmitting its basic ideals to mankind as a universal heritage. And when the artificial barriers fall, it will continue to retain its universality throughout the course of history. Let us, therefore, look back with joy on our former life as a nation, as being an essential transitional era in our history, and on our language, through which the life of that Jewish nation took root in spiritual soil!

Christianity put in its very first appearance as a universalist faith; but precisely in this lack of a national origin and individual language lies its weakness. Its concepts and sentiments are characterized by great vagueness; they conflict with every definite national trait. They are mere phantoms which deny all real life. Dreams of a disembodied existence, they widen the chasm between body and soul and view the destruction of all things physical as the greatest attainable bliss. Christianity arose under the influence of the disintegration of noble civilizations, the Jewish and the Greek; it was garbed in decaying languages; it had the seeds of morbidity implanted in it, as it were—a morbid state under which it labors to this day. Christianity is the true mother of mysticism and romanticism. Judaism is lucid, concrete, vital, and affirmative. Judaism is permeated with spirituality; it does not deny the earthly world, but instead transfigures it. It is rooted in one particular people with a language and history of its own, and yet it embraces all of mankind.

. . . The Science of Judaism is the study of the particular orientation of the spiritual life through which, within one particular sphere, Judaism was founded, developed, broadcast, and preserved in full vigor down to our time. Our interest in this spiritual force grows as we perceive that it did not operate within narrow limits and far away from the world of reality. On the contrary, its spiritual power has manifested itself almost at all times in the very midst of the mightiest spiritual movements in world history, at the very focal points of important cultural developments. It was, in fact, receptive to stimuli emanating from the centers of culture, so that it never shut them out; but it was not absorbed by them. It succeeded rather in assimilating them to its own manner, thus giving evidence of its independent vitality. This evidence is corroborated even more effectively by the telling influence which the spirit of Judaism has continuously exerted on human progress as a whole and which—as its vitality permits us to hope—it will continue to exercise in the future. At three important crossroads in world history, Judaism had an important part in guiding the development of spiritual and intellectual life. At the close of the era of antiquity, Judaism gave birth to Christianity; during the Middle Ages, it brought Islam to life and nourished it with its essential content; and at the opening of the modern era, it provided the intellectual background for Spinoza and thus the first momentum for a complete revolution in the theories of philosophy. These worldwide forces did not continue to have an effect on Judaism, but the spirit of Judaism continued to be manifest within them. It is significant, too, that Judaism survived and took root in those countries which long before had produced the first fruits of civilization: Egypt, Phoenicia, Syria, Assyria, and Babylonia. Judaism maintained the closest possible ties with these countries and thus certainly was in no position to ward off their intellectual influences. Nevertheless, Judaism remained independent of them. True, at a later date, it was exposed to the influences of Parsiism* which it assimilated in a fashion which was its very own; subsequently, it united with Hellenism to give birth to Alexandrianism;† and, eventually, it developed its own fullest potential in closest

*Zoroastrianism.

† The Greco-Jewish synthetic faith which developed among the Jews of Egypt.

union with Arab civilization. It was in this manner that Judaism made its contribution to the cultural movement and communicated to medieval Christianity the intellectual heritage of antiquity which it had rescued from oblivion in the Arab era. Hence the hope is quite justified that the time may not be distant when Judaism will once more impregnate and so transform the world of ideas, and at the same time independently assimilate the variety of outside cultural elements to which it is exposed.

Through this highly effective activity on the part of Judaism, both in giving and in receiving, the content as well as the scope of its "science" has developed into a mighty system. . . . All of the individual parts thereof constitute member organisms of one great whole. None of these may be ignored; by the same token, no one such element may be emphasized at the expense of the others. The sole task of the specialists, therefore, is to analyze the individual facets and then to relate them to the whole.

Even as any vital and viable idea falls into a threefold organic division of its own, so this entire wealth of material, too, may be separated into three major categories.

The idea became manifest in the physical world with all the vigor and freshness of youthful strength; however, it remained confined within the framework of the time and the space within which it was born. In naive elation at its victory, it overlooked the limitations inherent in it and, as it soared upward, it bore with it upon its wings the dust of the earthly conditions under which it had first come into being. . . . Its eyes were trained upon the utopian heights from which it felt called upon to envelop all things below, and yet it found itself compelled to go on existing within the narrow bounds of limited lowlands. It had the ability creatively to reflect a perfect image, and yet it remained so deeply rooted in its native soil that it could not detach itself from it.

Thus Judaism became firmly consolidated. Next, it sought to penetrate all outside conditions, to transform them. But, instead, it was itself modified and influenced by the very conditions which it had sought to affect. The further it reached out, the more one-sided it became; it squandered its strength and lost its intensity. The spiritual wealth which it gained was not always genuine, and the idea which inspired it grew superficial and was eventually spent, dissipated.

And then it attained the third phase. At this point it pulled itself together and reverted to its former intrinsic character; but with the difference that now it was changed by a wealth of experiences and acquisitions which it then purified and transfigured.

A HISTORY OF SPIRITUAL ACHIEVEMENTS

. . . Language is the articulation of the national idea; history is the idea in action. Language is more vital and more immediate than history; like a garment, it covers the whole spirit at one time. However, its first outpouring is connected with a definite stage of the people's development. Thereafter it will at best no longer be the expression of the spirit but only its handy tool; in most instances it declines and becomes petrified. History is different. History does not reflect the spirit completely and all at once; it is dependent also on many factors which lie outside the spirit of the nation to which it belongs. But it is precisely by means of struggle, by development, by conflict and by victory or defeat that the strength or the impotence of the spirit is revealed. Particularly in the case of Judaism, we find history revealing an inexhaustible wealth of possibilities for the unfolding and molding of spiritual and intellectual life.

It is self-evident that history, as an essential component of the Science of Judaism, can only be a study of the history of spiritual achievements. The outer facets of its history have value only as substrata, as conditions under which achievements could come into being and which either hindered or furthered the growth of such achievements. It should be remembered, however, that it is inherent in the very nature of the Jews that their history should primarily be a spiritual one and, as such, a process that helped shape the entire world, and that it should not be expressed either in civic policy or primarily in political or communal life. The Jews remain in a state of inner division which in turn gives rise to inner struggle and feats of spiritual heroism.

Such, in fact, is the fate of all highly gifted peoples. The empire of the ancient Greeks fell, after their short-lived world supremacy, their unity having been forged by the Macedonians, the most primitive tribe in their midst. As for the Italians, who are now in the process of being welded into one united nation by the crude

Piedmontese, they have yet to prove whether, as a united nation with a capital in Rome, they will be able to regain that historical significance which we must admit they had attained during the Middle Ages. It was not despite their own inner division, but, in fact, just because of it, that the Germans were able to give birth to the greatest discoveries, . . . to the free spirit of the Reformation and to the glory of a literature of worldwide import. It is our wish that the new united *Reich*, led by its imperial dynasty, may be able to record similar achievements. Such, too, has been the history of Judaism, and it is precisely to its independence from political status that Judaism owes its survival. Anything that enters into the life of a nation as a sudden thing, instead of as a tender sapling, gradually growing into a strong plant, is no longer history. Judaism, however, has sprouted into full bloom from the tenderest of seedlings; with this fact it demonstrates that it has a genuine history.

. . . As part of the Science of Judaism, a study of its history will, of course, remain subject to all those laws which history recognizes as science. Scientific, critical study must not be hindered by dogmatic assumptions. Judaism has no cause to fear an unbiased critical examination.

. . . The history of Judaism is wonderfully unique in that it spans a period extending from remote antiquity down to the immediate present. It is therefore not mere curiosity which acts as a spur to its study, not merely the desire to eavesdrop on the mystery of the origins of Judaism, but at least equally the desire to detect the extent to which all of its later development was essentially already inherent in the growth and flowering process of the original seeds. These beginnings are hidden, modestly and shamefacedly in dim obscurity; the scholar, however, cannot avoid this difficulty, but must remain dependent upon these prehistorical phenomena. Without the revelation which only such study of the ancient history of Judaism—even though the results may be mere approximations —affords, he can never succeed in gaining the proper insight into Judaism's subsequent history which lies more fully recorded before him.

The history of Judaism may be divided into four periods:

The first period is that of vigorous creation, unfettered and unhindered, of *Revelation*. It was an era of free, creative formation from within. This period extends to the close of the biblical era, which cannot be said to have ended at the time of Exile, for its outgrowths continued well beyond that date.

The second period is the era during which all this biblical material was processed, shaped, and molded for life; it was then that Judaism took root in the spiritual heritage of the past and at the same time still maintained a certain degree of freedom in its approach to that heritage. This was the period of *Tradition,* which extended from the time of the completion of the Bible to the completion of the Babylonian Talmud.

The third period is characterized by toilsome preoccupation with the heritage as it then stood. The spiritual heritage was guarded and preserved, but no one felt authorized to reconstruct it or to develop it further. No one dared go beyond the limits set long before. This was the period of rigid *Legalism,* of casuistry, the era which was devoted to the summing up of what had been handed down by tradition. It extended from the time of the completion of the Babylonian Talmud down into the middle of the eighteenth century.

The fourth period, the era of liberation, has been marked by an effort to loosen the fetters of the previous era by means of the use of reason and historical research. However, the bond with the past has not been severed. What is being attempted is solely to revitalize Judaism and to cause the stream of history to flow forth once again. This is the era of *Critical Study,* our own modern era.

THE SOUL OF ISRAEL

Inasmuch as Israel is and should remain unique, it is a spiritual bond which unites Israel. It is a spiritual life all its own which embraces all its members, and which will remain unchanged even under the most diversified circumstances—through all the changes of rushing events which crowd one upon the other, in the most distant lands and in the midst of differing ideologies and varying convictions. But if you should ask me, "What is the content of this ideal that binds us together with so indissoluble a bond?" I will have to answer you that man has not been endowed with the ability to give an exhaustive portrayal of a spiritual life. . . . What is true of the knowledge of God applies here also. Who would presume to set forth what God is, to seek to confine His essence into one single exhaustive concept? All we can say is that He exists and that He is the original cause of all of life. He is the All-Wise One. But it is only the traces of His infinite wisdom that we behold in that masterpiece which is the world. He is the Almighty. His rule is evident everywhere. It is He who maintains the Universe and provides it with power to continue growing and developing. Thus you may see God even if you are not capable of grasping His essence.

. . . Of Israel's spiritual life, too, we can only say that it exists and that it manifests itself as a basic force. . . . An emanation of the Divine spirit, Israel was imbued with a creative spirit all its own and has been so to this very day. The other religious creeds are its daughters . . . and the best that is in them they owe to the spirit and tradition of Israel. Israel worked as a basic force in history. Israel exists; at first it was a small family, then it grew into a tribe, and thereafter it became a whole state. And when its spirit became separated from the political state, might one not have assumed that it would vanish and that its body would disintegrate into its original components? But this never came to pass. It was only then that Israel's soul truly blossomed and entered into all parts of the world; and now the strength of Israel has proved itself everywhere. Even as it did not cease to grow in days of oppression, so it will not disintegrate in freedom; it will not dissipate itself into atoms to join alien configurations. To the outside, of course, in civic affairs, it will join with other elements and merge into the national life that surrounds it; but it will always retain its own spirit: it will continue to exist.

Of course, Israel is not like a stone which endures through millennia, rigid and unchangeable, which then is smashed and broken apart when the elements sweep over it. . . . No, Israel is wise; its life is a life of knowledge. Its faith, likewise, is not fixed, bound or rigid—for that would not be wisdom and eternal spiritual life. No, Israel heeded the call: "Know the God of your fathers and serve Him." Listen and choose for yourself; test it and see for yourself. It was not the outward, rigid law that made Israel indestructible; it was the winged message of the prophets that rendered Judaism inviolable. The lightning flashes of the spirit did not emanate from Sinai only; they flared also from Israel's great men, the prophets. In a world of paganism and idol worship, their message became a life-giving spiritual sun.

In later times, too, Israel remained loyal to that spirit and to knowledge, never attempting to confine freedom. . . . To be sure, the sons of Israel were part of the times in which they lived and could not rise above the level of their contemporaries in knowledge and perception. . . . But even in the darkest days, there was an inner strife and stirring which preserved the real life of Israel in strength and vigor . . . and was it not in the darkest ages that the brightest luminaries shone forth from Israel, of all peoples? That which a great medieval thinker plainly put forward was felt by all, even unawares: faith is not an empty phrase, a formula or an assertion which you must accept unquestioningly. . . . No, faith is an idea which, rooted deep within your heart, must constitute the foundations of your spiritual being, the flower of spiritual life, the noble fruit of genuine conviction. . . . Israel never gave recognition to any belief that would not be consistent with understanding; it never worshiped as a sacred mystery that which was in contradiction with what could be comprehended by human reason.

"Faith and Reason are two beacons," each shedding its own light, but both ultimately meeting and fusing into one bright beam. This is the doctrine of Israel; this is its wisdom and this is the guarantee for its continued survival. In our days, much that blossomed in times gone by has faded away, and minds frequently are divided. But do not despair, my friends, for Israel's spiritual life remains unified. Scholarship may move along the most divergent paths; trends may split up into a host of shadings and partisan factions; yet, do not lose courage; only one spirit is now and shall ever be within Israel. . . . Spiritual life undergoes manifold changes in its outer manifestations, and the Divine spirit, too, reveals itself in many different forms. But it is precisely the varied nature of its manifestations that marks the existence of a genuine spiritual life in the midst of Israel.

Third and last, my dear friends, Israel is "mighty." Israel is endowed with a vitality that ensures its survival. By this I do not mean the kind of might that relies on the strength of the arm. . . . Israel's vitality has always consisted in the endeavor to fight for that which is divine. . . . It has given its all, and suffered without flinching or hesitation for its God and for its faith. . . .

ISAAC MARCUS JOST

INTRODUCTION TO ISAAC MARCUS JOST

ISAAC MARCUS JOST (1793–1860) *was the first major historian of the Jews in the modern period. Though he has been overshadowed by the greater men who followed him, and his works—untranslated from the German and not reprinted—are today little read, his groundbreaking achievement deserves full acknowledgment.*

He was born at Bernburg in central Germany and received the usual traditional Jewish education before going on to university studies in Göttingen and Berlin. Most of his life was spent teaching in modern Jewish schools, especially at the progressive Philanthropin in Frankfort. For a time he edited two Jewish journals, one in German, and later another in Hebrew. As an educator, he also published textbooks on both Jewish and general subjects.

Jost was a schoolmaster with a sober, practical view of the world. Though he lived in the period of German romanticism, his outlook was considerably closer to eighteenth-century Enlightenment rationalism. In 1818 he began to write his comprehensive History of the Israelites, which appeared from 1820 to 1829 and in nine volumes covered the period from the Maccabees to the year 1815. In 1846–47 he added three more volumes dealing with his own time, and during 1857–59 a History of Judaism and its Sects. He wrote in simple language, hoping that the unlettered Jew as well as the Christian statesman and scholar would be among his readers. His work is characterized by its apologetic character and its definite rationalist bias. But it also manifests a high degree of impartiality and erudition.

The selection given below is taken from the Introduction to the least known of Jost's historical works today, a two-volume condensation of his larger Jewish history called General History of the Israelite People (1832). It is here that Jost most fully expresses his idea of Jewish history. Here, too, he deals specifically with the problems of biblical historiography since this shorter work, unlike the earlier nine volumes, includes the biblical period.

Jost's introductory essay raises questions and poses themes which recur among Jewish historians thereafter with great frequency. He declares that the Jewish people is historically unique because it was able to outlive other nations in whose cultures it participated while maintaining its cohesion as a separate and distinctive entity. Though Jost regards this survival as an indication of Divine Providence, he does not allow the attribution to interfere with his methodological reflections on Jewish historiography. He shows his awareness of the problems that must be solved if Jewish existence in the Diaspora is to be properly understood. He realizes that it possesses a special character: Jewish history does not present the panorama of political and military activity which is common to other histories. "Can there be a history of a slave?" he asks, and then proceeds to discuss the peculiar difficulties which beset an historian of the Jews. He sees, too, that it is hard for the scholar to free himself of religious bias, to gain the necessary tools of research, and finally to arrive at a convincing synthesis. Above all, he distinguishes sharply between theology and history, pointing out the differing goals and methods of the two disciplines and declaring "solely and resolutely" for history.

THE RIGORS OF JEWISH HISTORIOGRAPHY

We view the Israelite people as historically unique. It grew from a family into a people, achieved statehood, succumbed to the change in its lot like all states, and its mighty structure finally collapsed; but it arose again from its ruins with renewed strength. It was not reduced to being a component of other peoples; although no longer playing a role in world events, it remained a vibrant image of times gone by. It saw states established, blossom, and wither; it saw national constitutions change, heard nations called by new names; it accompanied peoples on their migrations from one part of the world to another and exchanged language and mode of thought with them. It was dragged hither and yon, terrorized, its fragments scattered in all directions, and yet, though dispersed everywhere, it always coalesced in times of tranquillity, striving toward a primordial form which constitutes its inner essence. Ever feeling ill at ease, ever dissatisfied with a bleak present, it finds comfort in recollection and strength in hope. Thus it outlives world history. What monument devised by human skill compares with this one? Does any more intensely arouse our astonishment? Where could we find a more powerful stimulus to reflection on the higher guidance of human affairs than here, where the frail endeavors of human effort visibly miscarry and yield to an inner, spiritual force?

What a beautiful and instructive task it is for every thinker to seek out and penetrate the reason for this wondrous unity, this endless perseverence, this confidence in battle against superior forces, this defiance of the almighty power of fate! Nonetheless, we may claim with certainty that this task, however often set, has yet to be accomplished, and that it can never be accomplished except through closer familiarity with Israelite history. But this history remains shrouded in a dense fog. The few points of light that glimmer forth afford no image of this field of knowledge, and indeed tend to lead astray. Although the importance of attaining a multifaceted view of this object has been abundantly felt and recognized, we had to be content until now with the description of individual prominent points which were regarded as the distinguishing mark of the whole. We did not descend into the depths of this realm to examine the coherence of the core, the powers which bind it from within, and to assay the external influences which operated to congeal or to dissolve. As a result, we collected so many superficial, distorted, groundless judgments for and against the Israelites themselves and so many useless, inappropriate measures for their treatment on the part of the states.

The task is indeed difficult, and the great obstacles which confront its accomplishment must temper our criticism of the one-sidedness of several otherwise thorough scholars. Indeed, they should make us grateful even for biased accounts of our subject, since from various unilateral views we may hope at length to achieve a multifaceted inquiry and certain knowledge.

But what are these obstacles? What is it that here more than in other scientific fields impedes the diligent scholar's research? First of all, there is the customary way of viewing the subject, namely with prejudice. In the entire civilized world, whenever the sources of religion are taught, the nature of the Israelites is necessarily discussed. Firmly held conceptions are interwoven with those of religion and thus rendered so unshakable that only a revolution in religious ideas could bring about a change. Whoever belongs to a denomination of the three major religions possesses these conceptions, adjusted to the principles of his particular group. If then, as a scholar, he proceeds to a closer examination of them, the warm ardor he feels for his denomination presses him to confirm the religious instruction he has received rather than to seek its opposite; the latter he rejects in advance as invalid. A freer thinker may indeed gain the insight that Israelite history, however much it is in general connected with the history of the Church, is deserving of treatment independent of religious dogmas and in fact demands scientific study, but he will not easily be able to gain acceptance for the results of his research. Every educated man, and even more every religious one, will find them contradictory to ideas authoritatively implanted in early youth, and hence he will reject them as irreligious. The historiography of no people is so beset with the pretentious and condemnatory views of dilettantes as is that of the Israelites, which everyone fancies to know from the relevant sources. Thus, no matter how carefully even sober thinkers attempt gently to drive prejudice away, to cleanse imbibed conceptions, to classify and define often uncertain notions more precisely—striving to unchain the captives arouses the multitude to severe grumbling and often even violent opposition.

This is what frightens so many scholars, who would like to shed some light, from casting their beams into such an obscure domain. Instead of cultivating this thankless soil, the learned man finds sufficient fertile acreage in lovelier regions of science where the earth more generously rewards his labors, where with less effort he may hope for agreeable prospects, configurations, and sweeter fruits which will attract the spirit and mind of the multitude. For this reason the history of the Israelites—insofar as it does not appear as a necessary supplement to the history of religion—for the most part lies fallow. It is simply brushed off as inherently arid or else not worthy of development. Rarely is a critical spirit drawn to it, and even then mostly for secondary reasons. For some it serves as a guide while wandering among the sources of religion. For others it must supply from its arsenals weapons to defend Judaism against Christianity and Islam, to defend the latter two against the former, or each of these against the other. Individual sects even use Israelite history in putting forward their claims against all other sects. Thus, just as the Israelite people is scattered, subjugated to all, and freely esteemed by few, so too its history has been reduced to bondage. It seldom finds a friend or loving care.

But can there be a history of a slave? Asking the question reveals a mighty obstacle. It is commonly held that where independent activity has ceased, there too history has ceased. It is thought that history directs its attention to the development of forces, to a description of the origins, emergence, creativity, and circumstances of a people, its entanglements with other powers, its wars and clashes up to the point of its collapse. The older historical sources of the history of the Israelite people do indeed constitute rich mines of choice experiences of this kind; the mind's eye may here enjoy a highly manifold development of forces, and we may draw from these sources serious and boundless instruction. But as these same sources dry up, we must forego any further hope of new enjoyment. What pleasing pictures, one asks, can the lot of the slave still offer us? What henceforth makes up the variety in his life, aside from the exchange of masters?

In view of these considerations, everyone turns away his contemptuous or pitying glance. Only rarely does a friend of humanity linger to detect even among the humbled a certain power of spirit, to ponder carefully that power's opposition to the all-powerful force of external circumstances, and to recognize that it indicates more than a fossilized existence. But oh, how easily freedom of judgment is here led astray! The investigator is overcome with warm sympathy, which he is scarcely able to suppress before it comes to determine his historical judgment. It influences him more strongly in evaluating a subjugated people than in dealing with an individual slave. If this sympathy takes the form of attachment, the observer pours out his saddened heart in laments over the cruelty, injustice, and implacability of fate—over the lack of understanding, the malice, spite, and arrogance of those in power, who, misusing their chance predominance, shamefully trample upon mankind. If, on the other hand, he feels lively admiration for physical energy and contempt for human weaknesses, then he will regard the sufferings of the oppressed simply as deserved punishment for their misdeeds, the consequences of abnormality and of the calamitous renunciation of independence. He will see in endurance only the degeneration of noble sentiments, in perseverence only an obstinacy and rigidity not worthy of charitable treatment. . . .

But for the honest and impartial friend of scientific study there are other difficulties which arise. Those presented by the peculiarities of the Hebrew religious texts are universally known. Neither translations nor exegeses suffice to make the spirit feel at home in antiquity. They may do for a church's determination of religious views and doctrines, but the historian must go back to their foundation. He must grasp with certainty the collective spirit of the language and the mode of representation used by the individual writers of an ancient people. He must compare their statements with each other and with additional information that concerns or touches upon the same matter. Via the strictest examination of their truthfulness and degree of reliability, independent of any denominational considerations whatever, he must open ways for the investigation of historical data. His goal is to achieve the lofty position from which he will be able to draw them together into general, comprehensive views and into composite portraits. He must even dismiss existing studies which mainly arrange the material or order it systematically for religious purposes; he must cleanse those same materials of all mortar in order to reexamine their value and to use them properly for the structure of history. In the process he will often enough come across new pieces which have remained unused and others which have been totally misconstrued or even deformed by those who worked on them. It will be his duty to call attention to them or to restore them. And yet, considering the scantiness of the historical material, one must expect in advance to find gaps and, nearly from the start, to be limited to the recognition of isolated complete segments; there is little hope of ascertaining a continuous national history which everywhere hangs together. The task of grasping everything clearly, ordering the configurations into an appropriate general impression, if possible presented so that it is recognizable in its individual parts and faithfully portrays its subject, is so difficult that it still requires many trial endeavors before it can be achieved to complete satisfaction.

As soon as we lay aside the Hebrew Scriptures, Israelite history assumes a totally different character. With the collapse of the ancient state, chaos sets in. The last sources vanish and a differently shaped world disentangles itself from the chaos. After a brief flash of the old spirit, darkness descends, and with the dawn of a new day we see fragile structures built on top of and among the ruins of an earlier people. They are poor replicas of earlier times, inhabited by the shadows of departed spirits who feast upon the insipid sources of a lax quest after fables and an ominous affected piety, until finally they are supplanted by the artificial constructions and abnormal figures of semieducated sons of Greece. If we had only the so-called Apocrypha and the two more important half-Greeks, Philo and Josephus, if we could not avail ourselves of other, better products of the spirit and of more certain guidance by a stronger hand, then we would likely have to despair of the history of the Second Temple and the period thereafter. But upon closer view, all these lifeless phenomena disappear and we see the older *Volksgeist,** whose existence is joined to the Deity, undergo a profound and significant development. We see it hold sway among the ruins, often bringing them to new life and arousing energy. We see it tarry here for yet a while as it begins to wind its arms around the entire globe. Thus, as soon as the deficient vitality of the expiring body is exhausted, it may emerge with new glory; it may inspire, instead of one single people, a world of peoples that is more or less prepared to accept it. It banishes from real life the dreams of an earlier time and awakens the whole world to a lively battle for truth and for the vocation of man, until at last, after long misunderstandings and severe disputes, a great reconciliation of mankind comes to prevail.

The Israelite people does not fail to recognize the great change

*Spirit of the people.

which the God of Israel had determined shortly before the people's collapse. It is deeply affected by the change and clings ardently to its God, striving in vain to restrict Him. But it has been decided otherwise in the counsel of the Almighty. Knowledge and veneration of Him shall no longer be limited to a land, to a people. The hitherto favored nation collapses, its glory departs, its pride has vanished. Yet with an unending love it clings to its God; scattered and dispersed, it follows Him into all lands with greater faithfulness than before. It feels itself overwhelmed, but it does not acknowledge itself as vanquished. Its true fatherland—its God and its religion —has not been lost; it has become even more precious with the loss of worldly joys. Here the defeated people feels strengthened anew to enter the lists with all nations in the battle for truth. In the common struggle to attain that final reconciliation, the Israelites, regardless of all the misery which became their lot on that account, remain master of the field through nearly two thousand years—and they have never laid down their weapons.

It is the task of the historian to describe this spiritual struggle, especially during the second half of Israelite history. But the task requires both great caution and deep insight which, insofar as possible, penetrates to details. The historian must grasp precisely, not merely the general positions of the parties, which change in different periods, but also the positions held simultaneously but affected by locality and other circumstances. Otherwise he cannot understand, evaluate, or judge fairly the choice of weapons, the type of battle, and the opposing attacks. This understanding requires long preparation, highly comprehensive studies, and uncommon candor. The historical sources are scattered far and wide; in part they are already quite obscure; and often they deliver only fragments, isolated kernels. Many of them are inherently dull and vapid, worthy of attention more as evidence of their time and place than by virtue of their content. The gathering of testimony, which justice demands, wears upon one's patience because of the endless contradictions and absurdities, the expressions and references whose meaning can often only be surmised. One is confronted by an immense number of deeds, speeches, laws, disputes, opinions, stories, poems, legends, and other phenomena affecting the lot of the Israelites. This is to say nothing of the many different places, times, and thinkers. One must consider as well human inclinations, cultural variations, historical setting, and in general the prevailing circumstances of entire nations, districts, and individuals, to say nothing of natural predispositions, emotions, and intellectual movements. All this is necessary to arrive at a certain historical understanding and to derive fruitful results and just evaluations.

Historiography, at least in regard to the object of our concern, has not yet developed to the point where it can regard the evidence as complete and can proceed to issue a verdict. It still remains the duty of the historian of the Israelites to gather and to order, but to forego any general and reliable judgment. Even if in his opinion he is sufficiently familiar with individual segments of history to trust himself with an evaluation of the proceedings, this awareness must not delude him into arrogant condemnation. Rather, his judgment becomes totally impartial only when he subjects his view to the examination of similarly impartial experts. This consideration is our guiding principle. Although we cannot avoid at times giving our judgment and at other times endeavoring via the narrative itself to engender or to substantiate an opinion, we are nevertheless guided throughout by the view that every effort of contemporary historiography can serve only as preparation and pathfinding for future, more solid, accomplishments. . . .

We take our stand solely and resolutely within the bounds of history. Those of theology remain foreign to us. It lies outside our task to consider how ecclesiastical faith or religious conviction, or even merely church institutions, should make use of the events of world history—and especially of Israelite history—in order to grant validity to each church's specific doctrine regarding the influence of divine providence on mankind and to confirm the ecclesiastical dogmas associated with it; in order, further, to bestow upon the individual harmony and peace of mind; and in order to endow ecclesiastical statutes with a basis in history. Every ecclesiastical society follows its own laws and traditions in these matters and establishes in its own way the inner consistency of its accepted system. Theology solves questions which history does not pose or must leave unanswered. If it derives data from history, it seeks not merely to disclose in them the causes and effects suggested by historical research, but rather the revelations of divine judgment and divine providence.

History, on the other hand, limits itself to representing what has occurred in accordance with the causes which disclose themselves to the observant eye and with the consequences that develop from them according to the laws of nature. Where it lacks the means to construct a great and conclusive chain of events, it may employ conjectures to fill in the missing links, but it must justify and support them. If, however, this proves impossible and theology therefore finds occasion to take over such facts—or miracles—which history has left aside as enigmatic and to connect them with the higher world order which is revealed to it, then we shall leave this lack of agreement inviolate on account of its beneficial influence: we are not in a position adequately to solve all the enigmas of antiquity.

From this vantage point, the freest which we believe we may choose, we cast a glance over the older historical sources. Since theology understands these sources differently, we would indicate in advance all the more specifically our own manner of utilizing them. We consider the entire collection of Hebrew sacred literature a source of history although it was not all intended to be historical and even the actual historical books do not proceed from an historical point of view. Indeed, we are relatively more justified in drawing our subject matter from this literature to the degree that the historical material is only, as it were, included by chance, but does not constitute a book's sole contents. For such sources which contain only the account of events are much sooner subject to doubt than those in which historical data appear as known and acknowledged, and are unconsciously repeated and supplemented. In the former instance, we must examine the author, his level of culture, and his intent with utmost care before we trust him. In the latter, we need only apply inner criticism in order not to misunderstand the individual datum torn from its context; the fact itself lives before our eyes and weaves itself into the life of the people, appears in all manner of forms, inspires poetry, and proves to be indisputable truth. In this sense, the Holy Scriptures of the Hebrews become wholly excellent sources of histroy. They constitute a collection of popular accounts, thoughts, laws, speeches, poems, seldom separated into genres but rather meshed and interwoven, nearly always producing a clear portrait of the totality. In every book, in every paragraph—one is tempted to say in every expression—one sees the entire spirit of the people with its traditions and its relationships, a complete world of its own which manifests itself in every special form and whose specifics can be understood only by seeing the whole. The more this world appears locked in upon itself, the more closely is everything within it tied together; even what it received from the outside was forced to adapt itself to its forms and to fuse with it. This inner unity is its truth for the historian.

The question as to what can be determined historically with regard to the higher origins of these writings is out of place here, since no conclusion can substantiate a supernatural revelation. The latter remains a positive dogma of religion, one of its starting points which is presupposed without question and does not require proof. Attempts to prove it have come to grief, and they cannot succeed. In fact they have so greatly strengthened unbelief that some writers have undertaken to topple the dogma by questioning individual manifestations and misinterpreting the simplest statement. By using external criteria they have been able to find, instead of higher, directly divine origins, not only falsehood, but even fraud, purposeful deception, priestly manipulation of the people, farcical superstition, and jejune examples of the most obtuse ignorance. All this and then some has been claimed outright by Voltaire,* by the author of the "Fragments" (Reimarus),† and more recently by Gramberg,‡ Leo,§ and others; a larger number, who speak less offensively, seem to presume it. Such claims, however, result from careless juxtaposition of times and peoples, from comparing facts which can never shed light on one another. In similar fashion it would be justified to condemn more or less all the creative works of antiquity, a judgment into which some scholars have indeed already been misled.

But religious belief, as all previous attempts attest, does cast the historian in chains, and thus there must be some arrangement from the start to free him from either relating facts which he cannot justify because he all too obediently follows the text, or breaking with faith. An accommodation is achieved through sound criticism, which faith must allow the scholar. It is the critical method which must guide the historian through the realm of history, and although he continually follows particular authorities, it must nevertheless stand by his side, advising, warning, and showing him the way. True faith, which is located in the mind, is not threatened by the transformed appearances of externals; it cannot be true if it shrinks

---

*Voltaire (1694–1778), the great French Enlightenment philosopher, wrote most disaparagingly and facetiously of biblical history.

†Hermann Samuel Reimarus (1694–1768) was among the most radical of the Protestant theologians of the German Enlightenment. In his posthumously published "Fragments" he denied biblical revelation and miracles.

‡K. P. W. Gramberg in 1823 published a critical history of the religious ideas in the Old Testament.

§Heinrich Leo's lectures on the history of the ancient Jewish state were published in 1828, four years before the appearance of Jost's essay.

from criticism of historical data. Criticism no more does harm to religion than a closer examination of the laws of nature and their variability threatens to shatter belief in the Creator. Moreover, religion has long, and often without admitting it, been a friend of criticism; for without its support every church must effect the dissemination of the most dangerous errors under the guise of revelation. Therefore, it itself leans upon the judgment of experts and deep thinkers as protection against whatever attacks may be launched against it. Aside from this, criticism also asserts itself insofar as religious works are no longer extant in quite their original form, insofar as even early copies are not available, and insofar as our careful examination is required to deal with variant readings and with the apparent contradictions and obscurities they produce. The results of this criticism must prepare the way for the historian and light his path.

NAHMAN KROCHMAL

INTRODUCTION TO NAHMAN KROCHMAL

AS THE CHALLENGE of Aristotelian philosophy had prompted Maimonides to write his Guide of the Perplexed in the twelfth century, so the challenge of a philosophically grounded conception of history, which consigned Israel to a past stage of spiritual development and denied it a future, prompted Nahman Krochmal (1785–1840) to address the perplexed Jews of his time. What he gave them was a philosophy of Jewish history which, far from affirming Israel's destined oblivion, anchored it in eternity even as it moved forward through historical time. His ideas, embodied in a Guide of the Perplexed of the Time (published unfinished in 1851, a decade after his death), exercised considerable influence upon Jewish thinkers in the nineteenth century and continues to be the topic of much discussion today in the State of Israel.

Krochmal lived his entire life in the Austro-Hungarian province of Galicia, where he was born into a pious, but not fanatical merchant family. Gradually, without a sudden break, he moved out of the closed spiritual world of most of his fellow Jews into a study of secular disciplines. He was particularly attracted to philosophy and soon became an adherent of post-Kantian Absolute Idealism. From this philosophical movement he accepted a conception of God as the Absolute Spirit whose nature is gradually revealed to human consciousness. *Krochmal identifies the Absolute Spirit with the God of Israel and tries to show that the insights of modern philosophy simply present a different, perhaps profounder understanding of teachings already contained in the Jewish tradition. But that tradition must be conceived of in terms of its historical development if it is to be harmonized with modern modes of thought.*

This is the point to which Krochmal devotes his Introduction (the first selection below). He argues that it is useless, in a generation which is learning to think historically, to assert the traditional view that David wrote the entire book of Psalms. Unless Judaism is presented as a developing entity, it will be summarily rejected by the growing number of young people who find a seemingly unbridgeable gulf between the authoritative assertions of tradition and the secular thought to which they are increasingly exposed.

The heart of Krochmal's conception of Jewish history is given in the other four selections, excerpted from the body of his work. Here we find his view of the difference between the history of the nations and that of Israel. All societies undergo successive periods of growth, blossoming, and decay. But while the nations of the world are doomed to extinction at the conclusion of the cycle, Israel's manifestation of the Absolute Spirit enables it to begin anew, fresh growth following the last stage of decay. Israel alone among nations is immortal.

Krochmal outlines three cycles which Israel traversed down to the middle of the seventeenth century. The first begins with Abraham, reaches its apogee with David and Solomon, and concludes with the destruction of the First Temple. The second runs from the Babylonian Exile to the failure of the final resistance to the Romans with the fall of Betar in 135 C.E. The final cycle, whose high point is connected with the period of Islamic efflorescence, concludes with the Chmielnicki massacres of 1648–49 in Poland. Krochmal was able to illustrate the historical developments of the first two cycles in some detail, but managed to indicate only the framework of the third. The excerpts given here have been chosen to present Krochmal's basic approach and the turning points in his cyclical conception. It is especially worth noting how he manages to interweave his radically untraditional approach to Jewish history with statements taken from the Bible and rabbinic literature, making it appear that his own views are prefigured in the tradition itself.

ONLY AN HISTORICAL APPROACH CAN PRESERVE JUDAISM

Know, my friend and reader, that the Lord, praised be His name, determines the generations in advance: each generation with its scholars, each generation with its sages. In His goodness He alters and changes the modes of investigation, of study, and of moral instruction to Israel. If at one time a method was known to be good, correct, and free of problems, it is quite possible that this method would by nature be inadequate to teach the members of another generation, distant from the first both in time and in character. Such is the case with the matter before us. Although the ancients considered it proper to ascribe an early date to the Writings* in order to teach the principle of prophecy and the prediction of a distant event, already at the time of the literal expositors among Spanish Jewry beginning with the days of R. Samuel ha-Nagid,† and even much more in our own times, the situation is the opposite; that is to say, we must inquire, investigate, and ascribe every matter to the proper time of its composition. For example, our Sages, when interpreting to their generation of Israel, saw fit to ascribe the entire book of Psalms to David and to his time, including even the psalm "By the Rivers of Babylon" (Ps. 137); they maintained that by virtue of the Holy Spirit David foresaw the Babylonian Exile and bewailed it. However, both for the Sephardic interpreters,‡ and even more so in our own time, such a view will not convince enlightened readers and listeners, nor the young people. That which had an effect on the earlier generation will not arouse hope, trust, and faith in this generation of [secular] learning. We, our teachers, and our interpreters, will achieve this desired end with greater success if we explain the psalm to them in this way: it was sung by a son of Levi, of the Levites who were singers in the Temple and were forced by the Babylonians to go into exile from their beloved land and Temple, into the desolate plains by the River Chebar. As they went, they

* The last part of the Hebrew Bible, beginning with the book of Psalms.

† Samuel ha-Nagid (993–1055) of Granada, in Spain, was not only a statesman and poet, but also a critical scholar and patron of Jewish learning.

‡ Those of Spanish origin, such as Abraham ibn Ezra.

carried the harps, which they loved more than anything else, upon their shoulders. And as they tired upon the way, they hung the harps not upon the cedars or pleasant trees which were in their land, but rather upon the stooped-over willows of Babylon. When the leaders of the Exile ask to hear something of the sacred music, one of them starts to sing, his heart burning and his spirit filled with sorrow over what has been lost, and he vows not to forget it in the distant land, desiring and hoping for vengeance against the evil ones who still have not left his fatherland. In this way all the words of the psalm concerning all the contemporary events which the exiles saw with their own eyes, become a flashing fire, a flame of the Lord, and a sure testimony to the magnitude and depth of their infinite love for their land, their people, and their God. All of this will have a sacred and beneficial effect even upon the hearts of this latter-day generation. It will engender within it every excellence, virtue, wisdom, and sense of justice, in accordance with the need of the present time. But this will not be accomplished at all by pushing the psalm back to the time of David, when the people and the state were beginning to reach their height of power, and when, if they heard of Babylon at all, it was only the faintest rumor. Especially the youth, who have already read abbreviated versions of world history, of which many are in their possession, will not only lose the beneficial effect which is to be gained by reading and studying this psalm, but their souls will have contempt for the way we explain and interpret it.

"R. Huna said in the name of R. Aha: Let not the words of the Torah be in your eyes like a man who has a grown daughter and wants to marry her off; rather, 'My son, if thou will receive my words and my commandments, lay them up with thee . . .'" (Prov. 2:1).* This passage means that the enlightened man who gives advice and moral instruction should not hasten to express what he has but recently learned, to teach today what he himself learned only yesterday, as we find among those who study for ulterior purposes and proclaim abroad their knowledge which has not had a chance to ripen sufficiently even within themselves. The above passage fittingly compares such an enlightened man to a person who wants to give his aging daughter to whomever comes along. This manner of study is likewise nicely hinted at in the Scriptural passages: "It is a tree of life *to them that hold fast to it*" (ibid., 3:18), and "If thou wilt

---

*Midrash *Leviticus Rabba* 25:1.

receive my words and my commandments, *lay them up with thee*" (ibid., 2:1). Even more aptly has the Scriptural passage, "ye shall have planted all manner of trees for food" (Lev. 19:23), been interpreted to refer to the study of Torah, and counsel has been derived from the continuation: "Three years shall it be as forbidden unto you . . . and in the fourth year . . . it shall be holy."*

Both extremes† lack the proper faith for this, our generation. What is common to both is that their conception of revealed religion is what they have been accustomed to thinking since their childhood. The difference between them lies only in this: the one group rejoices in finding occasion to cast doubt and suspicion upon that faith, while the other makes every effort to strengthen and support it with various imaginary and fanciful devices—means which cannot ever serve as a firm foundation in an enlightened generation. Thus they toil uselessly, serving no purpose.

THE NATIONS AND THEIR GODS

> For let all the peoples walk each one
> in the name of its god,
> But we will walk in the name of the
> Lord our God for ever and ever.
>
> Micah 4:5

We see that it was the plan of Divine Providence not to scatter the human race as completely separated individuals like the rest of the animal world, for whom solitary existence is the norm and association merely incidental, but rather to combine it into small and large groups beginning with the family, then the clan, the city, the district, and finally the largest grouping which is that of a complete and ordered national community, known as a people and a nation. This accords with the scriptural verse: "When the Most High gave to the nations their inheritance, when He separated the children of men . . ." (Deut. 32:8). The laws of Providence further

*The tradition must be fully absorbed before its sancity can be properly realized.

†Those who reject the tradition summarily and those who accept it uncritically.

determined that within these groupings there should gradually emerge beneficial and effective institutions operating to integrate each group. For example, occupations and trades necessary for existence will be divided among the members of the group according to individual inclination and experience. Thus the group reaches a greater or lesser degree of coherence. Legal norms then emerge, first instinctually within individuals or subgroups, but in the course of time evolving into a few legal statutes based on general principles. Gradually tendrils of love, tender feeling, and mercy, as well as honor, humility, modesty, and all the other virtues which are beyond the strict requirements of the law, begin to sprout, initially in the family, then in the community, and finally in the nation. Thereafter, manual skills rise from the level of necessity to those of usefulness and adornment: artists, flourishing, create various things of beauty, sing songs which stir the soul, play musical instruments, and in similar ways bring about aesthetic development. In addition, already at the beginning of this long period and during the course of it, sparks of religious fire, implanted deep in the soul of man—knowledge of God and cultic practices—start to flicker in the midst of the people.

After a time, the nation gains repose from the severe labor and trials that characterize the period of its establishment and territorial settlement. Thereupon more general principles are formulated; the language becomes richer in words and expressions, acquiring an aesthetic dimension; history is recorded; schools are established for young and old; mathematics and sciences appear; the political organization and legal system are carefully formulated; morality rises to the level of systematic thought and purity of intention. Finally, in this same gradual fashion the knowledge of God and the cult that is always associated with it, which existed within the nation from the beginning of its development, are refined and purified from their gross materiality and confused sensuality.

Note that all the arts, laws, virtues, language concepts, books of wisdom, and concepts of God, which we have said are diffused within each nation at various stages of development, are all spiritual attributes and characteristics which become the possession of the entire nation. They were at first potentialities in the souls of single individuals which emerged over a long period of time and within the context of a large and well-integrated society, joined together, generation after generation, by ties of mutual cooperation. These valuable attributes in some instances emerge after a long period within the nation as a whole; in others they are produced by a single tribe which for one reason or another reaches a superior level; and in still others they are produced by groups or individuals who enter the nation from another land and instruct it. Such individuals become "princes of God," sacred leaders like Abraham, our father, peace be upon him, and Melchizedek.*

And note further that all these attributes and characteristics, which together constitute the sacred spiritual treasure of every nation, differ *quantitatively*. That is to say, one branch of culture may be more highly developed than another. But since they all have a single root (namely the spirituality of the nation which develops from potentiality to actuality in the manner we have outlined above), all these branches will be *qualitatively* equal and uniform. For example, to the extent that the aesthetic concepts of beauty and splendor which spread within the nation are either sensual, or rational, or mixed, in the same manner will its basic legal and moral concepts vary as well. So, too, in congruency with all the above, the nature of its scientific knowledge and its religious conceptions will be defined uniquely and in a fashion different from every other nation.

In the Scriptures these attributes are termed spirit: spirit of grace and splendor, spirit of law and justice, spirit of courage and power, spirit of the good, spirit of wisdom and understanding, spirit of the fear of the Lord. In each instance, the quality is described as being Divine in order to indicate explicitly its spirituality. (We shall, for the most part, use the word "God" as an adjective, not a noun, as one today says "Divine" to refer to spirit in its essence. Note this.) With regard to these qualities the Scriptures say: Such and such a man was filled with the spirit of God, or God put His spirit upon him, or the spirit rested upon him, or cloaked him. Similarly, among latter-day thinkers the whole spiritual treasure, qualitatively unique and differing from people to people, is called the *Volksgeist* of the totality. The spirit of a nation develops very much like that of an individual. It reveals to the observer the unique mode of self-development which sets it apart from every other integrated and organized nation. This is true of its fine arts, mode of government, laws, education, and the like, and true, as well, of its worship and knowledge of God. In sum, with regard to all its actions in

---

*The king of Salem whom the Bible calls "priest of God the Most High" (Gen. 14: 18–20).

peacetime and in war and with regard to its historical development, each nation is clearly differentiable from the others. And yet it is difficult and uncommon for even an intelligent person to understand the interrelationship among the different branches of a single culture and how they share a common root.

But just as the spirit of a nation, in the way we have described, develops and reaches an apogee at the dawn of its existence and during the following important periods, so it is reduced and declines when the shadows of evening start to fall, until at length it hurtles downward, losing its favorable attributes one by one; humbled, it falls from its glory until finally it ceases to exist entirely. The reason for this is that as luxuries multiply so does the love of pleasure; productive creativity becomes subservient to the satisfaction of the senses; the spirit of grace and beauty which we mentioned becomes degenerate. As property and acquisitiveness increase, so do the pride and arrogance which some express toward others. Quarrels, violence, and pillage break out in the land, the legal system becomes corrupt, compassion and respect for the elderly disappear, as do all other moral virtues. In short, the above-mentioned spirits of justice and of goodness are destroyed. As emotional ties are rent apart so is the culture, which becomes subject to various foreign influences; characteristics alien to the nation and to its spirit of goodness during happier times flourish and spread among the people in these evil days. As satiety comes to compete with lust, as unnatural no less than natural passions come to prevail, hearts are weakened and courage evaporates. There is a fear of enemies near and far and an anxiety about the future. Individuals and the collectivity seek divination at the hand of soothsayers and seers; they foolishly accept every superstition and aberration. In sum, the spirit of intellect as well as the spirit of bravery and courage become startlingly corrupted. In one of his epistles,* Maimonides has written as follows: "It was because our fathers sinned (and they are no longer) that our kingdom perished and that our exile extends even to this day. They picked up numerous books dealing with divination and astrology (which matters constitute the essence of idolatry, as we have explained), and they erred by paying heed to them. They deemed them splendid arts and of great value. They ceased to engage in learning war and in conquering other lands. Instead, they

*To the Jewish community of Marseilles.

relied upon these arts. Therefore, the prophets called them foolish and senseless, which indeed they were."

As a result of all these corruptions, and with increasing force, the knowledge and worship of God become dim and confused, giving way to superstitious belief in evil spirits, demons, and gods who are not God. The plague spreads to all the realms we have listed: it begins with the nation's leaders, its judges, statesmen, and priesthood, until finally the rot and decay come upon everyone. All the basic principles and institutions, which were originally beneficial, become evil and pernicious. The prophets, with their righteous anger and fiery rebukes, painted these perversions before our eyes, as well as the retribution which, as a result, came upon our nation and some of the other nations associated with us by virtue of genealogy or location. In short: pleasure, pride, arrogance, and superstition—these are the four sore judgments which corrode the spirit of the nation until it perishes spiritually and physically, internally and externally, and it ceases any longer to be a nation.

From the above, we can now understand that although we considered the quality of spirituality to be created within a nation by means of the strong bond among its parts with regard to time and place, generation after generation, nonetheless it is only—and alone—that same manifestation of spirit which begets and sustains the bond all the days of the nation's existence. In truth, the essence of the nation as such is nothing other than the spiritual essence which it harbors (and every manifestation of spirit is self-caused, that is, its activity is its essence). Therefore, if we were to imagine the total absence of all the above-mentioned spiritual attributes in a particular collectivity, it would be unable to exist as a society of human beings—the bundle would instantly fall apart. But in fact this is impossible since man is created in the image of God, i.e., he is spiritual. Thus even among primitive desert folk some buds of spirituality have begun to sprout within family units and small aggregations; indeed, they make their composition possible.

Let us note further that although we have said that a nation does not perish completely until the spirit, which as we have explained comprises and sustains it, fails and disappears, nonetheless this will not contradict our basic postulate: that every spiritual manifestation possesses an enduring and unlimited mode of existence. This is so since its spirit will be extinguished only to the degree that it is bound in space and time, i.e., peculiar to a specific land or generation. In this respect the manifestation of spirit is likewise finite and no doubt perishes. But to the extent that it is spiritual in its essence, it will undoubtedly survive as legacy to another nation close to it in space or time. There is this difference: when a small nation ceases to exist, the spirituality it contained will not be recognizable to us, although in fact it does not disappear altogether. Only a great nation of manifold achievements will leave behind numerous traces of its spirituality which can be easily recognized for all generations. Thus its poetic and literary arts as well as its legal system become the inheritance of the entire human race and of its total fund of spirituality; thereby they continue to function for all time.

Having reached this theoretical standpoint, you can now understand how what we have called the composite spirit of each nation is what the Torah and the earlier prophets call in concrete language (which, as you know, is the language of our traditional religious concepts—not implying thereby, God forbid, any diminution of their excellence) the nation's god. The apocalyptists* and the aggadists,† who came later, called it: the nation's guardian angel. In other words, they took the total spirituality which pervades and dominates each nation and gave it material substance as a particular object with a name and attributes. They saw that just as the king of a nation binds it together and unifies it with regard to readily visible externals, so too the manifestation of the divine which it contains unifies and binds it together internally with regard to place and time, from generation to generation. Such would be the rational conception equivalent to the concrete notion just mentioned.

In accordance with our usual procedure, to elaborate matters only slightly and present brief hints to the man of wisdom and knowledge, let us take note of a few appropriate passages from the Scriptures and the Rabbis . . .: "And against all the gods of Egypt I will execute judgments" (Exod. 12:12); "I will punish Amon of No, and Pharaoh, and Egypt, with her gods" (Jer. 46:25); "And Chemosh shall go forth into captivity" (ibid., 48:7); "Malcam shall go into captivity" (ibid., 49:3); and this, too, is the deeper meaning of the saying of our sages: "The Holy One, Blessed be He, does not bring a nation to account until He first brings to account its gods." ‡

*The visionaries of the late biblical period, such as Daniel, as well as those not included in Scripture.

† The early rabbis who devoted themselves especially to nonlegal, moral, and religious exposition of Jewish teaching.

‡ Midrash *Deuteronomy Rabba* 1:9.

In each nation it is usually one of the spiritual attributes which we have mentioned that predominates, while the others are subordinated to it and determined by it. Thus also the god. or guardian angel, is chiefly characterized in terms of this spiritual quality. For example: the guardian angel of a nation which rules by the sword will be the spirit of physical might to which that nation will direct its worship. The same will be true for the spirit of art and industry, of beauty, justice, ingenuity, and science. For each of these individual attributes one of the nobler natural phenomena will usually be designated as its symbol. Most frequently the choice will fall upon one of the heavenly bodies close to the earth in accordance with its known or imagined properties. For example, the sun will be the actualizer of all hidden power; Saturn—intellect; Jupiter—spirit of justice; Mars—spirit of courage; Venus—spirit of beauty. The same nation may also represent each spiritual quality physically by means of paintings, sculptures, or other symbols: the image of a craftsman; the image of a hero capturing cities—Baal; a fertility image—Astarte;* the image of a person holding scales of justice, etc.

The Prophet has proclaimed: "Not like these is the portion of Jacob; for He is the shaper of all things, and Israel is the tribe of His inheritance; the Lord of hosts is His name" (Jer. 10:16). This means that God is the Absolute Spirit and there is none other beside Him. He alone is the source of all spiritual being and its totality. Individual manifestations of spirit, which are attached to the hosts of heaven and earth, are all finite and transient; they possess true reality and absolute existence only to the extent that they have their being in the Lord, Blessed be He, the Absolute Spirit, the Infinite One. This is the theoretical equivalent of the phrase "God of gods is the Lord" (Josh. 22:22)—all spiritual qualities are to be found truly and absolutely only in God. The same holds for the phrase "Lord God of hosts" (Ps. 80:5)—God is the true reality of all higher, complex beings, which encompass simpler phenomena; such beings, in particular, shed light on the manifestation of spirit and reveal its essence.

In the beginning, Divine Providence determined to choose our ancestors, the holy patriarchs, and to narrow the selection from their seed gradually to a single family—the twelve tribes of Jacob—which was made to grow into a complete nation with its own

*Baal and Astarte were gods worshiped by the Canaanites.

land and permanent boundaries; according to Scripture: "He set the borders of the peoples according to the number of the children of Israel" (Deut. 32:8). Then the Divine Wisdom determined to direct and perfect the nation so that it might become a Kingdom of Priests, i.e., teachers of the revealed absolute faith to the human race. It worked powerfully within the nation until, at length, the spiritual attributes, which were integrally related on account of their attachment to God and reliance upon Him for their truth, were manifest and took shape within it. That is to say, with every act of our nation and with every exalted and beneficent spirit that is revealed and manifest in our midst, we know in our hearts and we acknowledge with our mouths that God lives in our midst and that they come from His hand. In other words, they are rooted in Him and emanate from His spirit, for He is the totality of all spiritual manifestations. This is the mystical meaning, or in our terms the rational conception, of the words: "that I may dwell among them" (Exod. 25:8); "for I am with you" (Jer. 42:11); "and My spirit abideth among you" (Hag. 2:5). This is also the secret of the term "Divine Presence" and of the saying: "The Divine Presence rests in Israel." Thus, too, we may understand the meaning of the Rabbinic statement: "They were exiled to Babylon, exiled to Elam, and the Divine Presence was with them"; and the intent of the saying: "The Divine Presence does not rest on less than two thousand and two myriads of Israelites."* Note also the scriptural verses: ". . . the sun and the moon and the stars, even all the host of heaven, . . . the Lord thy God hath allotted unto all the peoples under the whole heaven. But you hath the Lord taken . . ." (Deut. 4:19–20). Finally, there is the verse: "And they went and served other gods, and worshiped them, gods that they knew not, and that He had not allotted unto them" (ibid., 29:25). So, too, the Rabbis said: "Israel is related to no constellation."† Therefore, we may definitely claim that it was only the sensual mode of representation of his generation which forced Daniel to posit the existence of a particular guardian angel for our nation as well. However, he called him by a name which does not point to any limited manifestation of spirit. He called him Michael [i.e., Who is like God?] (Dan. 10:21) to indicate

*The sayings are taken from Talmud *Shabbat* 22b; Talmud *Megillah* 29a; and Talmud *Yevamot* 64a.
†Talmud *Shabbat* 156a.

that there is no Absolute Spirit, infinite and truly existent in every respect, other than God alone; He is our portion and we are His.

To sum up the chapter: as the ancient nations became aware of the spirit which manifested itself within them during their formative period, its light came to prevail over them, its pleasantness captivated them, and their souls were inspired to awe, veneration, and worship. However, they confined themselves to the particularized spiritual manifestations and their hosts, the powers of heaven and earth. They achieved no clear comprehension of spirituality [as such]. Therefore, they did not realize that its truth and actuality are not contained in whatever is in essence particular, attached to a time and a place—for that aspect perishes completely—but rather in what is universal, possessing true reality in the Absolute Spirit. This Spirit is entirely a concept of pure reason and therefore cannot at all be grasped by the imagination or by common thought and understanding. On this account, except in the case of a chosen few, the truth was hidden to the multitude for whom the above-mentioned manifestations of spirit became dumb idols and demons, nongods. The cult, too, degenerated, especially during the period of decline, into great abominations. At length, spirituality ceased entirely and the people, too, was destroyed and perished.

However, God bestowed his grace upon the nation which He chose—a grace for which we can find the reason neither in ourselves nor in any of the preceding generations until we perforce go back to our original source, the patriarchs, and to what is related of them in the Torah. This supreme grace presented us with an idea that is supreme over all rational thought. We have always maintained this conception which is in some respects vast and difficult, though in others it is near and simple, especially after most of the people have grasped it. Now if it be your wish to know both the profundity and the simplicity of this idea, consider that even the great majority of Israel, when it stood at Mount Sinai and heard it, did not grasp it in its pure truth. Not until about the time of Israel's return from Babylon, i.e., until about a thousand years passed after the giving of the Torah, did it indeed become engraved upon the tablets of our hearts and no more depart from our history. Through it we have become teachers of the great multitude of nations; through it we continue to exist to this day; and with it we shall arise and be forever redeemed.

THE CYCLES OF JEWISH HISTORY

For I the Lord change not;
And ye, O sons of Jacob, are
not consumed.

Mal. 3:6

According to the workings of the natural order there are three periods through which each primordial nation passes from the time it comes into being until it passes from the scene and perishes:

1. The period of first growth, during which the spirit is born. As we mentioned,* this spirit transforms the material parts of the nation into organic units, integrated through all manner of ordered relationships, and it holds them together as a single entity, ready to receive every excellence and perfection. This period is called: *the stage of the nation's germination and growth.*

2. Thereafter, the spirit becomes fully actualized, all those beneficial institutions and spiritual attributes to which we have alluded reach their apogee, and after a longer or shorter lapse of time, the nation moves forward in all of them, gaining fame and glory. This period will be called: *the stage of power and achievement.*

3. However, in the case of every living thing, the cause of its withering and death is already contained within it. Thus, even during the course of the second stage, the seeds of corruption and degeneration begin to appear in the nation. Thereafter, they sprout, proliferate, and grow, dissolving all bonds and corrupting every beneficial usage, until gradually the nation's glory dwindles away, the nation declines and diminishes to the point of nonexistence. We shall call this period: *the stage of decomposition and extinction.*

This is the pattern for all the nations which possess a limited manifestation of spirit, one which is therefore finite and destined for extinction. But in the case of our nation, although we too have succumbed to the above-mentioned natural course of events with regard to material and tangible externals, the fact is, in the words of

*In the previous section.

the Rabbis: "They were exiled to Babylon, exiled to Elam, and the Divine Presence was with them.* That is to say, the universal spirit which is within us protects us and excludes us from the judgment that falls upon all mortals. And all this follows easily from what has been said above.

Even so, we have seen fit to mention the periods we have traversed since the nation's beginnings until this day in order to show clearly how the cycle of the three stages that we have mentioned repeats itself in our history, and how, when breakdown, decomposition, and decay have become complete, a new and reviving spirit always takes shape within us; though we fall, we arise invigorated—the Lord, our God, has not forsaken us. We shall note everything briefly since we assume the reader knows the subject. As is our custom throughout this work, we shall proceed at times by substituting explanations on the level of reason for what is related in our history in the language of simple conceptions. We have already reiterated that this latter is the level of cognition specific to the conceptions of the Torah and of our faith, since they are intended in equal measure for individuals and for the multitude, but this does not—Heaven forbid—detract from their excellence. The difference lies only in the manner of apprehension, not in the nature of the object, which is a single and true manifestation of spirit, and its activity is likewise single and true. Remember this always, gentle reader, and do not repay me with harm for seeking to benefit you—so, too, did Maimonides request of his readers.

THE FIRST STAGE OF THE FIRST CYCLE

From ancient times there were nations in the interior of Asia, to the northeast of Palestine, that reached a certain level of culture and were the recipients, as well, of certain refined religious concepts that remained with them from the days of Shem,† the ancestor and progenitor of all those nations. As the peoples journeyed from the

*Talmud *Megillah* 29a.

† According to the Bible (Gen. 10:21–31), Shem, one of the sons of Noah, was the ancestor of a number of Near-Eastern nations, among whom were the Hebrews.

east and were scattered to more western lands, the children of Eber*
were singled out from among them; they are the families that
journeyed into the more southwestern portion of Asia and settled
there. Most of them continued to live in tents and raise cattle, but
within fixed boundaries, wandering within their borders from place
to place in search of pasture. Some of them settled down in smaller
or larger groups and engaged in agriculture and in other economic
pursuits. . . . Their language and culture bear clear witness to the
single root of the descendants of Shem and to their close
connection with the children of Eber. Our progenitor Abraham
belongs in this setting. He, too, traveled with his ancestral families
during the last days of these great wanderings from the lands of the
northeast . . . and came afterward to the regions already inhabited by the various Canaanite clans and the Philistine people.† All
these were not of Hebrew stock, but rather of the children of Ham,‡
who came there from lands to the southwest of Palestine in a
portion of Africa. They had already been much corrupted by
idolatry and by evil practices and beliefs to the extent that shortly
thereafter they reached the point of engaging in abominations (i.e.,
their morality became so decadent that they perpetrated acts which
the soul abhors and from which it recoils, such as child-sacrifice,
cultic prostitution, and the mistreatment of strangers).

Our Sages have maintained that Abraham, on his own and
from the beginning, recognized his Creator and that he rejected the
worship of images, fetishes, and spirits, which were already
beginning to disrupt the acceptance of the pure concepts
originating with Noah, Shem, and Eber. Therefore, God was
revealed to Abraham and chose him to be the father of a multitude
of nations in southwestern Asia. Likewise his seed always retained,
to a greater degree than the rest of the Hebrews, pure religious
concepts which were more or less removed from complete idolatry.
Thus Muslim writers have related that even before the advent of
their prophet Muhammed, the tribe of Qureysh, into which he was
born, retained a worship pure of images as they kept their watch
over the Kaaba Temple in Mecca. Only shortly before the time of
Muhammed was an image erected there.

*Great-grandson of Shem and ancestor of Abraham.

†The Philistines were a people of Aegean origin who settled along the southern coast
of Canaan, though, as Krochmal was not aware, considerably after the time of
Abraham.

‡Another of the sons of Noah, whom the Bible regards as the ancestor of both
Canaanites and Philistines (Gen. 10:6–14).

However, the totally pure faith did not strike roots until Isaac. From his seed, as well, one family was excluded. Its worship was not pure, although it was better than that of the rest of Abraham's descendants. I refer to the people of Edom,* who created social and political institutions and lived in a settled state some time before our own nation, and whom alone the Scripture regards as our brother. Moreover, it would appear from the Bible that they did not possess idols in the full sense, nor any god of their own. When Moses sent messengers to them, he had the messengers say: "And we cried unto the Lord" (Num. 20:16), without specifying that he meant the God of our fathers. This would indicate that God's name was known to them from the days of the Patriarchs. . . .

Now from all the seed of Abraham and Isaac one family alone was singled out and chosen. In earliest times it was divided into twelve tribes according to the number and the names of the sons of Jacob. They alone kept the commandments of their ancestors— Abraham, Isaac, and Jacob—which forbade them from becoming absorbed by, or even uniting with, the Canaanites who held the land and were corrupt in their faith and in their actions. They did not even want to absorb others within themselves, as the descendants of Esau did with the Horites† who dwelled in the land and who merged with them; and it would seem that the remainder of Abraham's seed and the clans of Lot‡ did likewise. For this reason our ancestors did not want to settle down among the peoples at all, but rather to continue dwelling in tents and raising cattle in the plains of the land and in the wide valleys between the Canaanite settlements. Although they were compelled to purchase land for burial at full price, they trusted in the Lord and believed that in the end the land would be theirs and they would become a complete and integrated nation. They hoped that if they refrained from assimilating or fusing with the earlier inhabitants of the land, then those regions in which they presently dwelled would become their inheritance. . . . In special places—Gilgal, Shechem, Beth El, Moriah, Hebron, Beersheba—they called upon the name of the Lord; there they planted tamarisk trees and they set up pillars which, according to the Rabbis, were regarded favorably by God in

*The Bible identifies the Edomites, who inhabited the south of eastern Transjordan as descendants of Esau, the brother of Jacob (Gen. 36:1).

†The biblical Horites are the Hurrians, a non-Semitic ethnic group which was centered in Mesopotamia. The Edomites dispossessed them from southern Transjordan (Deut. 2:12).

‡The nephew of Abraham.

that early period. Therefore, those places became holy in later times and centers of great moral teaching as we find in Scripture: "For I have known him [Abraham], to the end that he may command his children and his household after him, that they may keep the way of the Lord, to do righteousness and justice" (Gen. 18:19).

The Lord is a God of knowledge and by Him actions are planned to guide and to direct history toward the spiritual goal. Thus Providence ordained that the holy family descend into Egypt and dwell for a time within its borders. Since that nation was even then spiritually more decadent with regard to beliefs and actions than were the Canaanites—about whom it is written: "The iniquity of the Amorite* is not yet full" (Gen. 15:16)—God was certain that Israel would not be absorbed within it. And who knows if the outcome would not have been different had they remained among the Canaanites for a longer period of time? This is one reason. A second is that, despite all of its abominations, Egypt was rich in buildings, crafts, useful and decorative arts, as well as sciences. Divine Providence thus desired that our nation dwell in their midst in order that it might become, according to the promise, a great nation, i.e., an integral nation possessing its full measure of assets and skills. Such would not have been the case had they remained among the Canaanites, who at the time of the Israelite settlement did not have fixed structures even for their idols.

Thus it was the spirit of the Lord that dwelt within the family, which had spoken to our first ancestor and guided him from distant lands to the chosen land, that also graciously drew Jacob to Egypt. . . . And now It says to him: "Fear not to go down into Egypt; for I will there make of thee a great nation. I will go down with thee into Egypt; and I will also surely bring thee up again" (Gen. 46:3–4). The intent of the verses, according to our mode of interpretation, is that Jacob was not to fear that his descendants might become absorbed within a large and integrated nation; it is also the promise that his seed would itself become a great nation, and that the universal spirit in its midst would save it from the fate of evanescence and extinction. . . . And thus it happened, that although they sojourned in that kingdom for a long time (according to the *Seder Olam* of Rabbi Yose, † which always picks the briefest

---

*The Bible closely identifies the Amorites with the Canaanites as one of the six pre-Israelite inhabitants of the land (Exod. 3:8).

† "The Order of the World," a Midrashic chronicle running from the Creation to the Bar Kokhba revolt against the Romans (132–135). Tradition ascribes it to Yose ben Halafta, a rabbi of the second century.

possibility—210 years), they lived together as cattle grazers in a single district near the border. Some tribes did indeed wander with their cattle into the nearby desert, but as is apparent from Scripture, they always returned to Egypt, the land of their permanent abode. The text plainly indicates that they observed circumcision, and we shall see clearly further on how the tribe of Levi, in particular, preserved certain very pure religious concepts and produced men worthy to be heads of the people and strong enough to serve in a royal palace. It seems further that their nature was vigorous and healthy, like any group which has not yet been weakened by self-indulgence. Therefore they were fruitful, multiplied, and became a mighty nation over a period of time which was not very long considering the extent of the growth. As the midwives said: "Because the Hebrew women are not as the Egyptian women; for they are lively" (Ex. 1:19). In short, with regard to the beginnings of all the capabilities required by a nation for its integration, they gained a great deal in Egypt. And what was the reason they did not disintegrate within a large and fortunate kingdom which exerted great pressure on strangers who came within its domain? The cause was none other than the memory of their homeland and single ancestor, the tradition which they possessed from their fathers, and the beneficial way of life which they bequeathed to them. It was this that bound them together and made them into a large people, ready to receive lofty and beneficial institutions as soon as a foreign people no longer ruled over them and they could establish their own political organization.

How well the metaphor of the Prophet fits the status of the nation at that time: "Thy breasts were fashioned, and thy hair was grown; yet thou wast naked and bare. Now when I passed by thee, and looked upon thee, and, behold, thy time was the time of love . . ." (Ezek. 16:7-8). The meaning of the passage is that the physical substance of the nation had already been completed and actualized—but its spirituality, although it existed potentially and sustained the material existence, had not yet appeared completely. Thus when "the time of love" came, it was the plan of Divine Providence that the people go forth to freedom by the force of many wonders, as it is recorded in the Torah. All of this verifies and teaches that the entire history of this people, its origins and its prosperity as well as its decline and fall, is explicable by an encompassing spiritual cause: the Divine Power which resides within our midst. We do not seek our benefit by the might of the sword alone, nor by the wiles of diplomacy or by becoming joined to a foreign people, nor yet solely by diligent craftsmanship, manual skills, or much physics and psychology—for the force and spirituality of all these is individual and ephemeral to the extent that they are limited manifestations. Every natural phenomenon is subject to corruption and decay, excepting only the great wonder which is the Spirit as it truly is, above the natural world of matter.

Thus, too, did God strengthen and consolidate the nation when, in a most wondrous and sublime fashion, He gave it teachings, laws, and righteous, embracing judgments, which served to perfect the individual and the group in the fullest possible way. And He promised the nation that by guarding its truth it would endure, that it would not perish; "For He is thy life, and the length of thy days, that thou mayest dwell in the land . . ." (Deut. 30:20). This faith was alive and strong within the nation during all periods, as it remained ever conscious of the Absolute Spirit in its midst. For that is the great principle: although a certain spirituality manifests itself within a particular nation, this is not sufficient until the nation becomes clearly conscious of it, realizing that what is coming into being in its midst is a manifestation of spirit and that it is this spirit which produces and sustains it. In the language of concrete thought this corresponds to its worship of God, as has been explained above. As for us, the children of Israel, it has been our basic principle that we always cling to the Lord, the totality and truth of all manifestations of spirit. . . .

The Lord carried out all these acts, that is, He crowned them with the Torah and united them by means of a single system of law and judgment. The tribes were organized about their tribal banners and in turn united with each other to become a single unit guided by the spiritual Providence which dwelt in the tent of meeting in the midst of the camps. The glory of God bound all together, shielding them and dwelling among the ten-thousands of the families of Israel. It was a further act of God's wisdom to turn the freely chosen wickedness of the desert generation—their despising of God—into good. He made them tarry in the desert until the generation which left Egypt died off, since they had not been sufficiently elevated from their low estate nor had their turbid spirit been cleansed of the Egyptian bondage. Then a second generation grew up in freedom, as powerful as young lions and as agile as deer upon the mountains. After all of this, after Divine spiritual Providence had nurtured us as a nurse does an infant, and after the great Gentile prophet [Balaam] had been astonished upon perceiving the people, until the spirit rested upon him and he spoke his exalted parables*—then the nation's first historical period was complete. The duration of this stage of germination and growth, according to the conservative calculation of the earlier-mentioned *Seder Olam,* amounts to 465 years, from the time that God was revealed to Abraham until the death of Moses, the faithful shepherd, may he rest in peace. . . .

[The chapter continues with a description of the second stage in the cycle: the period of power and achievement. This stage begins with Israel's entry into Canaan and reaches its climax with the reigns of David and Solomon; the stage of decline begins with the latter's death. Corruption and decay manifest themselves in religion, morality, and political life. At length the nation collapses, as much from within as by the force of external military might. With the death of Gedaliah, the last ruler of Judah, slightly after the destruction of the Temple by Babylonia in 586 B.C.E., the third stage is completed. Yet, amazingly, the now exiled people still maintains its national identity. At this point the following chapter begins.]

RENEWAL AFTER DECLINE

> And I will put My spirit in you, and
> ye shall live, and I will place you
> in your own land.
>
> Ezek. 37:14

With the above words the prophet of the Exile by the river Chebar in Babylon responded when the people said to him: "Our bones are dried up, and our hope is lost; we are clean cut off. . . . Can these bones live?" (Ezek. 37:11,3). And it did indeed appear that the question was justified, considering how Israel was scattered frightfully to all the regions of Asia, and how immediately after the Destruction they did not succeed in establishing a new society either in Palestine or in Egypt. They remained scattered in ones and

*Numbers 23:7–24:24.

twos; only in Chaldea* did they succeed from the start in forming an important society known as the Community of Exiles from Judah. It was hard for them to believe that from this small settlement a new national spirit should burgeon and gain sufficient strength to gather the dispersed, unite them into organized groups, and establish, insofar as possible, complete communities with some bond, despite their distance one from another and the degree of change they had undergone. Would it be able to reconstitute them as a great nation, as a people in the full sense, in some respects greater than it had been before, making it into a mighty spiritual entity possessing many and different limbs but united by the activity of their encompassing spirit? Now, as indicated earlier, all of this is not possible unless the spirit of the nation is strong and firm, lending vitality and vigor to the weary, arousing the lethargic, and joining together those who are severed. In response comes the promise of the prophet which we have set as motto: There is strength in the word of the Lord, i.e., in the spirit manifest within this exile, to achieve that great and much desired intent. He further replies to the wicked among them, who stubbornly maintain their belief in complete disintegration and oblivion among the nations: "And that which cometh into your mind shall not be at all; in that ye say: We will be as the nations . . ." (ibid., 20:32). . . . The days that follow and their consequences bear witness to the truth of these prophecies, for the word of the Lord does not return unfulfilled.

It is fitting that at this point we ponder the enormous difference between the character of the spiritual manifestation as it existed within the nation during the initial periods of its existence, which we discussed earlier, and its character now. We should further note how it gradually revealed itself and gained strength during the period presently under discussion—the period we shall call: the stage of the nation's germination and growth for the second time. Previously the life of the nation was dependent upon its dwelling in a single place, its settlement upon the land given by God, and the people's becoming a single society before Him with regard both to divine worship and to political legislation—these two areas being undifferentiated and undivided at that time. Moreover, the spirit and unity of the nation were increased also by means of wars with neighboring peoples. The nation was mainly concerned with throwing off every external yoke and avoiding any manner of

*Babylonia.

subjection to a foreign people. So deeply was the feeling of unity rooted in each and every Israelite heart that they called those who dwelled in the land, citizen; those who cleaved and were bound to the inheritance of God were the leafy branches upon the trunk of the nation. Whoever was banished from the land considered himself a worshiper of other gods and cut off from his people, a branch severed from the tree which gave it life. Moreover, there was prophecy, the Urim and the Thummim,* and the other ancient sancta; also the great number of books, the exalted poetry, and the sublime rhetoric which then existed in Israel, and especially from the time of Samuel and David. All these were a faithful source for the manifestation and reinforcement of the spiritual element in the elite of the nation, from whom it emanated to the rest of the people.

However, all these beneficial spiritual attributes exist only to a slight degree or not at all in this new stage. Thus, already at its beginning, prophecy diminished, and during the course of it disappeared altogether. Even the psalmody, the song, and the compositions in the holy tongue (which, as one would expect, among the exiles in Babylon, became mixed with Aramaic†) decreased more and more during this time until they ceased entirely in the middle of the following period. The Torah and the other holy books which remained in their hands by the great grace of God (after many of them, which had not been copied and were deposited in the Temple, were burned along with the building and permanently lost) became sealed to the people, requiring translation and commentary. This last was difficult since a great dispersion had begun with the exile of the Ten Tribes, and quite clearly had increased continually from Judah as well, beginning with the time of Josiah.‡ The Diaspora settlements were separated from one another by great distances. They ranged from the furthest points in Asia to the Egyptian border with Ethiopia, and in the west to the lands of Greece. All of them were subject to rulers of foreign peoples and to their political control. They joined in their cult and in their wars, at first under the Babylonians, then under the great Persian Empire, and finally under the rule of the Macedonian Greeks, who seized control from the Persians. Yet with all of this

---

*The device for obtaining oracles contained on the breastplate worn by the high priest (Exod. 28:15–30).

† The Semitic language, similar to Hebrew, spoken by the Jews of Babylonia.

‡ King Josiah reigned over Judah from 639–609 B.C.E.

detriment in comparison with the days of the First Temple, a great new spirituality now appeared within the nation, in each of the Diaspora settlements that made it up. It everywhere became "the spirit of wisdom and understanding, the spirit of counsel and might, the spirit of knowledge and fear of the Lord" (Is. 11:2). That is to say: "the spirit of wisdom and understanding"—to recognize the value of the precious treasure they possessed from their fathers as opposed to the vanities of the nations into whose lands they had come. "The spirit of counsel and might"—to establish their community, strengthen it, and crown it with revealed commandments and beneficial ancestral institutions which all became so very dear to them that they gave up their lives rather than be forced to abandon them. "The spirit of knowledge and fear of the Lord"—to gather, write down, and copy everything that remained to them of the holy books, to meditate upon them and explain them intelligently, until the Torah be strengthened in every place of exile, studied, understood, and observed everywhere to the extent possible in the various lands. This whole great prospect—which the more you consider it the more you are amazed—was already clearly promised in the Torah (Deut. 30): that after their rebellion and stubbornness they would bethink themselves in the lands of the nations to which they were driven and they would return to the Lord their God. Then God would circumcise their hearts and those of their descendants. That is to say, the time would come when the spirituality of the nation would increase to the point where it would achieve what it did not in the days of the earlier prophets.

All of this occurs in every place of dispersion without reference to signs and wonders, to revealed miracles. It does not even result from the force of arms and the might of the sword—for we have not found a trace of them among the chief communities of the dispersion during this period from the destruction of the Temple by Nebuchadnezzar to the beginning of Greek rule—but rather solely from tranquillity and the arousal of spirit among the elders and the people. They possessed a single heart to act, as we find in the story concerning the community of those returning to the land of Judah: "And the Lord stirred up the spirit of Zerubbabel . . . and the spirit of all the remnant of the people" (Hag. 1:14). Thus, too, Zechariah the prophet promised them Divine assistance and victory over every adversary and foe: "Not by might, nor by power, but by My spirit, saith the Lord of hosts" (Zech. 4:6).

[Krochmal continues to elaborate upon this second cycle in some detail. The stage of growth, which began with the Exile, concludes with the Macedonian succession to the Persian Empire. The following period of might and glory encompasses the Maccabean revolt and lasts until the death of Queen Salome Alexandra (67 B.C.E.), which inaugurates the third stage. The seeds of dissension, planted earlier, now begin to sprout vigorously as civil war breaks out between the rivals to the throne, Hyrcanus and Aristobulus. Thereafter, increasing political division is accompanied by spiritual decline and the eventual Roman domination of Palestine. The Temple is destroyed; the nation remains oppressed, unable to marshal its spiritual force. The Hadrianic persecution and the abortive revolt of Bar Kokhba (132–135 C.E.) bring the third stage of the second cycle to a close.]

THE THIRD CYCLE

We have therewith completed two major historical cycles, each containing three stages: growth, fruition, and decay. However, we are unable at present to carry on the narrative and analysis for succeeding generations, though, in our view, subsequent history, likewise, in a general way hinges upon this conception. The only difference is that the periods are longer, possess highly divergent characteristics, and are in every respect animated by a different spirit. We shall only hint that the third germination occurred in the days of the Antonine emperors* at the end of the horrible persecution [by Hadrian]. We have in the Rabbinic literature lovely accounts of this beginning: how the Rabbis first gathered in Yavneh,† and later for a time in Usha‡ to the north, where they

*Antoninus Pius, who succeeded Hadrian as Roman emperor in 138 C.E., reversed the oppressive policy which his predecessor exercised toward the Jews. His more tolerant attitude was continued by the Antonine emperors who followed him.

†A town on the coastal plain of Palestine which served as the center of Jewish life after the destruction of Jerusalem in 70 C.E.

‡A town in Lower Galilee where the principal institution of Jewish self-rule, the Sanhedrin, was reestablished in 140 C.E., shortly after the Hadrianic persucution.

enacted beneficial regulations according to the needs of the time and of the impoverished nation which had survived like a brand snatched from the fire; how the Academy and the office of Nasi* were reestablished with the descendants of Hillel,† so that the Nasi and the sages associated with him were ready to defend Judaism before the Roman officials in Caesarea,‡ and when the situation required, to undertake special journeys to Rome. There are many such accounts in the Talmud and the Midrash. Note also the passage: "'I will not reject them . . . to break My covenant with them' (Lev. 26:44)—in the days of the Romans, when I raised up for them the members of the house of Rabbi§ and the sages of the various generations" ‖

The third period of might and power began about the year 4500,¶ when the Muslims greatly expanded their empire, attaining important political and intellectual achievements. Hereupon, great geniuses arose also among us, writers of wisdom and literary skill who attained a remarkable degree of excellence in every way. In this regard, also, we may apply the pleasing and enlightening words of the Midrash [on Lamentations]. . . .: "Because Thou renewest us at the dawn of empires, we know that Thy faithfulness is great to redeem us."

Following this long period, the stage of decline came for the third time. Beginning with the death of Maimonides and Nahmanides**there was a tremendous darkness of night with only few flashes of light. At the start of the sixth millennium, persecutions, expulsions, and unlimited troubles came upon us frequently and continuously until after the year 5400.†† An investigation of all these matters is valuable and precious to the end that we may gain wisdom concerning our future. . . .

*The president of the Sanhedrin.

†Hillel the Elder, who lived at the turn of the era, was the most important of the sages during the Second Temple period.

‡A city along the northern coast of Palestine which served as the center of the Roman administration.

§Judah ha-Nasi, patriarch of Judea at the beginning of the third century and redactor of the Mishnah.

‖Talmud *Megillah* 11a.

¶740 C.E.

**Moses Nahmanides (1194–1270), Spanish rabbi, biblical commentator, philosopher, and mystic.

††1640, shortly before the time of the Chmielnicki massacres in Poland.

HEINRICH GRAETZ

INTRODUCTION TO HEINRICH GRAETZ

THE FIGURE OF Heinrich Graetz (1817–1891) dominates the Jewish historiography of the nineteenth century. Though frequently criticized by other scholars, his work has enjoyed a tremendous and lasting popularity. Graetz was born into an orthodox Jewish family in the German province of Posen where he received the usual traditional Jewish education; the young scholar was forced to pick up whatever secular learning he could on his own. In the course of time, he became disenchanted with the narrow Talmudism of his childhood environment, moving first to the modern orthodoxy of Samson Raphael Hirsch and eventually to the positive-historical Judaism of Zacharias Frankel, the founder of a very moderately reformist movement within German Jewry. When Frankel became the first president of the Jewish Theological Seminary in Breslau in 1854, Graetz was asked to join its faculty. Pleased with his position and well liked by his students, he served as a teacher there for the remainder of his life. Though he wrote frequent scholarly and some popular articles—including a large number devoted to biblical criticism—it was his History of the Jews, published in eleven volumes from 1853 to 1876, translated, and often reprinted, which made Graetz's conception of Jewish history the norm during the latter half of the nineteenth century and secured its continuing influence up to the present time.

To appreciate fully Graetz's conception of Jewish history it is necessary to read directly from his historical narrative, to note how he deals with the major events and personalities of the Jewish past and how he weaves his thread of historical connection among them. As, however, Graetz's History is widely available in English, what is presented here is not a sample of his historical account, but reflections on the structure and substance of Jewish history. These are drawn from Graetz's programmatic essay, "The Construction of Jewish History," which appeared in 1846 in a periodical edited by Frankel, and from some of the prefaces and introductions to the various volumes of his history. None of these has previously appeared in English.

The first selection given here is taken from the essay. Indirectly, it presents Graetz's rationale for becoming an historian: his conviction that only through the study of Jewish history can one truly know what Judaism is. Philosophers are able to give no more than partial and arbitrary answers; history is the only genuine and complete reflection of the Jewish idea. This is also where Graetz first tries to define what characterizes Judaism as an historical phenomenon and what makes it unique in world history.

The remaining selections all introduce individual volumes of Graetz's History. The Introduction to Volume One (the second selection) contains Graetz's clearest acceptance of Nahman Krochmal's view of the successive cycles of growth, blossoming, and decay which Israel undergoes time after time. Volume Four of the original German edition begins with an Introduction (the third selection) containing Graetz's famous definition of Diaspora Jewish history as comprising two elements: a history of suffering and a history of religious literature. It also contains his periodization of the Diaspora era as Graetz conceived it at this stage of his work, and it is an excellent example of the metaphoric richness of his style. The three concluding selections present Graetz's understanding and division of the Talmudic period; the less narrowly spiritual conception of Jewish history and the notion of successive unifying "focal points" of Jewish history which he had arrived at by the time he published Volume Five in 1860; and finally his distress at the stagnation and decay which he thought characteristic of Jewish history from the death of Maimonides in 1204 to the age of Mendelssohn in the eighteenth century.

JUDAISM CAN BE UNDERSTOOD ONLY THROUGH ITS HISTORY

What is Judaism? This seemingly absurd question is likely to perplex many a man who, steeped in the study of Judaism, fancies he has thoroughly exhausted its content, just as the question, What is truth? has proved embarrassing to many a man with an overweening confidence in its possession. What has not been passed off as Judaism since the time it first became the object of intellectual interpretation! How many different views of its basic nature have been circulated in recent years with claims of exclusive validity and with pretensions to have discovered the norms that govern the sphere of practical religion!

At times Judaism has been taken to be an elaboration of speculative theology, an early anticipation of Hegelianism, as it were, that runs through all dialectical processes (Samuel Hirsch);* and at times it has been represented as the exact antithesis of a priori thinking, as an a posteriori revelation of characteristic and apparently irrational dogmas which, by virtue of their manifest certitude, elicit the grudging acknowledgment of speculative reason (Steinheim).† Judaism has sometimes been regarded as a thoroughly coherent system designed to instill in its followers a sense of obedience, a docile compliance to an absolute divine will, having as its goal the inculcation of religiosity (Ben Uziel).‡ Then again Judaism has been taken as the very opposite of religion—a kind of shower bath, as it were, to chill the excessive ardor of the human heart, an antidote to the effects of a purely religious propensity, a practical system for the most part that serves as a dependable balancing pole to counteract the harmful consequences of

*Samuel Hirsch (1815–1889), German liberal rabbi, wrote a work interpreting Judaism in accordance with elements of the dialectical philosophy developed by the German philosopher Friedrich Hegel.

†Solomon Ludwig Steinheim (1789–1866), German Jewish religious philosopher, defined Judaism in terms of a supernatural revelation which did not merely confirm already present truths of reason.

‡The pen name under which Samson Raphael Hirsch (1808–1888), leader of German Neo-Orthodoxy, wrote his *Nineteen Letters on Judaism* (1836) defending the traditional faith.

one-sided and opposing inclinations (Isaac Mieses).* Judaism's characteristic expression has at times been taken to be that of a purely rational religion with ethical goals that do not extend beyond the prosaic rationalism of the workaday world and, at other times, as a mystical guide for those who seek refuge in a life of contemplation, a religion concerned with immortality and with preparations for the hereafter.

These diverse and often conflicting conceptions of Judaism's basic character draw upon the rich treasures of Jewish history to support their respective claims, and they all must contain some true elements that make them appear plausible since they all seek to gain credence by assuming a semblance of truth. Such divergent interpretations of Judaism, however, testify to the great wealth and immense range of its intellectual tradition. Taken as single instances of Judaism's absolute basic principle, all these different conceptions are true. They prove to be false, however, when they are advanced as mutually opposed and irreconcilable interpretations, for then we are left with a number of Jewish institutions that cannot be subsumed under this common denominator nor adequately explained, if at all, without doing violence to their essential nature.

Many different paths have been taken in the past in an effort to arrive at a deeper understanding of what constitutes the essential character of Judaism. At times its dogmatic and metaphysical nature—its ideal character—was stressed, and all other aspects were subordinated to this leading principle and regarded as the nonessential mold into which the idea is poured to make it accessible and familiar to the prevailing popular conception; or the concrete nature of Judaism—its legislative character—was emphasized, in which case it was conceived as an ethical system in the broader sense. Those who sought to demonstrate the speculative character of Judaism would confine themselves to the circumscribed world of biblical doctrine or they would range over the vast and luxuriant regions of Jewish literature to find support for their thesis, including the Midrash and philosophical exegesis, frequently unaware that the proofs they adduced bore the traces of alien origin and hence were invalid as criteria for determining the precise character of a purely Jewish system. Those who sought to demonstrate the practical nature of Judaism would either go back to the written word, thus eliminating all subsequent tradition, or take

*Isaac Mieses (1802–1883), German Jewish rationalist philosopher and scholar.

their stand in contemporary Judaism and consider the Judaism of their own day as the natural distillation of its immanent elements.

It is clear even from this brief analysis that these basic conceptions of Judaism must necessarily differ since they draw their inspiration from divergent points of view. The question, however, is whether the cause of this diversity may not reside in the complexity of the object itself whose innate nature is refractory to logical synthesis, in which case one must forever despair of ascertaining the true nature of the soul that animates and governs the organic life of Judaism. But before we abandon ourselves to such despair, we must employ other analytical methods in the hope that they might lead us closer to the basic idea on which Judaism reposes.

It is plain that all these attempts to capture the essence of Judaism share a common error: they fail to submit the totality of Judaism to their scrutiny, always confining their interests to one of its aspects. Thus, often neglecting the broader aspects of isolated factors, they frequently confuse cause and effect. The totality of Judaism, however, can only be understood through its history which alone can explain its character as a whole and the operations of its combined potencies. Every vital idea must create for itself a tangible existence; it must emerge from its slumbering ideal state and assert its ruling principle in the pulsating world of reality. History is thus not only the reflection of an idea, but also the criterion of its genuineness and demonstrability. The idea nourishes within itself an indestructible force that is not only able to withstand corruption in the perishable world of matter, but can rise above it and impress it with its own conquering impulse. Once the idea has broken through to reality and survived the entanglements of history, we must assume that it contained from the outset all its emergent configurations *in potentia*. For history brings to maturity only the seeds of the idea, and the manifold forms that history assumes are but the concrete manifestations of the idea.

This is not the place to enlarge upon these facts of the philosophy of history, a study that is still in its infancy. It can, however, be demonstrated that Jewish history in all its phases, even in its apparent aberrations and inconsistencies, exhibits a central idea and basic conception. If we survey Judaism in its broad outlines, in both its active and passive condition, and examine the turning points of its history, and if we remove the husk from the grain—the productive ideas from the gross facts—we would come upon the original vital impulses that are implicit in the very idea of

Judaism. We shall attempt to employ these methods in our interpretation of Jewish history.

Judaism began as a negation, a negation of paganism; it appeared on the stage of history as a kind of Protestantism. This truth was already recognized by Maimonides, although his observations were superficial. He viewed paganism from the outside as an isolated phenomenon and contrasted it, especially its obscene rites, with Judaism without penetrating the surface. His highly superficial view of the Jewish laws of sacrifice is well known. But even the excesses of paganism and its crude customs, which often offend our moral sense, go back to a primary notion; all manifestations of pagan life can be reduced to some basic idea. It is precisely to negate this idea within its narrow confines that constitutes Judaism's predestined vocation: to show the paucity of truth in paganism and its harmful effects on social morality, and to do so, not in a theoretical academic manner, but in the active world of experience. Once we succeed in drawing a fixed line of demarcation between paganism and Judaism, we can anticipate the basic idea on which Judaism rests. Nothing is easier than to determine this line that separates the two religious forms. For this we need not make extensive comparisons of their respective dogmas. . . .

Even a cursory glance reveals that the deep antagonism between paganism and Judaism is the same as that between nature and spirit. Nature in its widest sense, as an all-powerful immanent force, is the indispensable presupposition and condition of paganism that conceives God as coextensive with nature. Even during the period of his highest development, after he divested himself of his animal and plant aspects and took on human form, and even when Greek art, in support of religion, gave the inhabitants of Mount Olympus a more spiritual and elevated character of ideal perfection, the pagan god still remained nature idealized. The immortal gods of paganism were, just as ordinary mortals, subject to necessity and to the inexorable laws of nature; and Tyche, the blind goddess of fortune, was the mistress of both gods and men.

Without dwelling on the inevitable consequence of this pagan conception of God, namely, the ethical bondage of man in which human actions—whether good or bad, beneficient or injurious—are regarded as predestined by fate, like the immutable laws of nature, we shall now consider the reverse of paganism, Judaism. Here God alone is the sole Source of authority, determining and self-deter-mined. There is a clear division between the natural and the divine; nature is nothing over against God. It must first be brought into existence by the Divine Will, by a free act of creation, depending on God's breath for its existence and reducible by Him at any time to its original state of nothingness. The idea of God thus constitutes the crowning point of Jewish life; all activities and undertakings fall within the purview of the Divine and acquire value with reference to it. Jewish life is impregnated with God's glory and it retains its native vigor only when imbued with His spirit. Moral freedom or self-determination is therefore the immediate consequence of the Jewish principle. In the Jewish view, nothing is more repugnant than the worship of natural phenomena, and where this appears as an effective force it must be resisted as unwarranted, sacrilegious, and futile. A considerable number of legal ordinances in Judaism have this negative character and reflect the subordinate place assigned to man's natural condition. The life of nature, especially those natural elements introduced into human society to be appropriated and assimilated by the human organism, must therefore be subjected, as it were, to a process of consecration.

This fundamental distinction in the conception of the Divine may be amplified still further. The pagan perceives the Divine in nature through the medium of the eye, and he becomes conscious of it as something to be looked at. On the other hand, to the Jew who conceives God as being outside of nature and prior to it, the Divine manifests itself through the will and through the medium of the ear. He becomes conscious of it as something to be heeded and listened to. The pagan beholds his god; the Jew hears Him, that is, apprehends His will. From beholding to imitative representation is but one step, and the heathen cult of idolatry is a natural consequence of the pagan conception of God, however strange it may appear to Judaism to represent in an image the Divine "that has no form."

The two different conceptions of God also gave rise to distinct art forms. The sensuous conception of God in Greek paganism found its expression in sculpture, the alluring and fragrant blossom of the pagan attitude to life. Judaism, on the other hand, which perceived its God in the modulations of the alternate rising and falling of imageless tones and in the rhythm of sensuous sound, produced a musical art that was bound up with religious poetry corresponding to its conception of God. But even the special forms of poetry reveal the profound difference between the pagan and the Jewish spirit—a difference, however, that could only have been developed later.

This theme need not detain us any longer; it is reflected throughout Jewish history and is too apparent to require further corroboration. Judaism's determined opposition to paganism and to its two most conspicuous characteristics, idolatry and immorality, reflects the profound difference between the religion of the spirit and the religion of nature, between divine transcendence and immanence.

It is plain even from this preliminary sketch that the monotheistic idea is by no means the primary principle of Judaism, as has until now been erroneously assumed almost universally. Rather, it is the secondary consequence of the transmundane God-idea, just as polytheism (and idol worship) cannot be said to be the primary principle of paganism. For this reason the idea of monotheism does not exhaust the immense range and depth of Jewish tradition. Even the negation of nature worship is not the whole of Judaism, but only the beginning of a development that runs through the entire course of its history.

Judaism's task then is by no means confined to this negative oppositional aspect, but rather to exemplify in a positive manner its own peculiar God-idea. All its regulations and precepts express this double aspect, sometimes in negative and sometimes in positive form. Another pronounced characteristic of Judaism is its tendency to find concrete application for the most abstract and idealistic doctrine. Thus, the supramundane God-idea was not left in the ethereal region of vacuous abstraction, but sought concrete embodiment in the life of the people; an appropriate state constitution was the vital bearer of this idea which found expression in the customs of the people and in the attitudes of the individual. The revealed God-idea does not exist for its own sake so that it might be known merely theoretically, but has a practical aim, that of promoting temporal felicity: the God-idea was also a political idea.

It is customary to call the constitution of the Jewish state theocratic in the derogatory sense of the word. But in this, as in many other respects, Judaism has been misunderstood. At the head of the Jewish state is God, the cardinal point from which all its activities proceed and to which they bear constant reference. But although God is the alpha and omega of this "City of God,"* its primary goal is what Mieses in his original brochure *"On the Chaotic State of Present-Day Judaism"* has called, somewhat crudely but justly, eudaemonistic: "that it may be well with thee upofi the land which the Lord thy God giveth thee"–a phrase that recurs in the most diverse ordinances and which is also found at the conclusion of the ceremonial law of the "bird's nest" (Deut. 22:6)† as well as the ethical commandment to honor one's father and mother (Ex. 20:12). The view of Aher (Rabbi Elisha ben Avuyah)‡ that one who fulfills this commandment will be rewarded with prosperity or the view of Rabbi Jacob, his grandson, who interprets this reward as referring to the world to come (Talmud *Hullin* 142a), obviously rests on an erroneous exegetical interpretation. Judaism is not a religion for the individual but for the community as a whole, and the promises and rewards connected with the observance of the Law do not apply to individuals, who would soon lose faith in a religion that did not keep its promises, but rather to the entire people. The integrity of the Jewish state and its welfare depend on the observance or nonobservance of the laws. Nor does Judaism reward fidelity to the Law with the promise of eternal bliss in a future world. It is not concerned with immortality; the doctrine of the survival of the soul has as little place in Judaism as the dogma of transubstantiation, for example, and who knows whether this apparent weakness may not also be its strength. Judaism, we repeat, is not a religion for the individual but for the community as a whole, which is tantamount to saying that Judaism, in the strictest sense, is no religion at all—if we understand by religion the relation of mortal man to his Creator and his hopes for a good life on earth—but rather a political community subject to the laws of the state.

But these material social goals are in turn inbued with metaphysical notions, entwined and encased by dogmatic ideas. Judaism is by no means without dogmas, even though they do not appear as dry formulas and are not pursued with religious fanaticism. From this point of view Judaism may be said to have a religious character. It is precisely this double aspect, however, that

---

*A reference to the work of Saint Augustine (354–430) by this name.

†One may not take both the mother bird and its young. The mother must be let go.

‡A great sage of the second century C.E. who became an apostate when, according to one tradition, an incident which he witnessed shattered his faith in divine reward for obeying God's commandments.

constitutes the essence of Judaism: the knowledge of God and social felicity, religious truth and the welfare of the state—these are the two streams that interpenetrate and converge in Judaism. The dogmatic and the social, or in other words, the religious and political, are the two poles around which Jewish life revolves. The concrete expression of these abstractions is the revealed Law —Torah—and the Holy Land. The people's interests centered on these two previous gifts. The Law is the soul and the Holy Land the body of this peculiar political organism. The land, with its clearly defined borders, offers wider scope for the unrestricted development of laws that express the God-idea in its highest form, whereas the Law exists to promote Israel's social welfare. The Torah, the Israelite nation, and the Holy Land are, one might say, mysteriously related to one another, indissolubly linked by an invisible bond. Judaism without a political state structure resembles a hollow, half-uprooted tree that puts forth leaves only in its top branches but which is no longer able to send forth shoots and tendrils. You can subject Judaism to a process of sublimation, extract modern ideas from the vast storehouse of its traditions and proclaim them with specious rhetoric and brilliant catchwords as the real essence of Judaism, and then erect a church to preserve this sublimated, idealized Judaism *in nuce* and vow a solemn profession of faith—but you will only have embraced a shadow and taken the seared husk for the luscious fruit. You will have Judaism neither as it is unambiguously set forth in the Bible, as it developed in the three thousand years of its history, nor as it still lives in the unshaken conviction of the majority of its followers.

Judaism is not a religion of the present but of the future. Just as its patriarchs put their trust in divine assurances and regarded their own age as only a preparatory period for the future of their race, so also does Judaism struggle to create a present it does not possess and, conscious of this imperfection and its bleak present existence, looks back to Sinai's flaming bush and forward to the ideal future age proclaimed by the prophets, when the knowledge of God and the reign of justice and contentment shall have united all men in the bonds of brotherhood. Memory and hope are the pillars of cloud and fire that will lead Israel to its future. In the hope of obtaining the Promised Land where the knowledge of God would grow and flourish, the patriarchs wandered through the land on high camels, often meeting with hostility, and it was this same hope that consoled their children in Egyptian bondage and sustained the growing young tribes when they lived in tents as nomads in the Arabian desert, homeless and inglorious, lacking the most elementary political organization. This desert life of the tribal hordes was actually the embryonic stage of the future nations. The history of the Jewish people begins only at the last station of the desert; the Jordan river marks the transition from tribal organization to national political structure. A logical pattern can be discerned in the history of this people, and when viewed in larger units, it reveals the alternating activity of the two factors* which, in fact, constitute Judaism.

Jewish history, during the period on native soil, can be conveniently divided into two parts which are similar in only few respects. The first half, the pre-exilic period, has a predominantly political character, and the religious element is present at the beginning to only a slight degree. The second half, however, the post-exilic period of history, is characterized by its pronounced religious quality; and the political-social tendency, of which there are still some faint traces, is altogether absent by the time we reach the end of this period. The leading personalities of the first historical period are citizens of the state, renowned warriors and kings with only slight religious inclinations, whereas those of the second period are pious men, sages, teachers, students and sectarians with just a feeble interest in social problems. This basic difference is apparent at first glance, for the two periods are clearly distinguished by totally different characters and institutions, and this distinction in the nature of the two periods has misled one Jewish historian into dividing Jewish history into a history of the Israelites and a history of the Jews. But is there no connecting link between these two periods? Did not the prophets prepare the way for the religiosity of the second period? Judaism in both periods retains the same character and, despite differences in external experiences and inner changes, is conscious of constituting an indivisible unity.

It must therefore lie in the very nature of Judaism, in its root idea, to exhibit these two factors in its history, the religious and the social, at first separately or in casual conjunction but later as interdependent and mutually accommodating. The combination of the religious and the political, the unity of the supramundane God-idea and the political life of the state, may in another sphere lead to interminable conflicts and in the end seem to be impossible;

*The political/social and the religious.

in Judaism, however, these two elements were to merge in perfect union—the natural life of society, in its higher and lower functions, was to be elevated and transfigured by the God-idea. The vision of a political state with its Jewish institutions remains the ideal of Judaism transported to the distant future: the Messiah as he was conceived by the prophets, transmitted by tradition and assimilated by Jewish consciousness, is the keystone of Judaism. Our task . . . is to apply this criterion to the successive stages of Jewish history, their heights and depths, and to construe them in the light of Judaism's basic principle and of the universally acknowledged truth: history is the reflection of the idea. . . .

THE MIRACLE OF JEWISH SURVIVAL

Even a person who does not believe in miracles must admit that the course of Israel's history contains something resembling the miraculous. It reveals not merely, as in the case of other peoples, the transition from growth to blossoming and decay, but also the extraordinary phenomenon of decay followed once more by new sprouting and blossoming; moreover, this rise and fall occurs three times. The history of the crystallization of the Israelite clans into a people from the entry into the Land of Canaan up to the foundation of the monarchy constitutes the first epoch: the *growth*. The second epoch, the *blossoming*, is made up of the reigns of the two kings, David and Solomon, who raised the Israelite people to a state of the first magnitude. The period of blossoming was short; it was followed by a gradual diminution of strength and finally by the downfall of the national entity. But it arose again, grew gradually under the rule of Persians and Greeks, and thanks to the Maccabees, it again put forth resplendent blossoms, only to perish once more under the Romans. But it only seemed to perish, so that it might experience another resurrection in a different form. . . .

No less remarkable is the fact that this people twice began its growth while seemingly lifeless on foreign soil: the first time in Egypt, the second time in Babylonia, and, if you like, even the third time in the Roman and Parthian empires. One of the prophets of Israel describes the growth of the Israelite nation in Egypt with the

metaphor of a female infant who, left in an open field and covered
with blood and dirt, despite her abandonment and distress blossoms
into a lovely young woman.* Its growth in Babylonia is described by
another prophet using the metaphor of a hapless, mourning widow,
robbed of all her children, who is comforted by the sudden
assemblage from everywhere of her numerous offspring, and is
rejuvenated through them.† A fitting metaphor has also been
suggested for the third rejuvenation of the Jewish race.‡ Of course,
metaphors are not precise, but they do provide and approximate
conception of something which goes beyond the commonplace. In
any case, this people is an uncommon phenomenon. Originating in
gray antiquity, it still manifests youthful vigor; having experienced
numerous transformations, it has yet remained true to itself.

THE DIASPORA / SUFFERING & SPIRIT

This is the eighteen-hundred-year era of the Diaspora,§ of
unprecedented suffering, of uninterrupted martyrdom without
parallel in world history. But it is also a period of spiritual alertness,
of restless mental activity, of indefatigable inquiry. In order to
sketch a clear and appropriate picture of this period, one would
have to draw a two-sided image. One aspect would show humbled
Judah with the wanderer's staff in his hand, the pilgrim's bundle on
his back, his features grave, his glance turned heavenward; he is
surrounded by the walls of a dungeon, the implements of
martyrdom, and the red-hot branding iron. The other aspect is of
the same figure, bearing the earnestness of the thinker upon his
luminous brow, the mien of a scholar in the radiant features of his
face; he is in a study filled with a huge library in all the languages of
mankind and dealing with all branches of divine and human
knowledge. The external history of this era is a *Leidensgeschichte*, a
history of suffering to a degree and over a length of time such as no

*Ezekiel 16:4–14.
†Jeremiah 31:14–16.
‡Graetz does not tell us what the metaphor is or who suggested it.
§ The period from the destruction of the Jewish state in 70 C.E. down to 1850.

other people has experienced. Its inner history is a comprehensive *Literaturgeschichte*, a literary history of religious knowledge, which yet remains open to all the currents of science, absorbing and assimilating them; once again, a history unique to this one people. *Inquiring* and *wandering, thinking* and *enduring, studying* and *suffering*—these fill the long stretch of this era. Three times during this period world history changed its garb. Decrepit Rome languished and sank into the grave. Out of its decay the chrysalis of the European and Asiatic peoples took shape; these peoples in turn developed into the glistening, butterfly-like figures of Christian and Islamic knighthood; and, finally, from their incinerated castles arose the phoenix of civilized international relations.

World history was transformed three times, but the Jews remained the same; at most they merely altered their external appearance. Likewise the spiritual content of world history was transformed three times. From a developed but hollow state of civilization mankind submerged into barbarism and dismal ignorance, only to raise itself again from its ignorance into the bright spheres of a higher civilization. The spiritual content of Judaism remained the same; it only steeped itself in the substance and form of new ideas. While the Judaism of this era includes the most celebrated *martyrs,* compared to whom the persecuted sufferers of other nations and religions may almost be considered fortunate, it also produced towering thinkers who did not remain merely the pride of *Judaism* alone. There is likely no science, no art, no direction of the spirit in which Jews have not shared, in which they have not demonstrated equivalent ability. *Thinking* became as characteristic a feature of the Jews as did *suffering.*

On account of the largely forced, rarely voluntary, migrations of the Jews, the Jewish history of this era encompasses the entire inhabited earth: it stretches into the snowy regions of the north and into the blazing sun of the south; it traverses all oceans and establishes itself in the most remote corners of the world. As soon as a new part of the world is invaded by a new people, scattered Jews immediately appear, defying every climate and every hardship. If a new area of the world is discovered, Jewish communities are soon formed and grouped together here and there following an inner drive for crystallization which operates without worldly aid or external compulsion. Dispersed to all regions of the earth, the Jews form a huge circle that expands out of sight. Its periphery coincides with the ends of the inhabited world; at its center is the Temple, still sacred even in ruins. These migrations brought the Jewish people new experiences; homeless, they exercised and sharpened their gaze. Thus even the plenitude of their suffering contributed to broadening the horizons of Jewish thinkers. The Jewish history of this era witnessed, was affected by, and to an extent participated in all the overwhelming events of world history from the time when the full terror of the barbarians exploded upon the overrefined Roman Empire until the spark of culture was struck anew from the hard anvil of barbarism. Every storm upon the sea of world history also had an effect on Judaism, shaking it to its foundations without shattering it. The Jewish history of eighteen centuries presents a microcosm of world history even as the Jewish people has become a universal people; being nowhere at home, it is at home everywhere.

What prevented this ever-wandering people, these truly eternal Jews, from degenerating into brutish vagrants or a vagabond horde of gypsies? The answer is self-evident. During its desolate history of eighteen hundred years the Jewish people carried with it the Ark of the Covenant which placed an ideal striving in its heart and even transfigured the badge of shame on its garment with an apostolic radiance. The proscribed, outlawed Jew, pursued over the entire earth, felt an exalted, noble pride in bearing, and in suffering for, a doctrine which reflected eternity and by which the nations would eventually be educated to the knowledge of God and to morality, a doctrine from which the salvation and redemption of the world would go forth. The lofty consciousness of his glorious apostolic task kept the sufferer erect, even transformed his sufferings into an aspect of his exalted mission. Such a people for whom the present meant nothing while the future meant everything, which seemed to exist by virtue of its hope, is for that very reason as eternal as hope itself. The Law and the messianic hope were two protecting and consoling angels at the side of the humbled Jews, saving them from despair, from stupefaction, and loss of identity. The Law for the present, the messianic hope for the future, both mediated by scholarship and the effusions of poetic art—these poured balm on the grieved hearts of the unfortunate people. Since for this subjugated nation the world at large was reduced to a gloomy, filthy dungeon in which it was unable to satisfy its urge to act, the more talented among its members retreated to the inner world of ideas which expanded proportionately as the restraints of the outside world were drawn more narrowly around its mangled body. Thus appeared a doubtless rare phenomenon: the persecuted proved more than a match for his oppressor, the tormented almost pitied his tormentor, the prisoner felt freer than his jailer.

Jewish literature reflects this serious intellectual life and was bound to become the richer as it not only served the needs of the highly talented, but acted as a salve for the entire suffering people. As the Jewish people made itself at home all over the inhabitable earth, Jewish literature became truly a world literature. It makes up the kernel of Jewish history which the history of suffering has surrounded with a bitter husk. The entire people has deposited its treasure of ideas and its inner being in this immense literature. The teachings of Judaism are contained in it, refined, glorified, visible to the weakest eye. Only someone accustomed to reducing a lofty, imposing wonder of the world to the category of an everyday phenomenon will regard it as of little account. The consecutive data and events of Jewish history must be connected with the thread of this literature. It provides the pragmatic continuity and therefore must not be treated incidentally, as a mere appendix to the main history. The appearance of a new significant book is not just an interesting detail, but within its circle becomes a *deed* which has consequential ramifications. Jewish literature was born in pain and spasms of death; it is as manifold as the countries of its origin, variegated as the dress of the nations among whom it blossomed, rich and polymorphic as the recollection of its millennial experiences; it bears the unmistakable traces of a *single* progenitor, of Judaism. A single trait is imprinted upon all its configurations, every surface and edge reflecting the ideal whose rays they capture. Jewish literature thus constitutes the basic possession of this era which with regard to its active aspect can therefore justly be termed the *theoretical-religious* era. It stands in contrast to the era after the first exile, which had a *political-religious* character, and to the pre-exilic era, which was predominantly *political.*

Manifold and encompassing as this literature is, it is nonetheless possible to distinguish three main tendencies, three individual currents which, although they absorb inflows from other sources, are thereby only insignificantly diverted from their course. Each of these principal tendencies may be regarded as the *primary discipline* to which the remainder are related in *secondary* fashion. The predominant activities of this long era were: *study of the Talmud,* philosophical exegesis, and the independent *philosophy* of modern times. The era falls into three periods: the *Talmudic* the *rabbinical-philosophical,* and the *critical-philosophical . . . .*

1. The *Talmudic period* runs from the founding of the Sanhedrin in Yavneh to the decline of the Exilarchate* and the Talmudic academies of Babylonia (70–1040).
2. The *rabbinical-philosophical period* fills the span from the firm establishment of the rabbinical and philosophical schools in Spain, France, and Germany until their decline brought about by the school of Mendelssohn† (1040–1760).
3. The *philosophical-critical period* extends from the rise of the Mendelssohn school to most recent times (1760–1850).

THE TALMUDIC PERIOD

During this period of nearly a thousand years‡ Jewish history is primarily and almost exclusively concerned with the theoretical consolidation of the religious life, with the establishment of the doctrines received as tradition in all their ramifications and applications. It is true that at the beginning of this period there is a clear effort to make another attempt at restoring the lost political life. This effort produces clashes, revolts, wars, and new defeats. But soon the political movement recedes, leaving the entire field to purely spiritual activity. Here begins the assiduous task of gathering the tradition, sifting it, interpreting and applying it, ordering the recently accumulated interpretations and applications and making them into a whole, and finally of utilizing portions of this immense accumulation of material in daily life. This gigantic task of creating the Talmud required the full spiritual powers of more than twenty generations: teachers and students, officials and artisans, Palestinians as well as foreign Jews, all willing to sacrifice the physical pleasures of life for their work. It cannot be regarded as an intellectual game of leisured scholars or as the forging of a coercive instrument by power-hungry priests. Rather, it is the genuine national creation of spiritual energy in which, as in the construction of a national language, not simply a few individuals but the entire

*The nonrabbinical authority in the Jewish community of Babylonia.

†Moses Mendelssohn (1729–1786), the father of the movement for Jewish cultural integration in German society.

‡From 70 C.E. to 1040.

people take part. This is indicated, as well, by the new direction taken by the course of development of Jewish history, namely the coming to the fore of reflective activity and the deeper absorption in inquiry. *Transmission, explanation, comparison* and *distinction* —theoretical preoccupations—from here on provide the main direction for a millennium and nothing can alter or disturb the course that is set.

Momentarily suppressed, this drive appeared the more forcefully the greater the pressure that was applied from without. But the Talmudic activity in its first stage was so dominant and exclusive that no branch of knowledge, not even such as was suited to support it, could find any room alongside. Even exegesis, the proper understanding of the holy text and the awareness of formal grammar, was only superficially touched upon. A Jewish philosophy, a free inquiry into the essence of Judaism and into the eternally true and eternally valid in the Law, could not appear at a time when it was necessary to huddle together after the shipwreck and find protection against new storms; this although the Alexandrians, with Philo at their head, did lay several foundation stones for such a venture. In order to draw exegesis, Hebrew linguistics, and philosophy into the circle of those subjects deemed worthy of study, a stimulus from a new element, inimical to the Talmudic tendency, was required. Karaism* was this new element of ferment which brought forth new forms and attitudes. The first part of this era may therefore rightly be called Talmudic since the principal direction of Jewish history relates to the elaboration of the Talmudic teaching and of the Talmud as the basic work. Only at the end of this period, stirred and accelerated by the Karaite split, was a sense also awakened for auxiliary disciplines, for exegesis, grammar, and even for the development of Jewish philosophy—though without the prerequisites of genuine maturity. Inner and outer disturbances meanwhile appeared and guided the stream of Jewish history into another channel; externally and internally, Jewish history changed its form. Judea and Babylonia, the cities on the Jordan and the Euphrates, until now the only arena of Jewish history, lose their significance. Jewish spiritual activity wanders from the distant East to the distant West, from Babylonia to Spain, where it buds anew and brings forth new fruits. The first period of the era of the dispersion (Diaspora) with regard to content is *Talmudic*, while geographically it is *Judeo-Babylonian*.

*The Jewish sect rejecting rabbinic authority which arose in the eighth century.

The Talmudic period consists of 970 years and is divisible into four smaller segments or epochs:

1. The *Tannaitic epoch,* from the collapse of the state and the introduction of the Sanhedrin in Yavneh to the conclusion of the Mishnah (70–200).
2. The *Amoraic epoch,* from the conclusion of the Mishnah and the establishment of the Amoraic academies in Babylonia to the completion of the entire Talmud (200–500).
3. The *Savoraic epoch,* from the completion of the Talmud to the development of the Gaonate under the rule of the Arabs (500–650).
4. The *Geonic epoch,* from the beginning of the Gaonate to its decline (650–1040).

BODY AND SOUL

The Jewish nation had expired upon the bloody, smoking ruins of Jerusalem and Betar;* the community was formed from the dispersed remnants, held together and consolidated by insightful, dedicated leaders. The Jewish state collapsed under the repeated blows of the Roman legions; new centers of the Jewish Diaspora were established in the academies of Yavneh, Usha, and Sepphoris, and later by the shores of the beautiful Sea of Galilee. When victorious Christianity, armed with the Roman fasces, destroyed the last focal point in the land of Judea and abolished the Patriarchate which stood at its apex, new centers arose on the shores of the Euphrates, in the form of the academies at Nehardea, Sura, and Pumbedita. When the fanaticism of the magi† incited the otherwise tolerant Sassanian kings of Persia against the Jews and Judaism, a new period of martyrdom began. The power of resistance seemed broken, the communities dissolved into atomized units without focus, the demise of Jewish teaching was at hand. How could Jewish history still carry on through the long centuries? Is it, ever since the completion of the Talmud, a mere conglomeration of chance events, of persecutions and martyrologies? Or did it take on the

*Bar Kokhba's last stronghold, which fell to the Romans in 135 C.E.

† Zoroastrian priests.

character of a dry literary history, in which books and authors play the leading role? Does the sequence of post-Talmudic history lack all cohesion and focus? Does it take a unified, concentric course, or does it break up into more or less uninteresting individual units? Is it ruled by the chaos of chance or by the ordering hand of an inner law?

The historian and the reader, concerned with the answer to this question must always remember one thing when they examine the post-Talmudic era: Jewish history, like the Israelite history of the pre-exilic period, and like the Judean history of the post-exilic period, consists of *two basic factors*. On the one hand, there is the seemingly immortal Jewish *race* [*Stamm*] as the body, on the other, the seemingly no less eternal *teaching of Judaism* as the *soul*. The thread of history during the Diaspora era is woven from the reciprocal influence of the people's body and soul. The *corporal aspect* of post-Talmudic history consists of numerous components. They include: the lot of the Jews under the various nations to which the persecutor's hand drove them and the wanderer's foot led them; the manner and way in which individuals formed themselves into communities, like atoms governed by a force driving them to crystallization; how these communities, often despite great distances, sought and found a connection with the collectivity or with the kernel of the race; and this center itself—the circumstances under which it came into being, the nature of its attractive power, how it was transferred now to here, now to there, how it sometimes was represented by a community, sometimes by an individual.

The other aspect of the Diaspora era of Jewish history, its *spiritual side*, is made up of the formation and development of Judaism, shaped by the Bible and Talmud, gradually working its way upward out of the atmosphere of literalism and fixed statute to the light of ideas and of self-consciousness; the impediments and the support which it found through its close contact with the vicissitudes of world history; the scientific purification which it experienced as a result of clashes with the sects and parties that emerged from its midst; the science and poetry which it produced and which, in turn, exercised a formative and ennobling influence on it; and the personalities, who as the bearers, leaders, and living embodiments of its essence, traced new directions and goals for it. That leaves the organic collaboration of these two factors: how at times the body of the people was pulled down to earth by the leaden weight of the hostile environment, drawing its soul down with it into depth and darkness; and how this soul, when aware of its Divine origin, freed itself of the oppression and took its flight toward heaven, making the body, too, catapult upward—all this a pragmatic treatment of history must demonstrate.

The history of the post-Talmudic era, therefore, still possesses a *national character*. It is by no means the mere history of a religion or of a church. Its object is not simply the course of development of a doctrine, but also that of an independent people, which, though it possesses no soil, fatherland, geographical boundaries, or state organism, replaced these concrete conditions with spiritual powers. Though scattered over the civilized portions of the earth and attached to the land of their hosts, the members of the Jewish race did not cease to feel themselves a single people in their religious conviction, historical memory, customs, and hopes. As the history of an *ethnic group* [*Volksstamm*], therefore, Jewish history is far removed from being a mere history *of literature* or *of scholars* which it is branded by those given to ignorance and partiality. Rather, the literature and religious development, just like the highly tragic martyrdom which this race, or this fellowship, has had to record, are only individual elements in the course of its history and do not constitute its essence.

Yet this history is unique, just as the people which experiences it is unique and has no analogue in world history. In the same way as a mighty current, which flows through the midst of huge stretches of water, retains its own course and does not change its color, so, too, the Jewish race and the Jewish history of the Diaspora have retained their own character in the midst of the mighty flow of the nations, and have not been essentially changed. The Jewish race felt, thought, spoke, and sang in all the tongues of the nations which generously or grudgingly offered its hospitality; but it did not forget its own language; it loved, enriched, and ennobled it in relation to the cultural levels which the people attained together with the rest of mankind. It took part to a greater or lesser extent in the spiritual labors of the nations among which it settled, without on that account ceasing to develop its own literature and make it into a new means of furthering the cohesion of its scattered members.

The history of this race, of course, records no victories with bloody trophies, no battles won or lost upon corpse-laden fields of combat, no conquest of large territories or enslavement of subject peoples, but so much the more does it record victories and achievements of the spirit. While swords clattered outside, while the nations waged devastating war against each other, aroused, or at least supported by religious teachings, the House of Jacob was concerned only with maintaining the light of the spirit; it nurtured the lamp with the oil of science and poetry to make it burn more brightly, and to the best of its ability drove away the ghosts of darkness that had been conjured up by ignorance and superstition. In the midst of a world of crude morality and barbarism it cultivated noble religious expression, pure morality, and the sanctity of life. It even contributed elements to a new form of religion for which the inhabitants of three continents soon raved enthusiastically; and thereby it laid the first foundation of a highly consequential movement in world history which produced new configurations and forms of culture. A base way of thinking may find such laurels, gained without blood or clamor, to be contemptible; higher natures will not withhold their admiration.

History has yet to duplicate the example of a people which, having laid weapons aside, devoted itself entirely to the peaceful pursuit of learning and art; a people which having freed itself of the bonds of narrow self-interest, let its ideas soar heavenward in order to comprehend its own nature as well as its mysterious connection with the universe and with God. Now indeed, Jewish history in the so-called Middle Ages presents such an example in the form of the Jewish race. Reduced to servitude a thousand times, this race has on the whole known how to preserve its spiritual freedom; reviled and humbled, it did not degenerate into a horde of gypsies or lose its sense of the lofty and sacred; to the contrary, exiled and homeless it created for itself a spiritual fatherland. The Jewish history of the post-Talmudic period illustrates all of this unmistakably. It knows no Middle Ages in the odious sense of the term, laden with the features of intellectual torpor, coarse vulgarity, and religious delusion. Instead, during this very period, in these repulsive surroundings, it produced the most brilliant figures, imbued with intellectual greatness, moral idealism, and purity of faith. If a religion were to be judged by the conduct of its principal representatives, then Judaism, as it appears from the tenth to the thirteenth century would receive the palm. To the extent that moral greatness and the quest for truth are prized, many of the Geonim of Babylonia and most of the Rabbis of Spain and France can be presented as examples for every time and place of the highest degree of human perfection. The Rabbis of this epoch were no one-sided, obtuse Talmudists, but genuine personalities possessing a lofty nobility of spirit, cultivators of the sciences, often physicians, and frequently counselors and guides to princes. Of course this long period was not free of mistakes and weaknesses, either of leaders or of communities—and an impartial history may not pass over them in silence—but as against the great virtues they recede to the point of imperceptibility.

The Diaspora history of the Jews may best be characterized as predominantly a history of culture, borne not by individual outstanding figures, but by an entire people. Spiritual movements, which at some point emerged from its midst, stirred the interest of the whole Jewish race in the most remote communities. The liturgical poems which Jewish singers made to resound in Judea or Babylonia, on the Rhine or the Guadalquivir* soon became, without official compulsion and without hierarchical regulations or prescriptions, the common possession of nearly all communities and integral parts of the worship service. Writings of significant content, produced by gifted personalities, were copied in all lands of the Jewish Diaspora—read, studied, and made a part of life. When at some distant time the visions of the Jewish prophets will be fulfilled and no nation will make war against another, when the olive branch, not the laurel, will adorn the forehead of great men, and the achievement of noble spirits will find entry in huts and palaces, then the history of the nations will possess the same character as does the history of the Jews; its pages will not be covered with acts of war and victory gained by the wiles of diplomacy, but with the advances of culture and their realization in life.

One should not let oneself be deceived by the seeming lack of cohesion and unity displayed by post-Talmudic Jewish history when it is viewed from the outside, making the Jewish race appear to fall into as many entities as there were communities. I say this impression should not deceive one into believing that it possesses no ordered forward progress, no centric momentum, It has, on the contrary, established quite definite and prominent centers from which historical life flowed out to the widely extended periphery. "Though the members of the House of Israel be driven to all parts of the world, from north to south and south to north, from east to west and west to east, they are nevertheless always at the center," notes an ancient Jewish preacher.† The scepter had indeed departed from Judah, but not the influence of the Law upon its members. And the

*River in southern Spain.
†Midrash *Tanna de-Vei Eliyahu* 5.

remarkable thing is that the interpreters of the Law, who formed the focal point and point of connection of the communities, did not need to enforce this unity with criminal penalties or stripes. Instead, the groups more or less flew toward the point of unity, allowing it to provide them with a defined scope of action.

At first it was Jewish Babylonia, the successor of Judea, that served as the unifying focal point for the extensive Jewish Diaspora when it became the seat of the Gaonate. From the shores of the Oxus,* the Volga, the Danube, and the Rhine to the islands and surrounding shores of the Mediterranean, the eyes of the Jewish communities were turned to Babylonia, i.e., to the Gaonate that resided there. Not less than any king did the heads of the academies in Sura and Pumbedita enjoy obedience and love from millions, who were not their subjects but their brothers. The communities received from them not only religious and moral instruction, but also scientific and poetic stimulation. And even before the Geonic center was dissolved by disintegrative historical forces, in what one might call a wondrous way, a new focal point of more significant content and greater capacity took shape in Spain. Alongside it there gradually appeared another center, at first in Southern France and then in the Lotharingian lands,† the two related to each other as twin foci. Difficult trials, which emanated from different directions and afflicted the communities in the lands of Islam and Christianity, had almost ruptured the two centers of gravity and loosened the cohesion, when a highly gifted, powerful personality appeared and became the bearer of unity and the focal point. This individual, therefore, forms a watershed in Jewish history. The new turning point is represented by *Maimonides,* who concludes the period of high cultural achievement during the Diaspora era.

The period from the completion of the Talmud to the end of the Maimonidean age, or from the death of Ravina‡ to the death of Moses ben Maimon, falls into three epochs:

1. The transition from the Talmudic to the Geonic age, or the *Savoraic epoch* (500–640).
2. The *Geonic epoch* (640–1040).
3. The age of high cultural achievement, or the *scientific-rabbinic epoch* (1040–1204).

*River in central Asia; Amu Darya.

†Lands on the border of France and Germany; Lorraine.

‡Ravina II (d. 499), the last of the Talmudic rabbis.

The principal arena of history during this period is at first the Babylonian region which the Arabs call Iraq, then Southern Spain and Northern France.

DEBASEMENT AND DECADENCE

Despite its stateless existence and atomistic dispersion, the Jewish race had maintained an organic wholeness and unity; and during the three centuries from Saadiah,* the first of the medieval religious philosophers, to Maimonides, the great stimulator of ideas, it attained a high point of spiritual freedom as well as a scientific and poetic productivity which makes one forget that this phenomenon occurred in the Middle Ages. This period of rich spiritual harvest is followed by an ice-cold, ghastly winter. Internal and external events of a decidedly unpropitious nature work together to strip Jewish history of the greatness it had possessed hitherto, and to force upon its bearer, the Jewish people, the repulsive image of a serf. Having aspired to the heights of heaven, it sinks into the profoundest misery.

Can a man of our day fully comprehend the sufferings which this people endured from the time when the papacy and its deluded host of princes and peoples marked it with the badge of shame so that every sneering mouth might spit at it and every fist be clenched to strike it; a period which lasted down to the expulsion of the Jews from the Iberian peninsula and even thereafter, until the sun of national freedom arose for them as well? Take all of the misery which has been inflicted by temporal and spiritual despotisms assisted in their torments by individuals and by nations; measure, if you can, the streams of tears which men ever poured out over a marred existence, over crushed happiness, over dashed hopes; imagine the tortures which an overstrained fantasy depicted in thousands and thousands of legends of the saints as a horror to the souls of the believers—you will still not reach the full compass of the misery which the martyr-people experienced through several centuries, quietly, and with an attitude of imploring, patient

*Saadiah Gaon (882–942), greatest scholar and religious authority of the Geonic period.

endurance. Jews were attacked as if all the powers of the earth had conspired—and they had, in fact, conspired to that end—to eradicate them or to transform them into an animal-like horde. In addition to the wounds, the blows of the fist, the kicks, the pyres—there was derision. The same men who inflicted humiliation and death upon Israel, who dragged it through the mud, recognized its noble origin, extolled its past, placed its prophets and religious leaders alongside their "saints," sang its songs in their houses of worship, derived restoration and consolation from its teaching —but appropriated all of these glories as if they had always been their own. They tore the crown from the head of the Jewish people, put it on their own, and made themselves the inheritors of a still-living people. History must not pass over such scenes of misery in silence; to the contrary, it must conspicuously display them, not in order to sink a thorn into the breasts of the descendants of the persecuted victims and to awaken sentiments of revenge, but to arouse admiration for the great endurance of this people and to demonstrate, that like its ancestor Jacob, it fought with both gods and men, and prevailed.

Along with this debasement and subjugation came spiritual stagnation. The luxuriant leaves and blossoms of a glorious ascent of the spirit gradually fell to earth, exposing a coarse, brittle stump, entwined with the ugly threads of a hyperpiety robbed of spirit, a bewildering secret doctrine, and all manner of perversions. The gushing spring of wise ideas and deeply felt lyric gradually dried up, the gaily leaping heartbeat of an elevated disposition grew faint and weary, depression and dullness of spirit set in. Personalities of determinative and standard-setting significance and influence disappeared, as if the power of historical creativity had become exhausted after the greatness it brought forth during the centuries from Saadiah to Maimonides. The creative force making for new and original productions of the spirit was more and more replaced by a dominant drive to preserve and cultivate what was given. Ideas decreased in number and the thinkers who appeared from time to time during the post-Maimonidean period seldom embarked upon an original path, preferring to cling to the given or else going off in wrong directions. Scientific endeavor did for a long time retain its devotees and cultivators among the Jews, but it was gradually confined to pedestrian disciplines. The number of translations and commentaries, added to the literature already at hand, exceeded by far the number of independent works. The disgrace imposed from without was matched by decay from within.

Yet the course of history during the period from the death of Maimonides to the rejuvenation of the Jewish race, monotonous as it is, nevertheless discloses a kind of progress. The external history begins with the *systematic* debasement of the Jews, with the consistent pursuit of their exclusion from all honorable careers and from Christian society. The degradation increases to the point of a general slaughter of the Jews following the Black Death.* To the old lies a new one is added—that of poisoning the wells and the air—and it serves to make the Jews an object of general aversion. Meanwhile, the final act of this horror play is being prepared: the expulsion of the Jews from the Iberian peninsula, their third fatherland after Judea and Babylonia.

The inner stagnation, too, comes in stages. It begins with the fight over literalism of belief versus the philosophical elucidation of Judaism; it strides on until it reaches the proscription of every form of secular learning by a mindless orthodoxy and Kabbalistic initiates; and it reaches its climax in the belief that only ignorance assures salvation. Thus creative ideas, which originated in Judaism or were carefully nurtured by it, are banned. Free thinkers, such as Gersonides,† Narboni,‡ Hasdai Crescas,§ and Elijah Delmedigo, ‖ become ever rarer and are suspected of heresy. Even the likes of Albo¶ and Abrabanel,** who tend to superficiality, and who attach themselves to the given in all of its degeneration and defend it, are no longer favored. The words of the Bible lose their ability to refresh and to elevate because deeply rooted perversity of mind makes them reflect and sanction not the truth, but error. Had not the Talmud been for Jews east and west, north and south, the holy banner around which all could rally, they would have fallen victim to the

*The great plague which devastated Europe in the middle of the fourteenth century.

†Levi ben Gershom (1288–1344), philosopher of broad intellectual interests living in southern France.

‡Moses ben Joshua of Narbonne (d. 1362) wrote a commentary on Maimonides' philosophical work.

§Hasdai Crescas (d. c. 1412), Spanish philosopher and critic of Aristotle.

‖Elijah Delmedigo (c. 1460–1497), philosopher and Talmudist during the Italian Renaissance.

¶Joseph Albo (fifteenth century), Spanish philosopher and author of the systematic but unoriginal *Book of Principles*.

**Isaac Abrabanel (1437–1508), philosopher and biblical interpreter who attacked some of Maimonides' theories and believed strongly in the imminent advent of the Messiah.

fate that their enemies ordained for them; the Talmud protected them from spiritual dullness and moral depravity.

This period of Jewish history, of regressive movement toward cultural perversion and of gradual decay, is divisible into three epochs:

1. From the death of Maimonides to the beginning of the systematic degradation of the Jews in Spain (1205–1370).
2. From this time to the expulsion of the Jews from the Iberian peninsula along with its aftereffects (1370–1496).
3. From this time to Mendelssohn, or to the beginning of the emancipation and rejuvenation of the Jews (1496–1780).

SIMON DUBNOW

INTRODUCTION TO SIMON DUBNOW

IN NINTEENTH-CENTURY Germany, where modern Jewish historiography began, Jewish identity was defined for the Jews in religious terms. Even German liberals would allow them to claim only a religious difference if they desired recognition as citizens of the state. No form of Jewishness which was national or secular could flourish in such an environment. Therefore, too, the ideas of Jewish history which developed tended to stress the religious element even when their subject was the Jewish people. In Eastern Europe, however, where Simon Dubnow (1860–1941) spent the first 62 years of his life, national differences could not be ignored among the diverse peoples living in the tsarist empire. Nor was religion, whether Christian or Jewish, sufficiently flexible to prevent the frequent defections of intellectuals to various atheist or agnostic ideologies. Dubnow's national and secular historiography reflects this very different atmosphere.

Dubnow's education, like that of so many of his contemporaries, began with the traditional Jewish subjects and gradually, by his own efforts, widened to include secular disciplines. His break with orthodoxy came when he was still quite young—and it proved permanent. Attracted to the Russian positivist thinkers and, above all, to the writings of the English utilitarian John Stuart Mill, he became a confirmed nonbeliever and a universalist. For a time he ceased entirely to identify with the Jewish community, returning only after he came to feel that his cosmopolitanism had set him adrift, that he was both alienated from his Jewish origins and rejected by the Russian intellectual elite. He sought a new mooring, which he found first in his study of Jewish history: "The study of the Jewish past," he wrote, "binds me to something eternal." He also became a Jewish nationalist and an active advocate of his own particular version of it, "autonomism," an ideology which claimed that productive Jewish national life was possible in the Diaspora if the Jewish people were given cultural autonomy within the existing states. The large mass of Jews within the Russian empire seemed to possess great potential for such a creative and rounded Jewish existence.

Dubnow devoted much of his scholarly work to the history of the Jews in Eastern Europe. He wrote numerous articles on the subject in Russian; a three-volume History of the Jews in Russia and Poland, which appeared in English (1916–20); and later an important Hebrew history of Hasidism (1931–32)—a subject to which Graetz gave only abbreviated and disdainful treatment. His magnum opus, however, was his massive ten-volume World History of the Jewish People, written in Russian during the 1920's, translated into various languages, including, most recently, English.

In 1893, Dubnow published an essay expressing his conception of Jewish history as he had formulated it at that stage in his life. It was originally intended as the introduction to an abridged Russian edition of Graetz's History of the Jews, which did not see print. The influence of Graetz's views is most apparent in this essay, from which three sections are presented below. Here one may note especially a reflection of Dubnow's Diaspora nationalism in his definition of the Jewish people as "the most historical" of all peoples because of the length of its existence, because of its involvement in ancient and modern civilizations, and because—lacking a land—its national consciousness has depended upon maintaining an awareness of its history. One should note, too, Dubnow's belief in the inspirational value of studying the Jewish past and his conviction, reminiscent of Krochmal as well as of Graetz, that the spirituality of the Jewish nation renders it immortal.

Thirty years later Dubnow's conception of Jewish history had changed radically. His new views, formulated in the Introduction to his World History of the Jewish People and published in 1925, show how completely Dubnow was finally able to shake off Graetz's influence. This Introduction ("The Sociological View of Jewish History"), here presented almost in its entirety, is noteworthy especially for the new scheme of periodization which rejects the outline established by Graetz. The reader should note, too, Dubnow's plan for organizing his material, his insistence upon the scientific character of his methodology, and his admission that he will regard positively whatever has strengthened the solidarity of the nation, and evaluate negatively those forces which have served to weaken it.

The Range of Jewish History

To make clear the range of Jewish history, it is necessary to set down a few general, elementary definitions by way of introduction.

It has long been recognized that a fundamental difference exists between historical and unhistorical peoples, a difference growing out of the fact of the natural inequality among the various elements composing the human race. Unhistorical is the attribute applied to peoples that have not yet broken away, or have not departed very far, from the state of primitive savagery, as, for instance, the barbarous races of Asia and Africa who were the prehistoric ancestors of the Europeans, or the obscure, untutored tribes of the present like the Tatars and the Kirghiz. Unhistorical peoples, then, are ethnic groups of all sorts that are bereft of a distinctive, spiritual individuality, and have failed to display a normal, independent capacity for culture. The term historical, on the other hand, is applied to nations that have had a conscious, purposeful history of appreciable duration; that have progressed, stage by stage, in their growth and in the improvement of their mode and their views of life; that have demonstrated mental productivity of some sort, and have elaborated principles of civilization and social life more or less rational; nations, in short, representing not only zoologic, but also spiritual types.

Chronologically considered, these latter nations, of a higher type, are usually divided into three groups: (1) the most ancient civilized peoples of the Orient, such as the Chinese, the Hindus, the Egyptians, the Chaldeans; (2) the ancient or classic peoples of the Occident, the Greeks and the Romans; and (3) the modern peoples, the civilized nations of Europe and America of the present day. The most ancient peoples of the Orient, standing "at the threshold of history," were the first heralds of a religious consciousness and of moral principles. In hoary antiquity, when most of the representatives of the human kind were nothing more than a peculiar variety of the class Mammalia, the peoples called the most ancient brought forth recognized forms of social life and a variety of theories of living of fairly far-reaching effect. All these culture bearers of the Orient soon disappeared from the surface of history. Some (the Chaldeans, Phoenicians, and Egyptians) were washed away by the flood of time, and their remnants were absorbed by younger and more vigorous peoples. Others (the Hindus and Persians) relapsed into a semibarbarous state; and a third class (the Chinese) were arrested in their growth, and remained fixed in immobility. The best that the antique Orient had to bequeath in the way of spiritual possessions fell to the share of the classic nations of the West, the Greeks and the Romans. They greatly increased the heritage by their own spiritual achievements, and so produced a much more complex and diversified civilization which has served as the substratum for the further development of the better part of mankind. Even the classic nations had to step aside as soon as their historical mission was fulfilled. They left the field free for younger nations, with greater capability of living, which at that time had barely worked their way up to the beginnings of a civilization. One after the other, during the first two centuries of the Christian era, the members of this European family of nations appeared in the arena of history. They form the kernel of the civilized part of mankind at the present day.

Now, if we examine this accepted classification with a view to finding the place belonging to the Jewish people in the chronological series, we meet with embarrassing difficulties, and finally arrive at the conclusion that its history cannot be accommodated within the compass of the classification. Into which of the three historical groups mentioned could the Jewish people be put? Are we to call it one of the most ancient, one of the ancient, or one of the modern nations? It is evident that it may lay claim to the first description, as well as to the second and the last. In company with the most ancient nations of the Orient, the Jewish people stood at the threshold of history. It was the contemporary of the earliest civilized nations, the Egyptians and the Chaldeans. In those remote days it created and spread a religious world-idea underlying an exalted social and moral system surpassing everything produced in this sphere by its Oriental contemporaries. Again, with the classical Greeks and Romans, it forms the celebrated historical triad universally recognized as the source of all great systems of civilization. Finally, in fellowship with the nations of today, it leads a historical life, striding onward in the path of progress without stay or interruption. Deprived of political independence, it nevertheless continues to fill a place in the world of thought as a distinctly marked spiritual individuality, as one of the most active and intelligent forces. How, then, are we to denominate this omnipresent people, which, from the first moment of its historical existence up to our days, a period of thirty-five hundred years, has been developing continuously? In view of this Methuselah among the nations, whose life is co-extensive with the whole of history, how are we to dispose of the inevitable barriers between the most ancient and the ancient, between the ancient and the modern nations—the fateful barriers which form the milestones on the path of the historical peoples, and which the Jewish people has more than once overstepped?

A definition of the Jewish people must needs correspond to the aggregate of the concepts expressed by the three group-names, most ancient, ancient, and modern. The only description applicable to it is "the historical nation of all times," a description bringing into relief the contrast between it and all other nations of modern and ancient times, whose historical existence either came to an end in days long past, or began at a date comparatively recent. And granted that there are historical and unhistorical peoples, then it is beyond dispute that the Jewish people deserves to be called the most historical, *historicissimus*. If the history of the world be conceived as a circle, then Jewish history occupies the position of the diameter, the line passing through its center, and this history of every other nation is represented by a chord marking off a smaller segment of the circle. The history of the Jewish people is like an axis crossing the history of mankind from one of its poles to the other. As an unbroken thread it runs through the ancient civilization of Egypt and Mesopotamia, down to the present-day culture of France and Germany. Its divisions are measured by thousands of years.

Jewish history, then, in its range, or, better, in its duration, presents a unique phenomenon. It consists of the longest series of events ever recorded in the annals of a single people. To sum up its peculiarity briefly, it embraces a period of thirty-five hundred years, and in all this vast extent it suffers no interruption. At every point it is alive, full of sterling content.

The Significance of Jewish History

The significance of Jewish history is twofold. It is at once national and universal. At present the fulcrum of Jewish national being lies in the historical consciousness. In the days of antiquity, the Jews were welded into a single united nation by the triple agencies of state, race, and religion, the complete array of material and spiritual forces directed to one point. Later, in the period of homelessness and dispersion, it was chiefly religious consciousness that cemented Jewry into a whole, and replaced the severed political bond as well as the dulled racial instinct, which is bound to go on losing in keenness in proportion to the degree of removal from primitive conditions and native soil. In our days, when the liberal movements leavening the whole of mankind, if they have not completely shattered the religious consciousness, have at least, in an important section of Jewry, effected a change in its form; when abrupt differences of opinion with regard to questions of faith and cult are asserting their presence; when traditional Judaism developed in historical sequence is proving powerless to hold together the diverse factors of the national organism—in these days the keystone of national unity seems to be the historical consciousness. Composed alike of physical, intellectual, and moral elements, of habits and views, of emotions and impressions nursed into being and perfection by the hereditary instinct active for thousands of years, this historical consciousness is a remarkably puzzling and complex psychic phenomenon. By our common memory of a great, stirring past and heroic deeds on the battlefields of the spirit, by the exalted historical mission allotted to us, by our thorn-strewn pilgrim's path, our martyrdom assumed for the sake of our principles, by such moral ties, we Jews, whether consciously or unconsciously, are bound fast to one another. As Renan* well says: "Common sorrow unites men more closely than common joy." A long chain of historical traditions is cast about us all like a strong ring. Our wonderful, unparalleled past attracts us with magnetic power. In the course of centuries, as generation followed generation, similarity of historical fortunes produced a mass of similar impressions which have crystallized, and have thrown off the deposit that may be called the Jewish national soul. This is the soil in which, deep down, lies imbedded, as an unconscious element, the Jewish national *feeling,* and as a conscious element, the Jewish national *idea.*

It follows that the Jewish national idea and the national feeling connected with it have their origin primarily in the historical consciousness, in a certain complex of ideas and psychic

*Ernest Renan (1823–1892), French historian, Semitic linguist, and philosopher.

predispositions. These ideas and predispositions, the deposit left by the aggregate of historical impressions, are of necessity the common property of the whole nation, and they can be developed and quickened to a considerable degree by a renewal of the impressions through the study of history. Upon the knowledge of history, then, depends the strength of the national consciousness.

But over and above its national significance, Jewish history, we repeat, possesses universal significance. Let us, in the first place, examine its value for science and philosophy. Inasmuch as it is preeminently a chronicle of ideas and spiritual movements, Jewish history affords the philosopher or psychologist material for observation of the most important and useful kind. The study of other, mostly dull chapters of universal history has led to the fixing of psychological or sociological theses, to the working out of comprehensive philosophical systems, to the determination of general laws. Surely it follows, without farfetched proof, that in some respects the chapter dealing with Jewish history must supply material of the most original character for such theses and philosophies. If it is true that Jewish history is distinguished by sharply marked and peculiar features, and refuses to accommodate itself to conventional forms, then its content must have an original contribution to make to philosophy. It does not admit of a doubt that the study of Jewish history would yield new propositions appertaining to the philosophy of history and the psychology of nations, hitherto overlooked by inquirers occupied with the other divisions of universal history. Inductive logic lays down a rule for ascertaining the law of a phenomenon produced by two or more contributory causes. By means of what might be called a laboratory experiment, the several causes must be disengaged from one another, and the effect of each observed by itself. Thus it becomes possible to arrive with mathematical precision at the share of each cause in the result achieved by several cooperating causes. This method of difference, as it is called, is available, however, only for a limited number of phenomena, only for phenomena in the department of the natural sciences. It is in the nature of the case that mental and spiritual phenomena, though they may be observed, cannot be artificially reproduced. Now, in one respect, Jewish history affords the advantages of an arranged experiment. The historical life of ordinary nations, such nations as are endowed with territory and are organized into a state, is a complete intermingling of the political with the spiritual element. Totally ignorant as we are of the development either would have assumed had it been dissevered from the other, the laws governing each of the elements singly can be discovered only approximately. Jewish history, in which the two elements have for many centuries been completely disentangled from each other, presents a natural experiment, with the advantage of artificial exclusions, rendering possible the determination of the laws of spiritual phenomena with far greater scientific exactitude than the laws of phenomena that result from several similar causes.

Besides this high value for the purposes of science, this fruitful suggestiveness for philosophic thought, Jewish history, as compared with the history of other nations, enjoys another distinction in its capacity to exercise an ennobling influence upon the heart. Nothing so exalts and refines human nature as the contemplation of moral steadfastness, the history of the trials of a martyr who has fought and suffered for his convictions. At bottom, the second half of Jewish history is nothing but this. The effective educational worth of the biblical part of Jewish history is disputed by none. It is called sacred history, and he who acquires a knowledge of it is thought to advance the salvation of his soul. Only a very few, however, recognize the profound, moral content of the second half of Jewish history, the history of the Diaspora. Yet, by reason of its exceptional qualities and intensely tragic circumstances, it is beyond all others calculated to yield edification to a notable degree. The Jewish people is deserving of attention not only in the time when it displayed its power and enjoyed its independence, but as well in the period of its weakness and oppression, during which it was compelled to purchase spiritual development by constant sacrifice of self. A thinker crowned with thorns demands no less veneration than a thinker with the laurel wreath upon his brow. The flame issuing from the funeral pile on which martyrs die a heroic death for their ideas is, in its way, as awe-inspiring as the flame from Sinai's height. With equal force, though by different methods, both touch the heart, and arouse moral sentiment. Biblical Israel, the celebrated, medieval Judah, the despised—it is one and the same people, judged variously in the various phases of its historical life. If Israel bestowed upon mankind a religious theory of life, Judah gave it a thrilling example of tenacious vitality and power of resistance for the sake of conviction. This uninterrupted life of the spirit, this untiring aspiration for the higher and the better in the domain of religious thought, philosophy, and science, this moral intrepidity in night and storm and despite all the blows of fortune—is it not an imposing, soul-stirring spectacle? The inexpressible tragedy of the Jewish historical life is unfailing in its effect upon a susceptible heart. The wonderful exhibition of spirit triumphant, subduing the pangs of the flesh, must move every heart, and exercise uplifting influence upon the non-Jew no less than upon the Jew.

For non-Jews a knowledge of Jewish history may, under certain conditions, come to have another, humanitarian, significance. It is inconceivable that the Jewish people should be held in execration by those acquainted with the course of its history, with its tragic and heroic past. Indeed, so far as Jew-haters by profession are concerned, it is running a risk to recommend the study of Jewish history to them, without adding a word of caution. Its effect upon them might be disastrous. They might find themselves cured of their modern disease, and in the possession of ideas that would render worthless their whole stock in trade. Verily, he must have fallen to the zero-point of anti-Semitic callousness who is not thrilled through and through by the lofty fortitude, the saintlike humility, the trustful resignation to the will of God, the stoic firmness, laid bare by the study of Jewish history. The tribute of respect cannot be readily withheld from him to whom the words of the poet (Pushkin)* are applicable:

To die was not his hope; he fain
Would live to think and suffer pain.

When, in days to come, the curtain rises upon the touching tragedy of Jewish history, revealing it to the astonished eye of a modern generation, then, perhaps, hearts will be attuned to tenderness, and on the ruins of national hostility will be enthroned mutual love, growing out of mutual understanding and mutual esteem. And who can tell—perhaps Jewish history will have a not inconsiderable share in the spiritual change that is to annihilate national intolerance, the modern substitute for the religious bigotry of the Middle Ages. In this case, the future task of Jewish history will prove as sublime as was the mission of the Jewish people in the past. The latter consisted in the spread of the dogma of unity of creation; the former will contribute indirectly to the realization of the not yet accepted dogma of the unity of the human race.

*Alexander Pushkin, foremost Russian poet of the early nineteenth century.

The Teachings of Jewish History

Above all, Jewish history provides the student with the conviction that Jewry at all times, even in the period of political independence was preeminently a spiritual nation, and a spiritual nation it continues to be in our own days, too. Furthermore, it inspires him with the belief that Jewry, being a spiritual entity, cannot suffer annihilation: the body, the mold, may be destroyed; the spirit is immortal. Bereft of country and dispersed as it is, the Jewish nation lives, and will go on living, because a creative principle permeates it, a principle that is the root of its being and an indigenous product of its history. This principle consists first in a sum of definite religious, moral, or philosophic ideals, whose exponent at all times was the Jewish people, either in its totality, or in the person of its most prominent representatives. Next, this principle consists in a sum of historical memories, recollections of what in the course of many centuries the Jewish people experienced, thought, and felt in the depths of its being. Finally, it consists in the consciousness that true Judaism, which has accomplished great things for humanity in the past, has not yet played out its part, and, therefore, may not perish. In short, the Jewish people lives because it contains a living soul which refuses to separate from its integument, and cannot be forced out of it by heavy trials and misfortunes such as would unfailingly inflict mortal injury upon less sturdy organisms.

This self-consciousness is the source from which the suffering Jewish soul draws comfort. History speaks to it constantly through the mouth of the great apostle who went forth from the midst of Israel eighteen hundred years ago: "But call to remembrance the former days, in which, after ye were enlightened, ye endured a great conflict of sufferings; partly, being made a gazingstock both by reproaches and afflictions; and partly, becoming partakers with them that were so used. . . . Cast not away therefore your boldness, which hath great recompense of reward" (Epistle to the Hebrews, 10:32–33, 35).

Jewish history, moreover, arouses in the Jew the desire to work unceasingly at the task of perfecting himself; to direct his attention to his glorious past, to the resplendent intellectual feats of his ancestors, to their masterly skill in thinking and suffering. It does not lull him to sleep, does not awaken a dullard's complacency or hollow self-conceit. On the contrary, it makes exacting demands upon him. Jewish history admonishes the Jews: *Noblesse oblige.*

The privilege of belonging to a people to whom the honorable title of the veteran of history has been conceded, puts serious responsibilities on your shoulders. You must demonstrate that you are worthy of your heroic past. The descendants of teachers of religion and martyrs of the faith dare not be insignificant, not to say wicked. If the long centuries of wandering and misery have inoculated you with faults, extirpate them in the name of the exalted moral ideals whose bearers you were commissioned to be. If, in the course of time, elements out of harmony with your essential being have fastened upon your mind, cast them out, purify yourselves. In all places and at all times, in joy and in sorrow, you must aim to live for the higher, the spiritual interests. But never may you deem yourselves perfect. If you become faithless to these sacred principles, you sever the bonds that unite you with the most vital elements of your past, with the first cause of your national existence."

The final lesson to be learned is that in the sunny days of mankind's history, in which reason, justice, and philanthropic instinct had the upper hand, the Jews steadfastly made common cause with the other nations. Hand in hand with them, they trod the path leading to perfection. But in the dark days, during the reign of rude force, prejudice, and passion, of which they were the first victims, the Jews retired from the world, withdrew into their shell, to await better days. Union with mankind at large, on the basis of the spiritual and the intellectual, the goal set up by the Jewish prophets in their sublime vision of the future (Is. 2, and Micah 4), is the ultimate ideal of Judaism's noblest votaries. Will their radiant hope ever attain to realization?

If ever it should be realized—and it is incumbent upon us to believe that it will—not a slight part of the merits involved will be due to Jewish history. We have adverted to the lofty moral and humanitarian significance of Jewish history in its role as conciliator. With regard to one half of Jewish history, this conciliatory power is even now a well-established fact. The first part of Jewish history, the biblical part, is a source from which, for many centuries, millions of human beings belonging to the most diverse denominations have derived instruction, solace, and inspiration. It is read with devotion by Christians in both hemispheres, in their houses and their temples. Its heroes have long ago become types, incarnations of great ideas. The events it relates serve as living ethical formulas. But a time will come—perhaps it is not very far off—when the second half of Jewish history, the record of the two thousand years of the Jewish people's life after the biblical period, will be accorded the same treatment. This latter part of Jewish history is not yet known, and many, in the thrall of prejudice, do not wish to know it. But ere long it will be known and appreciated. For the thinking portion of mankind it will be a source of uplifting moral and philosophical teaching. The thousand years martyrdom of the Jewish people, its unbroken pilgrimage, its tragic fate, its teachers of religion, its martyrs, philosophers, champions, this whole epic will in days to come sink deep into the memory of men. It will speak to the heart and the conscience of men, not merely to their curious mind. It will secure respect for the silvery hair of the Jewish people, a people of thinkers and sufferers. It will dispense consolation to the afflicted, and by its examples of spiritual steadfastness and self-denial encourage martrys in their devotion. It is our firm conviction that the time is approaching in which the second half of Jewish history will be to the noblest part of *thinking* humanity what its first half has long been to *believing* humanity, a source of sublime moral truths. In this sense, Jewish history in its entirety is the pledge of the spiritual union between the Jews and the rest of the nations.

THE SOCIOLOGICAL VIEW OF JEWISH HISTORY

*World History of the Jewish People** is perhaps an unusual title, but it corresponds fully to the content and scope of this unusual segment of the history of mankind. It is customary to speak of world history in conjunction with the general history of highly developed nations, as distinguished from the history of single countries and peoples. The destiny of the Jewish people, however, has unfolded in such a way that it possesses a world history of its own in the literal sense of the word. It embraces in a physical sense almost the entire civilized world (except India and China) and it coincides chronologically with the whole course of the historical existence of mankind. Judaism represents a true historical microcosm, and thus

*The title Dubnow gave to his multivolume general history of the Jews to which this essay forms the introduction.

there is excellent justification for speaking of a world history of the Jewish people.

The dominant method for the world history of Jewry, as for the world history of mankind, must be that of synthesis. The major task of the historian is to clarify the general goals and paths of historical life in varying times and places, and to uncover the organic connection among the individual fragments of time and space, distributed over three thousand years of national development. The historian who follows the synthetic method, and deals with materials already collected and more or less analyzed, must not shirk the labors of independent analysis, of critical examination of the sources, and of a re-examination of the facts. On their long historical way, these sources were bound to diminish considerably in reliability and completeness, and without strict re-examination they are bound to cause distorted generalizations. Still, the chief task consists in bringing to the fore the main outlines of the historical process that lie behind the great mass of facts, to draw up a carefully worked out plan of procedure and then to erect the towering structure of history in keeping with the plan. The first condition for such a work of synthesis, however, is a clear general conception of Jewish history, a clear idea of its bearer or subject, the Jewish people, a conception that is not marred by dogmatic and scholastic concepts; and this in turn will determine in advance the pertinent methods of scientific research.

Until quite recently there were great obstacles in the way of such a scientific conception of the history of the most historical of peoples. With regard to the most ancient part of Jewish history, the part which occupies the exceptional position of sacred history, the theological conception still dominates the minds not only of the orthodox, who accept the religious pragmatism of the historical books of the Bible without reservations, but also of the advocates of free biblical criticism, who substitute their own, no less theological pragmatism, for that of the Bible. In the treatment of the medieval and modern history of the Jews, we likewise find the dominance of a one-sided spiritualistic conception that is based on the axiom that a people deprived of state and territory can play an active role in history only in the field of intellectual life, while elsewhere, in its social life, it is condemned to being a passive object of the history of the peoples among whom it lives. Jewish historiography initiated by Zunz and Graetz thus paid attention mainly to two basic factors in presenting the history of the Diaspora: it dealt mostly with intellectual activities and with heroic martyrdom (*Geistes- und Leidensgeschichte*).

The main content of the entire life of the people was thus usually reduced to a history of literature, on the one hand, and to a martyrology on the other. The horizon of history was confined within these limits. The division into epochs, too, was adapted to this one-sided view of post-biblical history. The periods set up were the Talmudic, Geonic, Rabbinic, Mystical, and Enlightenment periods—a periodization valid for the history of a literature, but not for the history of a nation.

Only recently have we arrived at a more comprehensive and more strictly scientific conception of Jewish history that may be termed "sociological." Basic to this conception is the idea derived from the totality of our history, that the Jewish people has at all times and in all countries, always and everywhere, been the subject, the creator of its own history, not only in the intellectual sphere but also in the general sphere of social life. During the period of its political independence as well as in its stateless period, the Jews appear among the other nations, not merely as a religious community, but with the distinctive characteristics of a nation. This nation, endowed with perennial vitality, fought always and everywhere for its autonomous existence in the sphere of social life as well as in all other fields of cultural activity. Even at the time of the existence of the Judean state, the Diaspora had already attained high development and had its autonomous communities everywhere. Later on, it also had central organs of self-administration, its own legislative institutions (corresponding to the Sanhedrin, the academies and patriarchs in Roman-Byzantine Palestine; Exilarchs, Geonim, and legislative academies in Babylonia; the *aljamas* and congresses of communal delegates in Spain; *kahals* and *vaads*, or congresses of *kahals*, in Poland and Lithuania, etc.). The latest national movement among the Jews, linked as it is with this historical process and combining the older heritage of autonomism with the modern principle of national minority rights, testifies to the immortality of this eternal driving force of Jewish history. Even during the epoch of assimilation and of revolutionary change in the life of the people, it has been able to assert itself.

The causes of the one-sided conception of Jewish history, which was still widespread in the recent past, are obvious. Scientific Jewish historiography originated in western Europe in the middle of the nineteenth century, when the dogma of assimilation held complete sway there. This dogma asserted that Jewry is not a nation, but a religious community. Jewish historiography was also carried away by the general current and therefore concerned itself more with the religion of Judaism than with its living creator, the Jewish people. Even an opponent of this universally accepted dogma, like Graetz, was not able to go counter to this current. The profound evolution of national consciousness which characterizes our age inevitably wrought a transformation in our conception of the historical process. The secularization of the Jewish national idea was bound to effect the secularization of historical writing, liberating it from the shackles of theology and, subsequently, of spiritualism or scholasticism. A new conception of Jewish history came into being, a conception much more appropriate to the content as well as the scope of this history. Slowly the awareness grew that the Jewish people had not been entirely absorbed all these centuries by its "thought and suffering," but that it had concerned itself with constructing its life as a separate social unit, under the most varied conditions of existence, and that, therefore, it was the foremost task of historiography to try to understand this process of building the life of the Jewish people.

The subject of scientific historiography is the people, the national individuality, its origin, its growth, and its struggle for existence. In the course of a succession of centuries, the initially amorphous national cell became differentiated from the surrounding milieu of the peoples of the ancient Orient, took on a firmly outlined national form, established its own state and then lost it again, integrated in its own way the elements of universal culture which it has absorbed and, while so doing, lifted its spiritual creativity to the heights of the prophetic movement. The movement toward the final formation of the national type coincided with that of the first political catastrophe (the Babylonian Exile), and the succeeding Persian, Greek, Hasmonean, and Roman epochs were marked by the rivalry between theocracy and the secular state. The second political catastrophe, brought on by the irresistible onslaught of Rome, gave rise to new forms of struggle by the dispersed people for its national unity. The indomitable urge to autonomous life and to the preservation of the greatest measure of social and cultural individuality while amid alien peoples found expression, not in political, but in other social forms. The entire spiritual vitality of the nation came to be directed to this goal. The religion of Judaism was fashioned in accordance with the image of social conditions of the nation's existence, and not the reverse. . . .

I am fully persuaded that the general conception presented here is the only possible presupposition for a scientifically objective methodology of Jewish historiography. This conception provides a way out for our historiography from the labyrinth of theological and metaphysical theories and places it upon a firm bio-sociological foundation. The subject of investigation is not an abstraction but a living organism which has developed out of an original biological germ, the tribe, into a complex cultural historical whole, the nation. The method of investigation is strictly evolutionary. The period of the formation of the national individuality is to be examined first; then, after this individuality has assumed a more fixed form, the period of its struggle for separate existence, for the preservation and unfolding of its characteristic national traits and of the cultural treasures it accumulated in the course of centuries. In presenting this dual process of individuation and struggle for the emerging individuality, we start from the basic assumption that a strong and clearly molded national collective personality as the product of historical evolution is not only a natural phenomenon, but also represents a high cultural value. This, however, by no means implies that the historian must consider as valuable all those direct or winding paths that led to the preservation of the collective personality. If, for example, he is forced to recognize normal separation as an indispensable condition of national existence, he must not fail, on the other hand, to point out those periods during which cultural isolation—even though it was often necessary for the purpose of self-preservation—led to deplorable excesses, culminating in the complete alienation of the Jewish people from the valuable achievements of universal culture. It is incumbent upon him to present a vivid description of the struggle between centripetal and centrifugal forces that no national organism can escape, as well as the tragic conflicts in the life of the people induced thereby. The historian, however, who starts with the firm acceptance of national individuality as a cultural value, will evaluate the end results of the centripetal and constructive efforts differently from the centrifugal and destructive tensions.

Another obvious postulate of the sociological method is that due consideration be given in historiography, not only to the social and national, but also to the socio-economic factors which were so badly neglected by the old school. This is not to be interpreted as a concession to the materialist interpretation of history, which seeks to reduce all historical facts to the evolution of the economic conditions of life. We do not reject the antiquated, spiritualistic conception of history only to become captives of the opposite doctrine, the no-less one-sided materialistic view of history which equally obscures all historical perspective. The economic order, like the cultural order, is but one element of the natural and social conditions of the nation's life. Commanding sovereignty over the life of the nation is exercised by the totality of all social and spiritual factors it creates. Consideration of the reciprocal relations between the individual factors shows that there is interdependence as well as conflict among them. We find nowhere, however, that all these varied functions of life are subordinate to any one single factor.

The full value of this new conception of Jewish history is especially apparent to those who, like the author of this work, had themselves previously strayed along the crooked path of the old Jewish historiography. I myself at one time acclaimed the generally accepted principles without reservation. I myself passed through all the above-mentioned phases of historical thinking, in my search for a comprehensive synthesis of Jewish history, a synthesis which I pursued unceasingly from the first day of my scientific research. . . . The deficiencies of the old method became increasingly clear to me only after I had spent many years in detailed examination of the sources of general Jewish history, and after I had to write a history of the Jewish nation and not only of its literature. At the same time, the frame of investigation and generalization was visibly broadened and the historical horizon opened up until what was once hidden behind the veil of scholastic mystification finally came to the fore. Then I undertook to check the results I had arrived at inductively by the opposite, deductive method, and I found that my conclusions, which had thus turned into assumptions, were fully confirmed when applied to the historical materials.

The new general conception which we have described also involves a new arrangement of the materials of Jewish history and a new classification of the periods of the historical process. The division of the history of the Jewish people into periods and epochs must follow national and social rather than religious or literary criteria. These criteria are suggested primarily by the historical environment of the Jewish nation in the various periods, and then by the hegemony of one or another segment of the nation emerging in the ever-changing national center. Thus the history of the period of statehood, which many writers still divide into the epoch of the First Temple and the epoch of the Second Temple, should rather be subdivided in accordance with political considerations and along lines that correspond to the changing position of Palestine amid the world monarchies of the ancient Orient: Egypt, Assyria, Babylonia, Persia, the Hellenistic kingdoms of the Ptolemies and Seleucids, and the Roman empire. The history of the stateless period, on the other hand, after the Jews had lost their unified center, must be subdivided in accordance with clear-cut geographical considerations and along lines corresponding to shifts in the center of national hegemony within the Jewish people. Each epoch is determined by the fact that the dispersed nation possessed within this period one main center, or sometimes two coexisting centers, which assumed the leadership of all other parts of the Diaspora because they were able to achieve far-reaching national autonomy and a high state of cultural development.

The world history of the Jewish people may, therefore, be divided into the following two main periods: (a) the Oriental period, when the chief national centers were located in the Near East and in North Africa, in Palestine, Syria, Mesopotamia, Egypt; and (b) the Western period, when these centers shifted to Europe where colonies of the Jewish Diaspora gradually began to flourish. Within the Oriental period three further epochs must be distinguished, which were determined by political and cultural conditions: (1) the epoch of purely Oriental milieu, which includes the periods of the conquest of Canaan, the kingdoms of Judah and Israel, and the supremacy of the three successive world-monarchies, Assyria, Babylonia, and Persia (1200–332 B.C.E.); (2) the epoch of mixed Oriental and Western environment and of Graeco-Roman rule, which includes the intermediate episodes of an independent Judea under the Hasmoneans up to the fall of the Jewish state (332 B.C.E.–70 C.E.); (3) the epoch of dual hegemony, of Roman-Byzantine Palestine and Persian-Arab Babylonia, between the two newly emerged world-historical forces, Christianity and Islam. In the latter epoch, after Judea's defeat in the struggle with Rome, the following changes in the hegemony of Jewish centers occurred: the hegemony of Palestine during the time of pagan Rome (second and third centuries C.E.) was replaced at first by the dual Palestinian-Babylonian hegemony, while Byzantium and the new Persia dominated the Orient (fourth to sixth centuries), and then by a single Babylonian hegemony during the great Arab Caliphate (seventh to ninth centuries). In the older historiography this sequence of epochs in the second millennium of Jewish history was usually treated under the general heading of "The Talmudic Period," and under additional scholastic subheadings of epochs of the Mishnah, the Gemara, the Tannaim, the Amoraim, the Savoraim, and Geonim. In reality it was determined by the great epoch-making turns in world history.

This second millennium of the Oriental period of Jewish history, which coincides with the first Christian millennium was, however, also a period of colonization for the European Diaspora, a period which paved the way for the shift of national hegemony from East to West. The eleventh century of the Christian era thus forms the dividing line between two great periods of Jewish history, the Oriental and the Occidental. National hegemony now starts its migration through the centers of great Jewish mass settlements in Europe. In the Middle Ages the hegemony of Judaism fell to the lot of the Jews of Arab and, later, Christian Spain (eleventh to fourteenth centuries). Concurrently the Jews of southern and, later, of northern France (eleventh to thirteenth centuries), and soon also the Jews of Germany (thirteenth to fifteenth centuries) took the lead. In modern times (sixteenth to eighteenth centuries), Germany and the autonomous Jewish center in Poland shared the hegemony. Finally, at the end of the eighteenth century, under the impact of the Enlightenment, the Jewish cultural hegemony assumed a dual form. German Jewry took the leadership of the progressive movement in the West, while Polish-Russian Jewry remained the citadel of the old, traditional culture until it, too, was swept into the vortex of the latest currents in the second half of the nineteenth century.

The recent history of the Jews (1789–1914) was marked by profound social and cultural crises. These were caused by the fact that, on the one hand, short periods of emancipation and reaction followed each other closely and continuously in the general civic life, and that, on the other hand, these were paralleled by conflicts between assimilationist and nationalist tendencies within the Jewish communities of western and eastern Europe. In the latest phase of this recent history (1881–1914), in the epoch of growing anti-Semitism on the one hand and of the Jewish national movement on the other, Jewish national life took a new and significant turn of fate with the beginning of the exodus from eastern Europe. One group of emigrants established a new great Diaspora center in America within the short span of three decades, while the other, numerically far smaller, laid the cornerstone for the revived national center in the old homeland, in Palestine. The devastation of the World War and the Russian Revolution (1914–1920) dealt a severe blow to the largest of the previous Jewish centers, the Russian center, and, now, at the new dividing line of history, the sphinx of the Jewish people's future raises its face, simultaneously looking toward the West and toward the East. In the wake of the two great periods of Jewish world history, the Oriental and the Occidental, the prospects for the future indicate, if not a total turn toward the Orient, in the form of a resuscitated Palestine, at least a rivalry for national hegemony between East and West, between Palestine and the European-American Diaspora. The historian must halt at this dividing line caused by the world conflagration of 1914; our *History* does not go beyond this point.

The organization of the materials, covering thousands of years of the history of the world-historical people presents special difficulties. In the case of the most ancient period, these difficulties can be overcome since we have to cope only with the synchronous existence of the kingdoms of Israel and Judah after the division of the realm, and with a limited Diaspora in the period of Persian rule. The difficulties increase with the further extension of the Diaspora, first in the Orient, then also in the West. Already in the Graeco-Roman period the historian's attention is divided between Judea and the "great Diaspora," as it is later, in the Roman-Byzantine and Persian-Arab periods, between the two centers of Palestine and Babylonia, on the one hand, and the ever-expanding European Diaspora, on the other. As we approach the history of the western period, the difficulties become immeasurably greater. Here we are faced with an enormous number of countries, in each of which the destiny of the Jewish population is intertwined with the most diverse political and cultural conditions. The historian has the choice between the two possible ways of presentation, both of which, however, appear equally inexpedient. He may arrange the history of the Jewish people according to the countries in which it was scattered, and thus present it as a purely external collection of monographs, or he may treat the history of the Jews in all countries concurrently and, converting the history into chronicle, he may present a chronological record of events that coincide in time but differ fundamentally in character and local conditions. The first master of Jewish historiography, Graetz, preferred, in the main, the latter method of synchronism. The sudden transitions from one country to the other within the same chapter often alienate the reader of his grandly conceived work. Although this artificial stringing together of heterogeneous events has something of the plasticity of synoptic tables, it nevertheless lacks what is indispensable for a scientific synthesis, a concatenation of events with local conditions. This is completely obscured in such a chroniclelike presentation. With Graetz the confusion is further augmented by his method of throwing together political, socio-economic, and literary data in the narrowest sense of the word into a single chapter.

The only way to avoid all these limitations is to divide the materials according to the threefold principle of time, place, and subject matter. The history of each epoch must be presented according to the country in which it occurs, and within each country according to the order of causal connections that link the external conditions with those of internal life. Within the limits of each period, the history of the different segments of the nation are presented in such a way that the main center of national hegemony comes first and is then followed by the other countries according to their importance for the total national history. Sometimes, however, it appears unavoidable to begin the presentation of a particular section with a central event, for example, with a political or social movement that affected several countries simultaneously and impressed its character upon an entire period. Examples of such events are the first crusades and their significance for France and Germany, the new settlements of the Sephardim after their expulsion from Spain, the spread of the Shabbatean messianic movement* from Turkey, the first French Revolution and the beginning of Jewish emancipation and, finally, the German anti-Semitism of the last decades of the nineteenth century. The treatment of each epoch in the present work is prefaced by a general survey, which presents the leading characteristics of the center of each period as well as of its peripheral areas. In the presentation proper, the external political events are distinguished as far as possible from the internal social phenomena, on the one hand, and from the data of literary history, on the other. In each chapter dealing with a particular center of the Diaspora, the material is usually arranged in the following way: political conditions,

*The largest and most significant of the Jewish messianic movements, centering about the figure of the Turkish Jew Shabbetai Zevi (1626–1676).

self-administration in the Jewish communities, intellectual life and literature. For purposes of a history of the Jewish people we are interested in literary history only in so far as it influenced the social dynamics or was itself a product of social movements. We are concerned far less with individual works of literature than with literary movements that are expressive of the general orientation of the national spirit. History of literature in the narrowest sense of the word is outside the scope of this work.

ELDER HISTORIANS OF
THE STATE OF ISRAEL

INTRODUCTION TO YEHEZKEL KAUFMANN

*Y*EHEZKEL KAUFMANN *(1889–1963) is best known today for his highly original work as a scholar of the Bible. Against the prevalent view that Israel's religion evolved gradually out of a pagan context, he argued that Israelite monotheism developed as early as the desert period, that it was not merely the faith of a select few, and that it appears in the Bible cleansed of all traces of polytheism and myth. Almost alone among scholars he held that the Torah was the product of the earliest stage of Israelite history and that the Priestly stratum of the text preceded all the other sources, originating well before the post-Exilic period to which it is usually assigned. Kaufmann published his theories on the ancient period in his* History of the Israelite Religion, *which he wrote in Hebrew and which remained incomplete in eight volumes at the time of his death in 1963.*

But Kaufmann's interest was not limited to Israel of ancient times. Indeed, he had begun his scholarly writing with reflections on the entire span of Jewish history, and especially the many centuries of the Diaspora. After a youth spent in Russia, he settled in Berlin following World War I, and there during the 1920's composed his two-volume Gola ve-Nekhar *("Diaspora and Alien Lands") which was published in Palestine in 1929–30. As a Zionist* he had migrated a year earlier to the Land of Israel where he first taught high school in Haifa for some twenty years and then received an appointment to the Hebrew University in Jerusalem. What Kaufmann in his later biblical work would emphasize as the great force which welded Israel together as a people, its monotheistic religious faith, appears in this early work as the power which sustains Israel in the Diaspora, despite the Jews' being scattered among foreign nations and subjected to a host of forces capable of eroding their identity.

The selection from Gola ve-Nekhar given here illustrates the centrality Kaufmann assigns to the religious factor in Jewish history. The unique (Kaufmann uses the term "idiographic") character of the Jews' historical lot poses difficult questions for the scholar seeking to shed light on the nature and dynamics of Jewish history. To be sure, Israel is subject to the general laws of historical development no less than other peoples, but these laws cannot explain why the Jews, the sole example of a people living among the nations, should have survived intact through the ages. It was not their national feeling which accounts for this feat—Jews were at times very much attached to the lands of their domicile—but religion. Indeed national consciousness in the Diaspora was dependent upon religious values. According to Kaufmann, it is only the force of the Jewish religious idea which can explain Israel's survival, even as it was this same idea which first forged it into a nation at Sinai.

The peculiar and remarkable lot of the people of Israel constitutes a problem of unparalleled difficulty for historical and sociological investigation. It is the fate of a people whose national foundations were all destroyed, that was exiled from its land and scattered among other nations, that assimilated to them culturally, and yet did not cease being a separate people, bearing a special history. As soon as we approach the study of this historical phenomenon and examine it, we immediately encounter a prior and difficult methodological question: Is it at all possible to investigate this historical phenomenon, to explain it historically and socially? The Exile of Israel with its remarkable history is a unique phenomenon, and there is none like it in the history of the world; the people of Israel is the *only* exilic people. How is it possible, therefore, to explain a phenomenon like the Jewish Exile, i.e., to get at the roots and causes of a singular, unparalleled, unquestionably idiographic phenomenon? The general answer to this prior question requires a consideration of historical causes; despite their special idiographic forms, historical phenomena possess a common and permanent basis which enables us to grasp them and to determine their causal connections. It is possible, therefore, to comprehend even the Exile by discerning its general social foundations, and in this way alone. But study of Israel's exilic existence must cope with a special difficulty, since here it is necessary to explain the general foundations of a unique phenomenon. Not only must the phenomenon itself be explained, but also why *only* the people of Israel took this road of life in a diaspora. One thing, however, is clear in any case: when we pose the question of Israel's fate as an object of historical or sociological inquiry, we desire to comprehend this situation from a consideration of its general social foundations. Precisely for this reason the question of Israel's lot is a difficult one from the viewpoint of history and sociology. . . .

In a scientific historical investigation it is impossible for us to see the history of Israel (or that of any other people) as a separate and closed realm of occurrences in which all events flow from its internal "law," from its "purpose," or its special "mission." The history of Israel is a part of general history, and many of its phenomena are explicable by external causes, by the independent operation of external forces upon the people of Israel. There is a *causal* connection between the history of Israel and the history of the nations with which the people of Israel comes into contact. This implies the recognition that the history of Israel, too, is subject to the same laws, to the same causal connections, to which all of history is subject. For in this sense, at least, there are historical "laws": the operation of forces and factors which function within history are bound by certain laws which possess validity in every human society without exception. Therefore we must also understand the history of Israel as the product of the combined action of internal and external factors. We must grasp this action not from a teleological, metaphysical point of view, but from an empirical one, which is based on causes and laws, like that from which we grasp human history in general.

Yet from historical laws alone it is impossible to explain the history of a people. In history (as in nature) there is always a *foundation of the given* which we do not know how to "explain" and which we see as a kind of primordial cause. In the end, we are unable to explain satisfactorily why, for example, in Greece there appeared such tremendous and varied powers of creativity, or why particularly in Egypt there should have emerged such a developed and lofty worship of the dead. We are unable to explain satisfactorily the vast differences among different human societies just as we cannot explain the differences among individual human beings. For history, basics of this kind are foundations of the given with which it begins. The idiographic character of historical events is rooted in these foundations of the given. But nonetheless, all historical phenomena also possess a common basis which can be examined with regard to the generalizations it may contain and which can be determined with the regularity of a law. Moreover, the special character of the history of every society flows from the meeting and intersection of various factors which tend to join in a variety of combinations. However, the nature of the factors themselves must be studied from the viewpoint of cause and law, according to the example of what we find also in the "history" of events in nature. Therefore, with all of the great and characteristic differences between the history of the people of Israel and that of the rest of the peoples, we are unable to comprehend and explain Jewish history except via a study of the general nature and rules of the factors which operated within it. It is not possible to explain fully *all* of the phenomena of the history of Israel. Here, too, there is, of course, a foundation of the given which serves us as a kind of "first cause." For example, we will not be able ultimately to explain why the Hebrew state was a small one, or why a unique belief in unity emerged within Israel. But a given foundation of this kind (which we cannot explain or need not explain) is to be found in the history of every people. It does not relieve history of its subjection to determination by general laws.

The singular history of the people of Israel consists of a unique combination of two basic factors: the *national* and the *religious*. Operative in this history were the qualities of its ethnic existence, a certain action of political forces, the laws of demography and of the extension of settlement, the laws of national assimilation, the in-influence of the religious basis upon the life of Israel and of the peoples in whose midst it lived and functioned. Although out of the operation of these factors there emerged a history which bears a unique and anomalous character, we can understand and explain this history empirically only by a study of the nature of these factors, by a study of their foundation which operates in human history in general. The Exile of Israel is a unique sociological phenomenon in the history of the world, but its roots are planted in the nature of the ethnic and the religious factors, and in the manner of their causal operation in the life of every people.

From such an empirical historical examination the question of Israel's fate takes on a new form which is totally different from that which was given it by the earlier religious outlook, whether Jewish or Christian. The religious outlook struggled with the question of the destruction of ancient Israel, the subjugation, the dispersion, the exile. Why did idolatrous nations destroy the kingdom of Israel and why were they allowed to subjugate Israel and to exile it from its land? The question was basically one of *reason* and *purpose*, and the religious outlook in its own way sought an answer. From the viewpoint of an empirical historical study the problem ceases to be a problem. The destruction and the dispersion in themselves are phenomena such as we find in the history of many nations. Assyria, Babylonia, and Rome did not destroy only the state of Israel or subjugate only the people of Israel. Therefore this destruction and this subjugation do not require a special explanation: the determining factor was the relation between the political forces of

Israel and those of its conquerors. But, on the other hand, there arises the difficult problem of a singular phenomenon which we find in the history of Israel and of no other people: *the existence of the people of Israel in its dispersion and exile.* For the religious, or teleological, conception, the explanation of this phenomenon is not very difficult. The existence of the people of Israel, the sole bearer of God's true teaching, has a clear purpose; this existence fits nicely into the Divine scheme embodied in history, into the view of history as a "Divine Comedy." Yet for the causal study of history it presents a difficult problem.

The basic question does not concern the war which the people of Israel waged for its physical existence during the generations of the Exile, the war for a loaf of bread or a place of rest. With all of its anomalous and unique conditions, this war is nevertheless not in itself a singular phenomenon. It is the war which every ethnic group wages with its surroundings. This struggle for existence, despite its exilic form, is essentially the same as the war of the people of Israel with its enemies in ancient times. Formerly, Israel fought its battle for life by the sword like every other people. During the generations of the Exile it gradually learned other modes of warfare. Not with a mighty hand, not with their sword and bow, did the Jews come to distant lands to seek a livelihood, but with their staff and their pack. When their neighbors made trouble in one country, they wandered to another. Their God dealt charitably with them in that he scattered them among the nations and taught them to wander from land to land. A people of one-time shepherds and farmers eventually became merchants in some places, and moneylenders in others. They possessed no noblemen or proud aristocrats living by the sword. But many of them succeeded valiantly with their money, and others turned to intellectual disciplines, thereby gaining both sustenance and honor. In place of ministers of state and heroes of war, there arose among them *shtadlanim** and *parnasim*;† in place of political organization there emerged inner unity and extensive solidarity. This entire war, together with its implements, is the natural and common war for existence which teaches living creatures to use all their abilities and to adapt as much as possible to the conditions of life. Although this struggle for existence is of

*Representatives of Jewish communities who pleaded their cause before the ruling authorities.

† Lay leaders of Jewish communities.

major importance, it is not the basic problem in the history of Israel. Since the people of Israel did not cease being a special ethnic group even after it went into exile, it was obviously required to wage the struggle for existence of every ethnic group, though under special conditions and in special ways, as demanded by the circumstances of life in the Exile.

The basic problem for historical inquiry is the phenomenon itself, which previously was not a problem at all—the very nature of Israel's national particularity in the Diaspora: Why did it not cease being an ethnic group? What is the reason for the fact that the people of Israel persisted in being a nation although faced with conditions of life such as always entail, without exception, national assimilation? It is a law that every nation and tribe defends itself against enemies which rise against it to destroy or to dispossess it. But it is also a law that every nation and tribe which is scattered or intermingled among other nations becomes swallowed up and absorbed by them. What, therefore, brought it about that the people of Israel should be a single people despite its being scattered and dispersed among the nations?

In order to be able to understand this problem fully, we must emphasize the *singular character* of Israel's existence in the Diaspora. When the people of Israel was scattered among the nations, it, too, went the way which was laid out for every scattered and dispersed people—the way of assimilation. The Jews were influenced by the culture of their neighbors, became attached and clung to the lands of their habitation, learned the ways of their neighbors, adopted their manners and customs, their clothing, food and drink, etc. That is, the nature of social reality drew Israel toward national absorption. The change of language, which the Jewish people underwent, is particularly important in this connection—language is a people's primary expression of ethnicity, and forgetting its language means the extinction of the ethnic group. Not the dispersion in and of itself is unique to exilic Jewry: many nations have a "dispersion," i.e., they are divided into smaller units which dwell in different parts of the world. But there is no people in the world which was scattered among other nations, adopted their languages, and nevertheless continued to exist. On the one hand, dispersion and linguistic assimilation, and on the other, national distinctiveness for numerous generations—this is the special quality of the people of Israel which makes its existence a singular and special problem in the history of the nations. . . .

If we examine the culture of Israel from its *general aspect*, its universal and secular content, we see that in this regard it deserves no special consideration nor does it possess any particular power which might be able to motivate men to struggle for many generations against the nature of reality for the sake of their national distinctiveness. Idolatry produced richer and deeper cultures than the culture of Israel. Babylonia, Egypt, Persia, Greece, and Rome produced grand and sublime works in philosophy, science, poetry, art, morality, law, and politics. In many respects these nations outdid Israel immeasurably in their creative powers; and in numerous other respects they at least approximated it. But what was the fate of those cultures and the fate of the nations which created them? Whatever was good and beautiful in these cultures became the legacy of all peoples. But as for the nations which produced the cultures, when their time came, they were either dispersed and perished or, due to the circumstances of the time, the special connection between them and their culture was broken. From this we learn that the spiritual wealth of a culture, its universal value and greatness, cannot save a group from extinction. Roman civilization, Latin language and literature, Roman law—even the Roman Empire—continued to exist for a long time after the Roman *people* disintegrated and perished. The peculiar force which united the scattered people of Israel and preserved its distinctiveness in foreign lands is therefore not to be found in its culture—however great—to the extent that the culture is a secular and universal creation.

It is even less possible to find this force in the national foundations of Israel's civilization, in its historical *forms*. To the degree that they served as bases for secular existence, there was no singular quality to Israel's land, language, customs, historical memories, or way of life. All the power of these foundations of life, in every instance, lies in their being forms of life which possess a natural existence, in their serving as a garment for the nature of reality. They influence the lives of men and nations and they arouse them to fight for them as long as they exist and *because* they exist. But a land *of the fathers*, a *dead* language, an *artificial* mode of life—all these no longer possess secular, natural, and normal force. Why should we suppose that the love of the Jews for their land, their language, their songs, their customs, their food and drink, their clothing—to the extent that each of these was the product of secular human life, ways of fulfilling physiological or spiritual needs—was singular and different from the normal love of every man for his ethnic mode of life? In any case, history proves that there is no basis whatsoever for this supposition. More than once the Jews clung to the lands of their exile with a faithful love. They learned the foreign languages, spoke them, thought and wrote poetry in them. As a living language, Hebrew was forgotten, and in more than one land the Jews' mode of life in every respect resembled that of their neighbors. Not here, therefore, should we seek the secret of the distinctiveness.

Entirely different from the secular cultural dimension is the dimension of religion. On the one hand, religion differs in its general character from the other components of culture. It is in the nature of religion to subjugate a person to its fixed values and to compel him to guard them well in all the circumstances of life. On the other hand, we find that religious creativity was embodied in Israel in a *singular form* like none other in the world. Therefore, it is in the operation of this unique factor, no doubt, that one must seek the secret of the special course of Israel's history.

Indeed, when we examine the people of Israel's national consciousness in the Diaspora, we see that all of the values to which it clung and by which it lived were *religious* values. The land, the language, the memories, the past with all of its heroes, its destiny, race, customs—all of these were not taken as secular matters; they were sublimated and became religious values. Of course, there were in its life secular national forces as well; vital biological forces were also operative. The wars of Israel with its enemies in the Hellenistic period and in the Roman period, as well as the struggle for existence in the Christian and Muslim worlds, are a people's secular conflicts. But the ultimate source of all such manifestations of life is religious. "Israel" itself is a religious concept. The highest ideal inscribed on the soul of the nation, the ideal for which it waged a desperate struggle—the existence of Israel—is a religious ideal. This is not Israel as a collection of the descendants of a single ancestor which at one time inhabited a single land and constituted a single state, but rather Israel as the bearer of the word of God, which lives by the commandment of God. Israel's genealogical consciousness is religious, not aristocratic and secular. "Abraham," the progenitor of the nation, is first of all a religious figure, and the feeling of attachment which binds the individual to the nation, the "love of Israel," is a religious sentiment. Of course this love contains, as well, an element of fraternal love which is racial and secular. But the particular thrill which accompanies this sentiment and augments it with a special force is religious: Israel is a *holy* nation. The fundamental aspiration which aroused the nation to struggle with its total environment, which aroused its conscious and instinctive forces and armed them for war, was the aspiration to establish Israel as the bearer of religious sanctity and religious goals. The idea, therefore, which operated in the depths of the nation's soul, which compelled it to walk on its special path and impressed its seal upon all the manifestations of its life, was a religious idea.

A *religious idea*—not religion as a regimen of laws and commandments, as one is accustomed to think. The religious idea began to play its special unifying role in the life of Israel as early as the Babylonian Exile, during the period when the religion had not yet crystallized into a fixed regimen of laws. It singled Israel out from the nations still before the Torah had become the people's book. Even before Ezra, even before the canonization of the Torah, it brought about the remarkable phenomenon of the return to Zion. Those scholars who consider Ezra the father of Jewish particularity and his commandments the beginning of the later Judaism ignore the fact that Ezra began his activity after about 150 years of particularity. The late laws and commandments did not create the attachment of the people to the religious idea; they were its natural result. The religion and its laws were not *means* which someone invented to preserve the people from extinction or the race from mixture, as one is accustomed to think; *their action was that of a primary cause.* Isolated commandments and ordinances were indeed established as a fence and shield against foreign influence. But here, too, the internal force which created these was the power of faith: the power of the fundamental idea of the existence of Israel, the bearer of the religion of God. Moreover, one must not think that religion was only *one* of the forces which sustained the nation, along with other factors. Of course, various forces operated in the life of Israel and in different periods left their mark upon it. The political lot of the people was of decisive importance in its life and it ultimately determined the lot of its religion. But all of these factors were joined to the religious factor. The one and only primary cause for Israel's individuality in the Diaspora was its religion alone. It constituted the cultural foundation to which the nation clung even after it lost its national treasures; it was an attachment which caused it to distinguish itself from its neighbors and to create for itself a particular kind of life. Thus religion was the sole source of its national will. In the workshop of its religion, that life was created for which the people struggled against the nature of reality. Its religion created the idea of Israel together with all its ramifications. Were it not for the operation of this primary force which fashioned and sustained the goal and purpose of Israel's struggle for its distinctiveness, there would certainly have been no place for this battle and for all of the auxiliary forces it embraced.

However, if at first religion functioned in the life of Israel as a positive faith, in the course of time it became a social force independent of faith in the narrow sense. The fact that the breakdown of faith in modern times has not reduced the stature of Judaism, nor put an end to the struggle of Israel with its surroundings, has provided historical scholarship with the possibility of ascribing the existence of Judaism to an objective factor aside from the religious one. But the truth is that the religion itself is the objective factor which operates even where there is no longer faith—religion in its broad sense, the religious factor in the full scope of its social function.

INTRODUCTION TO BEN ZION DINUR

No HISTORIAN cast Jewish history into a firmer Zionist mold than did Ben Zion Dinur (1884–1973), a scholar whose nationalist perspective exercised a profound influence on Jewish historical studies in the Land (and later the State) of Israel.

Dinur, who was born in Russia, combined Talmudic learning gained in various academies in Eastern Europe with a secular education acquired mostly in the West as the basis for a career of teaching. Personally committed to Zionism, he settled in Palestine in 1921 where he taught at, and later administered, a training college for teachers in Jerusalem. Together with his colleague Yitzhak Baer, whose idea of Jewish history closely parallels his own, he founded Zion, which still remains the leading Israeli journal of Jewish history. After the establishment of the State, he served for a time as a member of parliament and as Minister of Education and Culture, in addition to teaching at the Hebrew University. As an educator, Dinur held that knowledge of Bible and Jewish history must be the core of Jewish education in Israel—a view which has been embodied in the curriculum of the Israeli schools. After retiring from teaching and administrative responsibilities, Dinur remained active as a scholar, continuing research which during the span of his life ranged over the full extent of Jewish history from the biblical period to the modern age.

Of his numerous writings, Dinur's major contribution is his incomplete two-part historical work (in Hebrew): Israel in Its Land (one volume, 1938) and Israel in the Diaspora (nine volumes, 1958–71). Dinur does not attempt in these volumes to present a narrative history of the Jewish people. Instead, he assembles quotations from a variety of sources which provide information relevant to Jewish history. In addition to the excerpts themselves, he supplies introductions, explanatory footnotes, and more extended treatment of certain issues related to his sources. Within his separation of the material by periods, he organizes it according to a threefold division adapted with slight modifications from Dubnow: the status of the Jews, actions of the Jewish collectivity, and the world view of the individual Jew.

To the first of the Diaspora volumes, Dinur prefaced an essay in which he critically evaluates previous Jewish historians and sets forth his own idea of Jewish history. The selection given here is taken from that introductory essay; it omits what Dinur has to say about his predecessors but presents the essence of his own view. The reader should give particular attention to Dinur's arguments for the "complete and unbroken" national unity of the Jewish people, to the crucial significance which he attributes to the Land of Israel in maintaining that unity, and to his conception of Jewish history in the Diaspora as a wholly continuous process, which is subject, however, to the effects of alternating periods of stability and crisis in the historical environment.

ISRAEL IN THE DIASPORA

Our first task, before we can arrive at a proper understanding of Jewish history, is to clarify the following five fundamental points: (1) the unity of the nation during the period of its exile and dispersion; (2) the nature of this unity; (3) the nation's power of independent action in the Diaspora; (4) the reciprocal relations existing among the scattered Diaspora communities; and (5) the place occupied by the Land of Israel in the life of the exiled nation.

1. *The unity of the nation.* Were the Jews still really a single nation, even after they had been exiled from their land and dispersed over many countries, living among foreign peoples in a variety of different states? Can it be said, that even in these circumstances, the Jewish people still formed one organically united nation, the members of which were held together by permanent social bonds that drew their strength from a common life and destiny, and functioned in a social, national, and—however tenuous—organizational framework, in spite of exile, dispersion, homelessness, and oppression?

2. *The nature of the nation's unity in exile.* Would it not be more correct to regard the unity of the nation in the Diaspora as purely religious? Was the common life—insofar as it existed at all—in fact any more than the common observance of the precepts of the Law and the common heritage of religious rituals and practices? And can the common destiny be regarded as in fact anything more than the similar plight of the Jews in various lands resulting from the form and development of the social and political systems in those lands, which were, so to speak, external data in no way dependent on the Jews themselves? Should we not, therefore, regard Saadiah Gaon's statement that "our nation is not a nation, except in its laws"* as an expression of the fundamental change that occurred in the Diaspora in the character of the nation's unity, which was now a unity restricted to the confines of its laws—its religious beliefs and doctrines and the rituals and practices connected with them—and ceased to be an all-embracing, organic unity nurtured by a common life and a common destiny of which the laws were only a part?

*The Book of Beliefs and Opinions, Chapter 3.

3. *The nation's power of independent action in the Diaspora.* Is it at all possible to regard Jewish history in the Diaspora as the *history* of a *nation?* Is it not rather the record of the vicissitudes of separate Jewish communities living in different historical frameworks? Have we any right to speak of the history of the nation in exile when it was, in fact, deprived of all "power of independent political action"? Should we not, therefore, consider it perfectly natural that the nation's power of independent action in exile was limited to the spiritual spheres of religious thought and practice, the only spheres of life in which the persecuted and homeless Jews were still their own masters? And does not this also lead us to the conclusion that Jewish history in the Diaspora is essentially the history of the religious element in Jewish life, in all its various manifestations and trends?

4. *The reciprocal relations existing among the Jewish communities in the Diaspora.* The significance of the dispersion of the Jews does not lie only in their being scattered far and wide over many different countries. No less important than this is the fact that the separate settlements of Jews in these countries united to form whole communities, each one of which drew its strength from its own special common life and common destiny. To obtain a correct overall conception of Diaspora history we must, therefore, first form a clear picture of the part played by these different territorial groups of communities, and by the reciprocal relations between them, in determining the general character of the nation in exile and dispersion.

5. *The place of the Land of Israel in the life of the exiled nation.* The basic phenomenon of the period of the Diaspora, without any doubt, is the fact that the Jews were exiles from their own land, dispersed among the nations and living on foreign soil. Hence, in order to obtain a proper historical understanding of the Diaspora it is essential first to clarify the actual importance of this basic phenomenon as a formative factor in Jewish life. The best indications of this are to be found in the attitude of the Jews in the Dispersion to the Land of Israel and its Jewish population, and in the connection that existed between this attitude and their feeling of strangeness and homelessness among the Gentiles. . . .

[After discussing how a number of modern Jewish historians, beginning with Jost, have dealt with the issues he has posed, Dinur continues as follows.]

I therefore proceed to formulate my own replies to these questions:

1. Even after the destruction of the Jewish state, when the homeless Jews were scattered among the nations and had been absorbed by the various states in which they lived, the unity of the Jewish people still remained complete and unbroken. Only the external conditions of the nation's existence changed, not its essential character. Even in dispersion the nation formed a distinctive organic entity; that is to say, the various scattered Jewish communities were united by unique life processes which cannot be understood simply as the sum total of the lives of the individual members of the nation, or as the aggregate of the separate life processes of each single Diaspora community. The fundamental nature of this organic entity is not only socio-psychological, but also socio-political. In other words, its various parts are united into a single whole not only by a reciprocal psychological influence which is the source and mainstay of their emotional awareness of belonging to each other, but also by the close bonds forged in the struggle for survival which makes them present a united front to the outside world and sustains their political will and their power of concerted action.

The socio-psychological feeling of unity springs from the memories of a common past history and the consciousness of a common historical and cultural background. A nation is like an individual. It is only the thread of the individual's memories that constitutes his own personal ego and unites his separate experiences into a single, integrated psyche, so that if this thread of memories is broken he loses his separate individuality and becomes psychologically unbalanced. In the same way, the national ego also depends on the thread of the memories shared by all the nation, on the combination of thoughts and community of feelings which are peculiar to the members of that particular nation and which are bound up with the events and experiences of their common past. Not merely is it "incumbent on every Jew to regard himself as having personally taken part in the Exodus from Egypt," but his memories of the past actually make him a participant not only in the Exodus, but also in all the important events and decisive turning points in the nation's life. Hence, the individual Jew's sense of national unity with his fellow Jews is based on his awareness of their common past. The events of the past are an inseparable part of the national religious consciousness. Remnants of past history have been embodied in certain national customs and beliefs and the impression made by past events has given rise to the feeling of a common national destiny.

The socio-political feeling of unity springs from the living and deeply felt attachment to Palestine which nurtures the active messianic hopes of the people and their longings for redemption, and also deepens their sense of not belonging in the alien environment. This sense of strangeness is thus the source of the constant urge of the Diaspora communities to band themselves together in self-defense.

The socio-psychological awareness of national unity finds expression in static nationhood; that is to say, in cultural conditions common to all the dispersed Jewish communities, in the social and economic status of the Jews in the various lands of the Diaspora, in the Hebrew language (which was never completely dead, since it never ceased to perform socio-psychological functions in some particular community) and Jewish literature, in the Jewish household and Jewish domestic life, in forms of divine worship and religious ritual. The socio-political sense of unity, on the other hand, finds expression in dynamic nationhood; that is, in events resulting from the nation's capacity for concerted action—the waves of immigration to Palestine, the messianic movements, the social conflicts and the class struggle within the Jewish communities, the creation of forms of organization best suited to the unification and effective use of the nation's forces. But both these static and dynamic qualities of nationhood draw their being from the existence of the Jewish nation, which never ceased to be a single entity even in dispersion.

2. Even in the days when they were an independent nation living in their own land the Jews were not "like all other peoples." The Jewish people were given a special national character and a special religious mission right from the beginning of their history. The traditional account of Abraham's departure from his home and of his subsequent choice by God is stamped with an unmistakably religious character. Equally unmistakable are the religious implications of the name "Israel," which denotes the special national character of the Jews. Similar implications are also preserved in the other personal names taken by Jews and in the numerous personal epithets and appellatives used by them. The historical significance of this is that the social ties which bound the children of Israel together into the house of Israel are seen to have resulted not only

from public historical processes; they were also forged by the personal names chosen as a sign of their national identity by individual Jews who, out of their loyalty to the God of Israel, banded themselves together into the congregation of Israel and the community of Israel and in every generation, in one form or another, now to a greater now to a lesser extent, pledged themselves "to keep and perform" the laws and statutes given to the Jewish people. This religious element in Jewish nationhood gave a special aura of sanctity to the whole Jewish way of life and was one of the causes of the peculiar blend of religion and nationalism in Judaism. The extent to which these two elements were harmoniously fused together differed from generation to generation, since there was naturally a constant struggle between them for the dominant role in the molding of the nation's life. This tension and conflict are an essential part of Jewish history at all times, including the Diaspora period. True, the cessation of the nation's political life and its exile from its own land increased the importance of the part played by the religious element, but they did not put an end to the continued existence of the national and secular element. In this respect too the history of Jews in Diaspora is a direct continuation of the history of the Jews in their own land, although it follows different channels.

3. The limits of both the static and the dynamic nationhood of Diaspora Judaism are determined by the ethnic character, the social order, and economic system, and the political and administrative organization of the countries in which the various parts of the nation were dispersed, and also by the civic and cultural condition of the peoples in whose midst the Jews resided. All these factors together constituted the framework within which—and only within which—the vital forces of the nation were given a chance to create and act, to organize themselves, and come to terms with their environment.

The Arabs, for example, treated "heretics" with tolerance and even permitted them a large degree of automony. The Jews in Islamic lands were thus able to take advantage of the religious toleration accorded them to create organs of self-government. But the social and political status of the Jews under the caliphate, and the character, form, and organization of Jewish autonomy (with the Exilarchate corresponding to the former monarchy, and the sages to the former priesthood, etc.), were a purely Jewish development resulting from the inner dynamism of Jewish nationhood. Within the historical framework of the rise of the feudal system the Jews were in need of special protection by the authorities in the form of charters; but the legal contents and scope of these charters resulted from the concerted action of the Jewish communities in the lands of Christendom. The political framework created by the constant struggle in Spain between the Arab and Berber elements of the population made it possible for the Jews to take an active and large part in Spanish political life. But it did not dictate either the extent or the form of this participation, both of which are to be explained only by the interplay of the inner forces in Spanish Jewry. Obviously, the framework within which the Jews live does not remain the same in all periods, but constantly changes, expanding or contracting, in the course of history. However, its degree of stability depends on factors entirely outside the sphere of Jewish history. As long as the framework remains fixed, the Jewish life inside it also preserves a steady regularity: the dynamic forces of the nation are denied an outlet and only its static socio-psychological qualities find expression in firmly rooted cultural traditions and stable ways of life. Hence periods of general political stability are times when the scattered communities of the Diaspora can consolidate their positions in their countries of residence.

But in periods of general crisis and upheaval, when tremendous revolutionary changes occur in the alignment of the forces constituting the outer framework of Jewish life, the dynamic forces of Jewish nationhood break out from their confinement, throw off the chains of the established order and the fetters of a time-honored tradition, and strive to shape their own destiny. In most cases they also enter the arena of the general political struggle, in one form or another—sometimes by voluntary choice and sometimes by instinctive compulsion, sometimes with passionate fervor and sometimes with timid hesitancy. This step is usually forced upon the Jews by the nature of historical events. In times of revolutionary ferment there is usually a violent eruption of the pent-up anti-Jewish emotions that have accumulated in various circles of the indigenous population during the preceding period of stability. The former fixed and agreed framework within which the Jews could live their lives in peace and security now disintegrates into a lawless anarchy in which they are exposed to wanton attacks and are obliged to band together in self-defense. Periods of political revolution, national migrations, and ideological conflicts are thus critical times in the history of the Jewish Diaspora.

Epochal changes in general history must, therefore, of

necessity bring about fundamental changes in Jewish life. A new era in general history heralds a new era of Jewish history in the Diaspora.

But epochal historical changes do not long remain confined within the borders of a single country, nor can the rise, existence, and fall of regimes be insulated within a single nation. The Arab conquests and the emergence of the feudal system in Europe, the Crusades and the struggle between the Church and the Roman Empire, the rise of the medieval cities and the coming into being of the new empires, the Reformation and the great voyages of discovery, the French Revolution and modern democracy—all these decisive and epoch-making historical developments affected, to a greater or lesser extent, practically all the countries where Jews were living. For this reason, both the periods of stability and the periods of crisis in the history of the Diaspora were never confined to a single country, but were always the common lot of all the scattered Jewish communities.

4. It is certainly true that the various Diaspora communities were not of equal historical significance. It is also correct to maintain, as Dubnow did, that those communities "which were distinguished by the greater intensity of their inner life" dominated the others; and it is perhaps possible, with certain reservations, to call the dominant community "a center" in relation to those dominated by it, especially if the community in question was large in numbers and thus constituted, quantitatively as well as qualitatively, a considerable part of the whole nation.

At the same time, however, a careful distinction must be made between a "center" of authority and a "center" of influence, that is, between a community connected with all the others by certain organizational ties and unquestioningly accepted by them as their authority in religious matters, and a community that, while not connected with the rest of the Diaspora by any such organizational ties, has, in consequence of certain historical circumstances, come to serve as a social and cultural model to all the other communities which copy its example for a certain period of time.

Such a center of authority was Palestinian Jewry. All the communities of the Diaspora were dependent on it in such religious matters as the exact dates of the festivals and the intercalation of the year, and it maintained regular contact with them all through the emissaries of Zion and the pilgrims. Moreover, there was the great prestige of the land of Palestine as such, deriving from the ancient traditions of its religious sanctity. Babylonian Jewry was also, in some measure, a center of authority, enjoying a position of unquestioned preeminence due to its highly organized religious and national autonomy, which rested both on a hallowed religious tradition (the Talmud) and on permanent and frequent religious and cultural contacts with the other communities of the Diaspora (the *yeshivot** and their organization). But all the other centers listed by Dubnow were only centers of influence, the true nature of which cannot be properly understood without preliminary examination of the reciprocal influence exerted by the communities of the Diaspora on each other.

We have already seen that the unity of the nation was, throughout the period of the Diaspora, fostered by the special way of life which was common to all the scattered communities and which at all times found concrete expression in all the various forms and manifestations of the nation's creative spirit: its faith and religion, its language and literature, its customs and manners, its institutions and organizations, its trends and movements. Although this creativeness was shared alike by all the communities of the Diaspora, of whose lives it was the authentic expression, it nevertheless originated primarily in those lands in which the real tendency and true character of the given historical period—whether it was to be one of stability or one of crisis—were most clearly evident. Hence every period had its own particular centers of influence. In periods of stability, when the socio-psychological elements of the nation's unity are most prominent, the degree of influence exercised by the Jewish communities depends on the extent to which they are able to consolidate their own positions and integrate themselves into the foreign nation-states, and on their readiness to adapt themselves to their environment and give up their own distinctive individuality. This influence stands in direct relation to the stability of these communities and in inverse proportion to their adaption to their environment (Babylonia, Spain, and Germany in the nineteenth century). Conversely, in periods of crisis, when the socio-political elements of the nation's unity come to the fore, the permanent influence of the communities is in inverse proportion to the extent of the crisis and in direct relation to the strength of their political will and their capacity for concerted action (France and Germany at the time of

*Academies of Talmudic learning.

the Crusades, Russia during the years 1878–1914, and America today).

5. The unity of the Jewish nation in exile and dispersion was also the organized unity of a people living according to laws, customs, and practices of its own which regulated every aspect of public and private life to an extent that can hardly be paralleled even in the most highly organized states. The main importance of this does not lie in the fact that the Jews in certain countries were granted the "privilege" of being subject only to their own laws. What is still more significant is that the organization of the nation's autonomy was founded on a complete set of beliefs and ideas, a comprehensive ideology, which provided the basis for the individual Jew's readiness to observe these laws and to obey the authorities appointed in every community to guard the laws and customs of the whole nation. This ideology is, therefore, by its very nature, one of the spiritual phenomena in the life of Jewry in the Diaspora.

6. It is thus clear that the record of the various manifestations of the nation's spirit must occupy a larger place in the history of the Jews than in that of all other peoples. Even the socio-political element in the unity of the dispersed nation more often manifested itself as a desire or aspiration, a trend of thought or visionary movement, than in the form of concerted and militant action. This does not mean, however, that in writing Jewish history all we have to do is to give an account of the philosophical systems of the Jewish sages or a literary appreciation of Jewish poetry. These are matters for students of the history of philosophy or for the historians of Hebrew literature. The writer of Jewish history must deal with the manifestations of the nation's spirit, insofar as they became part of the soul of the average, ordinary Jew who carried on the tradition of the special way of life shared in common by all the communities of the Diaspora. The whole spiritual character of any given generation is determined by this historically anonymous, average Jew's view of life, his beliefs and opinions, his ways of thought and manners of expression, his emotions and dreams. It is by the width of the gap separating popular beliefs from philosophical views—the former static and the latter dynamic—that the spiritual character of the average Jew in every generation is to be determined; and the record of the variations in this gap from one generation to another constitutes the spiritual history of the whole nation. From this point of view the historian is more interested in the questions asked by Jewish philosophy than in its answers; the methods by which it

arrives at its conclusions are for him more important than the conclusions themselves. Similarly, in dealing with Jewish poetry, the historian must be more concerned with the poet's themes than with his beliefs; and in discussing the latter he must pay more attention to the character of the poet's symbols than to the artistic perfection of his imagery. The questions asked by Jewish philosophy and the methods by which it attempts to find an answer to them reflect the doubts and uncertainties, the intellectual conflicts and dilemmas of the generation in question; the themes and symbols of Jewish poetry reflect its cares and joys, its dreams and struggles.

7. Even during the period of the Diaspora, the Land of Israel and its Jewish population still played a part of general importance in the history of the nation. Nor was this only because the deep and continuing emotional influence of the past, and the longings for redemption that fortified the nation's spirit in times of oppression and persecution, were all inseparably connected with Palestine which still remained the Holy Land. The special importance of the Land of Israel in the period of the Diaspora was also a consequence of the unique position, historically and territorially, occupied by the *Yishuv* among the dispersed Jewish communities. This uniqueness of the Yishuv resulted from three basic facts: its historical continuity, its individual character, and its complete Jewishness.

(a) *Its historical continuity*. There never ceased to be a Jewish population in Palestine. Till the time of the Crusades it was very numerous; and even the wars of the Crusades, which resulted in the wholesale destruction of Jewish communities in Palestine, did not put an end to its continuity. The Yishuv continued to exist, and life returned to the devastated communities after a short time. This historical continuity made itself felt in many fields: in the durability of the Yishuv's religious tradition, despite the frequent changes in the composition of the Yishuv caused by waves of immigration; in the permanence of its forms of organization, despite the succession of foreign overlords; in its religious authority over the whole of Jewry, in spite of opposition from without and dissension from within; and in its high level of Jewish culture, in spite of the harsh material conditions of its existence and its very limited chances of social development, both of which might have been expected greatly to reduce its cultural level.

For many generations—down to the Crusades—the office of Nasi (Patriarch) continued to exist as part of the Yishuv's political organization. The Nasi preserved his full rights and status as at once the supreme authority in religious matters, the recognized national representative in dealings with foreign powers, the official leader of the Jewish community, the highest legal authority, the head of the *Great Yeshivah* and also as the surviving descendant of the house of David. Even many generations after the Crusades several attempts were made, in various ways, to restore the hegemony of Palestine. This historical continuity was also largely responsible for the cultural continuity of the Yishuv, which was most strikingly demonstrated in the community's knowledge of the Law and in the extent of its use of the Hebrew language.

(b) *The individual character of the Yishuv.* In almost every period of the Diaspora, the Jewish population of Palestine was dependent on the Jewish communities dispersed in other lands. The constant financial assistance given to the Yishuv by these communities was at all times an organic—and most important—part of the economic realities of Jewish life in Palestine. Indeed, the Jewish population in Palestine depended on the Diaspora for its actual physical survival. By ensuring a steady flow of Jews to Palestine, the successive waves of immigration made good the population deficit caused in every generation by the harsh conditions of life in the country and by emigration, which was just as constant as the reverse process, although, of course, to take a well-known example, the immigration of the three hundred rabbis* was noised abroad far more than the emigration of their sons. Politically, too, the Yishuv was always in need of the protection of the Diaspora. In times of grave crisis the persistent representations made by the Jewish communities in Cairo and Constantinople— and later also in the European capitals—would result in the central authorities' intervening to save the Yishuv from its numerous enemies. This assistance from the Diaspora—in the form of a steady supply of new immigrants and constant financial and political support—was thus essential to the very existence of the Jewish population in Palestine, but also made it largely independent of the local conditions of the country. The small, devastated, and impoverished state could not support an urban population of any numerical importance. At the same time, the prevailing political and administrative circumstances made it impossible to establish any Jewish agriculture or to set up Jewish industries and crafts on any serious scale, although several important attempts were made to

*Three hundred French and English rabbis settled in Palestine in 1210–11.

do both. All this means, that historically speaking, the Yishuv was not just a relic which survived by force of historical inertia, but neither did it resemble any of the Jewish communities of the Diaspora which were equipped by local conditions to absorb and settle Jewish migrants. The whole existence of the Yishuv was something *sui generis* resulting entirely from a ceaseless, generations-long struggle, carried on by the whole of Jewry, and from the repeated and constant efforts made by unknown individuals and organized groups who, by their unflagging determination, kept the Yishuv in being, despite all obstacles and in the face of all attacks. They saved the Land from being abandoned by Jews, they preserved its congregations from complete destruction, and they ensured that the Law should not be forgotten in the Land and that the return to Zion should still be fervently prayed for. The organization, scope, and effectiveness of these efforts were subject, it is true, to the actual conditions of political rule prevailing in Palestine at any given time; but the efforts as such were entirely independent of these external factors and depended solely on the Jewish people and the relations existing between it and its land.

It is in this respect that the Yishuv was unique. In no other land, throughout all the phases of the Diaspora, was there a Jewish community whose existence, to such an extent, was the result of an individual spiritual effort maintained for generations. From this standpoint it makes no difference which of the various sects contributed most to keeping the Jewish population of Palestine in existence and even to increasing its numbers—the "mourners of Zion"* or the messianic visionaries, those who "waited hopefully for the redemption" or "the keepers of the walls," Rabbanites or Karaites,† *Hasidim* or *Mitnagdim*,‡ and the like. What was common to all these groups was the effort made by numerous individual Jews not merely to preserve, but also to enhance, the special way of life of the Yishuv, an effort stimulated by the inner forces of the nation, and not by any favorable outward circumstances of the country itself.

*A Jewish sect devoted to settlement in the Land of Israel which flourished at various periods of Jewish history up to the twelfth century.

†The Rabbanites upheld the Oral Law of the Rabbis; the Karaites, beginning in the eighth century, challenged it.

‡The rise of the popular religious movement of Hasidism in Eastern Europe in the middle of the eighteenth century resulted in the formation of a faction of "opponents" (*Mitnagdim*).

(c) *The complete Jewishness of the Yishuv*. The Jewish population in Palestine was the element of the nation that remained most uncompromisingly and stubbornly loyal to its Jewish heritage. Hence the strongest forces in Judaism from the lands of the Diaspora were at all times drawn to Palestine. . . . .

The Land of Israel and its Jewish population are thus seen to be an intrinsic part of Jewish history in the Diaspora, and not just loosely connected with it by their association with the nation's past memories and future hopes. The Yishuv, as already stated, exercised a magnetic attraction on all those forces in Judaism that were bent on preserving the independence of the Jewish way of life and its historical continuity. The close connection between the Yishuv, on the one hand, and the waves of immigration and the constantly recurring messianic ferments, on the other, was a natural consequence of the character of the Yishuv. In periods when the influence of the Yishuv on the life of the whole nation was in the ascendancy, there was a corresponding rise in the intensity of Jewish life everywhere. The strength of this influence is not to be measured by the number of Jews living in Palestine, but rather by the inner character of the Yishuv—by the completeness and intensity of its Jewishness. Geographically, Palestine was part of the Near Eastern dominions, first of the Mamluks (1250–1516) and then of the Turks (1516–1917), and this geopolitical situation undoubtedly determined the external framework of Jewish life in the country. But historically speaking—in terms of the Yishuv's influence and its connection with Jewish history as a whole—its place in every period is in the heart of the Jewish struggle for survival, as the center of Jewish intensity and Jewish stubbornness in every generation.

INTRODUCTION TO RAPHAEL MAHLER

THE MAJOR JEWISH historians from Jost to Dubnow grossly neglected the economic component of Jewish history. Idealist suppositions, a focus upon religion, or an opposition to Marxism kept them from exploring the material basis of Jewish existence. For a variety of reasons—some practical, some ideological—they tended to minimize economically based tensions within the Jewish communities. It is the great contribution of Raphael Mahler that his work has brought these significant aspects of Jewish history to general attention.

Mahler, who was born in eastern Galicia in 1899, studied both in a rabbinical seminary and at the University of Vienna. After teaching for a number of years in Jewish secondary schools in Poland, he migrated to America in 1937 where he lived in New York and was closely associated with YIVO, the Yiddish Scientific Institute. He settled in Israel in 1950, serving for a number of years as a professor of Jewish history at the University of Tel Aviv until his recent retirement.

It was Ber Borochov, the organizer and chief ideologue of the socialist-Zionist Po'alei Zion movement in Eastern Europe who most affected Mahler's thinking and indirectly also his historiography. In his writings, the young Borochov had managed to bridge a seemingly irreconcilable antagonism between Marxist universalism and the national aspirations of the Jewish people. Adopting Borochov's socialism and Zionism, Mahler came to be guided in his historical writings by these two constituent elements of his own ideology. Jewish history, he was convinced, must be understood according to the general explanation of historical development which is offered by historical materialism; at the same time it must be viewed "from the beacon point of the aspiration of the people to return to its homeland."

Although Mahler published an important work on the Karaite movement of the Middle Ages, he has limited himself mostly to the modern period, with particular emphasis on the history of the Jews in Poland. His major and as yet uncompleted work is his History of the Jewish People in Modern Times. Five volumes have thus far appeared in Hebrew (covering the period from 1780–1815 and, in part, from 1815–1848) and, in English, a single-volume abbreviated version of the first period. The work represents an important contribution to Jewish historiography both for its emphasis on the neglected economic element and for its utilization of unfamiliar and unpublished sources. The first Hebrew volume opens with an introductory chapter in which Mahler offers his conception of modern Jewish history. This is followed by a division of the modern era (from 1789–1950) into periods according to political and economic developments in Europe, supplemented by the progress of Zionism and settlement in the Land of Israel. The selection which follows is a translation of the first part of this chapter, presenting Mahler's general approach. Among its salient character-istics are Mahler's understanding of Jewish Diaspora history in terms of the spiral of social progress and reaction which characterizes the history of the nations in which Jews live; the importance he ascribes to demographic and occupational changes; the multiple adverse effects he considers to have been produced by the structural abnormality of the Jews' nonterritorial existence; and his application of the "law of progress, the iron law of universal human development," to Jewish history as an explanation for the return of Israel to its land.

A word should also be said regarding the rhetorical tone of this selection. Mahler has a penchant for colorful, heroic images; he wants the reader to sense the struggle which must inevitably bring success to both Zionism and socialism. Thus his language, like that of many Marxist historians, is extremely popular while his analysis is *kept simple. But one must remember that Mahler is here trying to make his points as dramatically and as unconditionally as possible. When, in his History, he comes to dealing with specifics, his terminology is relatively more sober, his judgments more reserved and qualified.*

಼಼಼

> "They are new every morning;
> great is Thy faithfulness."
>
> Said R. Simon bar Abba:
> Because Thou renewest us at the morn
> of empires, we know that Thy
> faithfulness is great to redeem us.
>
> Midrash *Lamentations Rabbati* 3:21

The modern era constitutes a dramatic peak in the history of mankind. During the last 150 years and before, world-shaking revolutions have occurred in economics, technology, social and political relationships, and cultural expression. Yet the history of the Jewish people stands out because of its particular course. On the one hand, it is closely attached to world history—Jews have correctly been compared to a barometer which enables us, by their status in each period, to measure decisively the trend of development of mankind and even of every single state. And yet there is no people that resembles Israel in the uniqueness of its national history, its specific economic and cultural development, and its severe struggle for biological and national existence. There is no need to rely upon conjecture or history of bygone times when we have not yet forgotten the most tragic example, the horrible fate of the people during World War II, just as from a different perspective we can point to a fact without parallel in world history: the reestablishment of the people's political independence two thousand years after it was exiled from its land. Attachment to world history and uniqueness, the two lines in the history of Israel which seemingly contradict one another, are but two sides of a single phenomenon, namely the detachment of the Jewish people from the soil. According to the founder of Socialist Zionism, Ber Borochov (1881–1917), it is nonterritoriality that constitutes the basis of the specific conditions of the people's economy in all the lands of its Dispersion, the foundation of its peculiar social structure and its unique cultural situation. This same nonterritoriality is also the reason for the Jewish people's exceptional political weakness, which makes it more dependent than any other people upon the state of the nations of the world and the trends in their development. Due to the nonterritoriality of the Jewish people, it is possible to explain its historical development in any period only as running completely parallel with every period in world history. Each period of human progress means a period of ascent for the Jewish people, just as each turn toward reaction in the life of the nations of the world brings calamity and manifold sufferings upon a people lacking political power. The tremendous imbalance in socio-economic, political, and cultural development among the settlements of the Jewish Diaspora is the direct result of the imbalance in the development of mankind, especially in the period of capitalism. Just as this imbalance in general development is unable to conceal from our eyes the essential tendencies of world capitalism in every age, so, too, in determining the periodization of modern Jewish history, we must first look at the developmental tendencies of the people as a whole, scattered throughout the world, notwithstanding all of the considerable deviations in the many individual areas of Jewish settlement.

Progress is the basic law of development in the life of society, and at no time has progress made such giant strides in all phases of human life as in modern times. Such remarkable development of the productive forces, so tremendous an ascent of civilization and of culture—these can only be measured by the distance that separates feudalism, which still held man in chains at the outbreak of the French Revolution, from the rise of socialism in our days. Passing through unceasing class warfare, repeated bloody revolutions, and devastating wars, mankind during these stormy generations arose and reached the level which it has presently attained.

Along with the development of capitalism, the socio-economic foundations of the life of the Jewish people underwent noticeable change. A people of middlemen, a people of moneylenders and peddlers in Western Europe and of lessees, innkeepers, retailers, and artisans in Eastern Europe was largely transformed into a people that possessed a capitalistic economic structure and capitalistic class division. Commerce and industry became the basic branches of the Jewish economy; Jews came to play a role in the arts and professions which was more than proportionate to their numbers in the general population. The dispersion into small communities in obscure villages gave way more and more during the capitalist period to concentration in metropolises, especially in Western Europe and in the new center, the largest of all Jewish settlements in the world, America. The impoverished Jewish small-town dwellers do not move from one forgotten village to another, but from the typical Kasrilevke* to Kiev, Warsaw, Lodz, and on to Berlin, London, New York, Chicago, and Los Angeles, to Capetown, Sidney, and Melbourne. The socialist revolution, too, in its beginnings marked a new stage in the economic development of the Jewish people. With the rise of the Soviet Union, those who had been storekeepers, merchants, tailors, and shoemakers, entered factories in all branches of industry; the Jewish population, which for generations had been predominantly of the lower-middle class, was entirely transformed into a wage-earning class of workers and clerks.

The development of the legal and political status of the Jewish people in modern times is no less conspicuous. Under feudalism the Jewish people, except for the uppermost stratum of the wealthy, was subject to regulations governing place of residence and occupation; it bent under the heavy burden of special taxes, not to speak of its exclusion from the political life of the lands of its domicile. With the victory of bourgeois rule, the time became ripe for the emancipation of the Jews, for granting them legal equality with the other citizens of the land. As the bourgeois revolution progressed and spread, so did the emancipation of the Jews, embracing ever more lands and areas. The bourgeois revolution in America brought liberation, founded in the law, to its Jewish community. In its wake, the French Revolution and its extensions during the period of Napoleon brought civic rights to the Jews of Western Europe. The Revolution of 1848 proclaimed equality of rights for the Jews in Central Europe. With the stabilization of the bourgeois state of law at the beginning of the last third of the ninteenth century, the Jewish emancipation was complete in all of Europe with the exception of tsarist Russia, which was under an absolutist regime, and Romania, which remained subject to boyar† rule. The socialist revolution of 1917 for the first time brought civic equality, and during the first years also a measure of nationality rights, to the largest of the Jewish settlements in Europe.

Likewise the cultural ascent of the Jewish people during the last

*The fictitious town described by the Yiddish author Sholem Aleichem (1859–1916).
†The boyars were the privileged, landholding class in Romania.

centuries should certainly be measured by the same criteria of general development. During the period of the decline of feudalism the culture of the Jewish people, more than that of the other nations, stagnated in an outworn tradition, sank into a religious slumber and, what is most important, was separated as if by the Great Wall of China from the surrounding world. However, in the period of modern capitalism the gates of universal culture and general education are thrown open to the Jews. Famished for hundreds of years by lack of rights and cultural separation, the Jews enthusiastically leap into all the technological professions, sciences, art, and literature; their names shine brilliantly among the primary builders of human culture. These same generations witness a flowering of Jewish national culture in its various branches: the scientific study of Judaism, publicistic literature in Hebrew and Yiddish, plastic arts, and Jewish music. With the victory of the socialist revolution in Eastern Europe, new horizons are revealed —though to be sure, only briefly—for Jewish culture as well, fashioned by the ideas of the new regime and the new world view.

Nonetheless, a grievous curse haunted the Jewish people—the peculiarity of its national existence, brought about by nonterritoriality. Like a black shadow this abnormality accompanies the ascent of the people in all areas of life. Not only does it stand in the way of its aspiration for equality with the territorial peoples, but it also undercuts and sabotages all of its achievements; it distorts and mutilates them, and in the end it subjects the very existence of the rootless people to mortal danger.

The specific conditions of production of the Jewish people bring its economic development in capitalism up against an iron wall. Because of its detachment from the primary branches of production, and especially from agriculture, the Jewish people in all capitalistic lands resembles an abnormal pyramid of inverted components in its economic structure—commerce, or commerce and industry, forms the base on which rests an extraordinary quantity of professions, and a minimum of agriculture at the apex. Jewish industry is confined to a few branches of the consumer industries, essentially clothing and food. In eastern Europe, the great center of Jewish population, Jewish industry is so scattered that its installations are not very different from artisans' workshops. Even in America, the new center to which vast numbers of Jews migrate, and where at the beginning the concentration of the immigrants in large factories brings about a vigorous process of industrialization, Jewish industry does not deviate from the narrow framework of the traditional branches, and the Jewish people remains the people "of the scissors and the flatiron." This process of industrialization, too, ceases with the end of the mass immigration, and there then emerges a reverse process of constant de-proletarian-ization, of movement into commerce, the professions, and clerical work. Today, even in this great American center of the Jewish people, only remnants of a worker class remain, while in the new centers of Jewish migration (in the twentieth century)—Central and South America, South Africa, and Australia—this process reaches its climax: there a Jewish worker class practically does not exist.

The abnormality of the people's social structure is a conse-quence of the abnormal economic pyramid. Its outstanding characteristic is the decisive majority that belongs to the middle class in the countries of the New World and in Western Europe, and to the middle class and the petty bourgeoisie in Eastern Europe. An attendant phenomenon is the flimsiness of the Jewish worker class, which is chained into the narrow and stultifying framework of certain special branches of production. This same narrow framework, which constrains the productive powers of the Jewish people, is also the cause of the extraordinary poverty of the Jewish population in the backward capitalist lands of Eastern Europe. Moreover, the concentration of Jews in commerce and consumer industries in all capitalist countries, and especially in Central and Eastern Europe, subjects them to ever more severe competition with the middle class and the petty bourgeoisie of the host people, especially with the storekeepers and artisans who become increas-ingly impoverished due to the process of concentration of capital. This competition is evident not only in the economic sphere, where Jewish retailers and artisans are pushed out and severely impover-ished, it also serves—as it does in the arts and professions—as a socio-economic basis for the anti-Jewish propaganda of every political reaction to be found in capitalist society, and in the end it takes the form of an organized anti-Semitic movement.

The peculiar economic structure of the nonterritorial people works for the worst even in socialist countries. Today there are only a few phenomena which differentiate the economic structure of the Jews of the Soviet Union and the countries of popular democracy from their structure in capitalist countries: in the Jewish communi-ties under socialist rule there still exists a large number of artisans who are organized into cooperatives, and, most importantly, the majority—which engages in commerce, clerical work, and the professions—belongs entirely, as does the smaller number of workers, to the class of government employees.

The abnormal conditions of life of the scattered people are negatively evident, as well, in the development of Jewish culture during modern times. The homogeneous and harmonious national culture, which had been treasured and enriched by all parts of world Jewry in every generation and during every period of the long exile, encountered its first crisis as early as the beginnings of capitalism. For the nations of the world the bourgeois revolution brings about a new flowering of national culture borne by the new ruling class. The same is not true for the new Jewish bourgeoisie in Western and Central Europe. It needed only to catch a whiff of the new regime and its civic emancipation in order to make every effort to secure favor and honor from the host bourgeoisie by denying the very existence of the Jews as a people and by proclaiming that the Jews are no more than a *religious denomination*. The Jewish bourgeoisie moves heaven and earth in its aspiration to uproot traditional Jewish culture—and first of all the Yiddish language—from within the Jewish population, in order to spur the process of linguistic and cultural assimilation. Thus the rift is deepened and exacerbated between an increasingly assimilated West European Jewry and an East European Jewry which serves as a backbone of the people. In the course of time this same process of assimilation in the areas of developed capitalism also sucks into its whirlpool the large new center of the people in America. The masses of Jews who are concentrated in the backward capitalist countries of Eastern Europe preserve the language and the national tradition and they build the new Jewish culture—though here, too, the leadership of the bourgeois class persists in preaching assimilation on the model of Western Europe. However, even the marvelous renaissance of Jewish culture in Eastern Europe appears essentially only in the area of Hebrew and Yiddish *belles lettres*. A people not concentrated on its own soil lacks any possibility of including within its national culture *all* of the branches of cultural creativity. It is not only deprived of a political life of its own, but it is entirely removed from technology, land and sea transportation, natural sciences, medicine, (modern) law, and a number of other humanities, which, for the most part, are not even reflected in its language. The defectiveness, the dissonance, and the incompleteness of the Jewish people's culture under the conditions of nonterritoriality are most apparent—as is the danger of assimilation—precisely during the period of burgeoning capitalism.

All of the objective factors that influence socio-economic, political, and cultural development in capitalist countries, which destroy the spoken national language and undermine Jewish culture in the Diaspora as a creative national culture, operate more forcefully in countries that have a socialist regime. To make the tragedy worse, the quick process is hastened, especially in the Soviet Union, by a purposeful policy of forced assimilation. This policy was already clearly apparent before World War II. After the war, toward the end of the Stalinist period, a cruel blow was struck at the remnants of Jewish culture, accompanied, as a frightful symbol, by the imprisonment, and afterward the execution, of the finest Jewish writers. Thus, in the countries of Eastern Europe, violence was used to seal the spring of Jewish national creativity. As if it were not enough that the vast majority of the Jewish population had been annihilated at the hands of the Nazis, the Soviet authorities and several neighboring countries raised the ax of extirpation over the very existence of Judaism. The situation in those countries which are exceptions to this rule, such as Poland (until recently, when its regime openly embarked on a policy of anti-Semitism), Bulgaria, and Yugoslavia, proves clearly that the system of forced assimilation does not follow necessarily from the principles of the regime itself.

However, even without the cataclysm of the Holocaust on the one hand and the bitter compulsion of de-Judaization on the other, the grave crisis of the rift in our culture deepens continually. In the West the maintenance and nurture of Jewish culture has been left to the Jewish population itself, but even there, during the course of only a few decades, this culture has undergone a rapid decline. In all lands of the Diaspora national creativity has reached the climax of crisis. Yet even this decline is not an indication of the final and decisive assimilation of the people. Not only is the pace of assimilation slowed in the West by the efforts of the organized Jewish community, particularly in the realm of education; in all the countries of the Diaspora, whether in the capitalist West or in the socialist East, assimilation encounters the people's peculiar conditions of production, which are revealed especially in its socio-economic structure. Thus we find that even the majority of the people, which has already changed its language and become alienated from its cultural tradition, does not reach the final stage of assimilation: total absorption.

It is just this collision with the solid wall of objective conditions which proves assimilation to be entirely illusory as a solution for the Jewish question. Return to the fold of the people is therefore the only way open to its sons, and a full national cultural renaissance, based on the firm ground of an independent territory, is an historical necessity. The ingathering of the exiles is a necessity even from the standpoint of the people's physical survival alone: mankind's political development in the modern period, especially at the stage of the clash between capitalism and socialism, teaches the Jewish people the clear and bloody lesson that under the conditions of the Diaspora its physical life, too, stands in jeopardy.

As throughout the history of class society, so too in modern times, the progress of mankind does not resemble a steady ascending straight line but rather, to use the classic figure of Marxism, a spiral line with its downward curves indicating the temporary successes gained by the forces of social and political reaction. The hasty progress of mankind in modern times is accompanied, as well, by class warfare of unprecedented severity. The economic development of the last 150 years has been no more forceful than the succession of revolutions, each more radical than the last, and repeatedly opposed by counterrevolutions as the forces of reaction vainly attempt to halt the forward march of humanity by waves of bloody terror. The appointed scapegoat of the reaction, its often tested means of social and political diversion, is the Jewish people scattered throughout the world these two thousand years. The reason for its persecution is the consequence of its dispersion: its political powerlessness and its socio-economic peculiarity. In each generation of its Exile, the Jewish people has been chosen for sacrifice by every form of reaction. For good reason the chronicle of Jewish history from the days of the Temple's destruction has been called "The Book of Tears." However, in modern times the intervals between periods of trouble become ever shorter and the sufferings become ever greater until they reach the most dreadful holocaust in all history.

Even during the era of burgeoning capitalism the process of Jewish emancipation was halted in one place after another by times when Jews were deprived of rights and anti-Semitic movements arose. They parallel the periods of counterrevolution: the period of "Metternichian reaction"* against the French Revolution, and the

*Klemens Metternich, the Austrian minister of foreign affairs (1809–48), was the architect of the political reaction which prevailed in Europe following the defeat of Napoleon in 1815.

counterrevolution which squelched the "spring of the nations"* in 1848. The reaction of imperialism—the economic and political successor of liberalism—which begins with the cruel suppression of the Paris Commune,† is also the time when modern anti-Semitism is born and begins to spread; likewise it is the time of severe discrimination and pogroms directed against the Jews in tsarist Russia, the stronghold of European reaction. The greatest of these calamities was the wave of bloody pogroms which swept over Russian Jewry during the period of cruel terror directed against the revolution of 1905.‡

With the victory of the socialist revolution in Russia in 1917, a wave of reaction sweeps the capitalist world and reaches its climax during the years of fascist and Nazi consolidation in Europe. This time it is not a reaction of one camp against another within the propertied class itself, as in the days when feudalism and absolutism fought against the industrial bourgeoisie; it is a reaction of the world of private property, in whole or in part, against socialism which has attained power. It is therefore not surprising that this assault of the united forces of reaction, the most horrendous in history because it was directed against the very existence of the new socialist regime, and which inundated the worker class with bloody terror, brought calamities upon the Jewish people, which until that time had not been written in the book of its sufferings. The new chronicle of the people's agonies parallels in all of its chapters the stages of the most degenerate of the reactions: the attempted counterrevolution of the White Guard§ in the Ukraine, soaked with the blood of Jewish victims whose numbers range not in the hundreds, as during the tsarist pogroms, but in the tens of thousands. The transfer of power in Germany to the Nazis, the foot soldiers of world capitalism in preparing its war against the Soviet Union, brings the Jews of Germany and neighboring fascist countries to the abyss of suffering and mortal danger. After the Nazi invasion of most of Europe during World War II, the time arrived for the most hideous act in

*A name for the largely abortive political and social revolution which spread through much of Europe in 1848.

†The Paris Commune, set up by the Parisians in opposition to the national government after the Prussian defeat of France in 1871, was liquidated after a few months.

‡The revolutionary fervor in 1905 compelled Tsar Nicholas II to proclaim a constitution. This grudging act was followed by a series of attacks on the Jews.

§The anti-Communist force.

the tragedy of the Jewish people's exile: the cruel murder of most of European Jewry. Such a "Final Solution" to the "Jewish question" was devised by the dark brown mercenary army of fascism, the nurtured child of retreating capitalism—that same capitalism which in its youth abounded with rhetoric about the "eternal rights of man," about the emancipation of the Jews, and about the necessity of their assimilation. And withal—the period of the clash of the two social systems in the world has just begun. . . .

This too—the law of progress, the iron law of universal human development, works everywhere, skipping over no nation in the world, not even the Jewish people, despite its fearful trials. To the people of Israel, also, "history has commanded . . . the blessing," the blessing of the sweet singer of Israel*: "Life for ever" —there—"upon the mountains of Zion"—as "brethren dwell together in unity." It is precisely during the turbulent and fateful modern age that we are witness, indeed the entire world is witness, to the lofty work of the people of Israel, which, again, is unparalleled in the annals of other nations: the people's massive effort to solve the strange contradiction in the conditions of its life, the contradiction between its economic and cultural productive forces which press forward, and the conditions of production which lack roots; as also the contradiction between its instinct for human survival and its pronounced national consciousness versus the constant and imminent danger to its physical and national existence. The solution to these immense contradictions could only be the return to its historic territory, to its homeland. Every period in modern times is also a new stage in the deepening national consciousness of the people of Israel and a new achievement in its efforts to renew its days as of old in the land of its fathers.

In every generation of its protracted exile, longings for Zion and yearnings for redemption in its land have filled the hearts of the people. The idea of a return to Zion was the animating spirit of its cultural creativity and the essential direction of all its social and spiritual currents. However, under the economic, social, political, and cultural circumstances of feudalism it was impossible for this historical aspiration to find practical expression in fact as a real national task. All of the conditions necessary for its achievement, whether in the world as a whole or in the life of the people, were missing. There is a great rule which holds for every individual

*King David, according to tradition, the author of the book of Psalms.

nation as it does for mankind as a whole: in each period society sets for itself only those goals which it is capable of achieving (Marx). Only with the development of modern capitalism did those changes occur in economics, in society, in politics, and in world culture which provided the conditions for the practical proposal that the Jewish people build the Land of Israel. Even a *single* direct consequence of the capitalist development of the productive forces, namely transportation by rail and ship, played a substantial role among the conditions making for a large immigration to the Land of Israel. In the wake of advancing capitalism, there took place among the Jewish people as well, processes of economic and social development, of cultural ascent, and of popular social and political organization—conditions necessary for the appearance of an organized movement of national liberation, the modern Zionist movement.

At the dawn of modern capitalism, during the period of the American and French revolutions, and in the days of the Napoleonic Wars, there already appear political and practical programs for the restoration of the Jewish people to its land. With these programs, their authors, English and French (Napoleon) political leaders, connect their state's interests in the Middle East. These programs are enthusiastically received by the leaders of the Jewish community in America and by farsighted individuals among the Jewish intelligentsia in Western Europe; for them the victory of revolution in their countries has strengthened feelings of national pride and yearnings for the national liberation of their people. Zionist programs appear more frequently during the first half of the nineteenth century, whether in Jewish periodicals and essays in America and Western Europe, or in general political literature. There begins as well an effort of organized Jewish aid for the economic restoration of the older settlement in the Land of Israel (Moses Montefiore*). During the period of flourishing liberal capitalism, beginning with the year 1848, there arises, following the beginnings of the economic and political expansion of the major Western powers in the Middle East, a political movement in Western Europe, especially in England, for the settlement of the Land of Israel by the Jewish people. Under the influence of the national movement in Europe, national consciousness arises as well

---

*Most prominent leader of British Jewry in the nineteenth century and benefactor of Jewish settlers in the Land of Israel.

among Jewish intellectuals in Western Europe (Moses Hess*), and the first heralds of the "Love of Zion" movement† make their appearance.

All these phenomena are only the buds of the people's awakening, the harbingers of the national liberation movement to come. During this period of capitalist development the still great power of numerous factors that impede the advance of the people's national consciousness prevents the realization of its historical impulse for return to Zion. The imbalance in the development of world capitalism lies at the root of the circumstance that the Land of Israel, as a portion of the Turkish empire, is sunk in stagnant feudalism; it is closed to immigration and to settlement of the waste places, and entry to the country remains illegal even at the beginning of the twentieth century. The lack of balance in the development of capitalism is also responsible for the semifeudal backwardness of Eastern Europe. The Jewish population in this principal center of the scattered people will not quickly awaken from the religious slumber of the Middle Ages to national and social consciousness. On the other hand, the enlightened do not generally regard nonterritoriality as the source of abnormality in the life of the people. On the contrary, they do their best to convince their people that the more it extends its dispersion the more will it succeed in improving its situation. Nearly the entire Jewish bourgeoisie of Western Europe suffers under the illusion that precisely by cutting every tie with the historical homeland of the people, by denying its own national character, and by assimilation within the ruling bourgeoisie, will a definite solution be found for the problem of its existence. The movement for enlightenment among the new Jewish bourgeoisie and intelligentsia in Eastern Europe does not, indeed, go so far as to preach clear assimilation, but it too promotes a program for cultural, social, and political adaptation to the native population, and it ignores any connection between the Jewish people and the Land of Israel.

However, with the stage of imperialism, as the Jewish middle and lower-middle classes are increasingly ousted from their positions in the economy, as the modern anti-Semitic movement begins to spread, and as the Jews of Russia are afflicted with restrictive laws and bloody pogroms, modern Zionism emerges and

*Nineteenth-century German socialist and precursor of Zionism.

† The East-European pre-Zionist movement which began in Russia in the 1880's.

becomes an increasingly powerful mass national movement. To be sure, the difficult economic and political conditions operating against settlement in the Land of Israel cause the mass migration to flow to the United States, the spacious land of flourishing capitalism and of wide opportunities for absorption. The immigration to the land of Israel, which increased especially after the defeat of the first revolution in Russia in 1905, established in the people's homeland a normal settlement, grounded in the soil; but by the numbers of its population, it still did not constitute more than the basis for the massive immigration that was to come. The immigration and settlement of this period bear the character of a first pioneering effort—an historical necessity both on account of the situation in the country and because of the socio-economic development of the people during the era of the Diaspora. Extensive settlement was not possible until it had been prepared for by the pioneering work of transforming a wilderness into a land fit for habitation. Moreover, the people that for so long had been uprooted from the soil and from basic production was not prepared—despite all of its longings for its homeland and its continually deepening national conscious-ness—to abandon the occupations to which it was accustomed and to change to new areas of labor as pioneers, so long as it was not forced to do so by the pressure of its situation in the lands of the Diaspora (a pressure that was ever increasing). The pioneers of the new settlement, the men of the Second Aliyah,* were nearly all drawn from the pioneering element within the Jewish worker class, which, as against the majority party of this class,† included the liberation of the people in its homeland within its socialist program and within the class war.

The end of World War I, which fatefully produced the socialist revolution in Russia, began a new period in world history. With this new stage in the struggle of the nations for their liberation, a new period opened as well in the history of the national liberation of the people of Israel. In Jewish history, the previous epoch—that of the burgeoning of modern capitalism—was marked by the process of civic emancipation, which was halted during periods of reaction when its achievements were undermined or nullified completely.

*The second wave of modern immigration to the Land of Israel, beginning in 1904 and lasting until World War I.

† The non-Zionist Jewish socialists who formed an organization known as the "Bund."

The second epoch, the era of the greatest catastrophe in Jewish history because of the severe crisis of capitalism, is also the period of the autoemancipation of the people, as "children return to their own border" (Jer.31:17). During these generations of the advance of socialism in the world and the national awakening of the peoples on the continents of Asia and Africa, the fatherland of the people is renewed thanks to the pioneering courage of its finest sons and daughters, inspired by the idea of national and social liberation. It is transformed into the great central haven of its wanderings, and into the spiritual center of its dispersion. The frightful trials experienced by the people as a result of the clash between the old world order and the new, serve as stages in the growing immigration to its land and the building up of its security. The pogroms perpetrated by Petlyura's* bands in the Ukraine intensify the Third Aliyah;† the national oppression in Poland increases the Fourth; and the wave of Nazism and fascism in Central and Eastern Europe spurs the largest of the waves of immigration before the outbreak of World War II, the Fifth Aliyah.

The most dreadful holocaust in the history of Israel, which destroyed a third of the people, is the bloody price it paid for its two-thousand year existence in the Diaspora. The people, which during the nightmare of the Nazi hell rose to the courage of the ghetto rebels, shook itself free of the catastrophe to engage in the fight for independence in its homeland. The people that dwells in Zion purchased the freedom of its land with its blood, and in this struggle it was assisted by the political and oral aid of the forces of progress in the entire world. On May 14, 1948, the independent State of Israel was proclaimed by the people of Israel in the Land of Israel. The echo of the words of the people's great poet [Bialik] on the pogrom at Kishinev‡ sounds like a prophecy: "For the Lord called for a springtime and a slaughter together." The slaughter was brought about by the fascist reaction of the regime whose glory had departed; its springtime the most unfortunate of peoples gained by the sweat of its brow and by its sword during the gloaming of

---

*Simon Petlyura (1879–1926), Ukrainian nationalist leader whose battalions in 1919 and 1920 massacred Jews in various Ukrainian towns.

† The third wave of immigration, immediately after World War I (1919–23). It was followed by the Fourth Aliyah (1924–28) and the Fifth Aliyah (1929–39).

‡ About a year after visiting the town of Kishinev, where a dreadful pogrom had taken place in 1903, the great Hebrew poet Hayyim Nahman Bialik (1873–1934) wrote his powerful poem "In the City of Slaughter," from which this verse is taken.

humanity's rebirth. The people of Israel's intense desires throughout the generations for political freedom in its land were realized. A new chapter begins in the history of Israel, the period of gathering in the exiles of the wandering people, scattered and dispersed among the nations. The road to complete national rehabilitation is still long, and as difficult as the parting of the Red Sea; it is as hard as the severe struggle of an oppressed and suffering mankind for full liberation and for the establishment of world peace. But mighty as a rock is the future of the people which builds its national home on the foundations of a humanity that is toiling, fighting, and surging forward.

THREE DIASPORA CONCEPTIONS

INTRODUCTION TO SALO BARON

SALO BARON is the first Jewish historian to compose a major history of the Jews in English. His astounding erudition and immense scope render him one of the truly outstanding figures in the entire history of Jewish historiography.

Born in 1895 at Tarnow, Galicia, an Austrian town close to the Polish border, he received an advanced rabbinical and secular education in Vienna. From 1917 to 1923, in addition to ordination, he managed to accumulate three doctorates: in history, political science, and law. After a few years of teaching at the Jewish Teachers' College in Vienna, he was invited in 1927 by Stephen S. Wise to serve on the faculty of the Jewish Institute of Religion in New York. In 1930 he received an appointment to Columbia University where he remained until his retirement in 1963.

Baron's writings range over the entire span of Jewish history, though his earliest work relates to the modern period. He has shown a remarkable ability for integrating Jewish with general history, based on his vast knowledge of political and intellectual developments outside the Jewish community. In addition, he has brought to Jewish historiography a sociological orientation which has enabled him to shed light on certain phenomena neglected by most other historians; he has especially advanced our knowledge of Jewish demography and occupational distribution.

Baron's major work is A Social and Religious History of the Jews, which in its second and greatly expanded edition has already reached fifteen volumes, though it has not yet passed beyond the year 1650. It is the first attempt at a comprehensive treatment of the entire span of Jewish history to appear since Dubnow composed his World History of the Jewish People in the 1920's. Although Baron has written a number of articles dealing with the methodology of Jewish historiography and suggesting emphases for the future, a really comprehensive view of the Jewish past appears most prominently in the first chapter of his major work; an excerpt from three sections of this chapter has been selected here to illustrate his conception of Jewish history. Especially noteworthy are Baron's focus upon the close relation between religion and history as representing the unique characteristic of the Jewish people and his endeavor to account for the multiple inner conflicts within contemporary Judaism while at the same time giving reasons for his faith in its viability.

EMANCIPATION FROM STATE AND TERRITORY

The history of every people is unique, and some value this uniqueness as an extraordinary distinction. Hence the many "chosen peoples" of mankind. But Israel emphasized the importance of its history for its religion and vice versa, as has no other nation. The Exodus from Egypt was apparently a minor occurrence in the history of that time, so minor, indeed , that the nation most concerned in it next to the Jews themselves, the Egyptians, never took the trouble to record it. . . . But it was precisely this event that was made by Moses and the prophets the cornerstone of the new development, the point of departure for a new era in mankind. Time and again lawgivers and poets, priests and prophets, referred back to the deliverance from Egypt, because in it they saw the origin of the Jewish people, and the final conclusion of the covenant between the people and its God.

Since that time this *people* has had an unusual history. In the period of the conquest and settlement in Canaan, under its own kings, and to an even greater degree in the two and a half millennia of the Dispersion, the career of this people represents a remarkable interplay of the history of an individual nation and of that of many nations or of mankind at large. Situated between two of the greatest trade routes of antiquity, ancient Israel watched the endless procession of Egyptian and Assyrian soldiers, Babylonian priests, Phoenician merchants, and Arabian Bedouins. It saw itself constantly and irresistibly drawn into the whirl of world politics and commerce. Other ethnic and religious groups lived for long in the very heart of ancient Israel, just as, from the eighth century onward, the Jews began again to live in other lands among varied alien majorities. This cannot be a mere accident of history. To insist that peculiar destinies of individuals and nations happen precisely to those individuals and nations with an innate disposition for them, may seem to be reaching out too perilously into the realm of metaphysics. Under the same circumstances, however, many other peoples would certainly have perished and disappeared from history. That the Jews survived is largely due to the fact that they were prepared for their subsequent destinies by their early history.

The most striking corollary to the contrast between history and nature in the Jewish religion appears to be the contrast between nationality and state in Jewish history. For a relatively short time the Jews had a state or states of their own. Gradually the nation emancipated itself from state and territory. As the Jewish religion developed away from any particular locality, the Jewish people— and this certainly was a contributory cause of the former development—also detached itself more and more from the soil. Common descent, common destiny, and culture—including religion—became the uniting forces. . . . This development away from the soil has, of course, been attended by tragedies: after fifteen and more centuries of sojourn in a country, the Jews can be regarded as strangers to its soil even by peoples (for example, the Bulgarians) who settled there long after them.

This tragedy is a necessary consequence of the revolt of nature against history. Despite all that Judaism stands for and all that the Jewish people has lived through, it cannot be denied that, at least until the day of the Messiah, which can come only in a miraculous way, history will not have vanquished nature. Until then, nature is the necessary substratum for history, as is the soil for the life of a nation. This eternal conflict marks the *tragic* history of the Jews. Time and again the Jews have reverted to nature, time and again they were obliged to create their territory. . . . The slaves in Egyptian bondage conquered Canaan, the refugees in the Babylonian Exile soon established a new self-governing state, and settlers from all over the world are now building up, against tremendous odds, the new state of Israel. In the two millennia of the Diaspora the quasipolitical aspirations of the people have never ceased to be a living force. The very failures of all the messianic movements throughout the ages were, in their tragic grandeur, nothing but the continuous reaffirmation of that yearning for the return to the soil. The people's half-conscious wish to become again rooted in territory and state also found repeated expression in the various substitutes it devised. . . . [T]hroughout the ages the Jewish community organization partly replaced the missing state . . . ; the Jewish quarters of ancient Alexandria or under the caliphate, in North Africa or in medieval and modern Europe, were a surrogate, however poor, for Israel's territory.

These are not inconsistencies, they are rather necessary compromises in life. History in its realization needs nature, as any given moment in time is realized in space. This is a tragic conflict and in its attempts to resolve it the Jewish people has often suffered severely. We have just witnessed the greatest tragedy in Jewish history which accompanied the onslaught of a blood-and-soil ideology on the fundamentals of history-made Western civilization. It was scarcely surprising that Nazism's concentrated fury hit the people whose entire career had longer and more persistently than any other embodied these historic fundamentals. But this tragic destiny is, perhaps, the most magnificent feature of the history of the Jews! As Martin Buber* once remarked:

> The Jewish people has become the eternal people not because it was allowed to live, but because it was not allowed to live. Just because it was asked to give more than life, it won life.

Such persistence in living *despite nature* has often amazed and repelled external observers. Even in recent years, keen and liberal-minded historians of the rank of Mommsen† and Nöldeke‡ could not conceal their impatience with and disapproval of the "unnatural perseverance" of the Jews after the loss of their political independence. Much gratuitous advice has been proffered to them throughout the ages, bidding them give up their stubborn resistance to the "normal" ways of life, mingle with the nations and thus simplify a perplexing situation. In almost every generation, indeed, Jewish individuals and minor groups tread this road to easygoing regularity. Now, however, the people as a whole could not embark upon it, even if it wanted to do so. Apart from the powerful Aryan opposition to assimilation, a simultaneous mass conversion of all Jewry to Christianity and Islam, if it were at all feasible, would clearly lead to the immediate constitution of a Judeo-Christian and Judeo-Muslim group which would continue living the segregated unnatural life of present-day Jewry. This unnaturalness would be inordinately aggravated through the removal of what has thus far been the most constructive force: the common religious heritage.

The life of the Jews contrary to nature has also led to their characteristic polarity in action and in thought. The acknowledg-

---

*Jewish social and religious philosopher (1878–1965).

† Theodor Mommsen (1817–1903), German historian of ancient Rome.

‡ Theodor Nöldeke, nineteenth-century German Semitic scholar.

ment of the Exile as a temporary sojourn under foreign oppression might have been, in former days, the necessary complement to the belief in Israel's selection. Beyond the need for psychological compensation for the feeling of inferiority connected with the *Galut** by a sense of superiority as a chosen people, exilic existence was frequently hailed as a necessary instrument of the divine government of the world. Only as a dispersed people could the Jews serve as the light of many nations. In modern times the attempt to combine full political amalgamation with the maintenance of a separate ethnic existence has become more complex and has resulted in a dual allegiance so frequently assailed and still more frequently misunderstood. The necessity, through two millennia, of cultivating at least two languages (as Hebrew and Greek, Arabic, or English; or even Hebrew, Aramaic, and Greek; or Hebrew, Yiddish, and Polish) for daily routine and synagogue prayer, for business correspondence and literary pursuits, demonstrated to every Jewish youth the abnormality of his national existence. The great poet Judah Halevi was not altogether wrong when he placed bilingualism into the very cradle of Israel's history and stated that Abraham himself spoke Aramaic in his daily intercourse, but resorted to Hebrew for sacred uses (*Kuzari*, II, 68). We need but vary this statement, in accordance with our historical knowledge, and say that Abraham and his family probably long continued using their Accadian dialect from Haran,† while learning to converse with their Canaanite neighbors in the latter's Hebraic tongue. To clinch it all came the gradual elimination of the Jews from the soil of medieval Europe and their increasing concentration upon trade and moneylending. The pious expounders of the biblical prohibitions of usury and the Talmudic disparagement of all interest (even if charged to Gentile borrowers) were thus forced into a position of leadership as the chief "usurers" of the Western world. Later, too, the often sincere protagonists of ethical monotheism saw themselves inescapably involved in some of the most nefarious practices of modern economic exploitation.

Similarly, Jewish national character and religious thought became full of contradictions. The eyes even of casual onlookers have been caught by the contrast between the practical sense of the Jew and his unrestrained idealism; between his adherence to

*The Exile.

†City in northern Mesopotamia associated with the family of Abraham (Gen. 11:31).

tradition and his proneness to innovations; between his quick, intuitive grasp and endless, arid casuistry; between his commercial avidity and unlimited charitableness. In Jewish religion, since the days of the prophets, universalism and particularism have been logical antitheses persistently linked in a living unity. "For Judaism," says Leo Baeck,* "there exists no creed without moral teaching, no mystery without commandment, no distance without proximity, no recognition of the hereafter without a recognition of this world" (*The Essence of Judaism*, p. 187). Did not ancient Pharisaism accept determinism and free will, and the medieval Jewish philosophers, God's transcendence and immanence as coexisting realities in defiance of all logical consistency? All life is a compromise between irreconcilable logical contradictions, and every train of thought reflecting reality will end in unbridgeable antinomies. But the Jewish mind, following the logic of its extraordinary destinies, appears as an uninterrupted chain of antinomies and paradoxes.

The greater the discrepancy between theory and reality, the more tragic became the inner conflicts in the Jewish personality. The steady equanimity and cheerfulness of the ghetto days (hidden to the uninitiated behind a drab and gloomy appearance) vanished in the modern period, especially when the Jews became more conscious of this glaring discrepancy. Mankind as a whole was constantly losing faith in eudaemonistic progress. Gone, for the most part, was the enthusiastic belief of the Enlightenment that the pursuit of happiness would proceed untrammeled, if only a few political obstacles were removed. . . . As a Jew and as a European, the emancipated Jew suffered doubly from the shattering of his high hopes. Messianic expectations attached to the new era of freedom and equality in the early period of Emancipation had to be toned down in the face of ever-new complications. The tiny but solid bridge of the ghetto having broken down, a chasm between Jewry's exalted mission and sordid reality opened, abysmal and terrifying.

Many Jews, steeped in their cultural and ethnic heritage, have gazed without perturbation on the precipice and searched for new paths on which to continue their historic march. Others, less free from dizziness, have completely lost their balance. Some have become the harshest Jew-haters of modern times. The Jew's

---

*German Progressive rabbi and religious thinker (1873–1956), represented in the final selection.

proclivity to self-criticism, even self-irony, was strengthened by a long and venerable tradition, going back to the ancient prophets. The struggle with nature and reality produced a negativism, a denial of the existing modes of social and individual life, whose edge was pointedly aimed at Jewish realities and at the Jewish forces which supported them. Sometimes this negativism was wholly constructive, preaching the subjugation of the present to the superior aim of molding the future. In many instances, however, it became negativism, pure and simple—barren and unproductive—delighting in contradiction for contradiction's sake. Self-accusation has been magnified to satanic self-hatred, with which few men have ever been so deeply afflicted as some unbalanced modern Jews. Theodor Lessing,* in describing several such Jews who became an abomination unto themselves to the point of self-destruction (notably Weininger† and Trebitsch‡), rightly sensed that even these aberrations were merely distortions of the legitimate consequences of Judaism's historic emphases. Were not the Jews, even in their most constructive representatives, the yeast among the nations? Their undermining of existing institutions, although a wholesome and often absolutely necessary function, irritated not only those interested in the preservation of these institutions, but also the more neutral bystanders. As Mommsen accurately remarked, every process of decomposition spreads a bad odor, and the Jewish "element of decomposition" had no right to complain when even its salutary and often indispensable labors aroused widespread resentment.

With the Jewish denial of existing realities went the refusal to recognize the powers of the day. Power itself often became the cause of suspicion and resentment rather than of admiration and acquiescence. The exaltation of powerlessness in the Jewish religion found its counterpart in the evolution of a people without political power. It has been observed, that from the very beginning, most biblical leaders were not born into power, but were said to have been endowed with it by a special act of Divine grace. While biblical law, following widespread Oriental prototypes, acknowledged the natural superiority of the firstborn son, biblical legend and history

---

*German Jewish philosopher (1872–1933), author of *Jewish Self-Hatred* (1930).

†Otto Weininger (1880–1903), author of *Sex and Character* (1903), a work displaying clear Jewish self-hatred.

‡Arthur Trebitsch (1880–1927), writer and convert to Christianity who turned virulently against Judaism.

attached a higher importance to those younger sons whom God called to perform a service. In the long series of biblical heroes, Abel, Isaac and Jacob, Moses, David and Solomon were all younger members of their respective families who became qualified for membership in defiance of natural succession. In the ultimate supremacy of the defenseless, persecuted, suffering prophets over the mighty kings of Israel and Judah, the recognition that there exists a higher power than sheer political force found definite acceptance. Deutero-Isaiah's poems of the suffering servant of the Lord, in the prototype of a suffering powerless people which nonetheless comes out victorious in the end, reflected not only the actuality of the Babylonian Exile, but also the gradual emancipation from the natural category of power as equivalent to political expansion and state domination.

Jewish messianic humanitarianism and internationalism spring from the same root. There have been many German thinkers who, glorifying power as do the spokesmen of no other nation (the British and Americans, for example, quietly take it for granted that power is and should be theirs, but do not theorize about it), reiterated that humanitarianism is "a ruse of the weak," invented by the weak (especially the Jews) for their self-protection. The inherent fallacy of this contention in the face of powerful cosmopolitan currents within mighty empires . . . is of less consequence here. The Jewish people doubtless rationalized the lack of its political power in the face of vast empires. But it must have felt then that it possessed powers other than political, which were their full equivalent. Will not even those power worshipers who view human history only from the standpoint of success, and equate right with ultimate acceptance by those in power, admit that the Jewish people has manifested an extraordinary power to endure beyond all the mighty empires of antiquity? Early recognizing the ultimate futility of even the greatest human power, ancient Judaism exalted the omnipotence of God alone, appearing "not by might, nor by power, but by My spirit, saith the Lord of hosts" (Zech. 4:6). The religious and ethnic power of perseverance, rather than the political power of expansion and conquest, became the cornerstone of Jewish belief and practice. Such power was naturally defensive and passive, and mutual nonaggression was one of its major safeguards. Thus Jewish universalism and pacifism may have been the rationale of Jewish political impotence, but at the same time they flowed from the vast stream of a real, although nonpolitical, potency.

It is necessary at this point to correct an even more widespread fallacy. Political powerlessness has often been mistaken by foe and friend alike as the equivalent of the Jews' utter despondency and misery throughout the history of the Dispersion. In recent years one has heard more and more frequently of the age-old pariah existence of the Jews. This concept, based on a false analogy with the Indian untouchables, is wholly misleading. It is, indeed, flatly contradicted by all known historical facts, both objective and subjective. Neither under the Hellenistic, Roman, and Persian empires nor under Islam and Byzantium, nor even in the worst years of medieval persecution, did the status of the Jews warrant any such comparison. The Jews doubtless suffered a great deal in their millennial procession. Scores of thousands of their martyrs have sanctified the Name (of the Lord) in untold sufferings, and daily and hourly ordinary Jews have borne the brunt of arrogance and ill will in passive, but nonetheless heroic, fashion. They had, however, the great compensations which accompany every truly religious sacrifice. And were they the only people of the earth to suffer? Has not the lot of all men, especially in those dark and cruel ages of scarcity and horror, been to suffer indescribable agonies for, or—what is much worse—without a just cause? Who would dare weigh one suffering against another and prove that the scale of one group of men has, over a long period, dipped lower than that of other groups? It is quite likely, moreover, that even the average medieval Jew, compared with his average Christian contemporary, man by man, woman by woman, child by child, was the less unhappy and destitute creature—less unhappy and destitute not only in his own consciousness, but even if measured by such objective criteria as standards of living, cultural amenities, and protection against individual starvation and disease. And subjective-ly, as long as the Jewish religion was at all intact, the people never conceded final defeat nor acknowledged its own inferiority in any ultimate category.

The wide assumption of a pariah status of pre-Emancipation Jewry could never have arisen, were it not for the prevalent view of Jewish history in the Dispersion as one of incessant suffering and persecution. This view has an old and venerable tradition, with such diverse roots as the opinions of Graeco-Roman Jew-baiters, patristic polemists against Judaism and Talmudic sages. The arrogance of medieval ecclesiastics and nobles gave definite shape to the picture of the Jew as a harassed and universally despised creature. In a more realistic retrospect, however, one must never forget that these were the same people who heaped contempt and oppression, equally boundless and cruel, upon the majority of their fellow Christians, peasant serfs and villains. Even among them, the more serious-minded pondered the historic riddle of Jewish survival and, like the Muslim sages, composed endless treatises in defense of their own creed against the claims of Judaism. Certainly no such relationship can be conceived between pure-blooded Brahmans and pariahs in India as would permit of religious disputations. However fateful their consequences to the Jewish participants, these and the perennial attempts to induce the Jews by suasion and force to abandon their faith and to join the majority on a highly respected footing were essentially an admission of the basic equality of the synagogue with the church and mosque.

Moreover, unlike genuine pariahs, Jews could, severally and collectively, leave their group and, at their own discretion, join the dominant majority. At least until the rise of modern racial anti-Semitism nothing was formally easier for a Jew than, by an act of simple conversion, to become a respected, sometimes leading member of the Christian or Muslim community. . . . The fact that so many Jews throughout the ages repudiated this easy escape, indeed furiously resisted all blandishments and force, testifies to their deep conviction that they would lose, rather than gain, from severing their ties with the chosen people.

HISTORICAL LITERATURE

The intimate relation between the Jewish people and its religion was felt at the very threshold of the history of both. It is no accident that among the oldest literary documents of the people are not only war songs, legends, and tales such as are found in other civilizations, but, primarily perhaps, laws and religious and moral teachings. Probably one of the oldest parts of the Bible is the so-called Book of the Covenant,* containing essentially civil and criminal laws. The ancient, most probably Mosaic, Decalogue itself deals with fundamentals of creed only in the first two or three commandments, devoting all the rest to laws concerning the conduct of daily

*Exodus 20:22–23:33.

life. The first of the writing prophets, Amos, is chiefly concerned with the problem of justice, the main principle of overcoming nature by history, of controlling the innate powers of the strong by the power of an organized historical group. Justice, and especially social justice, remained throughout the ages the cornerstone of Jewish public life and theology.

Neither is it an accident that this people was also the first to *write* great history. Historical narratives, songs, and the like existed among all nations. But a consecutive historical literature with that fine combination of factual statement, pragmatic interpretation, and charming presentation, as composed by the Hebrew writers and compilers between the tenth and eighth centuries, finds no parallel whatever in other ancient literatures before the Greeks. Even the otherwise most distinguished Greek historians, such as Herodotus and Thucydides, lacked something of the historical perspective of the Israelitic historians. Deuteronomy is able to reproach the Jews with ingratitude toward God because they have failed to "remember the days of old, consider the years of many generations" (32:7). The historical novels such as Ruth, Esther, Tobit, and Judith,* referring to historical rather than to mythological events, played in Judaism a role unparalleled in the ancient world. Extraordinary events in the Jewish past, moreover, were interpreted in the light of their total significance for the destinies of all nations. Hence the universal aspect and also, in a sense, the universal treatment of history by these early writers. They start out with the admission that twenty generations preceded Abraham, and that many other peoples may regard themselves as direct descendants of the Jewish patriarchs. This catholicity was in sharp contrast to the assumptions of the Babylonians and the Egyptians that they were the first to be created by their gods. Nowhere else, at that time or before, was such a sympathetic treatment of world history possible as is found in Chapter 10 of the first book of Moses.

In view of this early historical bent, the fact, that during the Dispersion until about a hundred years ago, the Jewish people seems to have lost interest in writing even its own history, might appear doubly astonishing. That this cannot be fully ascribed to the influence of the peoples among whom the Jews lived, is obvious; the medieval Arabs and the modern European nations displayed a vivid interest in history and produced many able historians. There were

---

*The books of Tobit and Judith are contained in the Apocrypha.

many other reasons at work: among them, the lack of political history in the ordinary sense; the supreme power of the Law which steadily interrupted historical continuity and made increasingly difficult the preservation of historical records. But, even in those ages, the essential orientation of the Jewish people toward its past and future cannot be subject to doubt.

MENACE OF A NEW SCHISM

The intrinsic unity of Jews and Judaism has been somewhat obscured in recent generations. On the one hand, Reform Judaism, at least in its earliest formulations, tried to emphasize more and more strongly the universal element in the Jewish religion. In consequence, the Jewish people as a whole lost its essential standing within the Jewish creed, and became rather an outward means toward the realization of a universal religion in the whole world. He who as a matter of principle thinks that the fundamental teachings of Judaism are reserved for the Jewish people "denies the One and Only God of messianic humanity," said Hermann Cohen— undoubtedly the greatest Jewish thinker of the last generation—in trying to demolish the nationalist movement. Even more significantly, he and many of his confreres bowed their heads in reverence before the supremacy of the state. Abandoning the general liberalistic aloofness toward the state ideal, many of these religious liberals paradoxically proclaimed:

> However central religion appears to us modern men within the general compass of history, it is nonetheless merely a concentric specialty within the unity of ethical culture. It is the state which occupies, for us, the focal position in human civilization [H. Cohen, *Jüdische Schriften*, II, 323, 331].

Even Cohen's qualification, that the state realizes the moral aims of mankind "as the symbol of a league of states," could not conceal the radical departure of Jewish liberalism from traditional nonpolitical, more truly universalist Judaism. While this attitude, and even more general assimilationist tendencies, led toward a denial of the Jewish national entity, Zionism and other Jewish national movements laid increasing stress upon the secular aspects of the Jewish people, often trying to detach the national being of the Jews from their religion. In their own way they also emphasized the state idea or political action to safeguard the rights of the Jewish minority.

All these movements in their extreme tendencies appear to be based largely upon the application of certain general formulations to a specific case which they do not fit. According to the widest accepted definition of nationalism, a nation (in the ethnic, not the political sense) is a group of men linked together by common ties of destiny and culture. Even on the basis of this formula, the common Jewish fate and culture includes the past generations of primarily religious Jews and the past history of Jewish culture which, at least until recently, was mainly a religious culture. We know how deeply rooted are modern Jewish cultural movements in one or another religious experience of bygone days. Hebrew, the language adopted by a large part of secular Jewish nationalism, is permeated with religious content. Neither will Yiddish, it appears, be wholly purified from its religious ingredients in the near future. This evolution has not yet run its course and we certainly lack the perspective to judge what will be the ultimate resultant of the strong conflicting forces in contemporary Jewish life. In the opinion of numerous observers, however, it is very likely, that just as Jewish nationality represented a vital element in the Jewish religion of former days, the Jewish religious heritage will soon be more generally recognized, under one shape or another, as an integral part of Jewish nationalism.

In the past as well as in the present, the existence of the Jews has always been a peculiar one (whether this peculiarity is a reason for pride and a feeling of chosenness is, of course, a matter of individual judgment). All attempts to explain this phenomenon in general terms, without paying attention to specific elements, must necessarily fail. In fact, the hasty usage of analogous terms borrowed from the general situation to define Jewish developments has often been seriously misleading. "Political Zionism," for example, is, strictly speaking, a misnomer, inasmuch as its controlling trend is dominated by an humanitarian ideal. . . . It has thus come to pass that, through a perverse irony of history, the Jewish nationality, the first nationality (in the modern ethnic rather than political sense) to appear on the historical scene, was long denied the right to be classified as a national entity altogether. That this happened in the period of modern nationalism, at a time when, one might say, the ancient Jewish conception of nationality was finally accepted by the world at large, makes this paradox even more poignant.

At any rate, the middle course seems, at present, to be victorious in countries where the Jews constitute a comparatively small section of the population. Such are all the countries of central and western Europe, and of America, including the United States. The Jewish Reform movement, extremely anti-nationalist, anti-Zionist, and anti-Hebraic in its earlier history, is now more and more on the road to reconciliation with these traditional forces. On the other hand, Zionism and nationalism have failed in these countries to secularize Jewish life to any considerable extent. Even among the five millions of American Jewry all attempts to revitalize Judaism as "the Jewish way of life becomes necessarily secular, humanist, scientific, conditioned on the industrial economy, without having ceased to be livingly Jewish" (H. M. Kallen,* *Judaism at Bay,* p. 5) have thus far not progressed beyond the stage of dreams. Quite different, of course, was, until the recent tragedy, the situation in such countries of Jewish mass settlement as Russia and Poland. Should secular Jewish nationalism really prevail there in the end and for the first time in history divorce the Jewish people from its religion, the possibility of a deep schism in Jewry would become real.

Such a menace is perhaps enhanced by the relatively large number of Jews now living and the vast extent of their settlements. Twelve million Jews are an unwieldy mass, difficult to control and still more difficult to unify under the most favorable circumstances. Scattered all over the globe, participating in the economic struggles and cultural evolution of almost every nation, they can hardly achieve uniformity or unity of a positive nature.

Extreme Jewish individualism and the impossibility of any mass of Jews agreeing on almost any single course of action, on the other hand, in themselves partly the result of these historical and geographic divisions, may be regarded as obstacles rather than aids to serious schismatic ventures. However great the readiness on the part of many modern Jews to deviate from the road of official Judaism (if such a term still has any meaning today), they spend most of their energies in mutually combating one another's newly

*Horace Meyer Kallen, contemporary American Jewish humanist thinker and cultural pluralist.

chosen road to salvation. The various schismatic trends, one might say, are so heavily charged with electricity, positive as well as negative, that they are likely to neutralize one another for a long time to come. The growth of the new Israel center, aided by the unprecedented technological facilities for mutual communication, should also strengthen the centripetal forces. Jewish solidarity, moreover, at least in the face of a common enemy, may likewise for a while counteract the disintegrating forces of individualism —another living Jewish antinomy which has baffled outsiders and easily lent itself to exaggeration and misunderstanding.

Despite all these retarding influences, the deep divergences in Jewish outlook, the numerical and geographic expansion of the people, seem to indicate the proximity of a climactic break and the falling off of many sections now loosely connected with the main body. The Jewish people has on several occasions experienced such a violent upheaval after a period of rapid growth. The separation of Northern Israel and Judah after the great expansion under David and Solomon might perhaps have been avoided. The formation of numerous sects and the separation of Christianity, however, at a time when the Jewish Diaspora spread over many lands, and most likely included some eight million members, was doubtless an historical necessity. When Judaism, recovering from this eruption under the caliphate of Baghdad, again rallied under its flag millions of prosperous and self-reliant adherents, forces of disintegration again arose, threatening to disrupt the national body into warring sects. Only with supreme effort and at the price of losing some of its most advanced and influential sections, did official Judaism repel the onslaught of Karaism and other sects. Despite the newer ties of solidarity forged in the heat of a worldwide anti-Semitic onslaught and of the Palestine struggle, many distinct symptoms in our time appear to point toward some ultimate violent separations, perhaps of a magnitude unprecedented in Jewish experience.

Most remarkably, the Jewish people seems to view these prospects with perfect equanimity. Not only those who prefer the easygoing road of delusion and who try to minimize the dangers, but also those who courageously face them, appear sublimely unconcerned. Did not the prophets indoctrinate the people with the belief that it is not the masses that count, but a "saving remnant"? As far back as Amos, this term apparently carried a widely accepted popular connotation. Soon after, Isaiah called one of his sons by the symbolic name *She'ar Yashuv* (the remnant will return). Since

Amos and Isaiah, Judaism has learned more and more to stress quality above quantity. Increasingly realizing the necessity of a chosen people as an example, and the intricacies of its own nonpolitical power of self-preservation, it placed the true vital inner power of the chosen few above the fictitious and externally glamorous force of the many. It is little wonder that down to our own days many a Zionist has professed disinterestedness in the ultimate destinies of the Diaspora and many a radical orthodox has prayed for the total secession of the internal enemy. Even the suicidal dream of some extreme assimilationists and communists that the Jewish people will soon disappear from the stage of history is nothing but a truly Jewish negativistic inversion of the positive doctrine of the remnant.

By another paradox, however, Judaism has always been deeply interested in the preservation of its followers. In ancient times the economic and military importance of numbers was fully recognized. Like the other Oriental nations, Israel gloried in the host of its conationals and the size of its blessed families. To become "as the dust of the earth" or "as the sand of the sea" (Gen. 13:16, 32:13) was long a dream of the people. To have many children was the deepest yearning of the Israelitic mother. Psalms 127 and 128, although apparently of post-exilic origin, still reflect the religious inclination toward aggrandizement of family and nation. With the loss of political independence, emphasis was shifted to ethnic preservation, but the goal remained the same. Orthodox Judaism is still most insistent, in theory and practice, upon procreation and the maintenance of the biological strength of the people.

However large or small may be their number at the conclusion of the present turbulent period of their history and whatever should be the outcome of these inner conflicts, few Jews are concerned about the prospects for the survival of their people because of these internal difficulties. The preponderant instinct among the majority, in any case, still perceptibly tells them that the Jewish religion, buttressed by the Jewish nationality, and the Jewish nationality, supernationally rooted in the Jewish religion, will weather the forthcoming storms, too, and that together they will continue their historic march into the unfathomable future.

INTRODUCTION TO ELLIS RIVKIN

ALTHOUGH Ellis Rivkin's work lacks the vast scope and erudition of Baron's writing, he has brought to Jewish historiography perceptive insights into the dynamics of Jewish history, and stimulating challenges to generally accepted assumptions.

Rivkin was born in 1918 in Baltimore, Maryland, and received a traditional Jewish education in addition to his secular studies. After earning a doctorate in history from Johns Hopkins University, he served for a time as a research fellow at Dropsie College and then came to the Hebrew Union College in Cincinnati. He has taught Jewish history there since 1949. Rivkin's writings deal with such diverse subjects as Jewish heresy and its opponents in the seventeenth century, the Saadiah/David ben Zakkai controversy of eleventh-century Jewish Babylonia, and, in particular, the origin and identity of the Pharisees. Like Baron, Rivkin pays little attention to the actions of individuals, but in contrast to the elder historian, he does not employ a sociological approach. Instead, he endeavors to analyze the structure of a given historical situation and to determine the dynamics by which one configuration is transformed into another. In explaining this process, Rivkin—like Mahler— places particular emphasis upon economic factors, though his own predilections in the modern period are for capitalism rather than socialism. His confidence in the cognitive value of historical analysis, as he conceives it, leads him to consider historiography a science, though the complex variables militate against definitive solution.

In 1971 Rivkin published a brief historical interpretation entitled The Shaping of Jewish History. In the Introduction he calls attention to what he terms the "unity concept," an idea he thinks characterizes the Jews' view of the world in every age. Because they believed in this unity (expressing it in a variety of ways), the Jews were able to maintain their identity while repeatedly integrating new modes of thought. Again and again they responded successfully to potentially disintegrative challenges by encompassing diversity within a basic unity. The first portion of this Introduction, which explains the unity concept, is presented below.

THE UNITY CONCEPT

The entire range and sweep of Jewish history in all of its remarkable complexity becomes intelligible as the working through of a concept of the unity of all reality, which I call the unity concept. Jewish history reveals itself to have been a process of elaboration of this simple, fragile, tenuous concept, espoused by a group of seminomadic sojourners in the ancient Near East. As historical circumstances raised novel and unanticipated problems of survival, the original concept became more sophisticated and complex to underwrite the development of new forms of Jewish life, each connected with the others, together forming the entire sweep of Jewish history.

This concept accords with what appears to me to be the paradoxical nature of the great conceptual breakthroughs in scientific thought. The crowning accomplishment always seems to have been to arrange under a simple, single principle or formula the rich variety of the phenomena themselves. If variety and differentiation are explained by some simple principle in the world of atoms and in the world of biological beings, why should one not look for an equivalently simple source of the variety and differentiations and unique happenings in the history of man? Why should the discovery of a simple principle preclude complexity and variation in history any more than it does in the natural sciences? The paradox of a simple principle explaining phenomenal complexity is so rooted in the remarkable accomplishments of science that it ought to encourage us to look for such a principle in human history without the fear that the diversity of historical phenomena will dissolve as a consequence. It is this paradox that I have sought to transfer to the realm of the historical processes.

Jewish historical experience lends itself to such an enterprise. It is unique, not in any supernatural sense, but in a phenomenal sense; i.e., there is no other historical experience quite analogous to it. It is not simply the history of a religion or of a people or of a nation. It is rather interlocked with the emergence and development of Western civilization—a minority interlocking in reciprocal interaction with large, complex, and enveloping cultures, societies, and civilizations. For though each phase of Jewish history bears the stamp of the enveloping society, it is, nonetheless, highly differentiated from it. Its individuality *is* the outcome of successive interactions with the encompassing culture, society, or civilization. Unlike any other entity, it cannot be treated, even temporarily, in isolation. Ancient Near Eastern motifs, patterns, and modes of dealing with reality cannot be separated from Israel's without distorting our picture of ancient Israel. Yet Israel's distinctiveness keeps it separate from Egypt, Assyria, Babylonia, or Persia. Likewise, though one can write a history of England without simultaneously writing a history of Russia, one cannot write a history of the Jews without regard to English, or Russian, or French, or German, or American, or Ottoman, or Christian, or Islamic, or Roman, or Hellenistic, or ancient Near Eastern history.

This, I submit, has no historical analogue. Though it is true there have been, from time to time, minorities interlocked with phases of Western civilization, there is no continuous entity that has been so interlocked—from the dawn of civilization in the ancient Near East to the post-industrial era of our day. Jews have been interlinked with every phase, and without a single disruption of their individuality. Furthermore, though always a minority, Israel was neither passive nor inconsequential. It not only fashioned the notion of a single omnipotent deity out of the stuff of Near Eastern experience, but it spun off two world-girdling religions, Christianity and Islam. And it did not lose its generative powers after procreating two independent religious systems. In virtually every territory of medieval Christendom and Islam, Jews fashioned forms and structures of bewildering variety as individualistic responses to changing historical circumstances. Indeed, this quality of creative adaptation was so efficacious that not only do Jews throughout the world today sustain at least three basic denominational divisions, but they also sustain a wide variety of national and secular identities as well. And most significant is the fact that the State of Israel, created by westernized Jews in the twentieth century, is alive and vibrant and developing and grappling with the complex problems of the contemporary Middle East. An analogous phenomenon just does not exist.

The larger world thus can no more be extricated from the Jew than the Jew can extricate himself from the larger world. To reconstruct the history of the Jews in the ancient Near East, the historian is compelled to grapple with the interrelationships within that region, with the patterns, motifs, and events of its civilizational complex; to reconstruct the history of the Jews in the Hellenistic and Roman worlds, one must pay almost as much attention to the Greco-Roman framework as to what is distinctively Jewish. Similarly, one distorts the Jewish experience if one neglects either the Church or the Mosque, or the institutions of the caliphate and feudalism, or the basic developments in Christian and Muslim thought, or the evolution and development of capitalism and the modern system of nation-states.

The problems of Jewish history can be understood by means of the unity concept. For most of Jewish history, this concept was the affirmation that God was one and omnipotent. But though this God was believed to be one and omnipotent, the concept of Him changed, as changing historical circumstances confronted Jews with new problems. Each successive form of Jewish history represents a solution to problems posed to the idea of unity by changing historical circumstances. The unity concept became the source and justification for variation and even radical transmutation of Jewish life. Commitment to unity did not breed repetitive conformity, but creative diversity, for the idea of God's omnipotence was drawn upon to multiply and diversify His powers and His attributes. Indeed the unity concept proved to be so resilient that it was successfully elaborated and extended to embrace ever more complex systems in earth as well as in heaven.

Jewish history is thus the history of the evolution, development, and elaboration of the unity concept through a sequence of historically interrelated and interdependent forms, none of which is identical with any other. The unity concept became the organizer, systematizer, and processor of diversity, rather than its negation. The commitment to unity did not end with unity—it ended with diversity.

This can be illustrated by the fact that millions of Jews today publicly proclaim adherence to the unity concept, though they differ radically as to what they mean, and in no single instance is the concept identical—not even for the most orthodox Jews who believe that God gave the Pentateuch to Moses—with the unity concept that flourished in biblical Israel. Yet every one of today's differing concepts is the outcome of a sequence of interconnections that ultimately reaches back to the unity concept associated with the seminomadic patriarchs. Similarly there are hundreds of Christian variations of the unity concept, each of which, though reducible to prior Christian concepts, must trace its origins back to the birth of Christianity, and *then* must connect with pre-Christian Judaism through an historical sequence of interconnected forms, all adhering to the unity concept back to the book of Genesis.

I do not claim that the unity concept is a guarantee of the religious, moral, or ethical quality of Jews or Judaism. I have been a student of history for too many years to have any illusions that men, Jews or otherwise, are more than human. I know the embarrassing biblical texts as well as the elevating ones. I am firmly convinced that Jews are neither better nor worse than their fellowmen. But it is nonetheless true that they have had a different history. Whether their religion, or ethics, or morals, or ideas, or concepts were or were not at any given moment higher than those held by others is irrelevant. What is relevant is, that higher, lower, or in between, they were fashioned under the aegis of the concept of unity; and that we can learn something about historical process from examining how this concept worked in history. Polygamy was, at one time, as compatible with it as monogamy is in our own day. The total eradication of the Amalekites* was, at one time, as pleasing to it as was unbounded compassion at another. The simple revelation of God to Moses in a wilderness Tent of Meeting was neither more nor less a commitment to it than was the medieval philosophical belief that God was the Unmoved Mover.

It should also be stressed that the unity concept is in no way committed to the perpetuation of any of the content attached to it by any of the forms, or, for that matter, to the perpetuation of the forms themselves. Jewish history reveals that no law, idea, custom, or dictum has been preserved intact from the beginning. It further reveals, that far from sustaining any single form of the unity concept, Jewish history *is* the interconnected sequence of *changing* forms. Yet all content and all forms, however diverse, fit under the unity concept, which is simply the notion that reality, be it simple, complex, or changing, is amenable to a unifying idea.

The one stubborn empirical datum of Jewish history which is difficult to challenge, is that the Jews, and only the Jews, have actively participated in *every* phase of the development of Western civilization. If this can be shown to be causally related to the Jews' adherence to the concept of unity, then it is only appropriate to raise the question whether this concept affords greater survival

---

*Deuteronomy 25:19.

value than a concept that attaches some kind of independent power to every diversity in nature, man, and historical experience. I doubt whether any scientist, for example, operates as though he really believes that reality is a congeries of unrelated, unconnected, and independent items, however much he may vociferously insist that he has transcended metaphysics. I also wonder whether the survival of man in our own day might not be dependent on whether he can conceptualize reality as a "unity of diversity"—with individual, national, racial, intellectual, and other differences as necessary and legitimate consequences of unity. I raise these questions of larger meaning since Jewish history gives evidence, not of the triumph of a single form, belief, or set of practices, but of the proliferation of many forms, ideas, beliefs, and practices—as many as survival necessitated. Jewish history testifies that the unity concept generated diversity, rather than stifled it.

The unity concept is the *essential* differentiating feature of Jewish history and it is the *constant* in every situation in which the Jews were required to solve problems through the millennia. But it is not in and of itself a sufficient explanation of Jewish history. It was used to solve problems, but because the Jews lived within larger societies the problems themselves were generally set by extrinsic forces. Thus the threat of Assyrian and Babylonian imperialism posed the question of how omnipotent Yahweh really was. The answer given by Amos, Isaiah, and Jeremiah was that He was so omnipotent that He used the great imperial powers as the rods of His anger. The problem was raised by imperialism; its resolution was sought by expanding the scope of the unity concept.

The unity concept thus developed dialectically: the idea spawned new possibilities through interaction with the external world, and the new possibilities themselves brought about new interactions. The idea constantly responded to economic, social, and political forces. Indeed, the evolution and development of the unity concept was the outcome of that very "Challenge and Response" that Arnold Toynbee* set as his essential criterion of a civilization and of its power to survive. How ironic that the Jews, the one civilization which reveals this principle as empirically verifiable, are considered by Toynbee to be a fossil civilization. Toynbee, oddly, sees fossilization setting in at the very moment when the Jews were fashioning a form of Judaism, Pharisaism, that was to give rise to Christianity, endowing it with the Jews' own techniques of responding to historical challenge.

*Contemporary English historian, author of the multivolume *A Study of History.*

INTRODUCTION TO LEO BAECK

DURING HIS LONG and eventful life, Leo Baeck achieved eminence as a rabbi, theologian, and historical scholar. He was born in Posen in 1873, and he studied at both the Conservative seminary in Breslau and the Liberal Hochschule in Berlin. Devoted to the totality of the Jewish people, he achieved the respect of all political and religious factions and served faithfully as the leader of the entire German Jewish community during the difficult Nazi years. Miraculously surviving his imprisonment at the Theresienstadt concentration camp, he spent the final years of his life, until his death in 1956, in England and the United States.

In his theology, Baeck was greatly influenced by Immanuel Kant in whose religion of duty he found a continuation of the Jewish conception of commandment. Yet for Baeck, Kant was an exception among Christian thinkers. Baeck considered Christianity as a whole to be "romantic," given to emotion and concern with individual salvation, while Judaism was "classical," turned to moral action for the redemption of society. Though he remained a rationalist, in his later religious thought Baeck gradually came to a greater appreciation of mystery as no less important than commandment in describing God's relation to the world.

Baeck's historical writings deal with the development of the Jewish spirit rather than with the physical history of the Jews. This

People Israel, his last major work which he began in the concentration camp, lies on the border between theology and history. It is an historical account of an idealized Israel's answer to the question posed to it by God and of the perpetual renewal of His covenant. According to Baeck's own distinction, the work is toldot (in Hebrew: "generations") rather than historia, (in Greek: "investigation").

The relationship between theology and history concerned Baeck for many years. Before the war he wrote an essay on the subject in which he argued that in Judaism theology does not consist of dogmas but of understanding Israel's historical experience: studying theology therefore means studying history. But the historian of Judaism, in Baeck's sense, may not—despite the secular influences of his time—allow himself to become an historicist. That is to say, he may not take a position outside of Jewish history, relating to it only as an unengaged scholar. He must rather take his stance within that history and thus link himself and his generation internally to Jewish tradition.

The selection which follows contains the larger part of Baeck's essay. Within its brief compass it brings into view once again most of the major issues which have formed the basis of this volume. Bridging the religious and secular realms, and providing for both the continuity and the uniqueness of Jewish history, Baeck's idea of Jewish history, as he presents it here, consists of the Jews' continuing response to the incursion of the infinite divine imperative into the finite world of men, and to the tension in the human fiber which that incursion creates.

ॐ

THEOLOGY AND HISTORY

Those who seek to understand the essential doctrines of Judaism often express the desire to arrive at them through a theology of Judaism. Although this hope is usually uncertain and even vague, it expresses an unmistakable longing to overcome the historicism which dominated the nineteenth century and to escape the relativism it brought in its wake. . . .

In the Judaism of the nineteenth century an historicization had set in early and decisively, at times even fatefully. The old unified culture which was alive and active through a millennium had dissolved. In an often all too hasty development, culture, law, the mode of life, and also to a certain extent, as a consequence of the ideas of the Enlightenment, religion—all had become secularized. The collective European culture, this "Europeanism" into which the Jew wanted and had to enter, demanded a substantial part of his mental and also, eventually, of his spiritual being. The old tradition had until then always been experienced directly in every age, had always entered the consciousness anew, and, with its succession of teachers, had brought about and guaranteed an outer as well as an inner unity of Jewish teaching. Now it tore apart, rent by the revolution which Judaism experienced at that time in its exodus from the old culture. Later, a spiritual relationship to it was again sought and found. When one again sought to identify one's life with one's past, this relationship essentially consisted in taking an attitude of a practical or scientific kind toward the tradition, in other words, the attitude of one who had advanced beyond it. One no longer stood within the tradition, but rather looked at it from the outside. The place of the real tradition was taken by learned reconstruction, the place of historical continuity by historical science.

It is true that in this way a certain solid ground was established in the chaotic time after the incipient revolution, and that it helped somewhat. But the cost was high; historicism was the price the following generations had to pay. History began to mean more than its content. With so much history, often little remained of religion, of the spirit which had its own history. Judaism became historical in a sense different from that which the men around the young Zunz had had in mind when they first spoke of an historical Judaism. It was often regarded as merely an area for research, not a matter of concern, not a problem of the seeking, thinking human being. History was studied for its own sake. . . .

At the same time, the idea of evolution, which was now supposed to replace the old certainty of tradition, produced no equivalent vitality or unity. It failed, first of all, because what was designated as evolution by one individual was what he himself had just established or was about to come up with. For practical purposes, for the needs of the decade, selection was made from the tradition and then called evolution. It became the label on whatever one had adopted or wished to possess, and then sought to provide with historical justification—somewhat like the Karaites, who skipped over past centuries and asserted the direct continuation of a real or imagined earlier epoch. A tradition was to be artificially created. These historical ideas expressed much less an experience of history than a significant experience of the present with its often urgent demands. Moreover, history itself was now inserted into the present due to the unavoidable battle for Jewish rights.

Although it is not to be denied that in this, as in every battle for justice and its historical justification, a religious element was involved, the struggle resulted in the politicization of history and the consequent narrowing of its horizon. Of course, just like historicism, this corresponded, especially in Germany, to a general trend; a generation of the disciples of Ranke had turned to the writing of political history with political intentions. But among the non-Jewish historians there always remained something of Ranke's universalism with its wide expanse and its broad aims. Here this was generally missing; the conscious or unconscious purpose of advocating a political cause pointed to an immediate program and restricted the field of vision. With the exception of Graetz, there was often a lack of that which Schmoller* considered characteristic of the true historian: "a firm conviction regarding the relationship of the Deity to human history, the origin and purpose of historical development, . . . the final moral and political questions." It seemed as if historiography refused to concern itself with the ultimate meaning of this history of Judaism. What, after all, made delving into and writing it worthwhile?

Opposition was bound to appear against such a conception of

*Gustav Schmoller (1838–1917), German political economist and intellectual.

history, against the perplexity that was its final product and the pessimism that was about to follow from it. Such opposition is unmistakably operative already in the intellectual movement of Zionism, where, from the beginning, concepts of the philosophy of history and of theology lived side by side with secular political ideas. Then, in the Judaism of our day, this opposition merged into the common mood that began to rebel against historicism as well as against the Europeanism which it taught. Out of all this has emerged also that somewhat vague desire for a theology of Judaism. . . .

Judaism possesses its peculiarity—the basis of its origin and its inner motivation—in the wholly characteristic essential problem which emerged from within it, a problem which has since taken its place in human thought and which manifests the world-historical and universal elements of Judaism. Universalism does not consist of that absoluteness of which Protestant theology liked to speak, but rather of something entirely individual in its determinacy. It is realized where an idea emerges from a single or collective individuality as a living spiritual force which can now no longer be physically or intellectually removed from the collective life and thought of humanity. Not general acceptance, not what already exists and is static, is decisive here, but the significance lies in the dynamic element and the motive power.

This problem, through and on account of which Judaism in all of its particularity has become universal—this specifically Jewish problem of world history—is that of the incursion of the Infinite, Eternal, the One and Unconditional into the finite, temporal, manifold and limited, and of the spiritual and moral tension of the human fiber which is its result. Whatever ideas and hopes Judaism has created within its own sphere and beyond it emanate from here. The whole antithesis to classical antiquity is expressed in it. In all of the manifoldness of forms which antiquity produced, its character and peculiarity lay in the concept of the *eidos*, of the perfected, completed and finished, the transcendent ideal at which man blissfully gazes upward; looking, perceiving, worshiping. The mystery religions as well, into which antiquity increasingly flowed, intended to represent this finality, and only on this account could they become one and could the Church then constitute itself out of the union of *logos** and *mysterium, eidos* and sacrament.

The universal idea of Judaism stands opposed to that universal

*The rational principle in the world.

idea of the finished and perfected; a comparison reveals its full specificity and its own world-historical character. Its idea is the entry of the Infinite and Transcendent into the finite and human, the tension and the conflict which is grounded in it, and the never-ending battle with the task, the way and the future. In the tension of this idea opposites persist: self-sufficiency and belonging, the distance and the bond, the being-other and the being-one, creatureliness and freedom, grace and law, revelation and prophecy, immanence and transcendence, mysticism and ethics, retirement and challenge.

This idea with its problem may be traced through the entirety of Judaism, in its collective content as in its extension. It has variety and movement; it has again and again seized the searching human being, with the result that it was constantly revitalized, reshaped and born anew. Thus Judaism is provided with its development, its history, its tradition and its historical unity. Therein, it also possesses its principle, its norm, and the criterion for that which is peculiarly its own and constitutes its essence. The systematic reflection upon this problem, by which an age renders its account of its Judaism and by which it seeks to express its own connection with the basic problem and its forms—this is *theology* in Judaism. And this theology is at the same time the reflection of the present age upon the history and tradition of Judaism. For the totality of the teaching is always given only in the continuation of the teaching and thereby in the sum total of the teachers in their sequence down to the last of them and in the extension of this tradition to the present time. What is of concern here is not a mere up-and-down line, a coming and going, or an alternation of narrowing and widening, progress and regress, but rather the question of this recurrent revival of the fundamental idea, this inner historical unity. In this sense it might be said that the extension of the contents of Judaism at the same time means its temporal extension, that the teaching of Judaism is at the same time its history and its history at the same time its teaching. Only through an awareness of this idea can an historicism and likewise a lack of history in Judaism be overcome.

It is characteristic of Christian theology that it leads to or aims at a dogma; for it is in fact or in intention a theology of the Church. By contrast it is characteristic of Jewish theology that it is theology of the teachers. The authority to teach and the right to represent the tradition, which is the right to theology, is the due of every teacher. But the teacher is legitimized only if he binds himself securely to the fundamental problem of Judaism, if he personifies it, or at least provides it with a nuance. Only the fact of religious, Jewish individuality evidenced thereby assures him a place in the tradition, guarantees him, as it were, a right of inheritance in the succession of teachers.

In this way the concept of tradition in Judaism gains its significance. The last century, whether affirming or rejecting it, was inclined to understand by tradition only a continuity of the constitutional form which the Jewish community, and in a certain sense Jewish life, had developed since the close of antiquity. A very significant part of the "law," the statutes, the rules and practices, which were elaborated through the halakhah and minhag,* may be inserted into this concept of political organization. If the Jewish collectivity of the Middle Ages—a widely extended diaspora—possessed not only the unity and continuity of the law but also the unity and continuity of the essential direction of life, it is to be attributed to this constitution. In it the stability and vitality of tradition were always, and almost tangibly, experienced; so much so that at times the tradition was represented by it alone, and the tradition in its most proper sense, that of the fundamental religious problem, receded before it or vanished altogether.

Later, as a result of the exodus from the old community structure, which was at the same time an exodus from the old way of life, the political organization also began to totter. It had created the old way of life, and now its tottering shattered it; the old tradition seemed rent asunder.

Of course, even the real tradition, the profoundly religious one from which that other had always drawn its most vital strength, was affected to its core by the great change in the times. The old piety was communal piety with its communal morality, but it almost always possessed an ardent, vigorous bond with the Infinite and Eternal, and thus with that fundamental problem of Judaism. In this piety, the community and the transcendent were bound up together: the narrow Jewish street knew it was encompassed by the world of divine spheres; its wretched visible proximity was merged into the invisible All of the mystery. The world-to-come entered

*Minhag refers to customary Jewish religious practice, as opposed to the legally binding forms of the halakhah.

into this-world with all of its tension. But once the Jew was drawn into a new wide sphere of this world with its great this-worldly tasks and had to provide a way of life for himself in it, the realm of the transcendent withdrew more and more behind the new this-worldliness, often to disappear. Religiosity, whether in its attempt to retain the old form for itself or to fashion a new one, threatened to become purely a religiosity of this world. In Conservatism as in Reform, satisfaction with the finished and the fully realized, a dogmatic rationalism, usurped the place of tension. In producing a real interruption of the tradition it dealt the tradition a fateful blow, and so provided the most significant cause for historicism.

The critical reflection which renders account of the basis and justification of all tradition in Judaism is, therefore, especially today, the beginning of all theology in Judaism. The renewed revival of the old problem, and thereby the renewal of the real tradition, the religious tradition, is its ordained task. In this task Jewish theology will gratefully receive insights from other sources, not least those which are indicated by the problem and crisis of historicism. It must operate systematically, that is to say, with knowing and not with believing, or, to put it Platonically, with *episteme* and not with *doxa*. But it will be theology of Judaism—Jewish theology—only if it seeks to comprehend and to realize out of that which is its own and out of the historical whole of Judaism what are its universal idea and its particular tradition, what constitutes its individuality in world history.

SOURCES

II Maccabees: *The Apocrypha of the Old Testament, Revised Standard Version* (New York, 1956), pp. 227-29, 233-34.

Josephus Flavius: *The Jewish War*, in *Josephus* (Cambridge, 1967), II, pp. 3-17; *Jewish Antiquities*, in ibid., IV, pp. 3-13. Translated from the Greek for that series by H. St. J. Thackeray.

The Dead Sea Sect: *The Dead Sea Scriptures* (Garden City, 1957), pp. 43-46. Translated from the Hebrew for that volume by Theodor H. Gaster.

Talmudic Conceptions: *Gittin* 55b-56a, *Yoma* 9b, *Shabbat* 119b. In the Soncino Press translation.

Rashi: Commentary to Genesis 28:9. Translated from the Hebrew by the editor.

Abraham ibn Daud: *The Book of Tradition* (Philadelphia, 1967), pp. 3-4, 91-92. Translated from the Hebrew for that volume by Gerson D. Cohen.

The Chronicle of Ahimaaz: *Megilat Ahimaaz*, ed. Benjamin Klar (Jerusalem, 1944), pp. 20-23. Translated from the Hebrew by the editor.

The Crusade Chronicle of Solomon bar Simeon: *Hebräische Berichte über die Judenverfolgungen während der Kreuzzüge*, ed. A. Neubauer and M. Stern (Berlin, 1892), pp. 1-5, 14-16, 131. Translated from the Hebrew by the editor.

Samuel Usque: *Consolation for the Tribulations of Israel* (Philadelphia, 1965), pp. 198-200. Translated from the Portuguese for that volume by Martin A. Cohen.

Solomon ibn Verga: *Shevet Yehuda*, ed. A. Shochat and Y. Baer (Jerusalem, 1947), pp. 30-31, 127-28. Translated from the Hebrew by the editor.

Azariah dei Rossi: *Meor Enayim*, ed. David Cassel (Jerusalem, 1969), I, pp. 214-19 (with cuts). Translated from the Hebrew by the editor.

David Gans: *Tzemah David* (Jerusalem, 1966), pp. 6-7, 76, 91-92, 154, 167-68. Translated from the Hebrew by the editor.

Nathan Hannover: *Yeven Metzula* (Tel-Aviv, 1966), pp. 15-17. Translated from the Hebrew by the editor.

Immanuel Wolf: *Leo Baeck Institute Year Book*, II (London, 1957), pp. 194–204. Translated from the German for that volume by Lionel E. Kochan.

Leopold Zunz: *Miscellany of Hebrew Literature*, I (London, 1872), pp. 167–173, 217–18 (with cuts in both sections). Translated from the German for that volume by A. Löwy.

Abraham Geiger: *Abraham Geiger and Liberal Judaism*, ed. Max Wiener (Philadelphia, 1962), pp. 149–57, 262–64. Translated from the German for that volume by Ernst J. Schlochauer.

Isaac Marcus Jost: *Allgemeine Geschichte des Israelitischen Volkes* (Berlin, 1832), I, 2–15 (with one cut). Translated from the German by the editor.

Nahman Krochmal: *Kitve Rabi Nahman Krochmal*, ed. Simon Rawidowicz, (Waltham, Mass., 1961), pp. 5–6, 34–44 (with cuts), 50–52, 112. Translated from the Hebrew by the editor.

Heinrich Graetz: *Die Konstruktion der judischen Geschichte* (Berlin, 1936), pp. 5–21; *Geschichte der Jüden*, I (Leipzig, 1874), pp. xxxiv–xxxv; ibid., IV (Berlin, 1853), pp. 1–9; ibid., V (Magdeburg, 1860), pp. 1–8; ibid., VII (Leipzig, 1863), pp. 1–4. The selection from *Die Konstruktion* translated from the German by Noah Jonathan Jacobs; selections from the *Geschichte* translated from the German by the editor.

Simon Dubnow: *Nationalism and History*, ed. Koppel S. Pinson (Philadelphia, 1958), pp. 257–60, 265–71, 322–24, 336–50 (in each instance without the author's notes). The first two selections from the German according to the Henrietta Szold translation of 1903, reprinted in that volume; the third selection translated from the German for that volume by Koppel S. Pinson.

Yehezkel Kaufmann: *Gola ve-Nekhar*, I (Tel-Aviv, 1929), pp. 166, 168–71, 204–7. Translated from the Hebrew by the editor.

Ben Zion Dinur: *Israel and the Diaspora* (Philadelphia, 1969), pp. 14–16, 47–63 (in each instance without the author's notes). Translated from the Hebrew for that volume by Merton B. Dagut.

Raphael Mahler: *Divre Yeme Yisrael: Dorot Aharonim*, I (Merhavya, Israel, 1961), pp. 13–21 (with minor changes by the author). Translated from the Hebrew by the editor.

Salo Baron: *A Social and Religious History of the Jews*, I (New York, 1952), pp. 16–31 (with cuts and omission of author's notes).

Ellis Rivkin: *The Shaping of Jewish History* (New York, 1971), pp. 15–21 (with minor changes by the editor).

Leo Baeck: *Judaism*, XIII (New York, 1964), pp. 274–84 (with cuts). Translated from the German by the editor.

SUGGESTIONS FOR FURTHER READING (in English)

GENERAL CONCEPTIONS

Becker, Carl L., *Everyman His Own Historian* (New York: Crofts, 1935)

Carr, Edward Hallett, *What is History?* (New York: Knopf, 1962)

Collingwood, R. G., *The Idea of History* (New York: Oxford University Press, 1956)

Hughes, H. Stuart, *History as Art and as Science* (New York: Harper, 1964)

Kahler, Erich, *The Meaning of History* (New York: Braziller, 1964)

Löwith, Karl, *Meaning in History* (Chicago: University of Chicago Press, 1949)

Meyerhoff, Hans, *The Philosophy of History in Our Time* (New York: Doubleday Anchor, 1959)

Nash, Ronald H., *Ideas of History*, 2 vols. (New York: Dutton, 1972)

Smith, Page, *The Historian and History* (New York: Knopf, 1964)

Stern, Fritz, *The Varieties of History* (Cleveland: World, 1956)

Walsh, W. H., *Philosophy of History* (New York: Harper Torchbooks, 1960)

JEWISH CONCEPTIONS

Ahad Ha-Am, "Past and Future," *Selected Essays*, tr. Leon Simon (Philadelphia: Jewish Publication Society, 1912), pp. 80–90

Baeck, Leo, *This People Israel*, tr. Albert H. Friedlander (Philadelphia: Jewish Publication Society, 1965)

Baer, Yitzhak F. *Galut* (New York: Schocken Books, 1947)

Baron, Salo W., *History and Jewish Historians* [in addition to essays on own views, also contains articles on Rossi, Jost, Graetz, Steinschneider, and Herzfeld] (Philadelphia: Jewish Publication Society, 1964)

———, "New Horizons in Jewish History," *Freedom and Reason: Studies . . . in Memory of Morris Raphael Cohen*, ed. Salo W. Baron et al. (Glencoe, Ill.: The Free Press, 1951), pp. 337–53

Dinur, Ben Zion, "Jewish History—Its Uniqueness and Continuity," *Jewish Society Through the Ages*, ed. H. H. Ben-Sasson and S. Ettinger (London: Valentine, Mitchell, 1971), pp. 15–29

Dubnov, Simon, *History of the Jews*, tr. Moshe Spiegel, I–V (South Brunswick, New Jersey: Thomas Yoseloff, 1967–73)

Graetz, Heinrich, "Retrospect," *History of the Jews*, V (Philadelphia: Jewish Publication Society, 1895), pp. 705–31

——, "The Significance of Judaism for the Present and Future," *Jewish Quarterly Review*, I (1889), pp. 4–13; ibid., II (1890), pp. 257–69

Hacohen, Joseph, *The Vale of Tears*, tr. Harry S. May (The Hague: Martinus Nijhoff, 1971)

Halevi, Judah, *The Kuzari*, tr. Hartwig Hirschfeld (New York: Schocken Books, 1964), esp. Parts One and Two

Hannover, Nathan, *Abyss of Despair*, tr. Abraham J. Mesch (New York: Bloch Publishing Co., 1950)

Joseph ben Gorion, *The Wonderful and Most Deplorable History of the Later Times of the Jews* [Josippon], tr. J. Howell (London: T. Thackeray, 1694)

Katz, Jacob, "The Concept of Social History and its Possible Use in Jewish Historical Research," *Scripta Hierosolymitana*, III (1956), pp. 292–312

Kaufmann, Yehezkel, *The Religion of Israel*, tr. Moshe Greenberg (Chicago: University of Chicago Press, 1960)

Mahler, Raphael, *A History of Modern Jewry 1780–1815* (New York: Schocken Books, 1971)

Rivkin, Ellis, "The Diaspora: Its Historical Significance," *Studies of the Leo Baeck Institute*, ed. Max Kreutzberger (New York: Frederick Ungar, 1967), pp. 267–318

——, "Unitive and Divisive Factors in Judaism," *Civilisations*, VII no. 4 (1957), pp. 43–57

Rosenzweig, Franz, *The Star of Redemption*, tr. William H. Hallo (New York: Holt, Rinehart and Winston, 1971)

Scholem, Gershom, "The Science of Judaism—Then and Now," *The Messianic Idea in Judaism* (New York: Schocken Books, 1971), pp. 304–13

Talmon, J. L., "Uniqueness and Universality of Jewish History," *The Unique and the Universal* (New York: Braziller, 1966), pp. 64–90

SECONDARY WORKS

Abrahams, Israel, "H. Graetz, the Jewish Historian," *Jewish Quarterly Review*, O. S., IV (1892), pp. 165–94

Bamberger, Fritz, "Zunz's Conception of History," *Proceedings of the American Academy for Jewish Research,* XI (1941), pp. 1–25

Baron, Salo W., *A Social and Religious History of the Jews* (New York: Columbia University Press), VI (1958), pp. 152–234 (on medieval Jewish historiography)

Berlin, Charles, "A Sixteenth-Century Hebrew Chronicle of the Ottoman Empire: The *Seder Eliyahu Zuta* of Elijah Capsali and its Message," *Studies in Jewish Bibliography, History and Literature in Honor of I. Edward Kiev,* ed. Charles Berlin (New York: Ktav, 1971), pp. 21–44

Boman, Thorleif, *Hebrew Thought Compared With Greek* (Philadelphia: Westminster Press, 1960)

Buber, Martin, "The Gods of the Nations and God" [on Krochmal], *Israel and the World* (New York: Schocken Books, 1963), pp. 195–213

Cohen, Arthur A., "The Century of Uncertainty" [includes treatment of Jewish historians from Ibn Verga to Dubnow], *The Natural and the Supernatural Jew* (New York: Pantheon Books, 1962), pp. 10–67

Cohen, Gerson D., Introduction to Abraham ibn Daud, *The Book of Tradition* (Philadelphia: Jewish Publication Society, 1967), pp. xiii–lxii

Cohen, Martin A., Introduction to Samuel Usque's *Consolation for the Tribulations of Israel* (Philadelphia: Jewish Publication Society, 1964), pp. 3–34

Cohen, Morris R., "Philosophies of Jewish History," *Jewish Social Studies,* I (1939), pp. 39–72

Curtis, John Briggs, "A Suggested Interpretation of the Biblical Philosophy of History," *Hebrew Union College Annual,* XXXIV (1963), pp. 115–23

Dentan, Robert C., ed., *The Idea of History in the Ancient Near East* (New Haven: Yale University Press, 1955)

Deutsch, Gotthard, "Heinrich Graetz," *Central Conference of American Rabbis Yearbook,* XXVII (1917), pp. 338–64

Fishman, Samuel Z., "M. Y. Berdichevsky on the Meaning of History," *Judaism,* XXI (1972), pp. 104–109

Friedman, Philip, "Polish Jewish Historiography Between the Two Wars (1918–1939)," *Jewish Social Studies,* XI (1949), pp. 373–408

Glatzer, Nahum N., "The Beginnings of Modern Jewish Studies," *Studies in Nineteenth-Century Jewish Intellectual History,* ed. Alexander Altmann (Cambridge, Mass.: Harvard University Press, 1964), pp. 27–45

Grayzel, Solomon, "Graetz's *History* in America," *Das Breslauer Seminar,* ed. Guido Kisch (Tübingen: J. C. B. Mohr, 1963), pp. 223–37

————, "Graetz's Structuring of Jewish History," *Jewish Book Annual,* XXIII (1965/66), pp. 82–86

Herlitz, Georg, "Three Jewish Historians: Isaak Markus Jost—Heinrich Graetz—Eugen Täubler," *Leo Baeck Institute Year Book,* IX (1964), pp. 69–90

Liebeschütz, Hans, "Between Past and Future: Leo Baeck's Historical Position," *Leo Baeck Institute Year Book,* XI (1966), pp. 3–27

Meyer, Michael A., "Jewish Religious Reform and Wissenschaft des Judentums," *Leo Baeck Institute Year Book,* XVI (1971), pp. 19–41

———, *The Origins of the Modern Jew* (Detroit: Wayne State University Press, 1967), especially pp. 144–82

Muilenberg, James, "The Biblical View of Time," *Harvard Theological Review,* LIV (1961), pp. 225–52

Neuman, Abraham A., "Historical Studies" [on Josippon, ibn Verga, and Usque], *Landmarks and Goals* (Philadelphia: Dropsie College Press, 1953), pp. 1–132

Neusner, Jacob, "The Religious Uses of History: Judaism in First-Century A.D. Palestine and Third-Century Babylonia," *History and Theory,* V (1966), pp. 153–71

Pinson, Koppel S., "Simon Dubnow: Historian and Political Philosopher," in Simon Dubnow, *Nationalism and History* (Philadelphia: Jewish Publication Society, 1958), pp. 3–65

Rivkin, Ellis, "The Writing of Jewish History" [principally on Baron], *The Reconstructionist,* XXV no. 9 (June 15, 1959), pp. 13–18; ibid. no. 10 (June 26, 1959), pp. 24–27

Rotenstreich, Nathan, *Tradition and Reality: The Impact of History on Modern Jewish Thought* (New York: Random House, 1972)

Roth, Cecil, "Historiography," *Encyclopaedia Judaica,* VIII, pp. 551–69

Salzman, Marcus, *The Chronicle of Ahimaaz* (New York: Columbia University Press, 1924)

Schorsch, Ismar, "The Philosophy of History of Nahman Krochmal," *Judaism,* X (1961), pp. 237–45

Schreiber, Emanuel, *Historians of Judaism in the Nineteenth Century* (Chicago: Occident Publishing Co., 1894)

Shotwell, James T., *The Story of Ancient History* (New York: Columbia University Press, 1939. Reprinted as Columbia Paperback, 1961)

Steinberg, Aaron, ed., *Simon Dubnow: The Man and His Work* (Paris: World Jewish Congress, 1963)

Stern, Nathan, *The Jewish Historico-Critical School of the Nineteenth Century* (New York: Columbia University Dissertation, 1901)

Taubes, Jacob, "Nachman Krochmal and Modern Historicism," *Judaism,* XII (1963), pp. 150–64

Tcherikower, Elias, "Jewish Martyrology and Jewish Historiography," *YIVO Annual of Jewish Social Science*, I (1946), pp. 9–23

Thackeray, Henry St. John, *Josephus, the Man and the Historian* (New York: Ktav, 1968)

Wacholder, Ben Zion, *Nicolaus of Damascus* (Berkeley and Los Angeles: University of California Press, 1962)

Wallach, Luitpold, *Liberty and Letters: The Thoughts of Leopold Zunz* (London: East and West Library, 1959)

Waxman, Meyer, *A History of Jewish Literature*, 4 vols. (2nd ed.; New York: Bloch Publishing Co., 1938–41)

Wiener, Max, "Abraham Geiger and the Science Of Judaism," *Judaism*, II (1953), 41–48

———, "Abraham Geiger's Conception of the Science of Judaism," *YIVO Annual of Jewish Social Science*, XI (1956/57), pp. 142–62

Wilson, Edmund, *The Scrolls from the Dead Sea* (New York: Oxford University Press, 1955)

INDEX